Communications in Computer and Information Science 1641

More information about this series at https://link.springer.com/bookseries/7899

Jiageng Chen · Debiao He · Rongxing Lu (Eds.)

Emerging Information Security and Applications

Third International Conference, EISA 2022
Wuhan, China, October 29–30, 2022
Proceedings

Editors
Jiageng Chen 🄳
Central China Normal University
Wuhan, China

Debiao He 🄳
Wuhan University
Wuhan, China

Rongxing Lu 🄳
University of New Brunswick
Fredericton, NB, Canada

ISSN 1865-0929   ISSN 1865-0937 (electronic)
Communications in Computer and Information Science
ISBN 978-3-031-23097-4   ISBN 978-3-031-23098-1 (eBook)
https://doi.org/10.1007/978-3-031-23098-1

This Springer imprint is published by the registered company Springer Nature Switzerland AG
The registered company address is: Gewerbestrasse 11, 6330 Cham, Switzerland

Preface

This volume contains the papers that were selected for presentation and publication at the Third International Conference on Emerging Information Security and Applications (EISA 2022), which was organized by the School of Computer Science, Central China Normal University, China, and held during October 29–30, 2022. Due to COVID-19, EISA 2022 was held fully online.

With the recent evolution of adversarial techniques, intrusions that may threaten the security of various assets, including information and applications, have become more complex. In addition, coordinated intrusions like worm outbreaks will continue to be a major threat to information, system, and network security in the near future. The popularity of the Internet generates a large volume of different types of sensitive information. Therefore, there is a need for emerging techniques, theories, and applications to protect information and practical security. EISA aims to provide a platform for researchers and practitioners across the world to exchange their ideas. It seeks original submissions that discuss practical or theoretical solutions to enhance information and application security in practice.

This year's Program Committee (PC) consisted of 31 members with diverse backgrounds and broad research interests. A total of 35 papers were submitted to the conference. Papers were selected based on their originality, significance, relevance, and clarity of presentation as assessed by the reviewers. Most papers were reviewed by three or more PC members. Finally, 13 full papers were selected for presentation at the conference, resulting in an acceptance rate of 37.1%.

In addition to the regular program, EISA 2022 included four outstanding keynote talks: "Attribute-based Hierarchical Access Control with Extendable Policy" presented by Qiong Huang from South China Agricultural University, China; "Towards Balancing Privacy and Accountability in Multiuser Authentication Systems" presented by Khoa Nguyen from University of Wollongong, Australia; "Recent Trends in Post-Quantum Cryptography" presented by Yuntao Wang from Osaka University, Japan, and "Lightweight computation for secure evaluating and privacy-preserving federated learning in IoT environments" presented by Tran Viet Xuan Phuong from Old Dominion University, USA. Our deepest gratitude for their excellent presentations.

For the success of EISA 2022, we would like to first thank the authors of all submissions and all the PC members for their great efforts in selecting the papers. We also thank all the external reviewers for assisting the reviewing process. For the conference organization, we would like to thank the general chairs, Anthony TS Ho, Sokratis K.

Katsikas, and Weizhi Meng; the publicity chairs, Pei Li and Chunhua Su; and the publication chairs, Shixiong Yao and Wenjuan Li. Finally, we thank everyone else, speakers and session chairs, for their contribution to the program of EISA 2022.

October 2022

Jiageng Chen
Debiao He
Rongxing Lu

Organization

General Chairs

Anthony T. S. Ho   University of Surrey, UK
Sokratis K. Katsikas   Norwegian University of Science and Technology, Norway
Weizhi Meng   Technical University of Denmark, Denmark

Program Chairs

Jiageng Chen   Central China Normal University, China
Debiao He   Wuhan University, China
Rongxing Lu   University of New Brunswick, Canada

Steering Committee

Jiageng Chen   Central China Normal University, China
Liqun Chen   University of Surrey, UK
Steven Furnell   University of Nottingham, UK
Anthony T. S. Ho   University of Surrey, UK
Sokratis K. Katsikas   Norwegian University of Science and Technology, Norway
Javier Lopez   University of Malaga, Spain
Weizhi Meng (Chair)   Technical University of Denmark, Denmark

Publicity Chairs

Pei Li   Central China Normal University, China
Chunhua Su   University of Aizu, Japan

Publication Chairs

Shixiong Yao   Central China Normal University, China
Wenjuan Li   The Hong Kong Polytechnic University, China

Program Committee

Muhammad Rizwan Asghar	The University of Auckland, New Zealand
Francesco Buccafurri	University of Reggio Calabria, Italy
Yunhe Feng	University of Washington, USA
Debasis Giri	Maulana Abul Kalam Azad University of Technology, India
Shoichi Hirose	University of Fukui, Japan
Romain Laborde	Paul Sabatier University, France
Costas Lambrinoudakis	University of Piraeus, Greece
Giovanni Livraga	University of Milan, Italy
Wenjuan Li	Hong Kong Polytechnic University, China
Sjouke Mauw	University of Luxembourg, Luxembourg
Weizhi Meng	Technical University of Denmark, Denmark
Jun Shao	Zhejiang Gongshang University, China
Ketil Stoelen	SINTEF, Norway
Chunhua Su	Aizu University, Japan
Gang Tan	The Pennsylvania State University, USA
Je Sen Teh	Universiti Sains Malaysia, Malaysia
Hao Wang	Shandong Normal University, China
Haoyu Wang	Beijing University of Posts and Telecommunications, China
Licheng Wang	Beijing University of Posts and Telecommunications, China
Qianhong Wu	Beihang University, China
Zhe Xia	Wuhan University of Technology, China
Wun-She Yap	Universiti Tunku Abdul Rahman, Malaysia

Additional Reviewers

Dong Zhong
Qinglei Cao
Shangbin Han

Contents

Asymmetric Secure Multi-party Signing Protocol for the Identity-Based Signature Scheme in the IEEE P1363 Standard for Public Key Cryptography

Yang Liu[1,2], Qi Feng[1(✉)], Cong Peng[1], Min Luo[1], and Debiao He[1,2]

[1] Key Laboratory of Aerospace Information Security and Trusted Computing
Ministry of Education, School of Cyber Science and Engineering,
Wuhan University, Wuhan, China
`fengqi.whu@whu.edn.cn`

[2] Shanghai Key Laboratory of Privacy-Preserving Computation, MatrixElements
Technologies, Shanghai 201204, China

Abstract. The identity-based signature (IBS) is an essential cryptographic primitive for secure communication in electronic commerce and IoT network. Since there are various kinds of devices corresponding to diversified security requirements, it could be a worthwhile trade-off to preserve the secret key by signing in a multi-party setting. However, most multi-party setting solutions start with resetting their one-time secret subkey, which could be a potential leakage of sensitive information. To tackle this question, we proposed an asymmetric secure multi-party signing protocol for the identity-based signature in the IEEE P1363 standard. Specially, our multi-party signature scheme is proved to be secure against a static malicious adversary corrupting all-but-two parties under the Paillier encryption scheme's security assumptions. What's more, the performance will be presented in a theoretical analysis way to show our scheme holds reasonable communication traffic and computation cost.

Keywords: Secure multi-party computation · Identity-based signature scheme · Key protection · Internet-of-things

1 Introduction

The internet-of-things (IoT) is becoming one of the main impetuses of the digital economy. As a statistics report showing in 2022, the worldwide connected devices are forecast to almost double from 13.1 billion in 2022 to more than 29 billion IoT devices in 2030 [30], which means there could be nearly 10% growth each year. With the rapid growth in the industrial scale, the phenomenon seems to be reasonable and could be more obvious in developing countries like China. The Chinese IoT market grew by 12% in 2020 and the total market size reached 1.7 trillion CNY [27]. Moreover, the device connection may be regarded as significant

J. Chen et al. (Eds.): EISA 2022, CCIS 1641, pp. 1–20, 2022.
https://doi.org/10.1007/978-3-031-23098-1_1

support of the IoT economy. In 2018, the device connection scale has reached 3.3 billion over the country and it is forecast to be almost 20 billion by 2025 [26,28]. In the future, the growth could remain to be seen.

The IoT could receive more attention since the smart city strategy keeps in effect. Referring to the development of the AI and communication technologies, devices in the IoT will be supposed to become smart and unmanned. Generally, end sensors make data collection processes in the IoT and the authenticity of raw data might be guaranteed by signing, which is one of the main approaches to achieving authenticity. Essentially the security of these signature applications is determined by the privacy of the signing key. Since there are differentiated devices in this network, the leakage of the signing key might cause huge security damage. Actually, this security topic has been ongoing [2,25,29].

Identity-based signature (IBS) is one of the promising and user-friendly signature schemes. Comparing to the public key infrastructure (PKI) based digital signature, the parties are represented by one's customized string and their private keys are generated by a public authority. Moreover the relationship between user and public key becomes obvious and readable, so the certificates shown the old relationship have gone. The cooperation always stays in the IoT environments, which means a signature may be generated by a group of different manufacturers not a single one. A question extracted from this situation might be "how could these parties give a valid signature while private key keeps unknown for every parties". This description could be mostly sound like the multi-party computation (MPC). To protect the privacy of secret sign key among this group, the secure multi-party computation is a reasonable way.

MPC, first introduced by Yao [33], allows n parties to jointly reached a function $f(x_1, x_2, ..., x_n)$ with the secret input x_i of i-th party. This kind of protocol could be supposed to hold equity and privacy, which typically meets the requirements of peer manufacturers. Inspired by Yao's novel idea, plenty of MPC-based protocols have been proposed to tackle similar problems in different scenes [16,20,22,32]. For multi-party signature schemes, an efficient and ingenious approach is to focus on signing phase. In order to preserve the privacy of signing key bound to be input in signing phase, the Shamir's secret sharing protocol satisfies this requirement and appends a more practical threshold further. The (n, t) threshold holds the flexibility for dynamic parties in individual. The ECDSA threshold may be typical and inspiring works [17,18].

With the complement of MPC frameworks, the scenes are extended to multiple parties [3,5,8,21,23], which means the adversary ability and the security target could be more complex. To preserve equality and privacy, some cryptographic primitives like commitment, zero-knowledge proof and homomorphic encryption could be considered for construction. However, for these schemes based on Shamir's secret sharing protocol, a trusted third party dispatching secret pieces is necessary and the secret value should be regenerated at a new computation turn. What's more, some works reconstruct the private singing key in the signing phase or allow the complete reconstructed signing key to be controlled by a certain party, these design processes could result in equality of signing and private of key damages or even leak the private key.

1.1 Our Contributions

In this paper, we focus on the key protection of IBS in the IEEE P1363 and present an asymmetric secure multi-party signing protocol. Firstly, we design a new asymmetric multi-party signing protocol, in which the participate P_1 is regarded as the leader among this group. To guarantee equality, the senders could provide proof related to their inputs. At the end of the signing phase, the leader P_1 receives signature pieces from others and outputs the complete signature, which reduces the total communication and computation cost. Secondly, to show the efficiency of our scheme, we present the communication and computation cost both in theory. Since there are no complex algorithms, the analysis table presents feasibility and performance.

1.2 Paper Organization

We will organize this paper as following. In Sect. 2, we will review related works about two-party signing schemes and multiparty schemes. In Sect. 3, we will give the preliminaries used in this paper about pairing and homomorphic encryption. In Sect. 4, we will illustrate our multi-party signing protocol in detail. In Sects. 5, we perform the analysis on the security in the malicious adversary model. Then In the Sects. 6, we will present the performance of the proposed protocol about computation complex and communication traffic. Finally, Sect. 7 concludes this paper.

2 Related Work

The first two-party DSA signature scheme was proposed by MacKenzie and Reiter [20]. Typically they inspiringly adopted homomorphic encryption to reach the results like $(k_1^{-1}k_2^{-1})$ and (x_1x_2) while the tuple (k_i, x_i) is controlled by the i-th party. However there are heavy algorithms such as homomorphic encryption and zero-knowledge proof during construction. Gennaro and Goldfeder [14] presented a multi-party ECDSA-based threshold signature without the dealer key generation in order to tackle the key regeneration problem. Specifically their solution was against malicious adversary with a dishonest majority. In the meanwhile the decentralized generation of RSA key generation could be unpractical. Then Feng et al. [12] proposed a frameworks of distributed signing protocol for IEEE P1363 standard. They presented a novel approach for multi-party scalar multiplication that could bring much interest for the signature structure in this standard. Recently Xue et al. [32] proposed a scalable two-party signature for ECDSA algorithm. With the novel approaches like re-sharing of secret key and linear sharing of the nonce, their solution holds only once multiplicative-to-additive operation in the offline phase. They further extended the application to 2-out-of-n situation.

For the limitations in two-party signing protocols, there are also works aimed to the extended situation like bandwidth and multiparty signing. Doerner et al. [11] improved their previous works and proposed a new consistency check mechanism. Unlike linear increasing in Diffie-Hellman key exchange, this mechanism holds $log(n)$ increasing under arbitrary participants. Moreover it still hold performance drawbacks in some WAN setting in terms of logarithmic round. To tackle the high bandwidth cost in threshold signing, Castagnos et al. [6] proposed a variant trustless setup protocol inspired by works [14]. The variant solution adopted the CL homomorphic encryption [7] and got rid of heavy range proof. Actually the solution holds little advantages even disadvantages when security parameter $\lambda \leq 192$. Abram et al. [1] proposed the first threshold ECDSA signature protocol with logarithmic communication complexity. Inspired by the works of pseudorandom correlation generators [4], they achieved silent preprocessing, which could reduce much communication cost. Further they set a trusted dealer for seed distribution to simplify the setup phase. Unfortunately the bottleneck existed in code implement.

Except for theoretical research, the practical application could be also attractive for many researchers. For the key leakage issues in mobile devices, Zhang et al. [34] proposed a secure two-party signing protocol without recovering the signing key in mobile devices. The solution faces an extremely inefficient performance in AES-256 security. To relieve the key management in DNS operator, Dalskov et al. [9] presented a generic transformation to reach the threshold ECDSA protocol from multiparty computation protocols. By performing benchmarks with other state-of-the-art protocols, they showed the efficiency of this transformation. For the security of cryptocurrency wallets, Feng et al. [13] proposed the first two-party EdDSA signature scheme. Taking advantage of the EdDSA signature, their protocol holds an efficient signing phase and affordable communication cost on mobile devices. Aiming at the potential risk of assets embezzlement in exchanges, Wang et al. [31] proposed a dynamic threshold ECDSA signature protocol in blockchains. The dynamic threshold means a mechanism that allows trustees to join or drop off, which could be more applicable in cryptocurrency exchanges. Specifically the signature generation phase holds polynomial computation cost not linear. Liu et al. [19] proposed a collaborative SM9 signature protocol for the smart home. The key generation phase is completed by the KGC and the two key pieces are stored in the user mobile device and smart home terminal respectively. However the protocol contains heavy algorithms like homomorphic encryption and Zero-knowledge proof.

Above these reviews about related works, it remains to be done how to design a low bandwidth and lightweight two-party signature protocol. Actually this could be what we attempt to contribute in this paper.

3   Preliminaries

Firstly, we summarize the notations used in this paper. n denotes the number of participants. $\mathcal{P}_1, ..., \mathcal{P}_n$ denotes the participants of our protocol. ID is the common identity of participants. q denotes a large prime numbers. $\mathbb{G}_1, \mathbb{G}_2$ are two additive cycle groups with order q. Q_1, Q_2 are generators of $\mathbb{G}_1, \mathbb{G}_2$ while $\mathbb{G}_T$ is a multiplicative cycle group with order q. D_{ID}^{leader} denotes one partial private key for honest leader $\mathcal{P}_1$. $d_{ID}^{(2)}, \ldots, d_{ID}^{(n)}$ denotes the partial private keys for $\mathcal{P}_2, \ldots, \mathcal{P}_n$. s, P_{pub} are master secret key and public key of KGC satisfying $P_{pub} = s \cdot Q_2$. H_1, H_2 are two cryptographic hash functions. $e : \mathbb{G}_1 \times \mathbb{G}_2 \to \mathbb{G}_T$ denotes a bilinear pairing map. $\leftarrow_R$ denotes the randomly sampling operation. $E_{pk}(\cdot)/D_{sk}(\cdot)$ denotes Paillier encryption/decryption algorithms, respectively.

3.1 Bilinear Pairing

Let q be a large prime number. Let $\mathbb{G}_1$, $\mathbb{G}_2$ denotes two additive cycle groups with the order of q, and $\mathbb{G}_T$ be the multiplicative cycle group satisfying a special map $e : \mathbb{G}_1 \times \mathbb{G}_2 \to \mathbb{G}_T$. Suppose that Q_1, Q_2 are generators of $\mathbb{G}_1, \mathbb{G}_2$, we say that e is a bilinear pairing if it follows the below attributes:

- **Bilinearity:** Given two elements $U \in \mathbb{G}_1$, $V \in \mathbb{G}_2$ and two integers $s, t \in \mathbb{Z}_q^*$, then it will stand for the equation $e(s \cdot U, t \cdot V) = e(U, V)^{s \cdot t}$.
- **Nondegeneracy:** For some elements $U \in \mathbb{G}_1$, $V \in \mathbb{G}_2$, the inequation $e(U, V) \neq 1_{\mathbb{G}_T}$ holds.
- **Computability:** Given two elements $U \in \mathbb{G}_1$, $V \in \mathbb{G}_2$, there is at least one algorithm to compute $e(U, V)$ efficiently.

3.2 IEEE Standard for Identity-Based Signature

The standard is defined as follows. Let $\mathbb{G}_1$, $\mathbb{G}_2$ denotes two additive cycle groups with the order of q, and $\mathbb{G}_T$ be the multiplicative cycle group satisfying $e : \mathbb{G}_1 \times \mathbb{G}_2 \to \mathbb{G}_T$. Define the generators of $\mathbb{G}_1$ and $\mathbb{G}_2$ are Q_1 and Q_2, respectively, and $g = e(Q_1, Q_2)$. The master private key for KGC is a random number $s \leftarrow_R \mathbb{Z}_q^*$ and the master public key for KGC is an element $P_{pub} = s \cdot Q_2$. Furthermore, KGC chooses two cryptographic hash functions $H_1 : \{0,1\}^* \to \mathbb{Z}_q^*$, $H_2 : \{0,1\}^* \times \mathbb{G}_T \to \mathbb{Z}_q^*$. The system parameter is $params = \{P_{pub}, \mathbb{G}_1, \mathbb{G}_2, \mathbb{G}_T, Q_1, Q_2, g, e, H_1, H_2\}$ as public parameters, and the master private key is private parameter kept by KGC securely.

- **Extract:** When a user submits his/her identity $ID \in \{0,1\}^*$, KGC computes $d_{ID} = (s + H_1(ID))^{-1} \mod q$, $D_{ID} = d_{ID} \cdot Q_1$. Finally KGC outputs D_{ID} as the unique private key.
- **Sign:** The user with identity ID will carry out following steps to sign on message M using his/her private key D_{ID}:
  1. Generates a random number $r \in \mathbb{Z}_q^*$;
  2. Computes $u = g^r$;
  3. Computes $h = H_2(M||u)$ and $S = (r + h) \cdot D_{ID}$;
  4. Outputs $\delta = \{h, S\}$ as the final signature on message M.
- **Verify:** The verifier computes $u' = \frac{e(S, H_1(ID) \cdot Q_2 + P_{pub})}{g^h}$ and can accept a signature $\delta = \{h, S\}$ on message M if and only if $h = H_2(M||u')$ holds.

3.3 Number-Theoretic Assumptions

Then we will explain the assumptions about number-theoretic. These assumptions are the infrastructure of our proof.

Assumption 1 (Discrete Logarithm Assumption, DL Assumption). Define $\mathbb{G}$ as a group with the order of prime number q and generator of Q. The advantage to compute $x \in \mathbb{Z}_q^*$ from tuple $D = (Q, x \cdot Q)$ for any probability polynomial time (P.P.T) adversary $\mathcal{A}$ is negligible.

Assumption 2 (Computational Diffie-Hellman Assumption, CDH Assumption). Define $\mathbb{G}$ as a group with the order of prime number q and generator of Q. For unknown $x, y \in \mathbb{Z}_q^*$, the advantage to compute $x \cdot y \cdot Q$ from tuple $D = (Q, x \cdot Q, y \cdot Q)$ for any probability polynomial time (P.P.T) adversary $\mathcal{A}$ is negligible.

Assumption 3 (One-time Padding). The $x + r$ and $x \cdot r$ are uniformly random if r is a uniformly random element unknown to the adversary and is completely independent from x.

3.4 Additively Homomorphic Encryption

Our protocol is instantiated with the well-known additively homomorphic encryption scheme Paillier, which is indistinguishability under chosen plaintext attack (IND-CPA) based on the N-residuosity assumption. We recall the details as follows:

- **Key-Gen:** Given the secure parameter κ, this algorithm will generate two κ-bit prime numbers p, q, and computes $N = pq$. Sets $\lambda(N) = lcm(p-1, q-1)$ be the Carmichael function of N and chooses $\Gamma \in \mathbb{Z}_{N^2}^*$ whose order is a multiple of N. Finally, the public key is set as $\{N, \Gamma\}$ and the private key is $\{\lambda(N)\}$.
- **Encryption:** Let $E_{pk}(\cdot)$ denotes the encryption operation using the public key $\{N, \Gamma\}$ and given a message $m \in \mathbb{Z}_N$, the $E_{pk}(\cdot)$ is gone as follows with the :
  1. Generates a random number $r \in \mathbb{Z}_N^*$;
  2. Computes $c = \Gamma^m r^N \mod N^2$;
  3. Outputs $\{c\}$ as the final ciphertext of m.
- **Decryption:** Let $D_{sk}(\cdot)$ denotes the decryption operation using the private key $\{\lambda(n)\}$, and given a ciphertext $c \in \mathbb{Z}_{N^2}$, the message could be extracted as $m = \frac{\mathcal{L}(c^{\lambda(N)})}{\mathcal{L}(\Gamma^{\lambda(N)})} \mod N$, where $\mathcal{L}(u) = \frac{u-1}{N}$ over the set $\{u \in \mathbb{Z}_{N^2} : u = 1 \mod N\}$.
- **Homomorphic Properties:** Given two ciphertexts of $c_1 = E_{pk}(m_1)$ and $c_2 = E_{pk}(m_2)$, the homomorphic addition function $+_E$ is defined as $c_1 +_E c_2 = c_1 c_2 \mod N^2$ (which finally satisfies $D_{sk}(c_1 +_E c_2) = m_1 + m_2 \mod N$). Similarly, define the homomorphic scalar multiplication function $\times_E$ as $c_1 \times_E m_2 = c_1^{m_2} \mod N^2$ (which finally satisfies $D_{sk}(c_1 \times_E m_2) = m_1 \cdot m_2 \mod N$).

– **Indistinguishability under chosen-plaintext attack (IND-CPA):** The Paillier encryption scheme has proven to be IND-CPA security where for any probabilistic polynomial time (P.P.T) adversary, there exists an negligible function $negl(\cdot)$ s.t.,

$$\left\{ \begin{array}{l|l} Pr[\mathsf{PubK}^{\mathsf{CPA}}_{\mathcal{A},\Pi} = 1] & (params) \leftarrow \mathbf{Setup}(1^\lambda), \\ \leq \dfrac{1}{2} + negl(\lambda) & (pk, sk) \leftarrow \mathbf{Key\text{-}Gen}(params), \\ & c_i \leftarrow E_{pk}(m_i), \\ & \text{Sample } b \in_R \{0,1\}, c_* \leftarrow E_{pk}(m_b), \\ & \mathcal{A} \text{ guess } b', \text{ if } b' = b, \text{ then output } \mathsf{PubK}^{\mathsf{CPA}}_{\mathcal{A}} = 1. \end{array} \right\}$$

3.5 The Share Conversion Protocol $\mathcal{F}_{M2A}$

Assume that Alice and Bob hold two secrets $a, b \in \mathbb{Z}_q$ respectively which could be thought as two multiplication shares of a secret value $c = ab \mod q$. Our protocol relies on a special protocol, referred as M2A, presented in [14] for securely converting the multiplicative shares into additive shares of t_A and t_B for Alice and Bob respectively, where $t_A + t_B = c = ab \mod q$.

To be more specific, Alice holds the secret value a and is associated with the public key used in E_A. Bob holds the secret value b. Both of them follows the $\mathcal{F}_{M2A}$ as following:

1. Alice encrypts her secret value a as $c_A = E_A(a)$ and proves in zero-knowledge (ZK) that $a < k$ by a range proof. The Alice initializes the M2A protocol via sending Bob the ciphertext c_A as well as the ZK proof π_A.
2. Bob firstly checks the validity of π_A. If not, Bob aborts this session. Otherwise, Bob computes $c_B = b \times_E c_A +_E E_A(t'_B)$ (which indeed satisfies $D_A(c_B) = ab + t'_B$) where t'_B is chosen randomly from $\mathbb{Z}_n$. Bob sets $t_B = -t'_B \mod q$ and finally, responds to Alice with c_B along with the ZK proofs:
   – π^1_B that $b < k$;
   – π^2_B that "he knows b, t'_B satisfying $c_B = b \times_E c_A +_E E_A(t'_B)$".
3. Alice verifies whether π^1_B and π^2_B are correct. If so, she decrypts c_B to extract $t'_A = D_A(c_B)$ and sets $t_A = t'_A \mod q$. Otherwise, Alice aborts this session.

According to the analyses in [14], M2A protocol satisfies strong correctness and security when $n > k^2 q$. In particular, it will enforce both Alice and Bob to honestly use the correct secret values a and b respectively.

3.6 The Non-interactive Zero-Knowledge Functionality

Our maliciously secure protocol will have the parties send a non-interactive zero-knowledge (NIZK) proof of the statement. As in [10,11,17,18], we model this formally by a NIZK functionality F^R_{zk}, which is defined in Fig. 1. This functionality is associated with the following relations:

Functionality F_{zk}^R

This functionality runs with parties $P_2, \ldots, P_n$, and does:

- Upon receiving (**prove**, sid, i, x, w) from a party P_i (for $i \in 2, \ldots, n$), if sid has been previously used then ignore the message.
- Otherwise, send (**proof**, $sid, i, x, R(x, w)$) to all parties where $R(x, w) = 1$ iff $(x, w) \in R$.

Fig. 1. The NIZK functionality for relation R

1. *Knowledge of the discrete log within an additive cycle group*: Let

$$R_{DL} = \{((\mathbb{G}, P, W), w) | W = w \cdot P\}$$

define the relation of $W = w \cdot P$ within the given group $\mathbb{G}$. We utilizes the standard Sigma protocol [24]. Thus, the prover executes one exponentiation and the verifier executes two. The communication costs between them are one point in $\mathbb{G}$ and one integer in $\mathbb{Z}_q$.

2. *Knowledge of range proof for Paillier*: Define the relation:

$$R_{range} = \{((N, \Gamma, c, k), (a, r)) | c = \Gamma^a r^N \mod N^2 \wedge a < k\}.$$

where the prover wishes to prove that a encrypted in the Paillier ciphertext smaller than k. We refer to a combination of standard Schnorr proof [18]. Thus, the prover executes eight exponentiations and the verifier executes nine in totals. The communication costs between them are five integers in $\mathbb{Z}_q$, five integers in $\mathbb{Z}_N$ and one integer in $\mathbb{Z}_{N^2}$.

3. *Knowledge of range-bounded Paillier affine operation*: Define the relation:

$$R_{affine} = \{((N, \Gamma, c, d, k), (b, t)) | d = c^b \Gamma^t \mod N^2 \wedge b < k\}.$$

where the prover wishes to prove that the Paillier ciphertext d was generated from c by carrying our a homomorphic affine operation using value b, t in a given range (such an affine operation is defined bt $a \cdot b + t$ where a is the value encrypted in c). Similarly, We refer to a combination of standard Schnorr proof R_{DL} and range proof R_{range} for this. Thus, the prover executes ten exponentiations and the verifier executes nine in totals. The communication costs between them are four integers in $\mathbb{Z}_q$, seven integers in $\mathbb{Z}_N$ and one integer in $\mathbb{Z}_{N^2}$.

For clarity, we remove the parameters part (such as $\mathbb{G}$ or N, Γ) from the input below, with the understanding that these parameters relative to each party are fixed throughput.

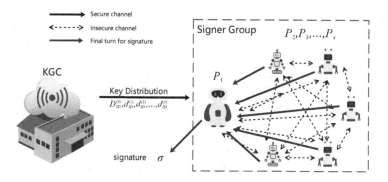

Fig. 2. The network model of our proposed protocol

4   Our Scheme

4.1   Network Model

We pay much attention to the asymmetric architecture of our scheme, for example, an IoT network. As shown in Fig. 2, assume that there are τ parties engaging in the computing process and involving two types of roles, i.e., the leading party, as well as the signing participant. In addition to parties, there will also be a key generation center KGC.

- KGC is a trusted key generation center to system setup and distributing the partial keys of parties. More specifically, according to common identity, KGC generates partial private key for each party while the total number of keys is n, which will also involving two types, i.e., one leading key and $n-1$ participant keys. Further the full private key could be reconstructed only if the all partial key are connected as they are totally independent.
- $\mathcal{P}_1$ represents a manage center in this asymmetric architecture that is responsible for launching a signing session, construct and publish the final signature. Remark that $\mathcal{P}_1$ need to be seen as a honest leading party, which means $\mathcal{P}_1$ must honestly transmit user's message to other participants, collect all the shares of signature and construct the valid signature.
- $\mathcal{P}_2 \ldots \mathcal{P}_n$ represents the subordinates in this asymmetric architecture that is mainly responsible for engaging in the signing process. Therefore, all of them can be seen as the signing participants and holds their own unique participant keys. Similarly, they must wait for $\mathcal{P}_1$'s initialization instruction and work jointly for a valid signature.

4.2   Setup Phase

In the setup phase, KGC will initialize the system as follows:

1. Chooses two additive cycle groups $\mathbb{G}_1, \mathbb{G}_2$, one multiplicative cycle group $\mathbb{G}_T$ with the order of a large prime number q.

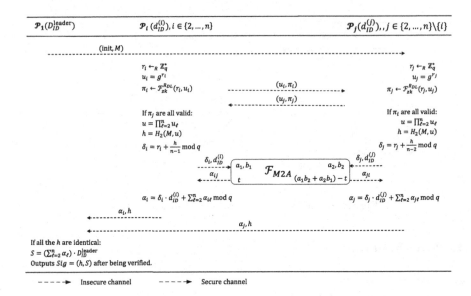

Fig. 3. Distributed signature generation phase

2. Chooses a bilinear map satisfying $e : \mathbb{G}_1 \times \mathbb{G}_2 \to \mathbb{G}_T$.
3. Generates two generators $Q_1 \in \mathbb{G}_1, Q_2 \in \mathbb{G}_2$ and calculates $g = e(Q_1, Q_2)$.
4. Chooses two cryptographic hash functions $H_1 : \{0,1\}^* \to \mathbb{Z}_q^*, H_2 : \{0,1\}^* \times \mathbb{G}_T \to \mathbb{Z}_q^*$.
5. Samples a random number $s \in \mathbb{q}_*$ as its master private key and correspondingly computes $P_{pub} = s \cdot Q_2$ as its master public key.
6. Publishes the system parameter $params = \{\mathbb{G}_1, \mathbb{G}_2, \mathbb{G}_T, Q_1, Q_2, g, e, H_1, H_2, P_{pub}\}$ and stores the master secret key s securely.

4.3   Key Distribution Phase

KGC will distribute partial private keys for parties $\mathcal{P}_1, \ldots, \mathcal{P}_n$ in this phase. When the leading party $\mathcal{P}_1$ registers with the common identity ID, KGC firstly computes $d_{ID} = (s + H_1(ID))^{-1} \mod q$. Then it chooses $n - 1$ independent random numbers $s_2, \ldots, s_n \in \mathbb{Z}_q^*$ and computes $s_1 = (\sum_{\ell=2}^n s_\ell)^{-1} \cdot d_{ID} \mod q$. Finally, KGC computes $D_{ID}^{\text{leader}} = s_1 \cdot Q_1$ as the leading key and sets $d_{ID}^{(i)} = s_i(i = 2, \ldots, n)$ as the participant keys. KGC sends $\{D_{ID}^{\text{leader}}\}$ to $\mathcal{P}_1$ and $\{d_{ID}^{(i)}\}$ to $\mathcal{P}_i$ $(i = 2, \ldots, n)$ respectively. For the distribution transmissions phase, the communication channels are assumed to be safe.

4.4   Signature Generation Phase

We now describe the distributed signature generation phase, which is run on the input of M (the message to be signed) and the outputs of key distribution phase described below. Specially, our protocol is based on the share conversion protocol $\mathcal{F}_{M2A}$ as recalled in Sect. 3.5 and standard Schnorr zero knowledge proof [24] (denoted as $\mathcal{F}_{zk}^{R_{DL}}$) for the knowledge of the describe log of a group element. Furthermore, in the description of the protocol, we denote $\mathcal{P}_i$ for all $i \in \{2, \ldots, n\}$ as the party executing the instructions and P_j for all $j \in \{2, \ldots, n\}\backslash\{i\}$ as the other parties, and we apply ℓ as a running index from 2 to n. As shown in Fig. 3, the details are as follows:

1. $\mathcal{P}_i$ generates a random number $r_i \in \mathbb{Z}_q^*$, calculates $u_i = g^{r_i}$, sends u_i to $\mathcal{P}_j$ for all $j \neq i$, and then submits $\{\mathbf{prove}, i, (g, u_i), r_i\}$ to $\mathcal{F}_{zk}^{R_{DL}}$.
   $\mathcal{P}_i$ receives $\{\mathbf{proof}, j, (g, u_j), \beta_j\}$ from $\mathcal{F}_{zk}^{R_{DL}}$, for all $j \in \{2, \ldots, n\}\backslash\{i\}$. If some $\beta_j = 0$ (which means the involving zero-knowledge proof is invalid), then $\mathcal{P}_i$ aborts this session.
2. $\mathcal{P}_i$ calculates $u = \prod_{\ell=2}^n u_\ell$, $h = H_2(M, u)$ and $\delta_i = (r_i + \frac{h}{n-1}) \mod q$.
3. Each pair of parties $\mathcal{P}_i$ and $\mathcal{P}_j$ engage in two $\mathcal{F}_{M2A}$ subprotocols:
   - $\mathcal{P}_i$ inputs $\{\delta_i\}$ and $\mathcal{P}_j$ inputs $\{d_{ID}^{(j)}\}$ to carry out the first $\mathcal{F}_{M2A}$ to get α_{ij}^1 and α_{ji}^1 respectively, which satisfying $\alpha_{ij}^1 + \alpha_{ji}^1 = \delta_i \cdot d_{ID}^{(j)} \mod q$;
   - Similarly, $\mathcal{P}_i$ inputs $\{d_{ID}^{(i)}\}$ and $\mathcal{P}_j$ inputs $\{\delta_j\}$ to carry out the second $\mathcal{F}_{M2A}$ to get α_{ij}^2 and α_{ji}^2 respectively, which satisfying $\alpha_{ij}^2 + \alpha_{ji}^2 = d_{ID}^{(i)} \cdot \delta_j \mod q$;
   - $\mathcal{P}_i$ adds up α_{ij}^1 and α_{ij}^2 to get $\alpha_{ij} = \alpha_{ij}^1 + \alpha_{ij}^2 \mod q$, similarly, $\mathcal{P}_j$ adds up α_{ji}^1 and α_{ji}^2 to get $\alpha_{ji} = \alpha_{ji}^1 + \alpha_{ji}^2 \mod q$. We can see that $\alpha_{ij} + \alpha_{ji} = \delta_i \cdot d_{ID}^{(j)} + d_{ID}^{(i)} \cdot \delta_j \mod q$ holds.
4. Each party $\mathcal{P}_i$ calculates $\alpha_i = \delta_i \cdot d_{ID}^{(i)} + \sum_{\ell=2}^n \alpha_{i\ell} \mod q$
5. All participants $\mathcal{P}_i$ send their α_i, $i = 2, \ldots, n$ and h to the leading party $\mathcal{P}_1$.
6. $\mathcal{P}_1$ checks if all the received h are identical. If any of them is inconsistent, $\mathcal{P}_1$ aborts this session. Otherwise, $\mathcal{P}_1$ calculates $S = (\sum_{\ell=2}^n \alpha_i) \cdot D_{ID}^{\text{leader}}$. $\mathcal{P}_1$ verifies $sig = (h, S)$ and message M using standard verification algorithm. If it returns unaccepted, $\mathcal{P}_1$ aborts this session; otherwise, $\mathcal{P}_1$ publishes this signature and ends the protocol.

4.5 Correctness

It is easy to get $u = g^{\sum_{i=2}^n r_i} \mod q$. As for another part of signature:

$$
\begin{aligned}
S &= \left(\sum_{\ell=2}^n \alpha_i\right) \cdot D_{ID}^{\text{leader}} = \left(\sum_{i=2}^n \delta_i \cdot d_{ID}^{(i)} + \sum_{i=2}^n \sum_{j=2}^n \delta_i \cdot d_{ID}^{(j)}\right) \cdot D_{ID}^{\text{leader}} \\
&= \left(\sum_{i=2}^n \delta_i\right) \cdot \left(\sum_{j=2}^n d_{ID}^{(j)}\right) \cdot D_{ID}^{\text{leader}} \\
&= \left(\sum_{i=2}^n (r_i + \frac{h}{n-1})\right) \cdot \left(\sum_{j=2}^n s_j\right) \cdot s_1 \cdot Q_1 \\
&= \left(\sum_{i=2}^n r_i + h\right) \cdot d_{ID} \cdot Q_1
\end{aligned}
$$

denoting $r = \sum_{i=2}^{n} r_i \mod q$. Therefore, if all of the parties holds honest behaviors , the signature $sig = (h, S)$ will be valid.

5   Security Analysis

Now we will give the clear proof for our proposed multi-party signing scheme to show the security. Here, we consider *2-out-of-n* security where if the leading party P_1 is always honest and at least one of the participants $P_2, \ldots, P_n$ is honest, the multi-party signing scheme is secure with static malicious adversary. It is feasible in IoT environment where P_1 can be set as the gateway.

Referring to the definitions in [14,15], where an adversary $\mathcal{A}$ could finally gives a complete signature against the multi-party signing scheme $\mathbb{P}$ with a non-negligible possibility ϵ. Therefore we adopt the simulator $\mathcal{S}$ and assume he could forge a original identity-based signature according to the interaction information from $\mathcal{A}$. To make sure that the protocol is secure, the adversary $\mathcal{A}$'s view must be indistinguishable for the simulation process of generation. Throughout the simulation, we denote that $\mathrm{Corrupt}(\mathcal{A}) \subset \{P_2, \ldots, P_n\}$ as the set of parties that are corrupted by $\mathcal{A}$, $\mathcal{P}_j, j \in \mathrm{Corrupt}(\mathcal{A})$ are corrupted parties and $\mathcal{P}_i, i \notin \mathrm{Corrupt}(\mathcal{A})$ is the honest party. To keep description simple, we denote the simulator algorithm as Sim. Then we could present the details of definition as following:

- $\mathrm{MPSign}_{\mathbb{P},\mathcal{A}}(\kappa; D_{ID}^{\mathsf{leader}}; \{d_{ID}^{(i)} | i \notin \mathrm{Corrupt}(\mathcal{A})\}) = \{V_j | j \in \mathrm{Corrupt}(\mathcal{A})\}, \{sig_i | i \notin \mathrm{Corrupt}(\mathcal{A})\}$ where κ is the security parameter, uncorrupted party $\mathcal{P}_i, i \notin \mathrm{Corrupt}(\mathcal{A})$ honestly participates in the signing process by holding key $d_{ID}^{(i)}$, and $\mathcal{A}$ could also obtain the inputs for corrupted parties. Let $sig_i = \{\alpha_i, h\}$ denotes the output of $\mathcal{P}_i$ and V_j denotes the view of corrupted parties (which consists of a tuple about the private keys, random variants and lists of transcripts received during the protocol).
- $\mathrm{Sim}_{\mathcal{S},\mathcal{A}}(\kappa; D_{ID}^{\mathsf{leader}}; \{d_{ID}^{(i)} | i \notin \mathrm{Corrupt}(\mathcal{A})\}) = \{V^* | \{sig_i | i \notin \mathrm{Corrupt}(\mathcal{A})\}$ where $\mathcal{S}$ executes the simulated protocol after learning the private keys $\{d_{ID}^{(j)} | j \in \mathrm{Corrupt}(\mathcal{A})\}$ from $\mathcal{A}$ who sets the inputs for the corrupted parties. Then, it computes $sig_2, \ldots, sig_n$ and gives V^* as the simulated views.

Theorem 1. *A multi-party signing protocol is secure if for any probabilistic polynomial time (P.P.T) adversary $\mathcal{A}$ there exists a simulator such that for all partial private keys of honest parties $\{d_{ID}^{(i)} | i \notin Corrupt(\mathcal{A})\}$, the distributions*

$$MPIBS_{\mathbb{P},\mathcal{A}}(\kappa; D_{ID}^{\mathsf{leader}}; \{d_{ID}^{(i)} | i \notin Corrupt(\mathcal{A})\})$$

and

$$Sim_{\mathcal{S},\mathcal{A}}(\kappa; D_{ID}^{\mathsf{leader}}; \{d_{ID}^{(i)} | i \notin Corrupt(\mathcal{A})\})$$

are indistinguishable in κ.

Then we construct a simulator S. We assume he could forge an original identity-based signature with a non-negligible possibility. indistinguishably, we set the simulation act as the honest parties P_i to communicate with corrupted P_j. Then S speaks first for every round of the proof with the rushing adversary A. Moreover the corrupted parties could receive the messages from the adversary after they get the honest parties' messages in *this* round. In this case there is no corrupted behavior in the key generation phase as we assume that KGC is a trusted party. So what the adversary A need to do is requesting the parties to sign messages $m_1, \ldots, m_K$, observing all the transcripts among the signing instances and outputting a forgery signature (h, S) on $m' \notin \{m_1, \ldots, m_K\}$ that could pass the verification.

In order to utilize the ability of A, we build a simulated protocol about the IEEE standard identity-based signature where S is a forger and A is a subroutine. Specifically when A requires a signature on fresh message m_k, S will obtain a valid signature (h_k, S_k) after he queries the sign oracle. Then it simulates the protocol with input m_k which reaches to the signature (h_k, S_k). The core indistinguishably between the simulation world and the real world will guarantee that it is the same possibility in both worlds for A to forge a signature. It required that the forged signature (h', S') about fresh m' has not been queried. We describe the details of simulation as follows.

- **Setting up:** The initialization of system could be done by KGC as we assume. Then KGC referring to the common identity ID^* to creditably distribute the partial private keys to the parties. During this process, the corrupted parties get keys, which adversary A could analyze from corrupted parties. Specifically what the A gets includes partial private keys $d_{ID}^{(j)}$ and Paillier keys $\{sk_j, pk_j\}$ used in $\mathcal{F}_{M2A}$ for $j \in \text{Corrupt}(A)$. Besides, honest parties' private keys are kept unknown to neither adversary A nor simulator S.
- **Signature generation simulation:** As the simulation goes, if some ZK proofs fail in Phase 1 and in $\mathcal{F}_{M2A}$, or the final verification in Phase 3 does not pass, S will abort just as required. The following process will take place if A require a signature of fresh message m_k:
  - Phase 1:
    1. S (acting as leading party P_1) invokes a multi-party signing instance by sending $\{\text{init}, m_k\}$ to all the parties $P_2, \ldots, P_n$.
    2. S receives the message $\{\textbf{prove}, j, (g, u_j), r_j\}$ that A sends to $\mathcal{F}_{zk}^{R_{DL}}$ for every $j \in \text{Corrupt}(A)$.
    3. S queries the signature oracle with input $\{m_k, ID^*\}$. Then he could obtain a signature $\{h_k, S_k\}$ from the oracle, thus S can compute

    $$u = g^{-h_k} \cdot e(S_k, h_1(ID^*) \cdot Q_2 + P_{pub}))$$

    (where $h_k = h_2(m_k, u)$).
    4. S selects random elements $u_i \leftarrow_R \mathbb{G}_T$ satisfying $\prod_i u_i = u \cdot \prod_j u_j^{-1}$ so as to reach h_k and S_k.
    5. S simulates $\mathcal{F}_{zk}^{R_{DL}}$ sending $\{\textbf{proof}, i, (g, u_i), 1\}$ to P_j for every $i \notin \text{Corrupt}(A)$ and $j \in \text{Corrupt}(A)$.

- Phase 2: All parties are supposed to join all the $\mathcal{F}_{M2A}^{\mathbb{G}_1}$ instances. At this point, $\mathcal{S}$ has known the values $\delta_j = r_j + \frac{h_k}{n-1} \mod q$ of corrupt parties. Therefore, $\mathcal{S}$ could always obtain one from $d_{ID}^{(i)}$ or the discrete logarithm of $\hat{u}_i$ (i.e., $\hat{r}_i = \log_g \hat{u}_i$), so that it cannot re-randomize or decrypt its shares during the process of $\mathcal{F}_{M2A}$ instances with $\mathcal{P}_j$. Thus,
  6. When executing the first $\mathcal{F}_{M2A}$ that supposes the inputs of δ_i and $d_{ID}^{(j)}$, $\mathcal{S}$ selects one random element in $\mathbb{Z}_{N^2}$ (acting as $E_{P_i}(\delta_i)$), sends it to $\mathcal{P}_j$ and receives ciphertext $c_{P_j}^1$ from $\mathcal{P}_j$;
  7. Similarly, when executing the second $\mathcal{F}_{M2A}$ that supposes the inputs of $d_{ID}^{(i)}$ and δ_j, $\mathcal{S}$ receives ciphertext $c_{P_j}^2$ from $\mathcal{P}_j$, selects one random element α_{ji}^2 in $\mathbb{Z}_q$, encrypts it using P_j's Paillier public key (acting as $d_{ID}^{(i)} \times_E c_{P_j}^2 +_E E_{P_j}(\alpha_{ij}^2)$) and returns it to $\mathcal{P}_j$;
  8. $\mathcal{S}$ sets α_{ij} as a random element in $\mathbb{Z}_q$;
  After all the execution of $\mathcal{F}_{M2A}$ instances, $\mathcal{S}$ could compute all the α_j of corrupt parties because $\mathcal{S}$ knows δ_j, d_{ID}^j, α_{ji}^2 and random tapes of corrupt parties.
- Phase 3: At this point, $\mathcal{S}$ verify the correctness of α_j and h that P_j sends to leading party $\mathcal{P}_1$ for every $j \in \text{Corrupt}(\mathcal{A})$ by checking two equations:

$$\alpha_j = \delta_j \cdot d_{ID}^{(j)} + \sum_{\ell \neq j} \alpha_{j\ell} \mod q$$

$$h = h_k$$

- Output: If no abort happens, $\mathcal{S}$ outputs $sig = (h_k, S_k)$ acting as the leading party $\mathcal{P}_1$.

Lemma 1. *Assuming that DDH and DL assumptions hold and the Paillier encryption utilized in the protocol is proven to be indistinguishability under chosen-plaintext attack (IND-CPA), then we can safely get the following two properties:*

- *A correct signature (h, S) or abort is issued according to given message m;*
- *Compared with a real execution, it holds fully indistinguishability.*

Proof. We will present the differences settings as follow.

In the first phase, after receiving the IBS signature (h_k, S_k) from oracle, $\mathcal{S}$ samples random elements u_i satisfying $\prod_i u_i = u \cdot \prod_j u_j^{-1}$ to reach (h_k, S_k). By this execution, it implicitly contributes fresh values $\hat{r}_i$ for honest parties $\mathcal{P}_i$ ($i \notin \text{Corrupt}(\mathcal{A})$) s.t. $u_i = g^{\hat{r}_i}$ and $\sum_i \hat{r}_i = r_k - \sum_j r_j \mod q$. Other transcripts associating with the $\hat{r}_i$ is the Paillier ciphertexts returned by $\mathcal{S}$ for $\mathcal{P}_i$ in the step 6) where $E_{P_i}(\delta_i) = \Gamma^{\delta_i} \gamma^N = \Gamma^{\hat{r}_i + h \cdot (n-1)^{-1}} \gamma^N$, $\alpha_i = \delta_i \cdot d_{ID}^{(i)} + \sum_{\ell \neq i} \alpha_{i\ell} = (\hat{r}_i + h \cdot (n-1)^{-1}) \cdot d_{ID}^{(i)} + \sum_{\ell \neq i} \alpha_{i\ell}$, where $\gamma, \alpha_{i\ell}$ are independently randoms. Under the assumptions of DL over $\mathbb{G}_T$, IND-CPA of Paillier's encryption and one-time padding, it obviously uncomputable for $\mathcal{A}$ to distinguish the real value of $u_i, E_{P_i}(\delta_i), \alpha_i$ from random elements. Furthermore, when putting α_i in the exponent of g, we have

$$g^{\alpha_i} = g^{(\hat{r}_i + \frac{h}{n-1}) \cdot d_{ID}^{(i)} + \sum_{\ell \neq i} \alpha_{i\ell}}$$

$$= g^{\hat{r}_i \cdot d_{ID}^{(i)}} \cdot g^{\frac{h}{n-1} \cdot d_{ID}^{(i)}} \cdot g^{\sum_{\ell \neq i} \alpha_{i\ell}}$$

$$= (u_i)^{d_{ID}^{(i)}} \cdot g^{\frac{h}{n-1} \cdot d_{ID}^{(i)}} \cdot g^{\sum_{l \in \mathrm{Corrupt}(\mathcal{A})} \alpha_{il}} \cdot g^{\sum_{j \notin \mathrm{Corrupt}(\mathcal{A})} \alpha_{ij}}$$

which means g^{α_i} is still un-distinguishable from a random elements at least one honest $d_{ID}^{(i)}, \alpha_{ij}$, which are unknown to the adversary. Similarly, when putting α_i in the exponent of Γ, we have

$$\Gamma^{\alpha_i} = \Gamma^{\hat{r}_i \cdot d_{ID}^{(i)}} \cdot \Gamma^{\frac{h}{n-1} \cdot d_{ID}^{(i)}} \cdot \Gamma^{\sum_{l \in \mathrm{Corrupt}(\mathcal{A})} \alpha_{il}} \cdot \Gamma^{\sum_{j \notin \mathrm{Corrupt}(\mathcal{A})} \alpha_{ij}}$$

$$E_{P_i}(\delta_i) = \Gamma^{\delta_i} \gamma_i^N = \Gamma^{\hat{r}_i} \cdot \Gamma^{\frac{h}{n-1}} \gamma_i^N$$

$$c_i = d_{ID}^{(i)} \times_E E_{P_j}(\delta_j) +_E E_{P_j}(\alpha_{ij}^2) = (\Gamma^{\delta_j} \gamma_j^N)^{d_{ID}^{(i)}} \cdot \Gamma^{\alpha_{ij}^2}$$

Obliviously it is un-distinguishable for $\mathcal{A}$ to distinguish Γ^{α_i} from a random value of $\mathbb{Z}_{N^2}$ under the DDH assumption.

During the $\mathcal{F}_{M2A}$ protocol, $\mathcal{S}$ firstly simulates $\mathcal{P}_i$ to encrypt δ_i to P_j. The instructions is $E_{P_i}(\delta_i)$ in the real protocol; and in the simulated protocol this ciphertext is chosen randomly by $\mathcal{S}$ from $\mathbb{Z}_{N^2}$. On the other hand, $\mathcal{S}$ simulates $\mathcal{P}_i$ to re-randomize the ciphertext from $\mathcal{P}_j$. The instructions is $c_i = d_{ID}^{(i)} \times_E E_{P_j}(\delta_j) +_E E_{P_j}(\alpha_{ij}^2)$ in the real protocol; and $\mathcal{S}$ also chooses random c_i from $\mathbb{Z}_{N^2}$ in the simulated protocol. It should be noted that according to the IND-CPA security assumption of Paillier encryption, we will get that the randomly selected ones obtain correct ciphertexts, which is completely computationally indistinguishable under the view of adversary $\mathcal{A}$.

Finally, the simulator $\mathcal{S}$ could always either output the correct signature (h_k, S_k) acting as the leading party $\mathcal{P}_1$ or abort if some verification fails. Since that (h_k, S_k) is a valid signature on m_k returned from the signature oracle, we can conclude that the output between the real execution and simulated execution are totally identical.

Theorem 2. *Under the assumptions of original identity-based signature scheme and Paillier encryption in the presence of static malicious adversary corrupting all-but-two parties. Protocol in Sect. 4 securely computes the identity-based signature in IEEE P1363 standard.*

Proof. Based on the **Lemma** 1, the $\mathcal{A}$ gets an indistinguishable view from the simulation $\mathcal{S}$. Then $\mathcal{A}$ could output the forgery with the same possibility ϵ as in real world. With the forgery from $\mathcal{A}$, $\mathcal{S}$ could learning from this forgery and output his fake in this asymmetric architecture with the same possibility.

As the security of the IEEE P1363 standard IBS scheme has been proven by decades, it must be negligible for $\mathcal{S}$ to forge successfully, which means that ϵ must also be negligible. Finally, there is no such $\mathcal{A}$ to forge our proposed multi-party signature generation protocol with non-negligible probability.

6   Performance Analysis

In this section, we will present the analysis of the asymmetric secure multi-party SM9 signing protocol. Specifically we give the comparison between the multi-party signature and the original signature. The related denotation are: C_{qadd} denotes the addition operation in $\mathbb{F}_q$. C_{qmul} denotes the multifunction operation in $\mathbb{F}_q$. C_{qinv} denotes the invitation operation in $\mathbb{F}_q$. C_{sm1} denotes the scalar multiplication operation in $\mathbb{G}_1$. C_{exp} denotes the exponentiation operation in $\mathbb{G}_T$. C_{mul} denotes the multiplication operation in $\mathbb{G}_T$. C_{h} denotes the secure hash operation. C_{M2A} denotes the operation of share protocol $\mathcal{F}_{\text{M2A}}$. C_{zkDL} denotes the operation of zero knowledge proof $\mathcal{F}_{zk}^{R_{DL}}$. C_{Verf} denotes the verification operation of original signature scheme. L_{Fq} denotes the size of element in $\mathbb{F}_q$. L_{ID} denotes the size of ID in key distribution phase. L_{G1} denotes the size of element in $\mathbb{G}_1$. L_{GT} denotes the size of element in $\mathbb{G}_T$. L_{M2A} denotes the size of output in share protocol $\mathcal{F}_{\text{M2A}}$. L_{zkDL} denotes the size of output in zero knowledge proof $\mathcal{F}_{zk}^{R_{DL}}$. Considering the obvious comparison, we analyze the differences in two dimensions and two phases. The dimensions are computation complexity and communication traffic. In detail, we display differences in the key distribution and signing phase as the setup and verification phases are a little trivial.

In the key distribution phase, participant $\mathcal{P}_1$ inputs the ID and the KGC distributes the participant keys. Specifically this process mainly includes the computation of d_{ID} and D_{ID}^{leader}. As the denotation is shown in Table 1. We obtain the computation complexity C_{KeyDis} and communication traffic L_{KeyDis} in this phase could be

$$C_{\text{KeyDis}} = C_{\text{h}} + nC_{\text{qadd}} + 2C_{\text{qinv}} + C_{\text{qmul}} + C_{\text{sm1}}$$
$$L_{\text{KeyDis}} = L_{\text{ID}} + nL_{\text{Fq}} + L_{\text{G1}}$$

totally. In conclusion, these two factors in this phase are both increasing approximately linearly with the number of participants n.

In the signing phase, the participants start or receive communication with each other. To reach the final complete signature, the intermediate results are sent to the participant $\mathcal{P}_1$. For example, we could analyze from the perspective of $\mathcal{P}_i$. After sampling a random number r_i and obtaining u_i, $\mathcal{P}_i$ computes the proof π_i. Then $\mathcal{P}_i$ could have communications with the remained participants. Next $\mathcal{P}_i$ obtains values u, h, δ_i before starting the process of share protocol $\mathcal{F}_{\text{M2A}}$. Finally each participant computes the last intermediate results and sends them to $\mathcal{P}_1$. We obtain the computation complexity C_{DisSig} and communication traffic L_{DisSig} in this phase could be

$$C_{\text{DisSig}} = C_{\text{exp}} + C_{\text{zkDL}} + (n-1)C_{\text{mul}} + (n-1)C_{\text{M2A}}$$
$$+ C_{\text{h}} + C_{\text{qmul}} + (n^2 - 1)C_{\text{qadd}} + C_{\text{sm1}} + C_{\text{Verf}}$$
$$L_{\text{DisSig}} = nL_{\text{GT}} + nL_{\text{zkDL}} + nL_{\text{M2A}} + (n-1)L_{\text{Fq}}$$

totally. In conclusion, these two factors in this phase are both increasing approximately linearly with the number of participants n.

Table 1. Cost comparison analysis

Item	Ours	Original
Key distribution (computation)	$C_h + nC_{qadd} + 2C_{qinv}$ $+C_{qmul} + C_{sm1}$	$C_h + C_{qadd} + C_{qmul}$ $+C_{qinv} + C_{sm1}$
Key distribution (communication)	$L_{ID} + nL_{Fq} + L_{G1}$	–
Signing (computation)	$C_{exp} + C_{zkDL} + (n-1)C_{mul}$ $+(n-1)C_{M2A} + C_h + C_{qmul}$ $+(n^2-1)C_{qadd} + C_{sm1} + C_{Verf}$	$C_{exp}+C_h+C_{qadd}+C_{sm1}$
Signing (communication)	$nL_{GT} + nL_{zkDL}$ $+nL_{M2A} + (n-1)L_{Fq}$	–

Finally the whole comparison is shown in Table 1. As we can see, the key distribution phase is nearly closed to the original one. The multiparty signing phase could be approximately linearly increasing in terms of computation complexity and communication traffic. The performance could be influenced by the detailed construction of the sharing protocol.

Moreover, we implement this scheme based on the MIRECL and our environment of evaluation is Windows 11(Intel(R) Core(TM) i7-9700 CPU @ 3.00 GHz 3.00 GHz). Initially we start with the two-party situation and extend to the multiparty cases. In addition we adapt our scheme into semi-honest model and malicious adversary model to show the performance. About the zero-knowledge proof and sharing protocol, we will take references in works [18] and [14]. What we should underline is that we implement this in a simple single-thread way for the limitation of experiments.

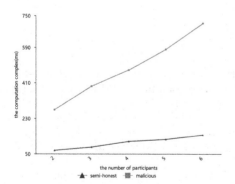
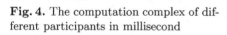
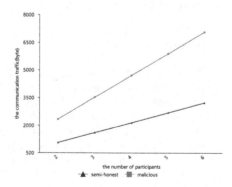

Fig. 4. The computation complex of different participants in millisecond

Fig. 5. The communication traffic of different participants in byte

Every evaluation item is executed 1000 times in order to reduce the error range. Our evaluations include computation complex and communication traffic. Firstly, we run these evaluations about computation complex in these two models, in which our scheme is presented in Sect. 4. The evaluation is presented in Fig. 4 and Fig. 5. For the malicious adversary model, our scheme gets about 712.94 ms time for 6 participants, about 475.53 ms for 4 participants and about 275.13 ms for 2 participants as shown in Fig. 4. As a comparison, our scheme gets about 147.40 ms for 6 participants, about 113.93 ms for 4 participants and about 68.46 ms for 2 participants in the semi-honest model. The performance could present the feasibility and practicability of our scheme.

As for the communication traffic, we could get the size of the element in $\mathbb{G}_1$, $\mathbb{G}_2$ and $\mathbb{G}_T$ is 64, 128 and 384 bytes respectively. As shown in Fig. 5, the communication traffic in the malicious adversary model could increase linearly with the number of participants.

7   Conclusion

Since the IoT keeps rapidly increasing, the ending devices could be more smart and multifunction. During the process of guaranteeing data authenticity, key management could be the main building block of privacy protection. Therefore, a secure multiparty signing protocol is an efficient and reasonable solution to tackle this situation. To reduce the communication cost, the final complete signature is generated by a specific participant based on the intermediate results of all participants in our protocol. As a potential direction of research and future works, we will evaluate this protocol in a simulated or real IoT environment and explore lower communication cost multiparty signing protocols meanwhile.

Acknowledgments. We would like to thank the anonymous reviewers. The work was supported by the National Key Research and Development Program of China (No. 2018YFC1604000) and the National Natural Science Foundation of China (Nos. 61972294, 62172307, 62202339).

References

1. Abram, D., Nof, A., Orlandi, C., Scholl, P., Shlomovits, O.: Low-bandwidth threshold ECDSA via pseudorandom correlation generators. In: 2022 IEEE Symposium on Security and Privacy (SP), pp. 2554–2572. IEEE (2022)
2. Alharbi, F., Alrawais, A., Rabiah, A.B., Richelson, S., Abu-Ghazaleh, N.: {CSProp}: ciphertext and signature propagation {Low-Overhead}{Public-Key} cryptosystem for {IoT} environments. In: 30th USENIX Security Symposium (USENIX Security 21), pp. 609–626 (2021)
3. Araki, T., Furukawa, J., Lindell, Y., Nof, A., Ohara, K.: High-throughput semi-honest secure three-party computation with an honest majority. In: Proceedings of the 2016 ACM SIGSAC Conference on Computer and Communications Security, pp. 805–817 (2016)
4. Boyle, E., Couteau, G., Gilboa, N., Ishai, Y., Kohl, L., Scholl, P.: Efficient pseudorandom correlation generators: silent OT extension and more. In: Boldyreva, A., Micciancio, D. (eds.) CRYPTO 2019. LNCS, vol. 11694, pp. 489–518. Springer, Cham (2019). https://doi.org/10.1007/978-3-030-26954-8_16

5. Boyle, E., Gilboa, N., Ishai, Y., Nof, A.: Practical fully secure three-party computation via sublinear distributed zero-knowledge proofs. In: Proceedings of the 2019 ACM SIGSAC Conference on Computer and Communications Security, pp. 869–886 (2019)
6. Castagnos, G., Catalano, D., Laguillaumie, F., Savasta, F., Tucker, I.: Bandwidth-efficient threshold EC-DSA. In: Kiayias, A., Kohlweiss, M., Wallden, P., Zikas, V. (eds.) PKC 2020. LNCS, vol. 12111, pp. 266–296. Springer, Cham (2020). https://doi.org/10.1007/978-3-030-45388-6_10
7. Castagnos, G., Laguillaumie, F.: Linearly homomorphic encryption from DDH. In: Nyberg, K. (ed.) CT-RSA 2015. LNCS, vol. 9048, pp. 487–505. Springer, Cham (2015). https://doi.org/10.1007/978-3-319-16715-2_26
8. Chandran, N., Garay, J.A., Mohassel, P., Vusirikala, S.: Efficient, constant-round and actively secure MPC: beyond the three-party case. In: Proceedings of the 2017 ACM SIGSAC Conference on Computer and Communications Security, pp. 277–294 (2017)
9. Dalskov, A., Orlandi, C., Keller, M., Shrishak, K., Shulman, H.: Securing DNSSEC keys via threshold ECDSA from generic MPC. In: Chen, L., Li, N., Liang, K., Schneider, S. (eds.) ESORICS 2020. LNCS, vol. 12309, pp. 654–673. Springer, Cham (2020). https://doi.org/10.1007/978-3-030-59013-0_32
10. Doerner, J., Kondi, Y., Lee, E., Shelat, A.: Secure two-party threshold ECDSA from ECDSA assumptions. In: 2018 IEEE Symposium on Security and Privacy (SP), pp. 980–997. IEEE (2018)
11. Doerner, J., Kondi, Y., Lee, E., Shelat, A.: Threshold ECDSA from ECDSA assumptions: the multiparty case. In: 2019 IEEE Symposium on Security and Privacy (SP), pp. 1051–1066. IEEE (2019)
12. Feng, Q., He, D., Liu, Z., Wang, D., Choo, K.K.R.: Distributed signing protocol for IEEE P1363-compliant identity-based signature scheme. IET Inf. Secur. 14(4), 443–451 (2020)
13. Feng, Q., He, D., Luo, M., Li, Z., Choo, K.K.R.: Practical secure two-party EdDSA signature generation with key protection and applications in cryptocurrency. In: 2020 IEEE 19th International Conference on Trust, Security and Privacy in Computing and Communications (TrustCom), pp. 137–147. IEEE (2020)
14. Gennaro, R., Goldfeder, S.: Fast multiparty threshold ECDSA with fast trustless setup. In: Proceedings of the 2018 ACM SIGSAC Conference on Computer and Communications Security, pp. 1179–1194 (2018)
15. Hazay, C., Lindell, Y.: Efficient Secure Two-party Protocols: Techniques and Constructions. Springer, Heidelberg (2010). https://doi.org/10.1007/978-3-642-14303-8
16. He, D., Zhang, Y., Wang, D., Choo, K.K.R.: Secure and efficient two-party signing protocol for the identity-based signature scheme in the IEEE P1363 standard for public key cryptography. IEEE Trans. Dependable Secure Comput. 17(5), 1124–1132 (2018)
17. Lindell, Y.: Fast secure two-party ECDSA signing. In: Katz, J., Shacham, H. (eds.) CRYPTO 2017. LNCS, vol. 10402, pp. 613–644. Springer, Cham (2017). https://doi.org/10.1007/978-3-319-63715-0_21
18. Lindell, Y., Nof, A.: Fast secure multiparty ECDSA with practical distributed key generation and applications to cryptocurrency custody. In: Proceedings of the 2018 ACM SIGSAC Conference on Computer and Communications Security, pp. 1837–1854 (2018)

19. Liu, S.G., Liu, R., Rao, S.Y.: Secure and efficient two-party collaborative SM9 signature scheme suitable for smart home. J. King Saud Univ.-Comput. Inf. Sci. **34**(7), 4022–4030 (2022)
20. MacKenzie, P., Reiter, M.K.: Two-party generation of DSA signatures. In: Kilian, J. (ed.) CRYPTO 2001. LNCS, vol. 2139, pp. 137–154. Springer, Heidelberg (2001). https://doi.org/10.1007/3-540-44647-8_8
21. Mohassel, P., Rosulek, M., Zhang, Y.: Fast and secure three-party computation: The garbled circuit approach. In: Proceedings of the 22nd ACM SIGSAC Conference on Computer and Communications Security, pp. 591–602 (2015)
22. Nicolosi, A., Krohn, M.N., Dodis, Y., Mazieres, D.: Proactive two-party signatures for user authentication. In: NDSS (2003)
23. Patra, A., Ravi, D.: On the exact round complexity of secure three-party computation. J. Cryptol. **34**(4), 1–77 (2021)
24. Schnorr, C.P.: Efficient identification and signatures for smart cards. In: Brassard, G. (ed.) CRYPTO 1989. LNCS, vol. 435, pp. 239–252. Springer, New York (1990). https://doi.org/10.1007/0-387-34805-0_22
25. Shim, K.A., Park, C.M., Koo, N., Seo, H.: A high-speed public-key signature scheme for 8-b IoT-constrained devices. IEEE Internet Things J. **7**(4), 3663–3677 (2020)
26. Slotta, D.: Annual growth rate of internet-of-things (IoT) connections in China from 2016 to 2018 with a forecast until 2025. https://www.statista.com/statistics/1194809/china-growth-of-iot-connection-number/. Accessed 3 Aug 2022
27. Slotta, D.: Market size of internet-of-things (IoT) in China from 2009 to 2020 with an estimate until 2025. https://www.statista.com/statistics/972077/china-internet-of-things-iot-market-size/. Accessed 3 Aug 2022
28. Slotta, D.: Number of internet-of-things (IoT) connections in China in 2015 and 2020 with estimates until 2025. https://www.statista.com/statistics/1026076/china-number-of-iot-connections/. Accessed 3 Aug 2022
29. Sun, J., Su, Y., Qin, J., Hu, J., Ma, J.: Outsourced decentralized multi-authority attribute based signature and its application in IoT. IEEE Trans. Cloud Comput. **9**(3), 1195–1209 (2019)
30. Vailshery, L.S.: Number of internet of things (IoT) connected devices worldwide from 2019 to 2030. https://www.statista.com/statistics/1183457/iot-connected-devices-worldwide/. Accessed 3 Aug 2022
31. Wang, H., Ma, W., Deng, F., Zheng, H., Wu, Q.: Dynamic threshold ECDSA signature and application to asset custody in blockchain. J. Inf. Secur. Appl. **61**, 102805 (2021)
32. Xue, H., Au, M.H., Xie, X., Yuen, T.H., Cui, H.: Efficient online-friendly two-party ECDSA signature. In: Proceedings of the 2021 ACM SIGSAC Conference on Computer and Communications Security, pp. 558–573 (2021)
33. Yao, A.C.: Protocols for secure computations. In: 23rd Annual Symposium on Foundations of Computer Science (SFCS 1982), pp. 160–164. IEEE (1982)
34. Zhang, Y., He, D., Zeadally, S., Wang, D., Choo, K.K.R.: Efficient and provably secure distributed signing protocol for mobile devices in wireless networks. IEEE Internet Things J. **5**(6), 5271–5280 (2018)

A Multi-task Mobile Crowdsensing Scheme with Conditional Privacy Preserving for Vehicle Networks

Zhe Xia[1,2]($\boxtimes$), Shiyun Liu[1], Yichen Huang[1], Hua Shen[3], and Mingwu Zhang[3]

[1] School of Computer Science and Artificial Intelligence,
Wuhan University of Technology, Wuhan, China
`xiazhe@whut.edu.cn`
[2] Hubei Key Laboratory of Transportation Internet of Things,
Wuhan University of Technology, Wuhan, China
[3] School of Computer Science, Hubei University of Technology,
Wuhan, Hubei, China

Abstract. Mobile crowdsensing recruits a group of users and utilizes their sensing devices to accomplish the sensing task. It can offer a flexible and scalable sensing paradigm with low deploying costs. As the development of vehicle networks, many works in the literature have investigated how to use vehicles as the sensing units for mobile crowdsensing. However, the majority of these works suffer some limitations. First, they can either achieve privacy preserving or supervision, but not both. Second, they mainly consider a single sensing task and overlook the management of users' reputations across multiple tasks. To address these limitations, we propose a multi-task mobile crowdsensing scheme with conditional privacy preserving for vehicle networks. In our proposed scheme, the privacy preserving requirement and the supervision requirement can be harmonized, achieving a property called conditional privacy preserving. Moreover, each vehicle can participate in multiple sensing tasks at the same time. Specifically, privacy protection covers identity privacy, location privacy and reputation privacy simultaneously. And the reputation center does not need to store any internal information (e.g. random numbers or ephemeral keys) when updating the vehicles' pseudonyms, reducing the risks of Denial-of-Service (DoS) attacks. Therefore, it provides a more secure and practical solution for mobile crowdsensing. Security analyses prove that our scheme achieves the desirable security requirements, such as correctness, conditional privacy preserving and authentication. And efficiency analyses demonstrate that our scheme can be used efficiently in multi-task mobile crowdsensing.

Keywords: Mobile crowdsensing · Conditional privacy preserving · Reputation management · Vehicular networks

J. Chen et al. (Eds.): EISA 2022, CCIS 1641, pp. 21–36, 2022.
https://doi.org/10.1007/978-3-031-23098-1_2

1   Introduction

With the development of mobile Internet and the wide deployment of intelligent devices with sensors, the concept of mobile crowdsensing (MCS) [1] has been introduced. Due to its abilities in perceiving, collecting, and analyzing information about the surrounding environment, MCS has become a very attractive technique that has been widely used in various areas, such as transportation, medical treatment and healthcare. Recently, vehicles are equipped with more sensors and become more intelligent, and it is natural to use them as sensor nodes in mobile crowdsensing [2,3]. Moreover, vehicular networks enjoys many advantages, such as high mobility, low energy consumption, convenient installation and maintenance. Hence, their use in MCS has attracted more and more attentions both in the academia and industry. In vehicular networks, the MCS architecture mainly consists of three entities: *data requesters, a cloud server,* and *sensing vehicles.*

The sensing vehicles can perform sensing tasks when they moving round the rural and urban areas [2], which makes them suitable for applications with the mobility requirement. However, the openness of vehicular networks makes them vulnerable to various attacks. For example, the sensors and controllers of the vehicle might be controlled or tampered by adversaries. Malicious sensing vehicles can not only forge and tamper the data, violating the authenticity and integrity of data, but also steal sensitive information such as identity and location, decreasing users' acceptance about this new technology. To address this issue, the reputation value is often used to evaluate the trustworthy of the vehicles [4–6]. This value is normally issued and managed by the reputation center as follows: the cloud server evaluates the trustworthy of the vehicle through the accuracy of the sensing data, and it sends the feedback report to the reputation center, who then updates the reputation value of the vehicle accordingly. However, when the sensing vehicle participates in multiple sensing tasks simultaneously, it will become more challenging to manage the reputation value. Besides, achieving privacy protection in location and identity already cause large overheads in communication and computing. If the reputation value is also protected, the system may become even more complex.

In recent years, many MCS schemes have used the reputation value to evaluate the trustworthy of participants. However, most of these schemes only consider privacy protection of vehicle's identity [7] and location [8], but the reputation value was not considered [8,9]. The consequence is that malicious adversaries may use the reputation value to infer the vehicle's trajectory or even its identity. Besides, most existing schemes only consider a single sensing task, and they cannot be used in multi-task sensing. Moreover, in the existing privacy protection schemes based on pseudonyms, the cloud server needs to store the random numbers when updating pseudonyms. This not only causes large storage overheads, but also makes the system vulnerable to the denial-of-service (DoS) attacks.

Apart from the above issues, conditional privacy preserving is also a crucial requirement in vehicular networks [10]. On one hand, adversaries may intercept the communications to derive many sensitive information, which may cause serious consequences on privacy leakage. On the other hand, the trusted authority needs to perform effective supervision, e.g. extract the real identity of some vehicle if necessary [11]. Therefore, conditional privacy preserving should be provided to harmonize the privacy preserving and the supervision requirements in vehicular networks. This stringent requirement requires that the trusted authority must be the only entity who can extract the real identity, location, and reputation value of a vehicle.

To address the above challenges, we propose a multi-task mobile crowdsensing scheme with conditional privacy preserving for vehicular networks. The major contributions of this paper are summarized as follows:

- The proposed scheme can be used in multi-task sensing, and it achieves conditional privacy preserving for identity, location, and reputation value simultaneously.
- When updating the pseudonyms of the sensing vehicles, the reputation center does not need to record any internal status (such as random numbers or ephemeral keys), which not only reduce the risks of DoS attacks, but also lowers the storage overheads.
- Security analyses prove that our scheme achieves the desirable security requirements, such as correctness, conditional privacy preserving and authentication, and efficiency analyses demonstrate that our scheme can be used efficiently in multi-task mobile crowdsensing.

The rest of the paper is organized as follows. Section 2 reviews some related works. Section 3 describes some preliminaries that will be used in our proposed scheme. Section 4 introduces the system and security models, and Sect. 5 presents our proposed scheme. Section 6 provides security and efficiency analyses. Finally, conclusion and discussion are included in Sect. 7.

2   Related Works

To achieve privacy protection in mobile crowdsensing based on vehicular networks, many existing schemes have considered identity and location privacy. Ni et al. [5] have used matrices to record the sensing area and sensing task, then randomized matrix multiplication is used to obtain matching of sensing tasks. Wang et al. [8] have proposed a novel area obfuscation mechanism by combining ε-differential-privacy with δ-distortion-privacy in sparse MCS to tackle the privacy protection for vehicle's location. Sun et al. [9] have used homomorphic encryption to achieve privacy protection. Zhao et al. [12] have assured statistics privacy using zero-knowledge proofs. However, the communication and computation overheads are quite heavy in these schemes, failing to meet the demands in real-world applications.

In order to evaluate the trustworthy of sensing vehicles, many researchers suggest to use the reputation value. Then, one can judge whether some vehicle is qualified to participate in the sensing tasks. In particular, some schemes have adapted the mechanism to update the reputation value in real time, e.g. at the end of each sensing task, the vehicle will be given a corresponding reputation value. However, these schemes have not considered the multi-task environment [13]. Afterwards, some reputation value management schemes suggest that one should not only update the reputation value of a single task, but also calculate the weight of the new reputation value based on the reputation feedback report and the vehicle's original reputation value [14–16].

Obviously, vehicles' reputation values also need to be protected. Otherwise, if this information is leaked, the adversaries may use it to infer the trajectory and driving pattern. However, most existing schemes in the literature have not considered the protection of reputation values. For example, Liu [16] has proposed a reputation management scheme, in which the reputation value is used to collect high-quality sensor data, but it is easy to be intercepted or tampered with. Although the scheme in [5] has suggested to transmit and store the reputation value in a threshold fashion, the protection can only be enhanced to some extent and the reputation value still may be inferred by adversaries. Afterwards, the scheme in [17] replaces each reputation value with a hash value to achieve lightweight privacy preserving for reputation value. But since hash function is deterministic, adversaries can still learn some information of the reputation value if its space is limited.

Regarding the conditional privacy preserving requirement, Raya [11] has proposed a conditional privacy preserving authentication scheme with anonymous certificates. Many public/private key pairs and the corresponding certificates are pre-loaded into vehicles' OBUs to protect the identity. But this scheme suffers some disadvantages. First, both the vehicle and the trusted third party need large storage space to store the data. Second, when a malicious vehicle sends a faulty message, it takes a long time to recover its identity. To address these weaknesses, Lu et al. [10] have proposed a modified CPPA scheme using anonymous certificates, in which the vehicle obtains a temporary anonymous certificate when it drives pass an RSU. To achieve conditional privacy preserving, each vehicle has to request a new anonymous certificate from an RSU frequently, as the adversary can trace a vehicle if the certificate is used over a long period. Zhang et al. [7] have presented a novel CPPA scheme by leveraging pseudonyms. And the ID-based signature tied to pseudonymous is used to guarantee the entities' privacy in [19].

To sum up, the existing schemes still suffer some limitations. First, either they have not considered conditional privacy preserving, or the protection has not covered the reputation value. Second, they mainly consider a single sensing task and overlook the management of users' reputation across multiple tasks. To address these limitations. We propose a multi-task mobile crowdsensing scheme with conditional privacy preserving for vehicle networks. Hence, it provides a more secure and practical solution for mobile crowdsensing.

3   Preliminaries

In this section, we review some preliminaries that will be used to design our proposed scheme, including homomorphic encryption [20], and the BCP encryption scheme [22].

3.1 Homomorphic Encryption

Paillier' s cryptosystem [20] is one of the most widely used encryption scheme with the additive homomorphic property. Suppose we have N encrypted data under the same public key pk, denoted as $[m_i]_{pk}$ $(i = 1, 2, \ldots, N)$. The additive homomorphic encryption ensures that the following equation always holds

$$D_{sk} \left(\prod_{i=1}^{N} [m_i]_{pk} \right) = \sum_{i=1}^{N} m_i$$

where $D_{sk}()$ represents the corresponding decryption algorithm with private key sk. Liu [21] has proposed some extensions that can be used as toolkit for processing encrypted data, including *Secure Less Than* Protocol (SLT) and *Secure Equivalent Testing* Protocol (SEQ). Given two encrypted numbers $[x]_{pk}$ and $[y]_{pk}$, the SLT protocol can compute a bit in the encrypted form, depending on whether $x \geq y$ or $x < y$. And the SEQ protocol can compute a bit in the encrypted form, depending on whether the plaintext of the two encrypted data are equal (i.e. $x = y$).

3.2 The BCP Encryption Scheme

The BCP encryption scheme [22] works as follows:

KeyGen: Given two large primes p, q, and $n = p * q$. Let g and h be two elements of maximal order in G, where G is the cyclic group of quadratic residues modulo n^2. Note that, if h is computed as $g^x \bmod n^2$, where $x \in \left[1, \lambda\left(n^2\right)\right]$ and $\lambda(*)$ is the Euler function, then x is coprime with $\mathrm{ord}(G)$ with high probability, and thus h is of maximal order. The public parameters are n, g and $h = g^x \bmod n^2$, and the secret value is $x \in [1, \mathrm{ord}(G)]$

Enc: Given a message $m \in Z_n$, choose a random number r in Z_n^*. The ciphertext is computed as $[m] = (T, T') = \{h^r(1 + mn), g^r\} \bmod n^2$.

Decryption With Weak Private Key (WDec): with the secret key x, the plaintext m can be retrieved as follows: $m = L\left(T / (T')^x \bmod n^2\right)$, where $L(u) = (u - 1)/n$.

Decryption With Strong Private Key (SDec): any ciphertext can be decrypted with the strong private key $SK = \lambda(n)$ by calculating:

$$T^{\lambda(n)} \bmod n^2 = g^{xr\lambda(n)}(1 + mn\lambda(n)) \bmod n^2 = 1 + mn\lambda(n)$$

Then, m can be recovered as follow:

$$m = L\left(T^{\lambda(n)} \bmod n^2\right) \cdot \lambda(n)^{-1} \bmod n$$

4 Models and Definitions

In this section, we describe the system model, security model, and security requirements.

4.1 System Model

The system model is shown as in Fig. 1 that consists of five entities: data requester, cloud server, reputation center, roadside unit, and sensing vehicle.

Fig. 1. The system architecture of proposed scheme.

Data Requester: It can be a management department, a service department, or an authorized individual. It assigns the sensing tasks in order to obtain some valuable information, such as road information, weather information, congestion level, etc.

Cloud Server: It collects, stores, and computes the encrypted sensing data. In addition, the cloud server evaluates the trustworthy of vehicles based on the accuracy of their submitted sensing data, and it generates the reputation feedback report. The cloud servers typically have strong storage and computing capabilities.

Reputation Center: It is responsible for verifying, storing, and distributing the reputation values and pseudonyms to each sensing vehicle. In addition, the reputation center updates the vehicles' reputation values based on the reputation feedback reports.

Roadside Unit (RSU): It is deployed on both sides of the road that is responsible for data transmission. Specifically, the RSU provides data transmission services between cloud servers and sensing vehicles, as well as between reputation centers and sensing vehicles.

Sensing Vehicle: It is generally equipped with various sensors, that are responsible for collecting and storing many types of environment data. Each sensing vehicle is also equipped with an on-board unit OBU [23,24] that can store secret information, such as secret keys, identities, locations, etc.

4.2   Security Model

The data requester, the cloud server, and the RSUs are all assumed to be honest-but-curious, i.e. they will follow the protocol, but they may try to obtain information beyond their authorization. For example, in the mobile crowdsensing environment based on vehicular networks, these honest-but-curious entities may intend to learn the location, identity, and reputation information of the sensing vehicles, called *inference attack* (includes location inference attack, identity inference attack, and reputation inference attack). Besides, if a malicious adversary intercepts a series of reputation values with respect to the same sensing vehicle, she may infer some other information such as its driving mode, and this attack is denoted as *reputation linkable attack*.

The reputation center is assumed to be fully trusted. The majority of the sensing vehicles are assumed to be honest, while the minority of dishonest vehicles may implement the following attacks:

- *Data pollution attack.* Malicious sensing vehicles may submit false sensing data, which may pollute the sensing results.
- *Sybil attack.* Malicious sensing vehicles may submit the same data many times or use fake identities in order to obtain a higher reputation or destroy the sensing results.
- *Reputation tamper attack.* Malicious sensing vehicles with low reputation value may tamper with the reputation value, so that they can participate in the sensing task that they are not authorized to.

4.3   Security Requirements

The following security requirements are considered in our proposed scheme:

- *Correctness.* If all participants execute the protocol honestly, the protocol will generate correct outputs.
- *Conditional privacy preserving.* Privacy protection are enforced on identity, location and reputation value from the adversaries, and this information can be retrieved by the trusted authority if necessary. In particular, identity privacy means that during the communication between the sensing vehicle and other entities, the adversaries cannot extract its real identity. Location privacy means that malicious adversaries cannot learn about the locations of sensing vehicles through messages. Reputation value privacy ensures that vehicles' reputation values should not be exposed or linked. However, the trusted authority can extract the real identity, location, and reputation value from the exchanged messages in a multi-task environment when necessary.
- *Authentication.* The exchanged messages cannot be tampered or fabricated by the adversaries without being detected.
- *Resistance to other attacks.* The proposed scheme is able to withstand various attacks in real-world applications, including the inference attack, reputation linkable attack, data pollution attack, Sybil attack, and reputation tamper attack.

5   The Proposed Scheme

In this section, we first give an overview of our proposed scheme, then its technical details are described. The proposed scheme consists of six phases: system initialization, task assignment, vehicle recruitment, data submission, data verification and information update, information tracing. The notations used in our proposed scheme are summarized as follows (Table 1):

Table 1. Formalized notations involved in the scheme

Notation	Definition
t_i	The ith sensing vehicle's reputation value
t_0	The threshold of sensing task's reputation
m	The content of a sensing task
$[m]$	The ciphertext of m
d	Sensing data
d_0	Sensing data's standard value
Δd	Sensing data's error threshold
PK_{DR}, SK_{DR}	Data requester's key pair
PK_{RC}, SK_{RC}	Reputation center's key pair
x, y	Sensing task's coordinate
r	Sensing task's radius
TSK	The sensing task list
RID	The real identity of a sensing vehicle
PID	The pseudonym of a sensing vehicle
T	The list that a sensing vehicle participate in

5.1   Overview of the Proposed Scheme

To simply the description, we first give an overview of the proposed scheme. We assume that there is a sensing task in an urban area. If the sensing vehicles desire to participate in the sensing task, their locations and reputation values should satisfy the location requirement and reputation threshold of this sensing task. For example, we assume that the data requester assigns a task and initializes the threshold for reputation as t_0. This means that the sensing vehicle's reputation value t should be no less than t_0, In addition, the position of the sensing vehicle should belong to the circle with radius r specified by the sensing task. As shown in Fig. 1, the proposed scheme includes the following steps:

- **System initialization.** The data requester and reputation center generate the system parameters and key pairs for the homomorphic encryption scheme. The reputation center initializes the reputation value for each vehicle, and sends each vehicle's pseudonym and reputation value to the corresponding sensing vehicle. All these transmitted messages are also signed by the reputation center.

- **Task assignment.** The data requester assigns a sensing task to the cloud server, along with the location requirement and reputation threshold for this sensing task. Then, the cloud server broadcasts this sensing task to the sensing vehicles via RSUs.
- **Vehicles recruitment.** Each sensing vehicle verifies that its current position is within the effective area of this task. If the verification is satisfied, the cloud server will send the corresponding task to the sensing vehicle.
- **Data submission.** The sensing vehicles submit the sensing data to the cloud server via RSUs.
- **Data verification and information update.** The cloud server verifies the legitimacy of the sensing data submitted by each sensing vehicle, generates a reputation feedback report and sends it to the reputation center. The reputation center then updates the pseudonym and reputation value of the sensing vehicle.
- **Information tracing.** The reputation center retrieves the location, identity, and reputation information of the sensing vehicle using a master private key when necessary, e.g. when some vehicle is found malicious and the court demands this vehicle's information to be revealed.

5.2   Technical Details of the Proposed Scheme

Step 1. System Initialization

- **Initialization of system parameters and generation of key pairs:** Given a security parameter κ, two safe primes p, q are selected, such that $p' = (p-1)/2$ and $q' = (q-1)/2$ are also primes. Denote $n = pq$ and g_1 is with maximal order in $\mathbb{G}_1$, where $\mathbb{G}_1$ is the cyclic group of quadratic residues modulo n^2. The data requester and the reputation center select secret parameters $a \in [1, \mathrm{ord}\,(\mathbb{G}_1)]$ and $b \in [1, \mathrm{ord}\,(\mathbb{G}_1)]$ and generate their key pairs as $(PK_{DR} = g_1^a, SK_{DR} = a)$ and $(PK_{RC} = g_1^b, SK_{RC} = b)$.
- **Vehicle's pseudonym assignment:** The reputation center starts the registration phase, while the sensing vehicles' real identities are RID_i for $i = 1, 2, \ldots, m$. The reputation center selects a cyclic group $\mathbb{G}_2$ with order q, and g_2 is a generator of $\mathbb{G}_2$. For each vehicle with RID_i, the reputation center chooses a random number $w_i \in \mathbb{Z}_q^*$ and a secret value $x \in \mathbb{Z}_q^*$. Then, it uses ElGamal encryption to generate the pseudonym $PID_i = \{PID_1, PID_2\}$, where $PID_1 = g_2^{w_i}, PID_2 = RID_i \cdot h_{pub}^{w_i}$ and $h_{pub} = g_2^x$. As follows, the reputation center chooses a random number $r_i \in [1, n/4]$, and uses the BCP encryption algorithm to generate the ciphertext for the reputation value $[t_i]_{PK_{RC}} = \{T_i, T_i'\} = \{PK_{RC}^{r_i} \cdot (1+n)^t, g_1^{r_i}\}\,(\mathrm{mod}\,n^2)$. Then, the reputation center generates a signature for $[t_i]_{PK_{RC}}$ as $\sigma_i = h^{x_i}$, where $x_i \in \mathbb{Z}_q$ is the signing key, $h = H\left([t_i]_{PK_{RC}}\right)$ and H is a cryptographic hash function. The reputation center publishes the system parameter $\{n, g_1, g_2, \mathbb{G}_1, \mathbb{G}_2, h_{pub}, H, y, PK_{DR}, PK_{RC}\}$ and sends $\{PID, [t_i]_{PK_{RC}}, \sigma_i\}$ to the vehicle with the real identity RID_i through RSU.

Step 2. Task Assignment

- **Standard value assignment:** The data requester releases the sensor task data m, and uses the proxy re-encryption to calculate the initial ciphertext $[m]$, and then uses its own public key and BCP encryption algorithm to generate ciphertexts $[d_0]_{PK_{DR}}$ and $[\Delta d]_{PK_{DR}}$, where

$$[d_0]_{PK_{DR}} = \{T_{d_0}, T'_{d_0}\} = \{PK^r_{DR} * (1+n)^{d_0}, g^r_1\} \,(\mathrm{mod}\, n^2)$$
$$[\Delta d]_{PK_{DR}} = \{T_{\Delta d}, T'_{\Delta d}\} = \{PK^r_{DR} * (1+n)^{\Delta d}, g^r_1\} \,(\mathrm{mod}\, n^2)$$

- **Generation of the task list:** The data requester divides the entire area into n task ranges. For the ith task block, The reputation center first initializes the key pair (PK_{Ti}, SK_{Ti}) of the task block. Then, the data requester uses the corresponding private key and BCP encryption algorithm to encrypt the central point coordinates (x_0, y_0), the range radius r, and the reputation threshold t_0, obtaining the ciphertext $[x_0]_{PK_{Ti}}$, $[y_0]_{PK_{Ti}}$, $[r]_{PK_{Ti}}$, $[t_0]_{PK_{Ti}}$. After the current task is initialized, the data requester adds the task TSK_i to the task list TSK. Finally, the task list $TSK = \{TSK_1, TSK_2 \ldots TSK_n\}$ is generated, where $TSK_i = \{[x_0]_{PK_{Ti}}, [y_0]_{PK_{Ti}}, [r]_{PK_{Ti}}, [t_0]_{PK_{Ti}}, PK_{Ti}\}$ for $i = 1, 2, \ldots, n$.
- **Broadcast the tasks:** After all tasks are initialized, the data requester sends $I_d = \{[m], [d_0]_{PK_{DR}}, [\Delta d]_{PK_{DR}}, TSK, PK_{DR}\}$ to the cloud server. After receiving I_d, the cloud server broadcasts $I_c = \{PK_{DR}\}$ in the crowdsensing area.

Step 3. Vehicle Recruitment

- **Location Match:** The sensing vehicle receives I_c and obtains the current position coordinates (x, y), and uses the data requester's public key and BCP encryption algorithm to obtain the ciphertext $([x]_{PK_{DR}}, [y]_{PK_{DR}})$ of the position coordinates. Where:

$$[x]_{PK_{DR}} = \{T_x, T'_x\} = \{PK^r_{DR} \cdot (1+n)^x, g^r_1\} \,(\mathrm{mod}\, n^2)$$
$$[y]_{PK_{DR}} = \{T_y, T'_y\} = \{PK^r_{DR} \cdot (1+n)^y, g_1{}^r\} \,(\mathrm{mod}\, n^2)$$

After that, it sends $I_v = \{PID, [t_i]_{PK_{RC}}, \sigma_i, ([x]_{PK_{DR}}, [y]_{PK_{DR}})\}$ to the cloud server.
- **Vehicle selection:** After receiving I_v, the cloud server first verifies whether the pseudonym PID and signature σ_i are legal. If the verification fails, the communication with the vehicle will be terminated. Otherwise, the cloud server determines which tasks the vehicle is participating in, and verifies whether the vehicle reputation value t meets the threshold t_0. Specifically, for the task $TSK_i = \{[x_0]_{PK_{Ti}}, [y_0]_{PK_{Ti}}, [r]_{PK_{Ti}}, [t_0]_{PK_{Ti}}\}$ in the task list TSK, the cloud server uses the additive homomorphic property and Secure Less Than Protocol (SLT) [21] to compare whether $[t_i]_{PK_{RC}}$ and $[t_0]_{PK_{Ti}}$ satisfies the following relationships:

$$\begin{cases} t_i \geq t_0 \\ (x - x_0)^2 + (y - y_0)^2 \leq r^2 \end{cases}$$

If the location and reputation value of the vehicle is legal, the cloud server adds the task sequence number i to the current vehicle's task list T.

- **Re-assign task:** After filtering the task list T, the cloud server re-encrypts the task message $[m]$ into the final ciphertext $[m]'$ using the proxy re-encryption algorithm. Finally, the cloud server sends $I_c = \{[m]', T\}$ to the sensing vehicle.

Step 4. Data Submission. The sensing vehicle receives the ciphertext $[m]'$ and decrypts it, obtaining the task information m. The sensing vehicle starts the sensing task and generates the sensing data d, and uses BCP encryption to generate the ciphertext of the sensing data $[d]_{PK_{Ti}}$. Finally, the sensing vehicle sends the $I_v = \{PID, [d]_{PK_{Ti}}, T\}$ to the cloud server.

Step 5. Data Verification and Information Update

- **Sensing data verification:** After receiving I_v, the cloud server first verifies the authenticity of the vehicle's pseudonym. If it passes the verification, the cloud server compares d' and Δd through $[d']_{PK\Sigma}$ and $[\Delta d]_{PK_{DR}}$. Specifically, the cloud server first calculates:

$$[d']_{PK\Sigma} = \begin{cases} [d - d_0]_{PK\Sigma} & d \geq d_0 \\ [d_0 - d]_{PK\Sigma} & d < d_0 \end{cases}$$

Then, the cloud server compares d' and Δd through $[d']_{PK\Sigma}$ and $[\Delta d]_{PK_{DR}}$. If $d' \leq \Delta d$, it means that the sensing data is valid. Otherwise, the cloud server refuses to receive this sensing data.

- **Generate reputation feedback report:** According to the verification result of sensing data, the cloud server generates a reputation feedback report F for each sensing vehicle and sends $I_c = \{PID, F\}$ to the reputation center, where

$$F = \begin{cases} 1 & d' \leq \Delta d \\ 0 & d' > \Delta d \end{cases}$$

- **Update reputation value and pseudonym:** the reputation center first verifies whether the PID is valid, if it is valid, the reputation center updates the reputation value of each sensing vehicle. Specifically, the reputation center calculates Δt of the vehicle's reputation value variation, and then calculates the updated reputation value as follows:

$$[t'_i]_{PK_{RC}} = \begin{cases} [t_i + \Delta t]_{PK_{RC}} = [t_i]_{PK_{RC}} * [\Delta t]_{PK_{RC}} \\ [t_i - \Delta t]_{PK_{RC}} = [t_i]_{PK_{RC}} * [\Delta t]_{PK_{RC}}^{n-1} \end{cases}$$

The reputation center generates a signature σ'_i for $[t'_i]_{PK_{RC}}$, and then updates the pseudonym of the vehicle as $PID' = \{PID'_1, PID'_2\}$, where $PID'_1 = g^{wi'}, PID'_2 = RID_i \cdot h_{pub}^{wi'}$. Finally, the reputation center sends $\{PID', [t'_i]_{PK_{RC}}, \sigma'_i\}$ to the sensing vehicle whose real identity is RID_i. The sensing vehicle then updates its own identity and reputation value.

Step 6. Information Tracing

- **Identity tracing:** The vehicle's real identity RID is encrypted within $PID_i = \{PID_1, PID_2\}$, where $PID_1 = g_2^{wi}$, $PID_2 = RID_i \cdot h_{pub}^{wi}$, $h_{pub} = g_2^x$. Using the private key of the system, the reputation center can compute g_2^{wi*x} and $RID_i = PID_2 \cdot g_2^{-wi*x} = RID_i \cdot h_{pub}^{wi} \cdot g_2^{-wi*x}$ to extracts the real identity of the sensing vehicle.
- **Reputation value tracing:** to trace the reputation value of sensing vehicles in multi-task crowdsensing, e.g. $[t_i]_{PK_{RC}} = \{T_i, T'_i\} = \{PK_{RC}^r * (1+n)^t, g_1^r\} \pmod{n^2}$, using the master private key of the system $\lambda(n)$, the reputation center can first calculate $T_i^{\lambda(n)} \bmod n^2 = g_1^{b*r*\lambda(n)}(1 + n)^{t*\lambda(n)} \bmod n^2 = (1 + tn\lambda(n))$. Denote $L(x) = \frac{x-1}{n}$, the reputation center can calculate $t = L\left(T_i^{\lambda(n)} \bmod n^2\right) \cdot \lambda(n)^{-1} \bmod n$ to extracts the reputation value.
- **Location tracing:** to trace the location information of sensing vehicles in multi-task crowdsensing, we take $[x]_{PK_{DR}}$ as an example, using the master private key of the system $\lambda(n)$, the reputation center can calculate $x = L\left(T_i^{\lambda(n)} \bmod n^2\right) * \lambda(n)^{-1} \bmod n$. Similarly, the reputation center can calculate y and r to extracts the location information of the sensing vehicle.

6   Security and Efficiency Analysis

6.1   Security Analyses

In this section, we prove that our proposed scheme can achieve the desirable security properties, such as correctness, conditional privacy preserving and authentication.

Correctness: the detailed proof for this property is omitted because of page restriction. At a high level, one can easily see that encryption can be correctly decrypted and legitimate signature can be validated. Hence, if all participants are honest, the protocol will generate correct outputs.

Conditional Privacy Preserving: regarding this property, we prove that any vehicle's sensitive information, such as location, identity and reputation value, can be protected from the adversaries, and the trusted authority can retrieve this information if necessary.

- *Location privacy:* in the proposed scheme, the adversary $\mathcal{A}$ can obtain the message $I_v = \{PID, [t_i]_{PK_{RC}}, \sigma_i, ([x]_{PK_{DR}}, [y]_{PK_{DR}})\}$ sent by the sensing vehicle. Although $\mathcal{A}$ acquires the encrypted ciphertexts, she cannot derive the specific location coordinates of each sensing vehicle. In the tasks assignment and vehicle recruitment phases, BCP encryption is used to encrypt the location information. It has already been proved that BCP encryption is semantically secure under the DDH assumption over $\mathbb{Z}_{n^2}$. Hence, $\mathcal{A}$ cannot obtain the location of each sensing vehicle. Furthermore, during the sensing task matching, the cloud server selects vehicles by comparing the vehicle's current location with the location required by the task. However, $\mathcal{A}$ cannot get the specific location of each sensing vehicle during this phase neither. Therefore, $\mathcal{A}$ cannot learn any information about the sensing vehicle's location. In other words, the proposed scheme can preserve location privacy.

- *Identity privacy*: In our proposed scheme, $\mathcal{A}$ may intend to learn the real identity RID of the sensing vehicle. The vehicle's real identity RID is encrypted in PID_i generated by the reputation center, where $PID_i = \{PID_1, PID_2\}, PID_1 = g_2^{wi}, PID_2 = RID_i \cdot h_{pub}^{wi}$ and $h_{pub} = g_2^x$. However, $\mathcal{A}$ cannot extract RID from $PID_2 = RID_i \cdot h_{pub}^{wi}$, because she does not have the corresponding secret key. Therefore, based on the DDH assumption over $\mathbb{Z}_{n^2}$, the proposed scheme preserves identity privacy.

- *Reputation value privacy*: In the proposed scheme, $\mathcal{A}$ may steal the sensing vehicle's reputation value t and sensing task's reputation threshold t_0, where $t_0 < t$. Specifically, from the task list TSK initialized by the data requester, $\mathcal{A}$ acquires the ciphertext but not the specific reputation value of each sensing task. Because the BCP encryption is semantically secure, $\mathcal{A}$ cannot learn any information about the sensing vehicle's reputation value, i.e. the proposed scheme can preserve reputation value privacy.

- *Traceability*: The vehicle's real identity RID is involved in pseudonym $PID_i = \{PID_1, PID_2\}$, where $PID_1 = g_2^{wi}, PID_2 = RID_i \cdot h_{pub}^{wi}, h_{pub} = g_2^x$. Using the private key of the system, the reputation center can compute g_2^{wi*x} and $RID_i = PID_2 \cdot g_2^{-wi*x} = RID_i \cdot h_{pub}^{wi} \cdot g_2^{-wi*x}$ to extracts the real identity of the sensing vehicle. Similarly, the trusted authority can extract the location and reputation value of the proposed scheme. Therefore, the proposed scheme could provide traceability.

Authentication: in the proposed scheme, all transmitted messages are digitally signed by their sender. And the receiver will only accept the received messages if the verification of signature is valid. Based on the security of digital signature, the adversary cannot tamper or fabricate messages without being detected. Hence, our scheme achieves the authentication property.

Resistance to Other Attacks: our proposed scheme can resist the inference attack, reputation linkable attack, data pollution attack, Sybil attack, and reputation tamper attack.

- Based on the above analyses, the proposed scheme can prevent the data requester, the cloud server, and the RSUs from suffering location inference attack, identity inference attack, and reputation inference attack. In addition, because the reputation value is encrypted using a randomized encryption. The proposed scheme can resist the reputation linkable attack.

- In the real multi-task crowdsensing environment, malicious sensing vehicles may submit false sensing data, which may lead to unreliable sensing results. Specifically, the cloud server compares d' and Δd through $[d']_{PK\Sigma}$ and $[\Delta d]_{PK_{DR}}$. If $d' \leq \Delta d$, it means the sensing data is valid. Otherwise, the cloud server refuse to receive this sensing data. Hence, our scheme can resist data replacement attack.

– Because the pseudonym PID of each sensing vehicle is distributed and updated by the reputation center, a malicious sensing vehicle is unable to forge multiple identities. Thus, our scheme can resist the Sybil attack. To verify the reputation value of every sensing vehicle, the cloud server uses the additive homomorphic property and Secure Less Than Protocol (SLT) to compare whether $[t_i]_{PK_{RC}}$ and $[t_0]_{PK_{T_i}}$ satisfies the relationship $t_i \geq t_0$. Hence, the sensing vehicle cannot pass the verification if the reputation value is less than the reputation threshold. This implies that our scheme can resist the reputation tamper attack.

6.2   Efficiency Analyses

In the system initialization step, one first selects two large safe primes. This can be done via the Miller-Rabin algorithm and it only needs to be executed once. Then the data requester and the reputation center compute a key pair, each requires one exponentiation in G_1. As follows, the reputation center generates an ElGamal ciphertext and a BCP ciphertext. The former requires two exponentiations and one multiplication in G_2, while the latter requires three exponentiations and one multiplication in G_1. In the task assignment step, the data requester generates six BCP ciphertexts, requiring eighteen exponentiations and six multiplications in G_1. In the vehicle recruitment step, the sensing vehicle generates two BCP ciphertexts, requiring six exponentiations and two multiplications in G_1. In information tracing, identity tracing needs one exponentiation and one multiplication in G_2. In reputation value tracing, it needs one exponentiation and one multiplication in G_1, and in location tracing, it needs three exponentiations and three multiplications in G_1. All these computations can be done efficiently, hence the proposed scheme is generally efficient in pratical use.

7   Conclusion

In this paper, we have proposed a multi-task mobile crowdsensing scheme with conditional privacy preserving for vehicular networks. The conditional privacy preserving property covers identity privacy, location privacy, and reputation privacy simultaneously. And each sensing vehicle can participate in several sensing tasks at the same time. Besides, when updating the pseudonyms of sensing vehicles, the reputation center does not need to store any internal status (such as random numbers and ephemeral keys), which can effectively reduce the risks of DoS attacks. Moreover, theoretical analyses show that the proposed scheme overcomes the weaknesses in existing schemes and it is efficient for multi-task mobile crowdsensing. In the future, we plan to consider a more severe security model, removing the assumption that the data requester, the cloud server, the RSUs are honest-but-curious, and providing verification mechanisms for these entities.

References

1. Ganti, R.K., Ye, F., Lei, H.: Mobile crowdsensing: current state and future challenges. IEEE Commun. Mag. **49**(11), 32–39 (2011)
2. Chen, X., et al.: PAS: prediction-based actuation system for city-scale ridesharing vehicular mobile crowdsensing. IEEE Internet Things J. **7**(5), 3719–3734 (2020)
3. Huang, C., Lu, R., Choo, K.-K.R.: Vehicular fog computing: architecture, use case, and security and forensic challenges. IEEE Commun. Mag. **55**(11), 105–111 (2017)
4. Ma, L., Liu, X., Pei, Q., Xiang, Y.: Privacy-preserving reputation management for edge computing enhanced mobile crowdsensing. IEEE Trans. Serv. Comput. **12**(5), 786–799 (2019)
5. Ni, J., Zhang, K., Xia, Q., Lin, X., Shen, X.S.: Enabling strong privacy preservation and accurate task allocation for mobile crowdsensing. IEEE Trans. Mob. Comput. **19**(6), 1317–1331 (2019)
6. Dai, M., Su, Z., Xu, Q., Wang, Y., Lu, N.: A trust-driven contract incentive scheme for mobile crowd-sensing networks. IEEE Trans. Veh. Technol. **71**, 1794–1806 (2021)
7. Zhang, C., et al.: TPPR: a trust-based and privacy-preserving platoon recommendation scheme in VANET. IEEE Trans. Serv. Comput. (2019)
8. Wang, L., Zhang, D., Yang, D., Lim, B.Y., Han, X., Ma, X.: Sparse mobile crowdsensing with differential and distortion location privacy. IEEE Trans. Inf. Forensics Secur. **15**, 2735–2749 (2020)
9. Sun, G., Sun, S., Yu, H., Guizani, M.: Toward incentivizing fog- based privacy-preserving mobile crowdsensing in the Internet of Vehicles. IEEE Internet Things J. **7**(5), 4128–4142 (2019)
10. Lu, R., Lin, X., Zhu, H., Ho, P.-H., Shen, X.: ECPP: efficient conditional privacy preservation protocol for secure vehicular communications. In: Proceedings of the 27th Conference on IEEE INFOCOM, pp. 1903–1911 (2008)
11. Raya, M., Hubaux, J.-P.: Securing vehicular ad hoc networks. J. Comput. Secur. **15**(1), 39–68 (2007)
12. Zhao, B., Tang, S., Liu, X., Zhang, X.: PACE: privacy-preserving and quality-aware incentive mechanism for mobile crowdsensing. IEEE Trans. Mob. Comput. **20**(5), 1924–1939 (2020)
13. Gao, S., Chen, X., Zhu, J., Dong, X., Ma, J.: TrustWorker: a trustworthy and privacy-preserving worker selection scheme for blockchain-based crowdsensing. IEEE Trans. Serv. Comput. (2021)
14. Hu, H., Lu, R., Zhang, Z., Shao, J.: REPLACE: a reliable trust- based platoon service recommendation scheme in VANET. IEEE Trans. Veh. Technol. **66**(2), 1786–1797 (2016)
15. Hu, H., Lu, R., Huang, C., Zhang, Z.: TripSense: a trust-based vehicular platoon crowdsensing scheme with privacy preservation in VANETs. Sensors **16**(6), 803 (2016)
16. Liu, Z., et al.: BTMPP: balancing trust management and privacy preservation for emergency message dissemination in vehicular networks. IEEE Internet Things J. **8**(7), 5386–5407 (2021)
17. Liu, Z., et al.: LPPTE: a lightweight privacy-preserving trust evaluation scheme for facilitating distributed data fusion in cooperative vehicular safety applications. Inf. Fusion **73**, 144–156 (2021)
18. Cheng, Y., Ma, J., Liu, Z., Wu, Y., Wei, K., Dong, C.: A lightweight privacy preservation scheme with efficient reputation management for mobile crowdsensing

in vehicular networks. IEEE Trans. Dependable Secure Comput. (2022). https://doi.org/10.1109/TDSC.2022.3163752

19. Nkenyereye, L., Islam, S.R., Bilal, M., Abdullah-Al-Wadud, M., Alamri, A., Nayyar, A.: Secure crowd-sensing protocol for fog-based vehicular cloud. Futur. Gener. Comput. Syst. **120**, 61–75 (2021)

20. Paillier, P.: Public-key cryptosystems based on composite degree residuosity classes. In: Stern, J. (ed.) EUROCRYPT 1999. LNCS, vol. 1592, pp. 223–238. Springer, Heidelberg (1999). https://doi.org/10.1007/3-540-48910-X_16

21. Liu, X., Deng, R.H., Choo, K.R., Weng, J.: An Efficient Privacy-Preserving Outsourced Calculation Toolkit With Multiple Keys. IEEE Trans. Inf. Forensics Secur. **11**(11), 2401–2414 (2016). https://doi.org/10.1109/TIFS.2016.2573770

22. Bresson, E., Catalano, D., Pointcheval, D.: A simple public-key cryptosystem with a double trapdoor decryption mechanism and its applications. In: Laih, C.-S. (ed.) ASIACRYPT 2003. LNCS, vol. 2894, pp. 37–54. Springer, Heidelberg (2003). https://doi.org/10.1007/978-3-540-40061-5_3

23. Engoulou, R.G., Bellaïche, M., Pierre, S., Quintero, A.: VANET security surveys. Comput. Commun. **44**, 1–13 (2014)

24. Guette, G., Heen, O.: A TPM-based architecture for improved security and anonymity in vehicular ad hoc networks. In: 2009 IEEE Vehicular Networking Conference (VNC), pp. 1–7. IEEE (2009)

25. He, D., Zeadally, S., Xu, B., Huan, X.: An efficient identity-based conditional privacy-preserving authentication scheme for vehicular ad hoc networks. IEEE Trans. Inf. Forensics Secur. **10**(12), 2681–2691 (2015). https://doi.org/10.1109/TIFS.2015.2473820

Towards Low-Latency Big Data Infrastructure at Sangfor

Fei Chen[1,2(✉)], Zhengzheng Yan[1], and Liang Gu[2]

[1] Shenzhen Institutes of Advanced Technology, Chinese Academy of Sciences,
Shenzhen, China
fei_chen_2013@hust.edu.cn
[2] Sangfor Inc., Shenzhen, China

Abstract. As a top cybersecurity vendor, Sangfor needs collects log streams from thousands of endpoint detection devices such as NTA, STA, EDR and identifies security threats in real-time way everyday. The discovery and disposal of network security incidents are highly real-time in nature with seconds or even milliseconds response time to prevent possible cyber attacks and data leaks. In order to extract more valuable information, the log streams are analyzed using stream processing with pattern matching like CEP (Complex Event Processing) in memory, and then stored in a persistent storage systems such as a data warehouse system or a search engine system for data scientists and network security engineers to do OLAP (Online Analytical Processing). Sangfor needs to build a low-latency big data platform to meet the challenges of massive logs.

More and more open source systems are proposed to solve the problem of data processing in a certain aspect. Many decisions must be made to balance the benefits when designing a real-time big data infrastructure. What's more, how to architecture these systems and construct a one-stack unified big data platform have been the key obstacles for big data analytics. In this paper, we present the overall architecture of our low-latency big data infrastructure and identify four important design decisions i.e. message queue, stream processing, OLAP, and data lake. We analyze the advantages and disadvantages of existing open source system and clarify the reason behind our choices. We also describe the improvements and optimizations to make the open-source stacks fit in Sangfor's environments, including designing a real-time development platform based on Flink and re-architecting Apache Kylin, Clickhouse and Presto as a HOLAP system. Then we highlight two important use cases to verify the rationality of our infrastructure.

1 Introduction

With the development of 5G, IoT and cloud technologies, more and more real-time big data with 4V characteristic (i.e. Volume, Velocity, Variety and Value) is generated from large numbers of sensors and person. Along with the explosion of data, there are various requirements of data processing and a wide ranger of big data use cases. At high level, the form of big data processing is mainly divided into four areas, i.e. message queue, stream processing, OLAP, and data lake. Message queue platform provides temporary message storage when the destination program is busy or not connected,

J. Chen et al. (Eds.): EISA 2022, CCIS 1641, pp. 37–54, 2022.
https://doi.org/10.1007/978-3-031-23098-1_3

allows applications to communicate by sending asynchronous messages between producers and consumers. Stream processing framework models a streaming application as a directed acyclic graph (DAG), executes computational logic on stream elements (called tasks) transparaently. OLAP (OnLine Analytical Processing) organizes large business databases, supports complex analytical queries, extracts business intelligence information from the data. Data Lake is a storage repository that holds a vast amount of raw data in its native format, including structured, semi-structured, and un-structured, it uses a flat architecture to store data, primarily in files or object storage.

In these areas, many distributed computing systems have been designed to deal with these challenges from the beginning of MapReduce [16]. For message queue, there are Kafka [19], Samza [28], Pulsar [5], RabbitMQ [8], RocketMQ [9]. Flink [25], Storm [29], Spark Streaming [32], Heron [21], Millwheel [13]are representative of stream processing frameworks. In OLAP, the popularity of Impala [3], Apache Kylin [4], Presto [27], Apache Druid [17], Spark SQL [22] and ClickHouse [6] is growing vigorously. Nowadays, data lake such as Apache Iceberg [2], Apache Hudi [1] and Delta Lake [23] have attracted much more attention and become the solid cornerstone of unified storage layer.

However, how to choose suitable component to architecture a unified big data infrastructure have been great challenges for many coporations [18,31]. There are two fundamental challenges within Sangfor. 1) *Data*: The volume of real-time stream data has been growing exponentially at a rapid rate from thousands of terminal devices. Due to the velocity of stream data, the unified data infrastructure has to cope with this data volume increase while providing SLA guarantees including low end-to-end latency, high throughput, and high availability; 2) *Use Cases*: As Sangfor's business grows, many use cases emerges from various application scenarios. Different business groups have varying requirements of data processing, such as streaming processing, SQL like queries, unified storage.

We depict the high-level data flow at Sangfor's infrastructure in Fig. 1. Various kinds of logs and network traffics from security devices are collected to message queue. In order to achieve low response latency, stream processing paradigm is introduced to tackle with these event streams. The results have two destinations, one is data lake for history storage and query, another is message queue providing real-time results for real-time applications such as security event alarm. There are also some source data coming from binlogs of traditional databases. These binlogs are integrated into data lake. On data lake, ETL (Extract-Transform-Load) on original data by batch processing is conducted to build a data warehouse. After that, data is normalized and layered. Security analysts make query plans and carry out statistics analysis through OLAP systems such as security event analysis.

In order to meet these various requirements of data processing, we propose a low-latency big data infrastructure which integrate message queue, stream processing, OLAP and data lake into one-stack unified big data platform. We improve the capability of stream processing by designing a real-time development platform based on Flink. And we also design a HOLAP system to support various query scenarios effectively by re-architecting Apache Kylin, Clickhouse and Presto. In summary, this paper makes the following contributions:

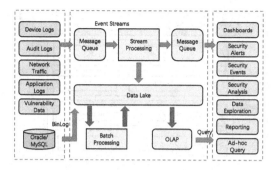

Fig. 1. The high-level data flow at Sangfor infrastructure

- We analyze and compare current open-source systems in message queue, stream processing, OLAP, and data lake. We identify the advantages and disadvantages of each system and clarify how to choose a suitable component according to data processing requirements.
- We present a low-latency big data infrastructure which integrate message queue, stream processing, OLAP and data lake into one-stack unified big data platform. Our infrastructure can support various use cases while achieving low latency and high throughput with large numbers of stream data.
- We propose the improvements and optimizations upon these open-source systems. We improve the capability of stream processing by designing a real-time development platform based on Flink and design a HOLAP system to support various query scenarios effectively by re-architecting Apache Kylin, Clickhouse and Presto.

The rest of this paper is organized as follows. In Sect. 2, we introduce the overview of high-level abstractions of our big data infrastructure. Section 3 describes system architecture, and compares the open source systems which we use in each layer of abstractions. More importantly, we clarify the improvements and optimizations on the open source solutions. In Sect. 4, we analyze the representative use cases in Sangfor's environment. We explains lessons we learned about architecting big data infrastructure in Sect. 5. Section 6 briefly surveys the related works. Finally, Sect. 7 concludes this paper.

2 Abstractions

Figure 2 illustrates the high-level abstractions of big data infrastructure and overviews the logical building blocks. The infrastructure mainly consists of the following parts (from bottom up): *Sorage*, *Compute*, *Library*, *API*, *Applicaitons*, *Metadata*, and *Manager*.

Storage. This contains: 1) stream storage which stores stream data temporarily for stream processing. There are two roles in stream storage systems, i.e. producer and consumer. Producer publishes messages to stream storage, and consumer which subscribes to this stream can consume the messages one event at a time. These systems

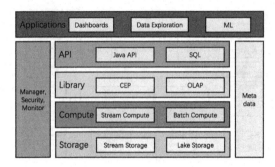

Fig. 2. The high-level abstraction of big data infrastructure and the overview of the components

support large numbers of reads and writes in very low latency. 2) lake storage which provides a object or blob storage to hold historical data for batch processing. It plays an important role in constrcuting a data warehouse, and also used as the storage tier of OLAP systems. These systems achieve better write performance usually by writing blocks one by one.

Compute. This provides the capability to perform arbitrary computation on the underlying stream and lake storage layers. It consists of two data processing patterns, i.e. stream processing and batch processing. Stream processing processes continuous infinite stream data immediately from stream storage in real-time way. Latency is the critical concern, and it usually takes few seconds or milliseconds to process data. Batch processing processes high volume of finite data in batch from lake storage within a specific time span. It focus on high throughput.

Library. This layer provides a set of functions customized for one particular requirement. We focus on CEP and OLAP libraries in our infrastructure. CEP (Complex Event Processing) is used to detect event patterns in an endless stream of events, for example security events detection. OLAP (OnLine Analytical Processing) executes analytical queries including filtering, aggregations with group by, order by in a low latency, high throughput manner.

API. This provides application programming interface for users to develop programs. It consists of native Java API and SQL. Fresh users who have good knowledges of databases can use SQL to construct their big data applications directly. However, it is not enough for advanced users whom mastering big data frameworks, especially when the complexity of business logics exceeds the expressiveness of SQL. Then native Java API is the best choice.

Applicaitons. This layer contains large numbers of applications from various kinds of scenarios, including real-time applications and analytical applications. For example, real-time applications detect security events, alarm to administrator and prevent security threats in time automaticlly. It takes few seconds through the whole process. Analytical applications query total security threats and their distributions in last week, in order to identify potential attack sources.

Metadata. This metadata connects data storage, data computation, data warehouse and data application, and records the whole process of data from generation to consumption. It describes the attributions of data such as schema, type, length. In our infrastructure, metadata can help application developer to find the data they care about conveniently, which can be used to guide data management and development work efficiently.

Manager. This layer provides the fundamental management of big data infrastructure, including the installation and deployment, the security and monitoring of each component. Due to the complexity of the whole infrastructure, it must be easy to installed and depolyed. The security includes authentication, authorization and audit. Monitor is responsible for collecting runtime metrics, checking the health state of each component.

3   System Design

In this section, we describe the system design of our big data infrastructure. We begin with an overview of the system architecture, followed by introducing the system details. Figure 3 shows the overview of big data infrastructure and the corresponding logical building blocks. We adopt Kafka as message queue, Flink as stream processing, Iceberg as data lake. In OLAP, we put Apache Kylin, Clickhouse and Presto together to support various query scenarios.

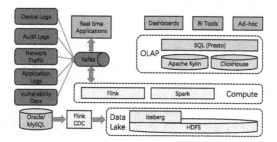

Fig. 3. The overview of big data infrastructure at Sangfor

3.1   Apache Kafka for Message Queue

Apache Kafka [19] is one of the most popular event streaming systems which is widely adopted in the industry. At its core, Kafka is designed as a replicated, distributed, persistent commit log that is used to power event-driven micro-services or large-scale stream processing applications. Clients produce or consume events directly to/from a cluster of brokers, which read/write events durably to the underlying file system and also automatically replicate the events synchronously or asynchronously within the cluster for fault tolerance and high availability.

There are numerous messaging systems out there with use cases for message queuing, distributed messaging, and high-performance event streaming systems. Following

we'll do a deep side-by-side comparison of Apache Kafka, Apache Pulsar [5], and RabbitMQ [8] on system throughput and latency, the primary performance metrics for event
streaming systems in production. Besides the performance, there are some other key
features to take into consideration such as ease of use, availability, semantics, message
replay, open-source ecosystem maturity, scale of open-source community.

We use the OpenMessaging Benchmark Framework (OMB) [7] to evaluate the performance of Kafka, Pulsar and RabbitMQ. We focused on two important metrics, i.e.
system throughput and system latency. In particular, the throughput test measures how
efficient each system is in utilizing the hardware, specifically the disks, the memory
and the CPU. The latency test measures how close each system is to delivering real-
time messaging including tail latencies of up to p99.9th percentile, a key requirement
for real-time and mission-critical applications as well as micro-services architectures.
Figure 4 shows the evaluation results. We conclude that: 1) Kafka provides the highest
throughput of all systems, writing 15x faster than RabbitMQ and 2x faster than Pulsar; 2) Kafka provides the lowest end-to-end latencies (5 ms at p99) up to the p99.9th
percentile at higher throughputs. RabbitMQ can achieve lower end-to-end latency than
Kafka, but only at significantly lower throughputs (30K messages/sec versus 200K mes-
sages/sec for Kafka), after which its latency degrades significantly.

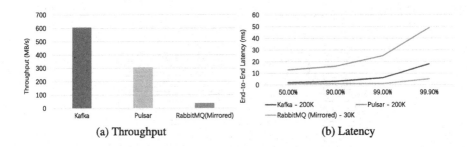

(a) Throughput   (b) Latency

Fig. 4. Performance comparison of Kafka, Pulsar and RabbitMQ

In summary, Kafka is a reasonable choice among the queuing and event streaming
systems. We adopt Kafka as our message queue systems.

3.2 Apache Flink for Stream Processing

Applications of stream processing technology attract a lot of attention in rencent years
[24]. Many stream processing systems have been designed to cope with challenge of
real-time stream data. Systems like Storm [29], Heron [21], Spark Streaming [32], Millwheel [13], and Apache Flink [25] first abstract streaming computations as dataflow
graphs (Directed acyclic Graph, DAG) and transparently execute data-parallel tasks on
distributed clusters. The Google Dataflow Model [14] introduce watermark mechanism
to deal with out-of-order processing [30] as Flink can do. We compare Storm, Storm-
Trident, Spark Streaming and Flink from streaming model, guarantees, back pressure,
latency, throughput, fault tolerance and stateful operations. Flink adopts native stream

processing model, guarantees exactly-once semantics, achieves high throughput, low latency, and light-weight fault tolerance. What's more, Flink has a mature ecosystem and community, and has been de facto of stream processing systems. In summary, we choose Flink as the stream processing engine.

Based on Flink, we build a real-time development platform for users to programming stream applications in a visual configuration way. At Sangfor, this platform is mainly used for CEP(Complex Event Processing) [20] rules to detect security threats. So, our improvements and optimizations focus on CEP library, such as rule configuration, new rules which open-source can not support, and auto-scaling when traffic load burst or resources are preempted. Figure 5 overviews the architecture of real-time development platform. It consists of three parts: 1) *rule configuration terminal*, which usually is a web providing tools or components to configure a CEP rule; 2) *DSL engine*, which transforms the CEP rules into a Flink program and submit to resource management platform; 3) *job monitoring terminal*, which is responsible for collecting jobs' metrics and makes auto-scaling decisions by evaluating these metrics.

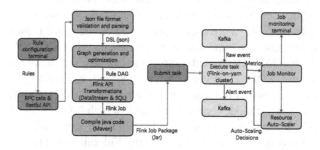

Fig. 5. The architecture of real-time development platform

The real-time development platform works as follows: 1) users draw a CEP program and configure rules' parameters in rule configuration terminal; 2) the program's blueprints are encapsulated into a JSON file which formalized as DSL format, then pass this file to DSL engine through RPC calls or Restful APIs; 3) DSL engine parses the JSON file and generates a program graph which describes the dataflow's sources, sinks and operations; 4) DSL engine optimizes the program graph such as merging multi operators which reading the same data source, de-duplicating two operators which has the same transformation logic; 5) when received the optimized graph, DSL engine transforms this graph into a Flink program using Flink API such DataStream API or SQL; 6) the Flink program is compiled into java code and packaged as a Jar, and then submitted to Yarn cluster; 7) job monitoring terminal collects job metrics such as resource utilization, source data lag, input, output and so on, checks jobs' health state; 8) if source data lags seriously, resource auto-scaler triggers auto-scaling decisions to scale out resource provision.

3.3   Put Apache Kylin, Clickhouse and Presto Together for OLAP

The research on OLAP databases systems explodes in recent years [15]. Considering the complexity of query scenarios such as aggregations query, ad-hoc query and details query, we suvery about popular OLAP systems including Hive, Spark SQL, Presto, Kylin, Impala, Druid, ClickHouse and Greenplum. These systems can be classified into two categories.

ROLAP. Relational OLAP stores data in columns and rows (also known as relational tables) and retrieves the information on demand through user submitted queries. A ROLAP database can be accessed through complex SQL queries to calculate information. ROLAP can handle large data volumes, but the larger the data, the slower the processing times. Because queries are made on-demand, ROLAP does not require the storage and pre-computation of information. However, the disadvantage of ROLAP implementations are the potential performance constraints and scalability limitations that result from large and inefficient join operations between large tables.

MOLAP. Multidimensional OLAP uses a multidimensional cube that accesses stored data through various combinations. Data is pre-computed, pre-summarized, and stored (a difference from ROLAP, where queries are served on-demand). It uses extra storage space to save query response time. The major disadvantages of MOLAP is that it lacks query flexibility than ROLAP, and cube expansion can take up a lot of storage space.

However, neither ROLAP system or MOLAP system can meet the query requirements of various scenarios at the same time. We need a HOLAP (Hybrid OLAP) system. The HOLAP storage mode connects attributes of both MOLAP and ROLAP. Since HOLAP involves storing part of your data in a ROLAP store and another part in a MOLAP store, developers get the benefits of both. With this use of the two OLAPs, the data is stored in both multidimensional databases and relational databases. The decision to access one of the databases depends on which is most appropriate for the requested processing application or type. This setup allows much more flexibility for query types.

We present the architecture of our HOLAP system (called Dipper) in Fig. 6. In Dipper, Apache Spark, Apache Kylin, ClickHouse and Presto are put together as the query engine layer. Apache Spark undertakes offline analysis and batch processing. Apache Kylin acts as the MOLAP, constrcuts data cubes and pre-computes results of complex aggregation queries. ClickHouse plays a role of query cache, and stores part of latest data. Some detail queries or aggregation queries are first routed to ClickHouse. If cache misses, Dipper triggers data update, and migrates the lastest data to ClickHouse. Dipper introduces Presto to execute ad-hoc query. If both cube and cache miss, then queries are send to Presto. The router is the key component which parses SQL statements to identify query types, then routes different queries to different engines. All metadatas are managed by Hive Metastore. There are one or more rest servers accepting SQL statements from applications through Rest APIs and JDBC/ODBC interfaces.

We evaluate Dipper's performance and compare it with Spark. We use the Star Schema Benchmark (SSB) [26] which is based on the TPC-H benchmark [11] and is devised to evaluate database system performance of star schema data warehouse queries. The SSB dataset has 1 billion records, 15 dimensions, 4 measures and 199 indexes. The cluster has 3 machines of each with 2 Xeon E5-2650 2.2 GHz CPUs and

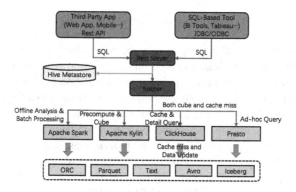

Fig. 6. The architecture of dipper

256 GB memory. Table 1 presents the results. The results show that Dipper behaves much better in a variety of query scenarios, and can achieve a 10x improvement in terms of query performance when compared with Spark.

Table 1. The comparison of query performance between dipper and spark

Query	Dipper(s)	spark text (s)	spark orc(s)
1 (Q1.1)	0.45	33.7	21.8
2 (Q1.2)	0.39	27.4	19.6
3 (Q1.3)	0.41	27	20.6
4 (Q2.1)	1.29	73.3	81.4
5 (Q2.2)	0.42	63.1	55.5
6 (Q2.3)	0.37	60.9	50.1
7 (Q3.1)	0.54	64.3	59.8
8 (Q3.2)	0.4	67.4	56
9 (Q3.3)	0.42	55.8	40.5
10 (Q3.4)	0.89	45.5	36.6
11 (Q4.1)	0.6	68.2	54.5
12 (Q4.2)	0.69	62	56
13 (Q4.3)	1.07	63.3	46.2

3.4 Apache Iceberg for Data Lake

Apache Hudi, Apache Iceberg, and Delta Lake are the current best-in-breed formats designed for data lakes. All three formats solve some of the most pressing issues with data lakes: 1) *Atomic Transactions*-Guaranteeing that update or append operations to the lake don't fail midway and leave data in a corrupted state. 2) *Consistent Updates*-Preventing reads from failing or returning incomplete results during writes. Also handling potentially concurrent writes that conflict. 3) *Data & Metadata Scalability*-Avoiding bottlenecks with object store APIs and related metadata when tables grow to the size of thousands of partitions and billions of files. We compare these three open-source systems in Metadata, ACID Transactions, Multiple Versions, Performance and

SQL, and conclude that no system can meet all requirements and performs over other systems.

In partition evolution, Iceberg is currently the only table format with partition evolution support. Partitions are tracked based on the partition column and the transform on the column. Hudi and Delta Lake do not support partition evolution or Hidden Partitioning. The ability to evolve a table's schema is a key feature. All three table formats support different levels of schema evolution. Both Iceberg and Delta Lake can support add, drop, rename, update and reorder operations on column while hudi can only support add and delete operations. As to ACID transactions, Iceberg provides snapshot isolation and ACID support. Beyond the typical creates, inserts, and merges, row-level updates and deletes are also possible with Iceberg. Hudi also has atomic transactions and SQL support for CREATE TABLE, INSERT, and Queries. But for Deletes it has to rely on the engine's (Spark/Flink) API. Delta Lake also supports ACID transactions and includes SQL support for creates, inserts, merges, updates, and deletes. For time travel, every time an update is made to an Iceberg table, a snapshot is created. We can specify a snapshot-id or timestamp and query the data as it was with Iceberg. The Hudi table format revolves around a table timeline, enabling us to query previous points along the timeline. Each Delta file represents the changes of the table from the previous Delta file, so we can target a particular Delta file or checkpoint to query earlier states of the table. In the matter of file format, only Iceberg can support Parquet, Avro and ORC.

We evaluate the performance of query, data load, update and incremental update between these three systems. We use the TPC-DS [10] as the benchmark, Trino [12] as the query engine, and Spark as the compute framework. Figure 7 compares the query performance between Iceberg and Hudi. From the results, we can conclude that: 1) Compared with Iceberg and Hudi, the performance of these two systems is similar if they are in Parquet file format, but there is a little difference in performance compared with the original Parquet format table, mainly because there is an extra layer of tabular transformation; 2) For ORC tables, due to the ORC optimization of Trino itself, the performance of Iceberg is better than that of Hudi Parquet tables, which is close to the performance of native ORC tables; 3) Hudi has indexing mechanism, but it is not used for query; Iceberg uses column-level statistics to filter data and performs better than Hudi.

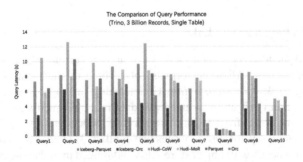

Fig. 7. The comparison of query performance between Iceberg and Hudi

We show the comparison of data loading performance between Iceberg, Hudi and Delta Lake in Fig. 8. The data loading performance of Hudi is far behind that of Iceberg and Delta. When using Upsert with 3 billions records, the performance gap is even larger due to indexing and sorting.

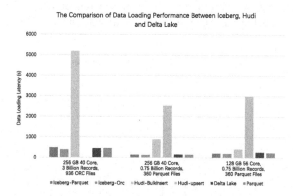

Fig. 8. The comparison of data loading performance between Iceberg, Hudi and Delta Lake

In Fig. 9, we depict the comparison of update performance between Iceberg, Hudi and Delta Lake. According to the experimental results, Spark provides the best performance for Delta Lake than Iceberg and Hudi. For single record update, Iceberg is slightly better than Hudi, mainly because Iceberg optimizes the query. However, for multiple records update, Hudi has better update performance than Iceberg because of its index. Because updates with a large amount of data involves data scanning and the MOR table has small files, Hudi's scanning performance is worse than Iceberg's. Therefore, totally the difference is not obvious. If running on servers of little poor configuration, the gap is relatively large. The impact of small files is a big problem.

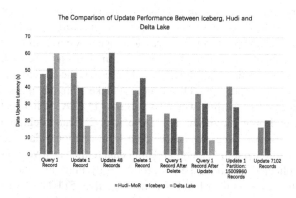

Fig. 9. The comparison of update performance between Iceberg, Hudi and Delta Lake

The comparison of incremental update performance between Iceberg and Hudi is shown in Fig. 10. We draw the following conclusions. 1) In Hudi, the incremental update performance of MOR (Merge On Read) is better than COW (Copy On Write). 2) The performance difference of incremental update between Hudi COW and Iceberg COW is about 2 times. 3) The full data loading performance of Hudi is twice worse than that of Iceberg; the upsert gap was even larger, 20 times. 4) Compared with Hudi, the update performance of Hive achieves worse performance as with the more files updated.

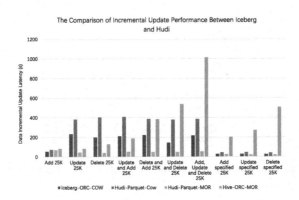

Fig. 10. The comparison of incremental update performance between Iceberg and Hudi

Of the three table formats, although Delta Lake supports much more features and achieves good performance, it is the only non-Apache project and is hard to become the industry standard because of smaller communities. In summary, we choose Iceberg as the table format of data lake.

3.5 One-Stack Rule Them All

The big data infrastructure uses a unified stack to support various types of data processing. It organizes message queue, stream processing framework, OLAP system and data lake systems into a whole platform. Uses can leverage this platform to cover the development requirements of big data applications. A complete end-to-end data processing pipeline can be drawn on this platform. Figure 11 presents the unified stack which rules message queue, stream processing, OLAP and data lake all in one infrastructure.

This data processing pipeline works as follows. 1) CDC (Change Data Capture) synchronization tool pulls binlog through Debezium; 2) Data integration tool such as Sqoop, FlinkX or DataX integrates source data from relational databases to Hive; 3) CDC logs are synchronized to Iceberg, updating data to the latest version; 4) Real-time stream data is collected to kafka, then is processed by Flink and the result one hand is written back to kafka, another hand is written to Hive; 5) ETL (Extract-Transform-Load) operations are conducted over Iceberg table using Spark; 6) Pre-compute queries need to build data cubes using Spark; 7) The metadata is managed in Hive metastore; 8) Presto can query Iceberg table; 9) Applications monitor data quality in Iceberg; 10)

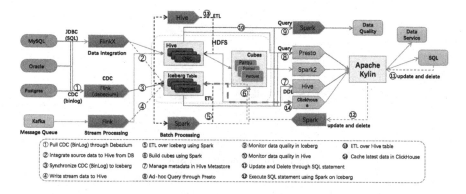

Fig. 11. The unified stack rule message queue, stream processing, OLAP and data lake all

Applications monitor data quality in Hive; 11) SQL editor provides the interface to update and delete tables through SQL statements; 12) Spark engine executes SQL statements on Iceberg; 13) ETL (Extract-Transform-Load) operations are conducted over Hive table using Spark; 14) Latest data is cached in ClickHouse.

4 Use Cases

In this section, we present several big data use cases among message queue, stream processing, OLAP and data lake in production at Sangfor, and show how our big data infrastructure can help them to achieve their business goals.

4.1 Security Application: Security Operation Center

With the growing number of cyber security threats affecting the business environment of many organizations, especially the IT environment, managed protection systems including SOC (Security Operation Center) are high sought after. A SOC is generally a platform set up to maintain the security of an organization. With the development of emerging technologies, SOC platform also needs to cope with the challenges of large numbers of big data.

Data collection, data processing, correlation analysis, and visualization are the four major components of SOC architecture. Figure 12 shows the SOC architecture. Data is collected from security devices such as VPNs, firewalls, routers, intrusion detection systems, and servers in the form of asset logs and security incidents via Simple Network Management Protocol (SNMP) and SYSLOG. The data processing unit is comprised of three main processes: data filtering, data merging, and data formatting. Data filtering eliminates redundant data, reducing duplicated incidents. Data merging is the process of combining several related pieces of data according to predefined rules. Data formatting converts disparate types of data into standard format. Correlation Analysis is used to identify possible risks across multiple events. Visualization displays the findings of security incidents.

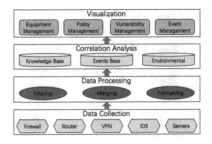

Fig. 12. The architecture of SOC

Under this scenario, data collection uses message queue for stream data, and data lake for historical data. Data processing and correlation analysis for stream data adopts Flink as the computing engine. OLAP system provides statistics results for visualization.

4.2 IoT Application: Smart Factory

Industry 4.0, Smart Factory and Industrial Internet are some of the terms used to describe the social and technological revolution that promises to change the current industrial landscape. The central asset management application can serve as the bridge between the power tools and the ERP (Enterprise Resource Planning) and MES (Manufacturing Execution System) systems that control the manufacturing process. Such a production system can benefit hugely from big data technologies that allow the aggregation of large volumes of heterogeneous, multi-structured data about the production process, including legacy data from many different systems.

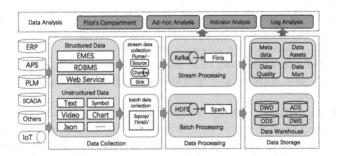

Fig. 13. The architecture of IoT in smart factory

Similar with the scenario of SoC, data collection, data processing, data storage and data analysis are the four key processes of IoT architecture. We present the architecture of IoT in smart factory in Fig. 13. Multiple-structured data is collected from various production control systems such as ERP, APS, PLM, SCADA and others. There are two data collection manners, one is stream data collection using Flume and another is batch data collection using Sqoop or FlinkX. The data processing includes stream processing and batch processing. For data storage, a data warehouse needs to be constructed with clear hierarchy which contains ODS (Operation Data Store), DWD (Data Warehouse Details), DWS (Data Warehouse Service), and ADS (Application Data Service). Data Analysis includes ad-hoc analysis, indicator analysis, and log analysis.

To support this scenario, data collection and storage use message queue for stream data, and data lake for batch data. Data processing adopts Flink as stream processing framework and spark as batch processing engine. OLAP system provides analytical tools for data analysis.

5   Lessons Learned

We have learned a lot in building the big data infrastructure at Sangfor. Many of the experiences are about service management: it is far from being enough to provide a framework for users to write applications. An easy-to-use unified platform encompasses deployment, development, monitoring, debugging and maintenance.

5.1   No Single System Can Rule All

There is no single system that is right for all use cases. For example, there is no OLAP system that can meet the query requirements of various scenarios. The fundamental reason is that no system can be perfect in data volume, performance and flexibility at the same time. Every system needs to make a trade-off between these three aspects when making designing decisions, as well as the stream processing. Providing a hybrid architecture which takes advantages of candidate systems' strength seems to be a good choice.

5.2   Ease of Deployment and Monitoring

Developing and running big data applications require more than writing the application code. The ease of deployment and monitoring is equally important. Due to the complexity of big data technology stack, deploying all the systems and applications takes a lot of work. The whole stack contains more than a dozen components or subsystem from the bottom up. It is necessary to construct a management platform aimed at provisioning, managing, and monitoring distributed clusters.

5.3   Ease of Development and Debugging

Developing big data applications is not an easy job for users. They must have a good knowledge of big data ecosystem. Only experienced programmers which master the APIs, architectures, principles of big data components can use native APIs to develop big data applications. However, the person using big data platforms are experts on their business areas, not big data technology. Providing a visual WebUI can help eliminate the barriers. Furthermore, the infrastructure should provide tools for debugging and failure handling.

6   Related Work

In this section, we conclude previous research work on message queue, stream processing, OLAP, data lake and big data infrastructure.

Message Queue. Traditional message queue systems such as Kafka [19], Samza [28], Pulsar [5], RabbitMQ [8], RocketMQ [9] have existed for a long time and play an important role as an event bus for processing asynchronous messages. Kafka is an open source distributed event streaming platform. At its core, Kafka [19] is designed as a replicated, distributed, persistent commit log that is used to power event-driven microservices or large-scale stream processing applications. Pulsar [5] is an open-source distributed pub/sub messaging system originally catered towards queuing use cases. It is designed as a tier of (almost) stateless broker instances that connect to a separate tier of BookKeeper instances. RabbitMQ [8] is an open-source traditional messaging middleware that implements the AMQP messaging standard, catering to low-latency queuing use cases.

Stream Processing. Many systems have been developed to process real-time streaming data such as Flink [25], Storm [29], Spark Streaming [32], Heron [21], Millwheel [13]. Flink [25] and Storm [29] model an application as a topology that defines operators (i.e. source, transform and sink) and the stream (i.e. the way which tuples flow between operators). Spark Streaming [32] proposes a discretized stream processing model, which follows a micro-batch model that structures stream processing as a series of batch computations generated periodically over small batch intervals. Millwheel [13] utilizes system-time watermarks [30] to determine when it is safe to garbage collect exactly-once deduplication data on the receiver side of a shuffle between two physical stages in the pipeline.

OLAP. OLAP systems have become more and more popular in recent years, including Impala [3], Apache Kylin [4], Presto [27], Apache Druid [17], Spark SQL [22] and ClickHouse [6]. Impala [3] raises the bar for SQL query performance on Apache Hadoop while retaining a familiar user experience. With Impala, users can query data, whether stored in HDFS or Apache HBase, including SELECT, JOIN, and aggregate functions in real time. By renovating the multi-dimensional cube and precalculation technology on Hadoop and Spark, Apache Kylin [4] is able to achieve near constant query speed regardless of the ever-growing data volume. Presto [27] allows querying data where it lives, including Hive, Cassandra, relational databases or even proprietary data stores. A single Presto query can combine data from multiple sources, allowing for analytics across your entire organization. Druid [17] merges key characteristics of each of the 3 systems i.e. data warehouses, timeseries databases, and search systems into its ingestion layer, storage format, querying layer, and core architecture.

Data Lake. Apache Iceberg [2] is a high-performance format for huge analytic tables. Iceberg brings the reliability and simplicity of SQL tables to big data, while making it possible for engines like Spark, Trino, Flink, Presto, and Hive to safely work with the same tables, at the same time. Apache Hudi [1] is a rich platform to build streaming data lakes with incremental data pipelines on a self-managing database layer, while being optimized for lake engines and regular batch processing. Delta Lake [23] is an open-source storage framework that enables building a Lakehouse architecture with compute engines including Spark, PrestoDB, Flink, Trino, and Hive and APIs for Scala, Java, Rust, Ruby, and Python.

Big Data Infrastructure. There are also some coporations building their real-time data infrastructure. Uber adopts open source technologies, constructs the real-time data infrastructure, and optimizes it for flexibility and scale for different user categories [31]. Facebook develops multiple, independent yet composable systems for real-time data processing based on Puma, Swift and Stylus [18].

7   Conclusion

This paper proposes a low-latency big data infrastructure which unifies various data processing in one platform. We compare current open-source systems in message queue, stream processing, OLAP and data lake and clarify the design decisions we made. We improve the capability of stream processing by designing a real-time development platform based on Flink and design a HOLAP system to support various query scenarios effectively by re-architecting Apache Kylin, Clickhouse and Presto. Experimental results show that our HOLAP system can improve query performance by 10x compared to Spark SQL. Also, our unified big data platform can cover all data processing requirements at Sangfor's business scenarios.

References

1. Apache hudi. https://hudi.apache.org/
2. Apache iceberg. https://iceberg.apache.org/
3. Apache impala. https://impala.apache.org/
4. Apache kylin. https://kylin.apache.org/
5. Apache pulsar. https://pulsar.apache.org/
6. Clickhouse. https://clickhouse.com/
7. Openmessaging benchmark framework. https://openmessaging.cloud/docs/benchmarks/
8. Rabbitmq. https://www.rabbitmq.com/
9. Rocketmq. https://rocketmq.apache.org/
10. Tpc-ds benchmark. https://www.tpc.org/tpcds/
11. Tpc-h benchmark. https://www.tpc.org/tpch/
12. Trino. https://trino.io/
13. Akidau, T., Balikov, A., Bekiroglu, K., Chernyak, S., Haberman, J., et al.: Millwheel: fault-tolerant stream processing at internet scale. In: Proceedings of the VLDB Endowment (VLDB 2013), pp. 1033–1044 (2013)
14. Akidau, T., Bradshaw, R., Chambers, C., Chernyak, S., et al.: The dataflow model: a practical approach to balancing correctness, latency, and cost in massive-scale, unbounded, out-of-order data processing. In: Proceedings of the VLDB Endowment (VLDB 2015), pp. 1792–1803 (2015)
15. Chaoqun, Z., Maomeng, S., Chuangxian, W., Xiaoqiang, P., et al.: AnalyticDB: real-time olap database system at Alibaba cloud. In: Proceedings of the VLDB Endowment (VLDB 2019), pp. 2059–2070 (2019)

16. Dean, J., Ghemawat, S.: MapReduce: simplified data processing on large clusters. In: The 6th USENIX Symposium on Operating Systems Design and Implementation (OSDI 2004), pp. 137–149 (2004)

17. Fangjin, Y., Eric, T., Xavier, L., Nelson, R., et al.: Druid: a real-time analytical data store. In: Proceedings of the 2014 ACM SIGMOD International Conference on Management of Data (SIGMOD 2014), pp. 157–168 (2014)

18. Guoqiang Jerry, C., Janet L., W., Shridhar, L., Anshul, J., et al.: Realtime data processing at Facebook. In: Proceedings of the 2016 ACM SIGMOD International Conference on Management of Data (SIGMOD 2016), pp. 1087–1098 (2016)

19. Guozhang, W., Lei, C., Ayusman, D., Jason, G., Boyang, C., et al.: Consistency and completeness: rethinking distributed stream processing in apache Kafka. In: Proceedings of the 2021 International Conference on Management of Data (SIGMOD 2021), pp. 2602–2613 (2021)

20. Jagrati, A., Yanlei, D., Daniel, G., Neil, I.: Efficient pattern matching over event streams. In: Proceedings of the 2008 ACM SIGMOD International Conference on Management of Data (SIGMOD 2008), pp. 147–160 (2008)

21. Kulkarni, S., Bhagat, N., Fu, M., et al.: Twitter heron: stream processing at scale. In: Proceedings of the 2015 ACM SIGMOD International Conference on Management of Data (SIGMOD 2015) pp. 239–250 (2015)

22. Michael, A., Reynold, S.X., Cheng, L., Yin, H., et al.: Spark SQL: relational data processing in spark. In: Proceedings of the 2015 ACM SIGMOD International Conference on Management of Data (SIGMOD 2015), pp. 1383–1394 (2015)

23. Michael, A., Tathagata, D., Liwen, S., Burak, Y., et al.: Delta lake: high-performance acid table storage over cloud object stores. In: Proceedings of the VLDB Endowment (VLDB 2020), pp. 3411–3424 (2020)

24. Paris, C., Marios, F., Vasiliki, K., Asterios, K.: Beyond analytics: the evolution of stream processing systems. In: Proceedings of the 2020 International Conference on Management of Data (SIGMOD 2020) pp. 2651–2658 (2020)

25. Paris, C., Stephan, E., Gyula, F., Seif, H., Stefan, R., Kostas, T.: State management in apache FlinK: consistent stateful distributed stream processing. In: Proceedings of the VLDB Endowment (VLDB 2017), pp. 1718–1729 (2017)

26. Pat, O.N., Betty, O.N., Xuedong, C.: Star schema benchmark (2009). https://www.cs.umb.edu/poneil/StarSchemaB.pdf

27. Raghav, S., Martin, T., Dain, S., David, P., et al.: Presto: SQL on everything. In: The 35th International Conference on Data Engineering (ICDE 3019), pp. 1802–1813 (2019)

28. Shadi A.N., Kartik, P., Yi, P., Navina, R., et al.: Samza: stateful scalable stream processing at LinkedIn. In: Proceedings of the VLDB Endowment (VLDB 2017), pp. 1634–1645 (2017)

29. Toshniwal, A., Taneja, S., Shukla, A., et al.: Storm @twitter. In: Proceedings of the 2014 ACM SIGMOD International Conference on Management of Data (SIGMOD 2014), pp. 147–156 (2014)

30. Tyler, A., Edmon, B., Slava, C., Fabian, H., et al.: Watermarks in stream processing systems: semantics and comparative analysis of apache FlinK and google cloud dataflow. In: Proceedings of the VLDB Endowment (VLDB 2021), pp. 3135–3147 (2021)

31. Yupeng, F., Chinmay, S.: Real-time data infrastructure at uber. In: Proceedings of the 2021 ACM SIGMOD International Conference on Management of Data (SIGMOD 2021), pp. 2503–2516 (2021)

32. Zaharia, M., Das, T., Li, H., Hunter, T., Shenker, S., Stoica, I.: Discretized streams: fault-tolerant streaming computation at scale. In: Proceedings of the 24th ACM Symposium on Operating Systems Principles (SOSP 2013), pp. 423–438 (2013)

Differential Cryptanalysis of Lightweight Block Ciphers SLIM and LCB

Yen Yee Chan[1], Cher-Yin Khor[1], Je Sen Teh[1]([✉]), Wei Jian Teng[1], and Norziana Jamil[2]

[1] School of Computer Sciences, Universiti Sains Malaysia, George Town, Malaysia
jesen_teh@usm.my
[2] Institute of Informatics and Computing in Energy, Universiti Tenaga Nasional, Kajang, Malaysia

Abstract. In this paper, we analyze the security of two recently proposed ultra-lightweight block ciphers, SLIM and LCB. SLIM is designed based on the Feistel paradigm, operating on 32-bit blocks and has an 80-bit key. The designers claim that SLIM is immune to differential cryptanalysis after they were only able to find a trail of up to 7 rounds by using a heuristic method. LCB is another ultra-lightweight block cipher with a 32-bit block and instead uses a 64-bit secret key. It was designed based on a hybrid of Feistel and substitution-permutation network structures. Although no concrete security analyses were performed, the designers claim that 10 rounds of the cipher is secure enough against various attacks including differential cryptanalysis. We verify these claims by proposing differential attacks on both ciphers. For SLIM, we first report optimal (i.e., having the best differential probability) trails for up to 32 rounds found using an SMT solver. We then propose practical key recovery attacks on up to 14 rounds that recover the final round key with time complexity 2^{32}. Next, a close inspection of LCB's design revealed a lack of nonlinearity, whereby its S-box could be modelled as a permutation. As such, differential trails that hold with probability 1 can be trivially derived for any number of rounds of the cipher. A trivial distinguishing attack can be performed with just one known-ciphertext. We fix this flaw and go on to show that LCB is actually more secure (against differential cryptanalysis) than SLIM given the same number of rounds. To the best of our knowledge, these are the first third-party cryptanalysis attacks against both ciphers.

Keywords: SLIM · LCB · Differential cryptanalysis · Lightweight block cipher · SMT

1 Introduction

In recent years, the protection of personal information has become one of the top priorities since the number of reported cases of data breaches have grown. Sensitive information being unintentionally transmitted or stored in unencrypted

© The Author(s), under exclusive license to Springer Nature Switzerland AG 2022
J. Chen et al. (Eds.): EISA 2022, CCIS 1641, pp. 55–67, 2022.
https://doi.org/10.1007/978-3-031-23098-1_4

form is one of the main reasons. As reported in late June 2019, a popular Internet of Things (IoT) software management company was found to have hosted an unencrypted database storing 2 billion entries of user data which was scraped from their customers' domestic appliances [6]. This incident shows that data confidentiality should be the prime concern when designing IoT or smart devices. However, encryption algorithms with high computational requirements are not suitable for such devices since they have limited resources in terms of processing capabilities and memory [2]. Therefore, there is a demand for lightweight cryptographic solutions that are not only efficient but require minimal computing resources.

To bridge this gap, the field of *lightweight cryptography* has seen a surge of popularity among researchers. Although the term lightweight is not strictly defined [4], with respect to block ciphers, it most often refers to cryptographic primitives with smaller block and key sizes, or reduced energy requirements [16]. PRESENT [5], Piccolo [14], LED [10] are some of the examples of well-known lightweight block ciphers. The challenge for designers is to find a balance between computational complexity and functionality [3]. For example, substitution-permutation network (SPN) ciphers like PRESENT and LED consume a relatively high amount resources. In contrast, small ciphers like KATAN [7] are more lightweight but rely on weaker round function components that are iterated a large number of times.

A block cipher is considered secure after it has been proven to be secure against various types of cryptanalysis attacks. Differential cryptanalysis is one of the main cryptanalytic attacks that cryptographers consider when designing ciphers. If a plaintext difference (usually an XOR difference) leads to a particular ciphertext difference with non-negligible probability, it can be used as a statistical distinguisher in a key recovery attack. To aid the search for these differential distinguishers, cryptanalysts have proposed automated search algorithms based on mixed-integer linear programming (MILP), Boolean satisfiability (SMT/SAT) solvers, branch-and-bound algorithms, and constraint programming which can significantly ease the search for good differential trails.

Apart from the earlier mentioned popular block ciphers, there have been many others that have been published in recent years [1,8,9,11,13,17]. However, unlike the former (which have been designed by known cryptographers), many of these ciphers have not been subject to third-party scrutiny. Further analysis of these lesser-known ciphers could either reveal highly secure or efficient designs that may have been overlooked by the cryptographic community or reveal serious flaws that can lead to security compromise if they were ever used in real-life applications. In this paper, we contribute to this endeavour by performing differential cryptanalysis of two relatively new block ciphers recently proposed in respectable peer-reviewed journals - SLIM (IEEE Access) [1] and LCB (KSII Transaction KSII Transactions on Internet and Information Systems) [13].

1.1   Contributions

SLIM and LCB are both 32-bit block ciphers with 80 and 64-bit keys respectively. Both are ultra-lightweight block ciphers meant for use in resource-constrained devices. SLIM's designers claim that the cipher is resistant to differential attacks after performing a differential trail search using a nested tree search. They only managed to find a 7-round trail that was not guaranteed to be optimal (in terms of differential probability) due to the heuristic nature of the approach. Based on this finding, the designers conclude that 32 rounds of the cipher is more than sufficient to resist differential cryptanalysis. In contrast, LCB's designers did not report any concrete cryptanalysis results for their cipher but claim that 10 rounds is sufficient to resist security attacks.

In this paper, we propose differential attacks on both ciphers to verify the designers' security claims. We used an SMT solver to find differential trails for SLIM while for LCB, cryptanalysis can be performed using pen-and-paper methods due to the linearity of its design. We found *optimal* differential trails[1] for all 32 rounds of the SLIM. We show that a *valid* 13-round trail exists that allows to perform a key recovery attack on 14 rounds of the cipher. Although our results do not threaten the security of the full cipher, it provides a more accurate estimate of the security margin for SLIM against differential cryptanalysis.

As for LCB, we first show that the cipher inherently linear due to a flaw in its substitution box (S-box) design. As such, there exists a differential distinguisher that holds with probability 1 for any number of rounds of the cipher, which can be used in a ciphertext-only attack. We then improve LCB by replacing its S-box with PRESENT's, and show that the cipher actually has better resistance to differential cryptanalysis as compared to SLIM. To the best of our knowledge, our attacks on SLIM and LCB are the first 3rd party cryptanalysis results for the respective ciphers.

2   Preliminaries

2.1   Notations and Abbreviations

In this paper, the index of rightmost nibble is 0, and increases from right to left (little-endian). Notations and abbreviations which mentioned in this paper are tabulated in Table 1.

2.2   Specifications of SLIM

SLIM cipher is a 32-bit Feistel-like block cipher designed to be implemented on resources-constraint devices such as RFID tags. Blocks are processed as 16-bit halves Li and R_i, where i denotes the ith round of encryption/decryption process. SLIM uses four 4-bit S-boxes (see Table 2) which were actually taken from

---

[1] An *optimal* trail is guaranteed to have the highest possible differential probability for a given round, but is not necessarily a *valid* distinguisher.

Table 1. Notations and abbreviations.

Symbol	Definition
n	Block size in bits
k	Key size in bits
R	Number of rounds
$\oplus$	Binary exclusive OR (XOR) operation
ΔP	XOR differences of plaintext (P) pairs
ΔC	XOR differences of ciphertext (C) pairs
L_i	Left halves of a input block i^{th} round
R_i	Right halves of a input block i^{th} round
K_i	Sub-key for i^{th} round

PRESENT [5]) and a bitwise permutation box (P-box) in its round function. The encryption process is summarized as follows:

$$L_i = R_{i-1}, \tag{1}$$

$$R_i = L_{i-1} \oplus P(S(K_i \oplus R_{i-1})). \tag{2}$$

Table 2. PRESENT's S-box used in SLIM.

x	0	1	2	3	4	5	6	7	8	9	A	B	C	D	E	F
$S(x)$	C	5	6	B	9	0	A	D	3	E	F	8	4	7	1	2

The P-box (see Table 3) of SLIM was designed to have no fixed point (every input bit is moved away from its original position), which the authors claim enhances resistance against linear cryptanalysis. One round of SLIM is shown in Fig. 1.

Table 3. SLIM P-box.

x	1	2	3	4	5	6	7	8	9	10	11	12	13	14	15	16
$P(x)$	8	14	2	9	12	15	3	6	5	11	16	1	4	7	10	13

SLIM has a complex key schedule which was not clearly defined in the original specification. Based on test vectors obtained from the designers themselves, details of the key schedule is as follows: The first five subkeys, $K_1...K_5$ are extracted directly from the 80-bit master key. The 80-bit key will then be processed by a nonlinear key schedule algorithm to generate the remaining subkeys.

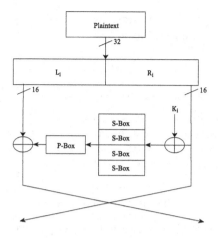

Fig. 1. 1 round of SLIM.

First, the 80-bit key is divided into two 40-bit halves, KeyMSB and KeyLSB, each with 10 nibbles each. The four least significant nibbles (nibbles 0 to 3) of both KeyMSB and KeyLSB are extracted. We denote the latter as MSB_{16} and LSB_{16} respectively. LSB_{16} will be circularly left shifted by 2 bits then XOR-ed with MSB_{16}, the result of which will be substituted by four S-boxes in parallel. Denote the intermediate 16-bit substitution output as SUB_{16}. MSB_{16} is then circularly left shifted by 3 bits and XOR-ed with SUB_{16}, the result of which is taken as the sixth round key, K_6.

K_6 and SUB_{16} will be used to replace the least significant nibbles of KeyMSB and KeyLSB respectively. The entire process is repeated in *windows* of of non-overlapping nibbles. If the key schedule has insufficient nibbles to process, it wraps around and continues from the least significant nibbles. For example, K_7 is calculated from nibbles (4, 5, 6, 7) while K_8 is calculated from nibbles (8, 9, 0, 1) and so on. The following equation summarizes the key generation process for one round:

$$K_i = S(MSB_{16} \oplus (LSB_{16} << 2)) \oplus (LSB_{16} << 3). \qquad (3)$$

2.3   Specifications of LCB

Light Cipher Block (LCB) is lightweight block cipher also designed for resource constraint devices. LCB's designers have opted to combine both Feistel and SPN design structures which would supposedly overcome the shortcomings of both design paradigms. As LCB was designed to be used in sensors, the designers focused on speed, power, memory, and storage when designing LCB. LCB processes 32-bit blocks with 10 rounds of encryption.

Each round, the plaintext block is divided into 16-bit halves, L_i and R_i, that will be processed by the round function called F-Block. F-Block supposedly consists of 4-bit S-boxes, 8-bit P-boxes, and a 16-bit linear box (L-box). After going through their respective F-Blocks, the two halves are swapped. The entire encryption process is summarized as follows:

$$Li = L(P(S(K_i \oplus R_{i-1}))), \tag{4}$$

$$R_i = L(P(S(K_i \oplus L_{i-1}))). \tag{5}$$

Upon closer inspection, we found that LCB's S-box was in fact a 4-bit permutation. As such, LCB is entirely linear (this was verified by using the test vectors provided by the authors in their specification [13]). The S-box for LCB in hexadecimal form is described in Table 4.

Table 4. LCB S-box.

x	0	1	2	3	4	5	6	7	8	9	A	B	C	D	E	F
$S(x)$	0	4	1	5	2	6	3	7	8	C	9	D	A	E	B	F

The P-box and L-box are 8-bit and 16-bit permutations respectively. Although their bit lengths are different, the S-box, P-box and L-box of LCB follows the same interleaving pattern where the left and right bits interleave one another as shown in Fig. 2. One round of LCB is shown in Fig. 3.

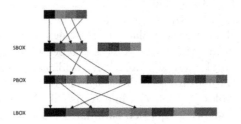

Fig. 2. S-box, P-box and L-box pattern.

The 64-bit master key is used to generate 16-bit subkeys in a straightforward manner: The 64-bit master key is simply divided into 4 equal parts, $K_1...K_4$ which are then fed into the different round functions sequentially during encryption.

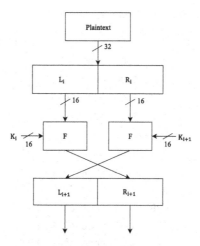

Fig. 3. 1 round of LCB.

3 Cryptanalysis of SLIM

3.1 SLIM Differentials

We perform differential cryptanalysis of SLIM verify its designers' security claims.

The differential behavior of SLIM was modelled and solved using an SMT solver [15] to find differential characteristics for all 32 rounds of the cipher. All trails found using the solver has the lowest possible weight (optimal). *Weight* is defined as $-\log_2(p)$, where p is the differential probability of the trail.

The input difference, ΔP, output differences, ΔC, and weights, W for rounds 1 to round 32 are tabulated in Table 5. From the results, differential trails of up to 13 round ($w = 31$) are *valid* differential distinguishers since $2^{-w} > 2^{-n}$, where n is the block size. The differential trail found is nearly twice the length of the one found by the designers themselves. We also discovered that SLIM does not have a significant differential effect. For example, other 13-round trails that share the same ΔP and ΔC as the optimal 13-round trail have weights of 42 or higher. Therefore, differential clusters lead to negligible improvements to the overall differential probability. 32 rounds of SLIM is secure against differential cryptanalysis ($w = 78$) with a security margin of more than double its block size.

3.2 Key Recovery Attack on SLIM Reduced to 13 Rounds

We use the best 12-round differential trail (0B82 000A $\xrightarrow{12}$ 0A00 801B) with probability 2^{-28} to attack 13 rounds of SLIM. Denote the input difference of the trail (which is also the plaintext difference) as $\alpha = \Delta P = $ 0B82 000A and the output difference as $\beta = $ 0A00 801B. We append one round to the 12-round trail,

Table 5. Differential trails of SLIM.

Rounds (R)	ΔP	ΔC	Probability p
1	0020 0000	0000 0020	1
2	4024 0090	0000 0090	2^{-2}
3	8D10 0400	0000 0D00	2^{-4}
4	1000 B000	1000 A008	2^{-6}
5	D804 0040	0040 D804	2^{-8}
6	0208 4700	8000 1D48	2^{-12}
7	09A6 001A	001A 4982	2^{-16}
8	9024 0090	9000 02D0	2^{-18}
9	0B82 000A	000A 0A82	2^{-21}
10	0020 00B0	0080 4823	2^{-24}
11	4827 0080	0020 08B4	2^{-26}
12	0B82 000A	0A00 801B	2^{-28}
13	A208 A000	A000 B208	2^{-31}
14	0290 9000	0090 9004	2^{-34}
15	0B82 000A	000B 0A00	2^{-36}
16	02D0 9000	0090 D004	2^{-36}
17	02D0 9000	9000 0290	2^{-41}
18	8900 0900	0900 8900	2^{-44}
19	0090 00B0	0090 00B4	2^{-46}
20	801B 0A00	000A 0B82	2^{-48}
21	9004 0090	0090 D004	2^{-51}
22	0900 0D00	0D00 0900	2^{-54}
23	0B82 000A	000B 0A00	2^{-56}
24	D004 0090	9000 02D0	2^{-58}
25	0109 000B	000B 010B	2^{-61}
26	D000 00D0	9000 02D0	2^{-64}
27	0090 D000	9000 02D0	2^{-66}
28	D004 0090	9000 02D0	2^{-68}
29	0B82 000A	000A 0A82	2^{-71}
30	D000 00D0	9000 1290	2^{-74}
31	A000 B000	A000 B208	2^{-76}
32	0B82 000A	0A00 801B	2^{-78}

the output difference of which is denoted as ΔC. ΔC has 12 active bits, which are unknown bits of ΔC after being masked by the subkey and the application of the S-boxes. The remaining 20 bits are inactive or fixed, and can therefore be used as a linear filter to discard wrong pairs. The attack procedures are as follows:

1. We encrypt 2^{30} pairs of plaintexts and expect to find at least $2^{30-28} = 2^2$ right pairs (4 pairs of plaintexts that conforms to the differential trail).
2. After 13 rounds, there are 20 inactive (or known) bits that can be used to filter wrong pairs. We expect $2^{30-20} = 2^{10}$ pairs to remain after filtering.
3. We prepare 2^{12} counters and guess the 12 subkey bits that correspond go the 12 active bits of the output difference.
4. Perform 1-round partial decryption for each pair using the guessed subkey bits and if the result matches β, increment its corresponding key counter. A total of $2^{10+12} \cdot 2 = 2^{23}$ partial decryptions are performed (or $\frac{2^{22}}{13} \approx 2^{18.3}$ full encryptions) towards the ciphertext pairs.
5. We expect 4 right pairs to vote for the correct 12-bit subkey while the remaining pairs will vote for a random subkey with a probability of $2^{10-12} = 2^{-2}$.

The overall time complexity of the attack is dominated by data preparation, where 2^{31} chosen plaintexts ($D = 2^{31}$) are encrypted ($2^{31}+2^{18.3} \approx 2^{31}$). Memory complexity is the size of the key counter. We have 2^{12} possible 12-bit keys, which requires $M = 12 \cdot 2^{12}/8 \approx 2^{12.58}$ bytes. With 4 right pairs, we expect the attack to succeed with probability $1 - e^{-2^{30-28}} \times 100 = 98.2\%$ to recover one round subkey[2]. The remaining key bits can be obtained via brute force or through auxiliary methods (e.g. repeating the attack on 12 rounds, which would be considerably faster).

3.3   Key Recovery Attack on SLIM Reduced to 14 Rounds

Next, we show that the 13-round differential trail (A208 A000 $\xrightarrow{13}$ A000 B208) with probability 2^{-31} can be used to attack 14 rounds of SLIM (albeit with lower success probability compared to the 13-round attack). Denote the input difference of the trail (which is also the plaintext difference) as $\alpha = \Delta P =$ A208 A000 and the output difference as $\beta =$ 0A00 B208. We append one round to the 13-round trail, the output difference of which is denoted as ΔC. ΔC has 12 active bits, which are bits of ΔC that have been masked by the application of the subkey and substitution layer. The remaining 20 bits are inactive or fixed and can be used as a linear filter to discard wrong pairs.

The attack procedure is the same as the 13-round attack since all parameters are similar. The time complexity of the attack is dominated by the data preparation step, which is around $T = 2^{32}$. Data complexity is $D = 2^{31} \cdot 2 = 2^{32}$ chosen plaintexts (full codebook). Memory complexity dominated by the key counter, which requires $M = 12 \cdot 2^{12}/8 \approx 2^{12.58}$ bytes. With 1 right pair, we expect the attack to succeed with probability $1 - e^{-2^0} \times 100 = 63.2\%$ to recover the final round subkey.

---

[2] Experimental verification of the attack is available at github.com/CryptoUSM/slim--cipher.

4   Cryptanalysis of LCB

Typically, the aim in differential cryptanalysis is to first obtain a high probability differential trail that can later be used in a key recovery attack. However, since LCB was found to be completely linear, we can trivially derive differential trails for any number of rounds with probability 1 that can be used in a distinguishing attack. A distinguishing attack attempts to differentiate encrypted data (coming from a particular block cipher) from a randomly generated data. The existence of an effective distinguisher, especially a distinguisher that spans all rounds of a cipher, implies that a block cipher is insecure [12].

For LCB, any input difference ΔP will transition deterministically to a particular output difference ΔC. Differential trails for LCB can thus be easily derived using pen-and-paper methods without the use of any automated tools. One example of a 10-round trail is illusrated in Table 6. Therefore, a successful distinguishing attack can be performed on the full LCB with just one known ciphertext as follows:

1. Obtain any 10-round ciphertext, C_1 and calculate $C_2 = C_1 \oplus \Delta C$.
2. Using any randomly selected master key, request the corresponding plaintext pair, (P_1, P_2) from the decryption oracle.
3. We expect that $P_1 \oplus P_2 = \Delta P$ with probability 1.

Table 6. 10-round LCB Trail with $p = 1$.

Rounds (R)	ΔP	Probability p
1	A1F6 0000	1
2	0000 D1E5	1
3	D372 0000	1
4	0000 836F	1
5	957C 0000	1
6	0000 B563	1
7	A1F6 0000	1
8	0000 D1E5	1
9	D372 0000	1
10	0000 836F	1

4.1   Improving LCB

Next, we make a slight modification to LCB by replacing its S-box then re-evaluating its security against differential cryptanalysis. The S-box plays an important role to introduce nonlinearity to a block cipher. Since LCB is linear, a straightforward improvement is to replace its S-box with a nonlinear one.

We opt for PRESENT's S-box because it has the added advantage of allowing a direct comparison with SLIM.

After replacing LCB's S-box, we performed a search for the best differential trails using an SMT solver and found that the optimal 10-round trail for LCB has probability 2^{-32}. As such, we recommend that LCB double its number of rounds to 20 to provide a comfortable security margin. At 20 rounds, the best differential trail has probability 2^{-68} as shown in Table 7. This implies that LCB requires fewer rounds to attain the same security margin against differential cryptanalysis as SLIM (20 rounds of LCB is as secure as 28 rounds of SLIM).

Table 7. Differential trails for the improved LCB.

Rounds (R)	ΔP	ΔC	Probability (p)
1	0000 0030	0101 0000	2^{-2}
2	0000 0070	0000 0041	2^{-4}
3	000D 0000	0000 4168	2^{-8}
4	0000 F009	0000 003C	2^{-12}
5	000F 0000	0000 0101	2^{-15}
6	0090 0000	4040 0000	2^{-18}
7	0090 0000	0000 0155	2^{-22}
8	0090 0000	1051 0000	2^{-26}
9	00F0 0000	0000 0101	2^{-29}
10	0000 0090	0000 1004	2^{-32}
11	0090 0000	0000 1055	2^{-36}
12	7009 0000	1055 0000	2^{-40}
13	0000 00F0	1010 0000	2^{-43}
14	0000 0009	0000 0041	2^{-46}
15	0790 0000	0000 0041	2^{-50}
16	700F 0000	00C3 0000	2^{-54}
17	0000 0090	0101 0000	2^{-57}
18	0090 0000	0404 0000	2^{-60}
19	0000 0009	0154 0000	2^{-64}
20	0009 0000	1051 0000	2^{-68}

5   Conclusion

In this paper, we report new differential cryptanalysis results for 32-bit lightweight block ciphers, SLIM and LCB. For SLIM, we provide the optimal differential trails for all 32 rounds. A valid differential distinguisher exists for up to 13 rounds with probability of 2^{-31}. We introduce key recovery attacks on SLIM reduced to 13 and 14 rounds, using 12 and 13-round differential trails respectively. The attacks have practical time/data/memory complexities of $2^{31}/2^{31}/2^{12.58}$ and $2^{32}/2^{32}/2^{12.58}$, and succeed with probability 98.2% and 63.2% respectively to recover the final round key. We also report a serious flaw with LCB's S-box which causes the cipher to be entirely linear. As such, differential trails with probability 1 can be trivially obtained from any input difference and be used in a distinguishing attack on any number of rounds in a ciphertext-only setting. We go on to show that by replacing LCB's S-box with the same one as SLIM, LCB is more secure than the latter by a factor of 2^{20} for the same number of rounds.

Acknowledgements. This work was supported by the Universiti Sains Malaysia, Research University Team (RUTeam) Grant Scheme (Grant Number : 1001/PKOMP/ 8580013) and the Uniten BOLD2025 Research Fund entitled "A Deep Learning Approach to Block Cipher Security Evaluation", Project Code J510050002/2021052.

References

1. Aboushosha, B., Ramadan, R.A., Dwivedi, A.D., El-Sayed, A., Dessouky, M.M.: SLIM: a lightweight block cipher for internet of health things. IEEE Access **8**, 203747–203757 (2020)
2. Al-Husainy, M.A.F., Al-Shargabi, B., Aljawarneh, S.: Lightweight cryptography system for IoT devices using DNA. Comput. Electr. Engi. **95**, 107418 (2021)
3. Banik, S., et al.: Midori: a block cipher for low energy. In: Iwata, T., Cheon, J.H. (eds.) ASIACRYPT 2015. LNCS, vol. 9453, pp. 411–436. Springer, Heidelberg (2015). https://doi.org/10.1007/978-3-662-48800-3_17
4. Beierle, C., et al.: The SKINNY family of block ciphers and its low-latency variant MANTIS. In: Robshaw, M., Katz, J. (eds.) CRYPTO 2016. LNCS, vol. 9815, pp. 123–153. Springer, Heidelberg (2016). https://doi.org/10.1007/978-3-662-53008-5_5
5. Bogdanov, A., et al.: PRESENT: an ultra-lightweight block cipher. In: Paillier, P., Verbauwhede, I. (eds.) CHES 2007. LNCS, vol. 4727, pp. 450–466. Springer, Heidelberg (2007). https://doi.org/10.1007/978-3-540-74735-2_31
6. Burkhalter, M.: Recent data leak highlights the importance of IoT back-end security (2019). https://www.perle.com/articles/recent-data-leak-highlights-the-importance-of-iot-back-end-security-40185881.shtml
7. De Cannière, C., Dunkelman, O., Knežević, M.: KATAN and KTANTAN — a family of small and efficient hardware-oriented block ciphers. In: Clavier, C., Gaj, K. (eds.) CHES 2009. LNCS, vol. 5747, pp. 272–288. Springer, Heidelberg (2009). https://doi.org/10.1007/978-3-642-04138-9_20
8. Chen, S., et al.: SAND: an AND-RX Feistel lightweight block cipher supporting S-box-based security evaluations. Des. Codes Crypt. **90**(1), 155–198 (2022)
9. Feng, J., Li, L.: SCENERY: a lightweight block cipher based on Feistel structure. Front. Comp. Sci. **16**(3), 1–10 (2022). https://doi.org/10.1007/s11704-020-0115-9
10. Guo, J., Peyrin, T., Poschmann, A., Robshaw, M.: The LED block cipher. In: Preneel, B., Takagi, T. (eds.) CHES 2011. LNCS, vol. 6917, pp. 326–341. Springer, Heidelberg (2011). https://doi.org/10.1007/978-3-642-23951-9_22

11. Guo, Y., Li, L., Liu, B.: Shadow: a lightweight block cipher for IoT nodes. IEEE Internet Things J. **8**(16), 13014–13023 (2021)
12. Knudsen, L.R., Meier, W.: Correlations in RC6 with a reduced number of rounds. In: Goos, G., Hartmanis, J., van Leeuwen, J., Schneier, B. (eds.) FSE 2000. LNCS, vol. 1978, pp. 94–108. Springer, Heidelberg (2001). https://doi.org/10.1007/3-540-44706-7_7
13. Roy, S., Roy, S., Biswas, A., Baishnab, K.: LCB: light cipher block an ultrafast lightweight block cipher for resource constrained IoT security applications. KSII Trans. Internet Inf. Syst. **15**(11), 4122–4144 (2021). https://doi.org/10.3837/tiis.2021.11.014
14. Shibutani, K., Isobe, T., Hiwatari, H., Mitsuda, A., Akishita, T., Shirai, T.: *Piccolo*: an ultra-lightweight Blockcipher. In: Preneel, B., Takagi, T. (eds.) CHES 2011. LNCS, vol. 6917, pp. 342–357. Springer, Heidelberg (2011). https://doi.org/10.1007/978-3-642-23951-9_23
15. Stefan Kölbl: CryptoSMT: an easy to use tool for cryptanalysis of symmetric primitives. https://github.com/kste/cryptosmt
16. Teh, J.S., Tham, L.J., Jamil, N., Yap, W.S.: New differential cryptanalysis results for the lightweight block cipher BORON. J. Inf. Secur. Appl. **66**, 103129 (2022)
17. Yeoh, W.-Z., Teh, J.S., Sazali, M.I.S.B.M.: μ ^{2}?: a lightweight block cipher. In: Alfred, R., Lim, Y., Haviluddin, H., On, C.K. (eds.) Computational Science and Technology. LNEE, vol. 603, pp. 281–290. Springer, Singapore (2020). https://doi.org/10.1007/978-981-15-0058-9_27

Parallel Validity Analysis
of the Boomerang Attack Model

Pei Li[ID], Liliu Tan[ID], Shixiong Yao[ID], and Jiageng Chen[(✉)][ID]

Central China Normal University, Wuhan 430079, Hubei, China
jiageng.chen@ccnu.edu.cn

Abstract. The boomerang attack is an extension of the differential attack that make it possible to theoretically construct a long quartet structured distinguisher with high probability from two unrelated short differential characteristics. This paper gives a quantitative analysis on the precision and effectiveness of theoretical probabilistic model of the boomerang attack and its extension (rectangle attack) by applying these two attack method on a lightweight block cipher KATAN32. The experimental result shows that the deviation between the theoretical and empirical probability of these two distinguishers is effected by length of the two unrelated differential characteristics in the quartet structured distinguisher. Furthermore, we design and implement a parallel cryptanalysis method in OpenCL to speed up the verification process by exploring the computational power of modern multi-core CPU and GPU.

Keywords: Differential cryptanalysis · Boomerang attack · KATAN32 · GPU · OpenCL

1 Introduction

A differential cryptanalysis attack is a chosen-plaintext attack that abuses a long and high-probability differential characteristic of the block cipher with a large number of plaintext pairs with the same specific difference and the corresponding ciphertext pairs to find the secret key which encrypted them [4]. This method is one of the most effective methods to attack iterative block ciphers and an important criterion of measuring the security of a block cipher. However, a long and high-probability differential characteristic which can cover nearly all of the block cipher is difficult to find in practice.

To overcome the above problem, Wagner proposed the boomerang attack [16] whose main idea is to connect two short differential characteristics with high probability and generate a long distinguisher of a "quartet" structure. The boomerang attack has provided new attack method for a lot of ciphers that were considered as safe previously from differential cryptanalysis [3]. Kelsey et al. improved the boomerang attacks and proposed amplified boomerang attack [11] that converts the adaptive attack model into nonadaptive chosen plaintext attack in 1999. Biham et al. made improvement to the amplified boomerang attack at

J. Chen et al. (Eds.): EISA 2022, CCIS 1641, pp. 68–86, 2022.
https://doi.org/10.1007/978-3-031-23098-1_5

the European Secret Conference and named it rectangle attack [2] in 2001. Rectangle attacks can aggregate multiple different differential paths, therefore, many limitations are eliminated when using the rectangle attack, which greatly reduces the complexity of the attack and increases the probability of the distinguisher.

The probability of the boomerang attack distinguisher is a theoretical probability calculated according to the boomerang attack model. There is currently no experiment to prove if this probability is accurate, since the verification process requires a large amount of chosen plaintexts and a lot of computational resources. Modern heterogeneous computing systems equipped with CPUs and GPUs provide a powerful platform to solve the computational intensive problem.

In this paper, we verify the effectiveness and accuracy of the boomerang attack model as well as those of the rectangle attack model. We will show how to search the differential characteristics according to branch-and-bound algorithm, and how to use parallel algorithm to accelerate the process of verification on heterogeneous architectures. To demonstrate the probability, we effectuate differential analysis on hardware-oriented Block Ciphers KATAN32, in addition, we use OpenCL [10] heterogeneous programming framework to accelerate the verification process on GPU. The discoveries and contributions of this paper are listed as follows:

(1) For KATAN32 ciphers, there may actually exist some correct quartet distinguishers which are theoretically invalid for the boomerang or rectangle attack model.

(2) A theoretically valid distinguisher could be inapplicable due to the two independent differential paths in the quartet structured distinguisher are mutually exclusive or incompatible.

(3) For KATAN32 ciphers, there is a deviation between the actual probability and the theoretical probability of boomerang attack and rectangle attack. Due to the rectangle distinguisher is constructed by aggregating the differential paths, while the boomerang distinguisher is constructed by selecting two specific differential paths. The overall deviation of the rectangle attack is less biased, compared to boomerang attacks.

(4) For KATAN32 ciphers, the deviation between the theoretical probability and the actual probability of boomerang attack and rectangle attack decreases as the number of rounds increases.

(5) This paper proposed a parallel cryptanalysis and verification algorithm for GPU to speed up the verification process, which has greatly accelerated the verification process compared with the serial CPU version.

This paper is organized as follows. Section 2 introduces the basic idea of differential analysis and boomerang attack, the structure of KATAN32, then followed with the GPU programming. The validity verification and parallel implementation scheme design of boomerang attack model are shown in Sect. 3. Section 4 presents and analyses the experimental results. Finally, we present conclusions and discuss the future work in Sect. 5.

2   Preliminaries

2.1   Differential Analysis

Differential analysis is a cryptanalytical method proposed for analysing DES by Eli Biham and Adi Shamir in 1990 [5]. It traces difference through the network of transformation, discovers the non-random behavior of the block cipher, and finally exploits such properties to recover the secret key. Several definitions involved in differential analysis are given below.

Differential Pair. Supposing that the difference of the two input plaintexts is $X \oplus X^* = \beta_0$, and the difference of the two corresponding cyphertexts after performing i round encryption is $Y \oplus Y^* = \beta_i$, then we have (β_0, β_i) as an i-round differential pair of the block cipher.

Differential Characteristic. A tracing path of highly probable difference through the various stages of encryption. For example, $\Omega = (\beta_0, \beta_1, \cdots, \beta_{i-1}, \beta_i)$ is an i round differential characteristic, also known as the differential path.

Given an ideal block cipher with n-bit output, the probability of any differential characteristic should be $DP(\Omega) = \frac{1}{2^n - 1} \approx \frac{1}{2^n}$. However, in practice, we can always find a differential characteristic as differential distinguisher whose probability is greater than $\frac{1}{2^n}$. Then the key recovery attack can be performed on block ciphers by exploiting the probabilistic property of the distinguisher with large amount of plaintexts and ciphertexts. Note that the longer the differential pair, the lower the corresponding probability. In the most circumstances, we can only find a distinguisher which has a long differential with low probability.

2.2   The Boomerang Attack's Quartet Structure

Instead of using a long differential with low probability, the boomerang attack [16] concatenates two short differentials with high probability to carry out the attack in order to achieve better effect than the traditional differential attack since it is much easier to find a short differential characteristic with high probability than a long one with high probability.

Figure 1 shows the structure of the boomerang attack. The n-bit block cipher with k-bit key, $E : \{0,1\}^n \times \{0,1\}^k \to \{0,1\}^n$, can be described as a cascade cipher $E = E_1 \circ E_0$. E_0 represents the first half of the cipher which exists a differential $\alpha \to \beta$ with probability p, and E_1 represents the last half which exists a differential $\gamma \to \delta$ with probability q. Both E_0 and E_1 are reversible.

(P_a, P_b) and (P_c, P_d) represent the plaintext pairs whose differential is α. (C_a, C_b) and (C_c, C_d) represent the corresponding cyphertext pairs whose differential is δ. The probability of the quartet distinguisher can be deduced as follow:

$$Pr(\alpha, \delta \to \delta, \alpha) = Pr(\alpha \to \beta) \cdot Pr(\delta \to \gamma) \cdot Pr(\delta \to \gamma) \cdot Pr(\beta \to \alpha)$$
$$= p \cdot q \cdot q \cdot p = p^2 q^2 \tag{1}$$

If $p^2 q^2$ is greater than 2^{-n}, then we can use this distinguisher to recover the secret key.

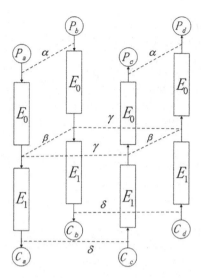

Fig. 1. The boomerang quartet

2.3 KATAN Block Cipher

The KATAN [7] is a family with small and efficient hardware-oriented block ciphers based on nonlinear feedback shift registers. The family consists of three variants according to the block size. KATAN32 is the smallest in the family with 32 bits, which means that the sizes of its plaintext and ciphertext are both 32 bits. The block sizes of KATAN48 and KATAN64 are 48 bits and 64 bits respectively. All variants utilize the same 80-bit LFSR-type key scheduling function. In addition, the nonlinear function of KATAN family and the number of encryption rounds are also identical.

The complete KATAN32 encryption requires 254 rounds of iteration, and the round function structure of KATAN32 which is similar to any of the KATAN variants as shown in Fig. 2. A plaintext with 32 bits is loaded into registers $L1$ and $L2$ whose length are 13 and 19 bits respectively in the round function. In each round, KATAN32 uses two nonlinear function $f_a(\cdot)$ and $f_b(\cdot)$. Then, these split bits are regenerated as follows including bit logical operations and bit shift operations.

$$
\begin{aligned}
f_a(L_1) &= L_1[x_1] \oplus L_1[x_2] \oplus (L_1[x_3] \cdot L_1[x_4]) \oplus (L_1[x_5] \cdot IR) \oplus k_a \\
f_b(L_2) &= L_2[y_1] \oplus L_2[y_2] \oplus (L_2[y_3] \cdot L_2[y_4]) \oplus (L_2[y_5] \cdot L_2[y_6]) \oplus k_b \\
L_1[i] &= L_1[i-1] (1 \leq i < |L_1|), \quad L_1[0] = f_b(L_2) \\
L_2[i] &= L_2[i-1] (1 \leq i < |L_2|), \quad L_2[0] = f_a(L_1)
\end{aligned}
\tag{2}
$$

In the above formulas, IR is an irregular feedback rule whose value is related to the number of encryption rounds. The operation of $\oplus$ is XOR and $\cdot$ is bitwise AND. k_a and k_b are two subkey bits that k_a is described to be k_{2i} whereas k_b

is k_{2i+1} for round i. $L[i]$ signifies the i-th bit of L. For each variant, the bits x_i and y_i are set independently [9], the particular parameters of KATAN family are listed in Table 1.

The key schedule of the KATAN32 cipher loads the 80-bit key into an LFSR whose chosen feedback polynomial is $x^{80} + x^{61} + x^{50} + x^{13} + 1$. The subkey of round i is extended by the primary key K according to the key scheduling function by the following linear operations.

$$k_i = \begin{cases} K_i & \text{for } i = 0 \dots 79 \\ k_{i-80} \oplus k_{i-61} \oplus k_{i-50} \oplus k_{i-13} & \text{Otherwise} \end{cases} \tag{3}$$

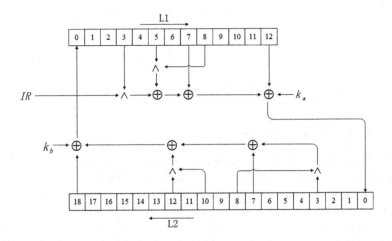

Fig. 2. Round function of KATAN32

Table 1. Parameters for KATAN family

Cipher	$|L1|$	$|L2|$	x_1	x_2	x_3	x_4	x_5	y_1	y_2	y_3	y_4	y_5	y_6
KATAN32	13	19	12	7	8	5	3	18	7	12	10	8	3
KATAN48	19	29	18	12	15	7	6	28	19	21	13	15	6
KATAN64	25	39	24	15	20	11	9	38	25	33	21	14	9

2.4 GPU and OpenCL

GPU (graphics processing unit) is a typical single instruction multiple data (SIMD) architecture which is good at large scale parallel computing. It is usually seen as a type of accelerator or a supplement to the CPU, which accelerates the graphics processing speed as much as possible. Modern GPU can performs general computing task as CPU. In addition, GPU contains multiple parallel processing cores and each one can run a large number of parallel threads. Therefore, the parallel operation capability of GPU is much greater than that of ordinary CPU, which is exactly what cryptanalysis requires.

OpenCL (Open Computing Language) [10] is the first open standard for parallel programming on heterogeneous systems that can consist of CPU, GPU, or other type of processor architecture. OpenCL is composed of two parts, one is the language used to redact kernels which is the functions running on OpenCL devices, and the other is the API used to define and control the platform. OpenCL provides task-based and data-based parallel computing mechanism. It greatly expands the application range of GPUs and makes them no longer limited to the graphics field.

The OpenCL program [10], like the CUDA program [8], is divided into two parts, one is running on the host with the CPU, and the other is running on the device with the GPU. The devices contain one or more computing units, and the computing units contain one or more processing elements [15]. The concepts are shown by a diagram in Fig. 3. The program running on the device is called a kernel function. OpenCL redacts the kernel function in a separate file, which is read and executed by the host code.

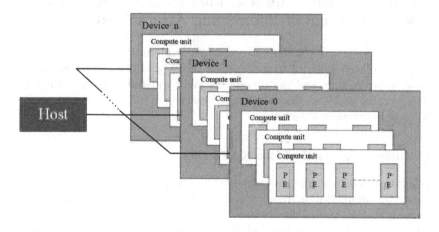

Fig. 3. Basic conception of OpenCL

In OpenCL C, the concurrent execution unit is called work-item. Each work-item executes the same kernel function. Work items can be organized into several work groups of equal size. The work-items in a work-group share a chunk of local memory. The hierarchical model of NDRange as shown in Fig. 4.

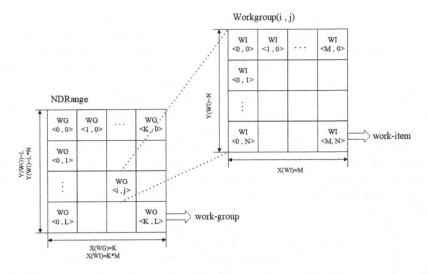

Fig. 4. The hierarchical model of NDRange (WG stands for work-group and WI for work-item)

3 Validity Verification and Parallel Implementation Scheme Design of Boomerang Attack Model

The boomerang attack combines two unrelated differential features with respectively probabilities p and q to form a new differential-like feature in the entire cryptographic system, and the theoretical joint probability is p^2q^2 which could be incorrect in practice. The following of the paper will analyse and verify the validity of boomerang attack.

3.1 Differential Analysis for KATAN32

Boomerang distinguisher is obtained by connecting two differential paths. Firstly, we perform differential analysis on KATAN32 and find two differential characteristics with high probability before verification.

Based on the branch-and-bound algorithm proposed by Matsui [13], we come up with the automatic search differential characteristics for KATAN32 without S-box in Algorithm 1. The algorithm utilizes the depth-first search algorithm to search for the best differential characteristic probability B_n of KATAN32 in n-round. Setting a proper initial value of $\overline{B_n}$ is critical to prune the bad branches [12]. When $\overline{B_n}$ is set too large, the differential path with the best probability will not be found. On the other hand, if $\overline{B_n}$ is too small, the search process will be very time-consuming.

KATAN32 is equipped with four nonlinear components AND, we will focus on analyzing the differential properties of these AND operations. Assuming that

---

Algorithm 1: Search algorithm for KATAN32

Input: ΔX_1: the input difference of round 1
$\overline{B_n}$: the initial value of early rounds
Output: ΔY_n: the output difference of round n
B_n: the best probability after n rounds

1 **procedure** *Round_1()*
   for *each candidate for* ΔX_1 **do**
2 | **for** *each feasible candidate for* ΔY_1 **do**
3 | | $p_1 = (\Delta X_1, \Delta Y_1)$ //
      | | $(\Delta X_i, \Delta Y_i) \stackrel{\text{def}}{=} \text{Prob}\{F_i(X_i \oplus \Delta X_i, K_i) = F_i(X_i, K_i) \oplus \Delta Y_i\}$
4 | | **if** $[p_1, B_{n-1}] \geq \overline{B_n}$ **then**
5 | | | *Round_i(2)*   // $[p_1, p_2, \dots, p_k] \stackrel{\text{def}}{=} \prod_{i=1}^{k} p_i$
6 | | **end**
7 | **end**
8 **end**
9 **end procedure**
10
11 **procedure** *Round_i(i)*
   $\Delta X_i = \Delta Y_{i-1}$
   for *each candidate for* ΔX_i **do**
12 | **for** *each feasible candidate for* ΔY_i **do**
13 | | $p_i = (\Delta X_i, \Delta Y_i)$
       | | **if** $[p_1, p_2, \dots, p_i, B_{n-i}] \geq \overline{B_n}$ **then**
14 | | | **if** $i+1 < n$ **then**
15 | | | | *Round_i(i + 1)*
16 | | | **end**
17 | | | **else**
18 | | | | *Round_last()*
19 | | | **end**
20 | | **end**
21 | **end**
22 **end**
23 **return** to the upper procedure
24 **end procedure**
25
26 **procedure** *Round_last()*
   $\Delta X_n = \Delta Y_{n-1}$
   $p_n = \max_{\Delta Y_n}(\Delta X_n, \Delta Y_n)$
27 **if** $[p_1, p_2, \dots, p_n] \geq \overline{B_n}$ **then**
28 | $\overline{B_n} = [p_1, p_2, \dots, p_n]$ // update the value of $\overline{B_n}$ to the max.
29 **end**
30 **return** to the upper procedure
31 **end procedure**

---

the expression in regard to the AND operation is $z = x \cdot y$, the input difference of the two operands are ΔX and ΔY, then the corresponding output difference is $\Delta Z = (x \cdot y) \oplus ((x \oplus \Delta X) \cdot (y \oplus \Delta Y))$. The relevant differential attributes are displayed in the Table 2, and we can notice that the probability of the output difference with value 0 or 1 is 2^{-1} when the input difference is not $(0, 0)$.

Table 2. Differential table of AND operation

Value of (x, y)	Difference of (x, y)		
	(0, 1)	(1, 0)	(1, 1)
(0, 0)	0	0	1
(0, 1)	0	1	0
(1, 0)	1	0	0
(1, 1)	1	1	1

We perform a differential search on the KATAN32 block cipher, and the optimal rectangle distinguisher constructed using the high-probability differential paths obtained by the search is shown in Table 3. In order to verify the validity of the boomerang attack and rectangle attack models, we will select different rounds and different probability differential paths to construct the corresponding boomerang distinguishers and rectangle distinguishers.

Table 3. The best rectangle distinguisher of KATAN32

α	0x08010000	$\hat{p}^2 = 2^{-16.2}$
δ	0x00210022	$\hat{q}^2 = 2^{-16.5}$
Probability	$\hat{p}^2\hat{q}^2 = 2^{-32.7}$	
Round	80 rounds	

Many research [1,6,14,17] has found better distinguishers. However, our purpose is to verify the validity of the basic boomerang attack model, not to find the optimal distinguisher of a specific round or the longest distinguisher. Thus, we will test the distinguishers of boomerang and rectangle attack models with different rounds and differential paths.

3.2 Design of Validity Verification Scheme for Boomerang Attack Model

Boomerang attack model consists of two differential characteristics, which are (α, β) and (γ, δ), and the probabilities corresponding to these two differential characteristics are $p = Pr(\alpha \rightarrow \beta)$ and $q = Pr(\delta \rightarrow \gamma)$, respectively. However, the rectangle distinguisher is aggregated from multiple paths, Where $\hat{p}^2 =$

$\Pr^2 (\alpha \to \beta_i) = \sum_{\text{forall } \beta} \Pr^2[\alpha \to \beta]$, $\hat{q}^2 = \Pr^2 (\gamma_i \to \delta) = \sum_{\text{forall } \gamma} \Pr^2[\gamma \to \delta]$, the theoretical probability of the corresponding rectangle distinguisher can be obtained by aggregating multiple differential paths through experiments.

We select the differential paths of 20, 25, 30 and 35 rounds, then randomly combine them into the longer quartet boomerang distinguishers and rectangle distinguishers of 40, 50, 60 and 70 rounds. We evaluate these distinguisher with following steps.

(i) Encrypt the plaintext pair (P_a, P_b) to obtain the corresponding ciphertext pair (C_a, C_b).
(ii) Calculate $C_c = C_a \oplus \delta$ and $C_d = C_b \oplus \delta$ to obtain another ciphertext pair (C_c, C_d).
(iii) Decrypt the ciphertext pair (C_c, C_d) to obtain the corresponding plaintext pair (P_c, P_d).
(iv) If $P_c \oplus P_d = \alpha$, then (P_a, P_b, P_c, P_d) is called the correct quartet.
(v) Count the number of all correct quartets.

Design of Serial Algorithm Based on CPU. The input size of the block cipher KATAN32 is 32 bit. Therefore, there are 2^{32} pairs of (P_a, P_b) that satisfy $P_a \oplus P_b = \alpha$. We perform the following operations on each plaintext pair (P_a, P_b) whose difference is α. Firstly, we encrypt the plaintext pairs to obtain the corresponding ciphertext pairs (C_a, C_b), and calculate $C_c = C_a \oplus \delta$ and $C_d = C_b \oplus \delta$ to obtain the ciphertext pairs (C_c, C_d). Then, we perform decryption operations for the new ciphertext pairs to obtain the corresponding plaintext pairs (P_c, P_d). If the difference of the two plaintext pairs satisfy $P_c \oplus P_d = P_a \oplus P_b = \alpha$, then (P_a, P_b, P_c, P_d) is called a correct quartet. Finally, we count the number of correct quartets and calculate the probability of the correct quartet. Algorithm 2 displays the entire process.

Design of Parallel Algorithm Based on OpenCL. The GPU has thousands of computing cores. We will make full use of the parallel computing power of GPU by OpenCL to accelerate the verification process of boomerang attack model.

The experimental code consists of two parts: the host code and the kernel code. On the host side, we firstly initialize the runtime, including obtaining platform information, accessing device information, creating a context to manage device, and creating a command queue for each device to be used. As the initialization operation completed, usually, we next will create one or more OpenCL program objects. Finally, we create kernel objects linked to the functions in the program by the created and built program.

Before running the OpenCL kernel, we initialize the data to be processed, and store them into the host memory. In order to avoid out-of-memory on GPU, we only allocate a chunk of GPU memory and process 2^{32} plaintexts in batches. For every batch, the OpenCL kernel will apply encryption, decryption and counting process in parallel. At the end of the program, we read the result data from the

---

Algorithm 2: Serial Algorithm for Validity Verification of the Boomerang Attack Model

---

    Input: α: the input difference of plaintext pair(P_a, P_b)
            δ: the output difference of E_0
            P_a: 2^{32} possible plaintext values
    Output: *count*: the number of correct quartets

1

2 **procedure** *statistic*()
    for *each plaintext P_a* **do**

3 | $P_b = P_a \oplus \alpha$;

4 | **encrypt** $P_a \rightarrow C_a$;

5 | **encrypt** $P_b \rightarrow C_b$;

6 | $C_c = C_a \oplus \delta$;

7 | $C_d = C_b \oplus \delta$;

8 | **decrypt** $C_c \rightarrow P_c$;

9 | **decrypt** $C_d \rightarrow P_d$;

10 | $P_c xor P_d = P_c \oplus P_d$;

11 | **compare** $P_c xor P_d$ with α ;

12 | **if** $P_c xor P_d = \alpha$ **then**

13 | | count++

14 | **end**

15 **end**

16 **end procedure**

---

device memory and free the allocated memory. Algorithm 3 displays the entire process.

4 Experimental Results

4.1 Experimental Setup

In our study, the experimental environment such as platforms and devices we used are described in Table 8. We investigate the boomerang attack model by using the parallel validity verification method presented in Sect. 3.2. We will also use the similar method to evaluate the validity of the rectangle attack model.

4.2 Analysis of the Experimental Results of the Validity Verification of the Boomerang Attack Model

Our scheme is to randomly select two KATAN32 differential characteristics for splicing. In our experiment, we connected two differential characteristics of 35 rounds, 30 rounds, 25 rounds and 20 rounds to obtain 70 rounds, 60 rounds, 50 rounds, 40 rounds boomerang distinguishers respectively. Then we build the corresponding rectangle distinguishers through path aggregation.

Since KATAN32 is a 32-bit block cipher, there are a total of 2^{32} possible plaintexts of KATAN32. Therefore, there are also 2^{32} plaintext differential pairs

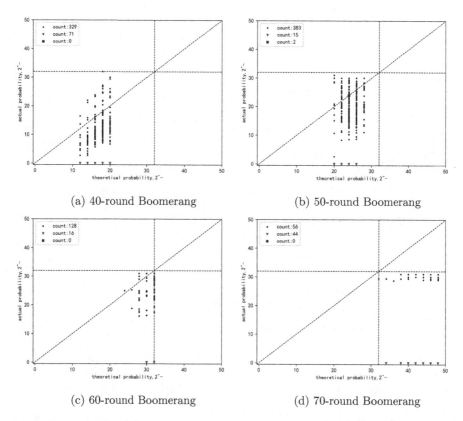

(a) 40-round Boomerang   (b) 50-round Boomerang

(c) 60-round Boomerang   (d) 70-round Boomerang

Fig. 5. The theoretical and actual probability comparison results of the 40-round, 50-round, 60-round and 70-round boomerang distinguishers.

and their corresponding quartets. Then, we use 2^{32} sets of plaintext pairs to test all boomerang distinguishers and rectangle distinguishers. Assuming that the number of correct quartets actually obtained is represented by $\#(P_a, P_b, P_c, P_d)$, then the probability of the correct quartets generated which is also the actual probability of distinguishers will be calculated by:

$$P_r = \frac{\#(P_a, P_b, P_c, P_d)}{2^{32}}$$

The theoretical and actual probability comparison results of the 40-round, 50-round, 60-round and 70-round boomerang and rectangle distinguishers are shown in Fig. 5 and Fig. 6, respectively. In these figures, the value of y-axis represents the theoretical probability of the boomerang or rectangle distinguishers, and the value of x-axis represents the actual probability calculated through experiments. The meanings of special marks and different types of discrete points in the figure are listed as follows:

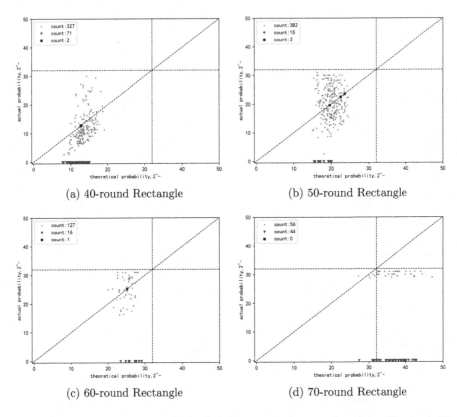

Fig. 6. The theoretical and actual probability comparison results of the 40-round, 50-round, 60-round and 70-round rectangle distinguishers.

Table 4. Average value of the deviation between the theoretical probability and the actual probability of different distinguishers

	40 rounds	50 rounds	60 rounds	70 rounds
Boomerang	3.3045e−3	4.9661e−4	1.2568e−6	5.4038e−10
Rectangle	3.2926e−3	4.9595e−4	1.2519e−6	4.6395e−10

- The diagonal dashed line means $y = x$.
- The dashed line perpendicular to the x-axis represents $x = 2^{-32}$.
- The dashed line perpendicular to the y-axis represents $y = 2^{-32}$.
- The dots represent ordinary discrete points.
- The inverted triangles represent discrete points where the probability that a valid distinguisher with theoretical probability greater than 2^{-32} actually obtains the correct quartet is 0.
- The squares represent discrete points on the dashed line $y = x$ where the theoretical and actual probabilitie are equal.

Table 5. Boomerang distinguishers with less deviation (partial samples)

α	β	γ	δ	Rounds	Theoretical	Actual
0x20040000	0x00000200	0x00410000	0x22000004	40	2^{-18}	$2^{-17.6}$
0x04008000	0x20000040	0x00104000	0x08800001	40	2^{-18}	$2^{-17.8}$
0x10020000	0x80000100	0x00202000	0x10000002	40	2^{-16}	$2^{-16.2}$
0x00410000	0x22000004	0x08010000	0x00000080	40	2^{-16}	$2^{-15.4}$
0x00000042	0x20002004	0x00040000	0x02101200	50	2^{-24}	$2^{-23.2}$
0x00200000	0x10801000	0x00808000	0x42000000	50	2^{-22}	$2^{-21.4}$
0x00208000	0x10801000	0x10020000	0xc4000008	50	2^{-24}	$2^{-24.7}$
0x00440000	0x21000000	0x00200001	0x00000080	50	2^{-26}	$2^{-26.3}$
0x02004000	0x08400800	0x08010000	0x21000000	60	2^{-26}	$2^{-25.3}$
0x00808000	0x02100200	0x00000042	0xa1000100	60	2^{-32}	2^{-31}
0x00202000	0x40840080	0x02004000	0x08400800	60	2^{-30}	$2^{-29.4}$

According to all the comparison results we can draw the following conclusions.

(1) From Fig. 5d and Fig. 6d, we can observe that some theoretically "bad" distinguishers whose probabilities are less than 2^{-32} actually are able to obtain some correct quartets and can be used in the key recovery process of KATAN32 in practice as the "good" distinguishers.

(2) Choosing two appropriate differential paths is critical to build a good boomerang distinguisher. A common method is to independently select two optimal short differential path and combine them into a long boomerang distinguisher. However, the selected two path could be mutual exclusive, that is, a theoretically valid distinguisher actually has actually 0 probability of obtaining a correct quartet. These case can be noticed from Fig. 5 and Fig. 6 where the points lie on the x-axis.

(3) We represent the expectation of the deviation between the theoretical and actual probabilities of all discriminators under the same number of rounds in Table 4.

From Table 4, we can intuitively observe that the deviation value corresponding to the boomerang distinguisher is always larger than that of the rectangle distinguisher in the same round. In theory, the boomerang distinguisher is composed of two specific differential paths, while the two parts of the rectangle distinguisher are aggregated through multiple paths. Therefore, compared to the boomerang distinguisher, the theoretical probability of the rectangle distinguisher is closer to the actual value.

(4) From Table 4, we can also observe that the average deviation between the boomerang distinguisher and the rectangle distinguisher decreases as the number of rounds increases. In theory, the more rounds a differential characteristic has, the lower its probability. Therefore, we can also verify that as the number of rounds increases, the deviation between the actual probability

and the theoretical probability of the distinguisher also decreases. Table 5 and Table 6 list some data samples where the theoretical probability and actual probability of boomerang distinguisher and rectangle distinguisher are close.

Table 6. Rectangle distinguishers with less deviation (partial samples)

α	δ	Rounds	Theoretical	Actual
0x20040000	0x00000020	40	$2^{-12.8}$	$2^{-12.8}$
0x00202000	0x42000000	40	$2^{-12.3}$	$2^{-12.2}$
0x10020000	0x88001010	40	$2^{-14.7}$	$2^{-14.6}$
0x00200000	0x20000040	40	$2^{-11.8}$	$2^{-11.7}$
0x00200001	0x08401800	50	$2^{-23.6}$	$2^{-23.6}$
0x00800000	0x81080100	50	$2^{-19.6}$	$2^{-19.6}$
0x00820000	0x80000100	50	$2^{-18.1}$	2^{-18}
0x40080000	0x42000200	50	$2^{-23.7}$	$2^{-23.6}$
0x00802000	0x20000004	60	$2^{-25.2}$	$2^{-25.2}$
0x00000042	0x40840080	60	$2^{-27.5}$	$2^{-27.2}$
0x00802000	0x08400800	60	$2^{-24.4}$	$2^{-24.6}$

(5) Our experiment not only compares the theoretical probability and actual probability of boomerang attack, but also tests the boomerang distinguisher with different keys. For each one of the 40-round, 50-round and 60-round boomerang distinguishers, 10 different keys were selected separately for the testing. The results are summarized in Table 10. As for the impact of the key, most of the randomly selected keys have very small impact on the actual probability.

4.3   Comparison of CPU and GPU Algorithm Results

Based on the validity verification experiment of the boomerang attack model, we propose a serial sequential implementation and a parallel implementation based on OpenCL. We tested the 40-round, 50-round, 60-round, and 70-round distinguishers in three different environments: CPU single-threaded, CPU multi-threaded, and GPU parallel. In the CPU multi-threaded environment, the tests were carried out with different threads with 32, 64 and 112 threads, respectively. The experimental execution time is shown in Table 9.

From Table 7, we can observe that the GPU-based parallel implementation is more than 360 times faster than the CPU single-threaded serial implementation. The CPU multi-threaded (112 threads) implementation is also more than 90 times faster than the CPU single-threaded implementation.

Table 7. The speedup compared to the single thread CPU method

	40 rounds	50 rounds	60 rounds	70 rounds
CPU multi-threaded (112 threads)	91.3	110.4	123	136.5
GPU parallel	360.2	429.2	475.5	513

5 Conclusion

In this paper, we proposed a parallel validity verification scheme of boomerang attack model. The experimental result shows that there is a difference between the theoretical and empirical probabilities for every distinguisher. Similar experimental results can also be observed from the rectangle attack model. We also noticed that the validity of a specific distinguisher is difficult to predict. Thus, we should use multiple distinguishers with different differential characteristics to increase the success rate of the boomerang attack, as well as that of the rectangle attack.

Appendix

Table 8. Device information of the CPU and GPU

	CPU	GPU
Name	Intel Xeon Platinum 9282	Tesla V100-PCIE-16 GB
Architecture	Skylake	Volta
CUDA cores	–	5120
Base clock	3600 MHz	1290 MHz
Boost clock	3800 MHz	1530 MHz
CPU cores	112	–
OpenCL	OpenCL 1.2	
System	Centos 7	

Table 9. Validation process execution time in different environments

	40 rounds	50 rounds	60 rounds	70 rounds
CPU single-threaded	54622.61 s	66920.10 s	75683.74 s	87013.79 s
CPU multi-threaded (32 threads)	1764.14 s	2035.25 s	2289.62 s	2656.61 s
CPU multi-threaded (64 threads)	906.29 s	1015.71 s	1170.02 s	1205.1 s
CPU multi-threaded (112 threads)	598.30 s	606.22 s	615.24 s	637.53 s
GPU parallel	151.64 s	155.93 s	159.15 s	169.61 s

Algorithm 3: Parallel Algorithm for Validity Verification of the Boomerang Attack Model

---

Input: α: the input difference of plaintext pair(P_a, P_b)
Output: *count*: the number of correct quartets

1 **procedure** *count*()
2   Initialize OpenCL runtime and Objects;
3   **for** *each batch of plaintexts P_a* **do**
4   **allocate** pinned memory on host device ;
5   **allocate** global memory on GPU device ;
6   **write** plaintexts P_a and key into the corresponding buffer ;
7   **copy** required information to GPU memory ;
8   **launch** *kernel_Encryption_Decryption*$(P_a, key, \ldots)$;
9   **copy** the XOR value of P_c and P_d from GPU to host memory ;
10   **launch** *kernel_statistic*$(P_c xor P_d, \ldots)$;
11   **copy** the number of rigth quartets from GPU to host memory
12 **end**
13   **count** all the rigth quartets ;
14   **free** the host memory ;
15   **free** the GPU memory ;
16   **release** all the runtime objects ;
17 **end procedure**
18
19 **procedure** *kernel_Encryption_Decryption*$(P_a, key, \ldots)$
20   **for** *each plaintext P_a* **do**
21       $g_{id} = get\_global\_id(0)$;
22       $P_b = P_a \oplus \alpha$;
23   **encrypt** $P_a \rightarrow C_a$;
24   **encrypt** $P_b \rightarrow C_b$;
25       $C_c = C_a \oplus \delta$;
26       $C_d = C_b \oplus \delta$;
27   **decrypt** $C_c \rightarrow P_c$;
28   **decrypt** $C_d \rightarrow P_d$;
29       $P_c xor P_d = P_c \oplus P_d$;
30 **end**
31 **end procedure**
32
33 **procedure** *kernel_statistic*$(P_c xor P_d, \ldots)$
34   **for** *each $P_c xor P_d$* **do**
35       $g_{id} = get\_global\_id(0)$;
36   **compare** $P_c xor P_d$ with α ;
37   **if** $P_c xor P_d = \alpha$ **then**
38   count++
39   **end**
40 **end**
41 **end procedure**

Table 10. Test of different keys (partial samples)

α	β	γ	δ	Rounds	Theoretical	Key	Actual
0x00202000	0x10000002	0x00040000	0x42000000	40	2^{-14}	0x9afff003ff	$2^{-13.2}$
						0xdaede4936f	$2^{-13.2}$
						0x5aada4976e	$2^{-13.2}$
						0xdae5a4956e	$2^{-13.2}$
						0xbae3b49a6e	$2^{-13.2}$
						0x2aa39c9ace	$2^{-13.2}$
						0x1bb3b49f4e	$2^{-13.2}$
						0x1d93bc9f4a	$2^{-13.2}$
						0xed93948f4b	$2^{-13.2}$
						0xe0da9c8e4b	$2^{-13.2}$
0x00208000	0x1080-1000	0x00802000	0x42000000	50	2^{-22}	0x26bffc00ffe6b	$2^{-21.8}$
						0x36bb7924dbe6b	$2^{-21.7}$
						0x16ab6925dba6b	$2^{-21.5}$
						0x36b969255ba6b	$2^{-21.6}$
						0x2eb8ed269ba69	$2^{-21.5}$
						0xaa8e726b3869	$2^{-21.5}$
						0x6eced27d3a69	$2^{-21.4}$
						0x764ef27d2a6d	$2^{-21.6}$
						0x3b64e523d2e6d	$2^{-21.4}$
						0x3836a72392eed	$2^{-21.3}$
0x0801-0000	0x21000000	0x02004000	0x08400800	60	2^{-26}	0x9afff003ff9b000	$2^{-18.8}$
						0xdaede4936f9ae00	$2^{-18.8}$
						0x5aada4976e9ad80	$2^{-18.8}$
						0xdae5a4956e9ad80	$2^{-18.8}$
						0xbae3b49a6e9a600	$2^{-18.8}$
						0x2aa39c9ace1a5a0	$2^{-18.8}$
						0x1bb3b49f4e9a5b0	$2^{-18.8}$
						0x1d93bc9f4a9b530	$2^{-18.9}$
						0xed93948f4b9b700	$2^{-18.8}$
						0xe0da9c8e4bbb500	$2^{-18.8}$

References

1. Ahmadian, Z., Rasoolzadeh, S., Salmasizadeh, M., Aref, M.R.: Automated dynamic cube attack on block ciphers: cryptanalysis of simon and katan. Cryptology ePrint Archive (2015)
2. Biham, E., Dunkelman, O., Keller, N.: The rectangle attack—rectangling the serpent. In: Pfitzmann, B. (ed.) EUROCRYPT 2001. LNCS, vol. 2045, pp. 340–357. Springer, Heidelberg (2001). https://doi.org/10.1007/3-540-44987-6_21
3. Biham, E., Dunkelman, O., Keller, N.: New results on boomerang and rectangle attacks. In: Daemen, J., Rijmen, V. (eds.) FSE 2002. LNCS, vol. 2365, pp. 1–16. Springer, Heidelberg (2002). https://doi.org/10.1007/3-540-45661-9_1
4. Biham, E., Shamir, A.: Differential cryptanalysis of des-like cryptosystems. J. Cryptology **4**(1), 3–72 (1991)

5. Biham, E., Shamir, A.: Differential cryptanalysis of the full 16-round DES. In: Brickell, E.F. (ed.) CRYPTO 1992. LNCS, vol. 740, pp. 487–496. Springer, Heidelberg (1993). https://doi.org/10.1007/3-540-48071-4_34

6. Chen, J., Teh, J.S., Su, C., Samsudin, A., Fang, J.: Improved (related-key) attacks on round-reduced KATAN-32/48/64 based on the extended boomerang framework. In: Liu, J.K., Steinfeld, R. (eds.) ACISP 2016. LNCS, vol. 9723, pp. 333–346. Springer, Cham (2016). https://doi.org/10.1007/978-3-319-40367-0_21

7. De Cannière, C., Dunkelman, O., Knežević, M.: KATAN and KTANTAN — a family of small and efficient hardware-oriented block ciphers. In: Clavier, C., Gaj, K. (eds.) CHES 2009. LNCS, vol. 5747, pp. 272–288. Springer, Heidelberg (2009). https://doi.org/10.1007/978-3-642-04138-9_20

8. Garland, M., et al.: Parallel computing experiences with CUDA. IEEE Micro **28**(4), 13–27 (2008)

9. Isobe, T., Sasaki, Yu., Chen, J.: Related-key boomerang attacks on KATAN32/48/64. In: Boyd, C., Simpson, L. (eds.) ACISP 2013. LNCS, vol. 7959, pp. 268–285. Springer, Heidelberg (2013). https://doi.org/10.1007/978-3-642-39059-3_19

10. Kaeli, D.R., Mistry, P., Schaa, D., Zhang, D.P.: Heterogeneous Computing with OpenCL 2.0. Morgan Kaufmann, Burlington (2015)

11. Kelsey, J., Kohno, T., Schneier, B.: Amplified boomerang attacks against reduced-round MARS and serpent. In: Goos, G., Hartmanis, J., van Leeuwen, J., Schneier, B. (eds.) FSE 2000. LNCS, vol. 1978, pp. 75–93. Springer, Heidelberg (2001). https://doi.org/10.1007/3-540-44706-7_6

12. Li, P., Zhou, S., Chen, J.: A CPU-GPU-based parallel search algorithm for the best differential characteristics of block ciphers. J. Supercomput. **77**, 1–21 (2021)

13. Matsui, M.: On correlation between the order of S-boxes and the strength of DES. In: De Santis, A. (ed.) EUROCRYPT 1994. LNCS, vol. 950, pp. 366–375. Springer, Heidelberg (1995). https://doi.org/10.1007/BFb0053451

14. Rasoolzadeh, S., Raddum, H.: Improved multi-dimensional meet-in-the-middle cryptanalysis of katan. Cryptology ePrint Archive (2016)

15. Stone, J.E., Gohara, D., Shi, G.: OpenCL: a parallel programming standard for heterogeneous computing systems. Comput. Sci. Eng. **12**(3), 66 (2010)

16. Wagner, D.: The boomerang attack. In: Knudsen, L. (ed.) FSE 1999. LNCS, vol. 1636, pp. 156–170. Springer, Heidelberg (1999). https://doi.org/10.1007/3-540-48519-8_12

17. Zhu, B., Gong, G.: Multidimensional meet-in-the-middle attack and its applications to katan32/48/64. Cryptogr. Commun. **6**(4), 313–333 (2014)

A Survey on Discrete Gaussian Samplers in Lattice Based Cryptography

Jiaxin Deng[1], Simin Chen[1], Jiageng Chen[1(✉)] [iD], and Weizhi Meng[2]

[1] School of Computer Science, Central China Normal University, Wuhan, China
chinkako@gmail.com
[2] Technical University of Denmark, Kongens Lyngby, Denmark

Abstract. Lattice-based cryptography is one of the most competitive algorithms in post-quantum algorithms. The discrete Gaussian sampler is a fundamental building block in lattice-based cryptography, but it is still challenging to construct a generic, efficient and secure discrete Gaussian sampler. In this work, we survey the existing discrete Gaussian samplers and summarize the characteristics and improvements of each sampler in detail. In addition, we discuss the evaluation criteria for samplers which we believe that a good scheme should use less precision to achieve the same level of security. The survey can help the reader to focus on the development of discrete Gaussian samplers and apply the discrete Gaussian sampler to lattice-based cryptography in a black-box manner.

Keywords: Lattice-based cryptography · Discrete Gaussian sampler

1 Introduction

Lattice-based cryptography has attracted more and more attention, not only within the cryptographic community, but also in the area of computer security in both research and industry, for at least two reasons: first, lattice-based cryptosystems are often algorithmically simple and highly parallelizable. Second, lattices allow to construct versatile and advanced cryptographic schemes that go beyond classical public key encryption, like identity-based encryption (IBE), fully homomorphic encryption (FHE), and attribute based encryption (ABE). Cryptographic primitives built on lattices, including digital signature schemes, IBE, and FHE, have been inspired by the Gaussian distribution reduction method proposed by [37]. Discrete Gaussian sampling was used for the first time by Gentry, Peikert, and Vaikuntanathan [23] as a trapdoor function, i.e. *preimage sampleable functions* (PSFs). They used PSFs to construct a hash-and-sign scheme, in which the message is hashed to a point in the lattice, and its signature is a nearby lattice point obtained by the sampling function. However, discrete Gaussian sampling occupies about 50% of the time in digital signature schemes [48]. Sampling with discrete Gaussian distribution is a fundamental problem that arises in almost every application of lattice cryptography, and it can be both time consuming and challenging to implement. Therefore, it is crucial to design an efficient discrete Gaussian sampler.

© The Author(s), under exclusive license to Springer Nature Switzerland AG 2022
J. Chen et al. (Eds.): EISA 2022, CCIS 1641, pp. 87–107, 2022.
https://doi.org/10.1007/978-3-031-23098-1_6

Existing samplers generally sample from a uniform distribution or other easy distributions (called approximate distribution) to obtain a target distribution (called ideal distribution). How good or bad the closeness of two distributions is determined by the relative error, and traditionally, most cryptographic schemes use statistical distance as a measure. Because the cryptographic scheme requires high quality, it is rigorous for statistical distance to be used in discrete Gaussian sampling with high quality.

There are two types of sampling algorithms: rejection sampling and inversion sampling. The rejection sampling algorithm first generates a sample x, and if x is greater than the probability of the target distribution, it will be rejected (otherwise accepted). The rejection sampling algorithm has many advantages, such as flexibility, and less memory, because the parameters of the discrete Gaussian distribution can change in real-time, and the memory consumed is independent of the parameters. The inversion sampling algorithm first computes the cumulative distribution table (CDT), then generates the random bits to look up the corresponding probability in the table, and finally inverses the cumulative distribution function to obtain the sampled value. We can divide the inversion sampling algorithm into two phases, namely the offline phase and the online phase. The CDT can be pre-computed in the offline phase, and the table can be directly looked up in the online phase without computing the complicated probability density function. Therefore inversion sampling is usually faster than rejecting sampling, but the former requires a huge pre-computed storage cost. Moreover, the pre-computed table is also related to the parameters of the Gaussian distribution, which makes inversion sampling less generic than rejection sampling (different schemes require different parameters). Recently, studies have shown that the execution time of the sampler can cause side-channel attacks [44], so the cryptographic scheme using discrete Gaussian sampling needs to consider the realization of constant time, but this is in conflict with efficiency. In other words, better use of discrete Gaussian sampling in cryptographic schemes requires a trade-off between memory consumption, sampling speed, parameter flexibility, and security. Over the two fundamental samplers, many works have improved these characteristics, generating a large number of new and more effective samplers.

Designing a generic, efficient, and secure discrete Gaussian sampler is a challenging task, and Gentry et al. [23] first adapted Klein's algorithm to a subroutine of their sampling algorithm, which is a randomized nearest-plane algorithm. Next, Peikert [41] proposed a randomized Babai's simple rounding-off algorithm, where the rounding operation used the inversion sampling. Buchmann et al. [8] proposed discrete ziggurat sampling, a rejection sampling algorithm with a time-memory trade-off. The discrete ziggurat sampling algorithm improves efficiency compared to the original [23] sampling algorithm, but it is still not a practical sampling algorithm because it requires large memory when the parameters are large, and the running time of the algorithm is not constant time. Karney [32] proposed a rejection sampling algorithm based on the von Neumann algorithm, which samples from the exponential distribution, does not require floating-point arithmetic, and the output distribution is exact. Recently, the (continuous) rounded Gaussian has been proved by Hülsing et al. [28] that it is secure for the cryptographic scheme. Compared with the discrete Gaussian, continuous Gaussian sampling has many useful algorithm libraries, such as the Box-muller algorithm. Dwarakanath et al. [18] adapted the Knuth-Yao algorithm to discrete Gaussian sampling for the first time. The algorithm is very efficient, but the disadvantage is that it relies on a pre-computed table and requires huge memory (when the standard deviation is large). Ducas et al. [14] proposed a Bernoulli-type sampling algorithm that first samples from a simple discrete Gaussian distribution and second performs rejection sampling on the sample values. The first step can be run in the offline phase and requires a relatively small amount of memory; The second step samples from a Bernoulli distribution without computing transcendental function. Because the sampler proposed by [14] is efficient and versatile, it has received a lot of attention, such as in terms of efficiency, generality, and security [3,11,13,27,43,46,49,51,53]. Micciancio and Walter [39] used the convolution-like technique in [41] to propose a significantly efficient and generic sampler. Inspired by the work of [4,39,50] improved the shortcoming of the gadget trapdoor in [38], that is, it can only be constructed on a power-of-q moduli lattice. Finally, [17] used a fast Fourier orthogonalization technique that greatly improves the sampling algorithm in [23] and applied it to the Falcon [21] signature.

Our Contribution: Our main contribution is to sort out the progress of discrete Gaussian samplers in the past ten years. We list the measures that Gaussian samplers need to use, as well as improvements in efficiency, generality, and security, as shown in Table 1. We divide Gaussian samplers into three types: rejection samplers, inversion samplers, and hybrid samplers. We believe that the survey of these samplers can help readers quickly study discrete Gaussian sampling, and provide some ideas for those interested in lattice-based cryptography.

Related Work: [20] surveyed some samplers, but it did not cover the variety of samplers, did not discuss the effect of measures, nor did it talk about constant-time improvements. [26] implemented a suite for testing discrete Gaussian sampling outputs, and [27] proposed a new test suite named SAGA. [6] investigated the hardware implementation for generating discrete Gaussian distributions, but we mainly discuss the algorithm and its improvements. [24] implemented a new sampling algorithm for lattice trapdoor, and also evaluated the recently improved Gaussian sampling algorithm, but it was not enough and the samplers were not sorted.

Organization of the Paper: We introduce some notions and discrete Gaussian distributions used in this paper in Sect. 2. We discuss measures for evaluating output distributions in Sect. 3. In Sect. 4, we extensively describe proposed samplers and their variants. Finally, we summarize the work of this paper in Sect. 5.

Table 1. Comparison between different sampler improvements: measures, efficiency, parameters, and security

Sampler	Memory	Speed	Centered	Fixed Deviation	Constant-Time	Measures
Rejection [16, 23, 35]	-/-/-	$(2\tau/\sqrt{2\pi})/6\tau/(2\tau/\sqrt{2\pi})$	✗/✗	✗/✗/✗	-/-/-	S/S/S
CDT [1, 10, 16, 29, 36, 41]	$O(\lambda\sigma)/O(\lambda\sigma)/O(\lambda\sigma)/$ $O(\lambda\sigma)/O(\lambda\sigma)/O(\lambda\sigma^*)$	$O(\lambda\log\sigma)/O(\lambda\log\sigma)/O(\lambda\log\sigma)/$ $O(\lambda\log\lambda)/O(\lambda\sigma^*)/O(\lambda\log\lambda)$	✓/✓/✗/✗/✓/✓	✓/✓/✓/✓/✓/✗	-/-/-/-/I	S/S/S/R/S/K
Discrete Ziggurat [7, 8, 25, 40]	var	var	✓/✓/✓	✓/✓/✓	-/I/-/I	S/K/S/S
Knuth-Yao [18, 25, 30, 31, 44, 45]	$O(\lambda\sigma)/O(\lambda\sigma)/O(\lambda\sigma)/$ $O(\lambda\sigma)/O(\lambda\sigma)/O(\lambda\sigma^*)$	$O(\lambda\log\lambda)/O(\lambda\log\lambda)/O(\lambda\log\lambda)/$ $O(\lambda\log\lambda)/O(\lambda\log\lambda)/O(\lambda\log\lambda)$	✓/✓/✓/✓/✓	✓/✓/✓/✓/✓/✓	-/-/I/I/I	S/S/K/K/S
Bernoulli-type [13, 14, 25, 43, 53] [3, 11, 27, 46, 49, 51]	$O(\lambda\log\sigma)/O(\lambda\log\sigma)/-/$ $O(\lambda\log\sigma)/O(\lambda)/O(\lambda)/$ $O(\lambda)/O(\lambda)/O(1)/O(1)$	$\leq 1.47/13/\approx 1.47/\leq 2/\leq 2/$ $\leq 2/\leq 2/\approx 1.47/\leq 3/\leq 2/\leq 2$	✓/✓/✗/✗/✗/ ✓/✗/✗/✓/✗/✓	✗/✗/✗/✗/✗/ ✓/✗/✗/✗/✗/✗	-/I/I/I/I /I/II/- /II/I/I	S/K/M/R/R/ R/R/S/R/R/R
Karney [12, 13, 32]	-/-/-	$\approx 2.03/\approx 1.47/\approx 3.68$	✗/✗	✗/✗	-/I/-	-/M/-
Convolution-like [4, 15, 19, 22, 29, 50]	var	var	✗/✗/✗/✗/✓	✗/✗/✗/✗/✓	I/I/-/I/-	M/S/K/M/R/M
Rounded-Gaussian [5, 7, 28, 51, 52]	-/-/-/-	-/2/-/-/2	✗/✗/✗/✗	✗/✗/✗/✗	I/I/I/I/I	R/R/R/R/R
Fast Fourier [17, 21]	$-/O(\sigma_{max})$	-/-	✗/✗	✗/✗	-/-	S/R

Table 1 summarizes the types of existing samplers, the memory used for sampling, the sampling speed (the time complexity of search algorithms or average iterations of rejection sampling), whether the center of discrete Gaussian is fixed, whether the standard deviation of discrete Gaussian is fixed, resisting side channel attack and the evaluation criteria between an ideal distribution and actual distribution.

▲ Bit precision is represented by the parameter λ.

▲ The Gaussian distribution's standard deviation is represented by the parameter σ.

▲ τ is the tail-cut of the distribution.

▲ "var" means memory or speed is variable.

▲ Smaller parameters are marked with *.

▲ Side channel attacks can be resisted by: Constant-Time (Type I) and Isochronous (Type II).

▲ There are four measures: Statistical distance (S), KL-divergence (K), Rényi-divergence (R) and Max-Log distance (M).

2 Preliminaries

2.1 Notion

We denote the integers by $\mathbb{Z}$, the rationals by $\mathbb{Q}$, and the reals by $\mathbb{R}$. We extend any real function $f(\cdot)$ to a countable set A by defining $f(A) = \sum_{x \in A} f(x)$.

We use bold lower-case letters (e.g., $\mathbf{x}$) to denote vectors in $\mathbb{R}^n$, for an undetermined positive integer dimension n that remains the same throughout the paper. A lattice Λ is a discrete additive subgroup of $\mathbb{R}^n$. In this work, we are only concerned with full-rank lattices, which are generated by some non-singular basis $B \in \mathbb{R}^{n \times n}$.

We use standard big-O notation to classify the growth of functions, and say that $f(n) = \widetilde{O}(g(n))$ if $f(n) = O(g(n) \cdot \log^c n)$ for some fixed constant c.

2.2 Discrete Gaussian Distribution

Definition 1. *For any center $c \in \mathbb{R}$ and Gaussian parameter $s \in \mathbb{R}^+$, let*

$$\rho_{s,c}(x) = e^{-\pi(x-c)^2/s^2}$$

be a Gaussian function centered in c scaled by a factor of s. This definition is sometimes formulated with the parameter $\sigma = s/\sqrt{2\pi}$. It is worth to mention that the integration of $\rho_{s,c}$ is $\int_{-\infty}^{+\infty} \rho_{s,c}(x) = s$. Therefore, we can define the continuous Gaussian distribution around c with parameter s by its probability density function

$$\forall x \in \mathbb{R}, D_{s,c}(x) = \frac{\rho_{s,c}(x)}{\int_{-\infty}^{+\infty} \rho_{s,c}(x)} = \frac{\rho_{s,c}(x)}{s}.$$

We extend Gaussian function to any countable set A by $\rho_{s,c}(A) = \sum_{x \in A} \rho_{s,c}(x)$. The discrete Gaussian distribution over the integers, denoted by

$$\forall x \in \mathbb{Z}, \mathcal{D}_{\mathbb{Z},c,s}(x) = \frac{D_{s,c}(x)}{D_{s,c}(\mathbb{Z})} = \frac{\rho_{s,c}(x)}{\rho_{s,c}(\mathbb{Z})}.$$

Naturally, we can extend the discrete Gaussian over the integer to the discrete Gaussian over the n-dimension lattice, where $\rho_{s,\mathbf{c}}(\mathbf{x}) = e^{-\pi\|\mathbf{x}-\mathbf{c}\|^2/s^2}$ and $\mathcal{D}_{\Lambda,\mathbf{c},s}(\mathbf{x}) = \frac{\rho_{s,\mathbf{c}}(\mathbf{x})}{\rho_{s,\mathbf{c}}(\Lambda)}$.

2.3 Smoothing Parameter

Definition 2 [37, *Definition 3.1*]. *For any $\epsilon > 0$, the smoothing parameter of the integers is the smallest $s > 0$ such that $\rho(s\mathbb{Z}) \leq 1 + \epsilon$.*

Lemma 1 [37, *Lemma 3.3*]. *For any integer $\mathbb{Z}$ and positive real $\epsilon > 0$, the smoothing parameter satisfies*

$$\eta_\epsilon(\mathbb{Z}) \leq \sqrt{\ln(2 + 2/\epsilon)/\pi}.$$

For example, $\eta_\epsilon(\mathbb{Z}) < 6$ is a relatively small constant for very small values of $\epsilon < 2^{-160}$.

We will use the following lemma to show how to limit the tail-cut τ,

Lemma 2 [23, Lemma 4.2]. *For any $\epsilon > 0$, any $s \geq \eta_\epsilon(\mathbb{Z})$, and any $\tau > 0$,*

$$\Pr_{x \leftarrow \mathcal{D}_{\mathbb{Z},s,c}} [|x - c| \geq \tau \cdot s] \leq 2e^{-\pi\tau^2} \cdot \frac{1 + \epsilon}{1 - \epsilon}.$$

It is too difficult or costly to sample from the ideal distribution, hence we expect the actual sampled distribution to be statistically close to the theoretical discrete Gaussian. There are several measures to keep the security proofs of the cryptographic schemes correct.

3　Measures

In this section, we overview the criteria for evaluating the output distribution of a sampler. Many security reductions for lattice-based cryptographic primitives assume that the primitive has access to samplers for ideal distribution. However, sampling from the ideal distribution is too difficult or expensive, so we just only sample from the approximate distribution. Traditionally, the quality between the approximation distribution and ideal distribution has been measured in terms of the statistical distance. Generally, the security required by a cryptographic scheme is $2^{-\lambda}$. In recent years, several statistical measures have been used to analyze the closeness of the approximate distribution to the ideal distribution. With the new measure, the analysis of cryptographic security becomes simpler and the same security can be achieved using fewer bits.

3.1　Statistical Distance

Definition 3. *The statistical distance between two distributions $\mathcal{P}$ and $\mathcal{Q}$ over the same support S is defined as*

$$\Delta(\mathcal{P}, \mathcal{Q}) = \frac{1}{2} \sum_{x \in S} |\mathcal{P}(x) - \mathcal{Q}(x)|.$$

The statistical distance is a naive and most commonly used measure. The following lemma uses statistical distance to show the relationship between the Gaussian distribution and the uniform parallelepiped.

Lemma 3 [37, Lemma 4.1]. *For any $s > 0, c \in \mathbb{R}^n$, and lattice $\Lambda(B)$, the statistical distance between $\mathcal{D}_{s,c} \bmod \mathcal{P}(B)$ and the uniform distribution over $\mathcal{P}(B)$ is at most $1/2\rho_{1/s}(\Lambda(B)^* \backslash \{0\})$. In particular, for any $\epsilon > 0$ and any $s \geq \eta_\epsilon(B)$, the statistical distance is at most*

$$\Delta(\mathcal{D}_{s,c} \bmod \mathcal{P}(B), U(\mathcal{P}(B))) \leq \epsilon/2.$$

Thus, to achieve λ-bit security, the accuracy of the statistical distance requires $\lambda + 1$ bits.

3.2 Kullback-Leibler Divergence

Definition 4. *Let $\mathcal{P}$ and $\mathcal{Q}$ be two distributions over a common countable set Ω, and let $S \subset \Omega$ be the strict support of $\mathcal{P}$($\mathcal{P}(i) > 0$ if $i \in S$). The Kullback-Leibler divergence, noted D_{KL} of $\mathcal{Q}$ from $\mathcal{P}$ is defined as:*

$$D_{KL}(\mathcal{P}\|\mathcal{Q}) \le 2\sum_{i \in S} \ln\left(\frac{\mathcal{P}(i)}{\mathcal{Q}(i)}\right)\mathcal{P}(i).$$

with the convention that $\ln(x/0) = +\infty$ for any $x > 0$.

Compared with statistical distance, KL-divergence has many good properties, such as additivity and non-decreasing. An important difference though is that it is not symmetric. The following lemma shows that KL divergence provides higher security,

Lemma 4 [42, *Lemma 1*]. *Let $\varepsilon^{\mathcal{P}}$ be an algorithm making at most q queries to an oracle sampling from a distribution $\mathcal{P}$ and returning a bit. Let $\epsilon \ge 0$, and $\mathcal{Q}$ be a distribution such that $D_{KL}(\mathcal{P}\|\mathcal{Q}) \le \epsilon$. Let x (resp. y) denote the probability that $\varepsilon^{\mathcal{P}}$ (resp. $\varepsilon^{\mathcal{Q}}$) outputs 1. Then, $|x - y| \le \sqrt{q\epsilon/2}$.*

We give an example below to illustrate the advantages of KL divergence in terms of security. Let $\mathcal{B}_c$ be the Bernoulli variable that returns 1 with probability c, then we have $D_{KL}(\mathcal{B}_{\frac{1-\epsilon}{2}}\|\mathcal{B}_{\frac{1}{2}}) \approx \epsilon^2/2$ (by Definition 4). Note that one requires $q = O(1/\epsilon^2)$ samples to distinguish two distribution with constant advantage rather than $q = O(1/\epsilon)$ queries for the statistical distance.

Many works use KL-divergence instead of statistical distance, see Table 1 for details. Pöppelmann et al. [42] first use KL-divergence to improve the convolution Lemma of Peikert [41] and construct a sampler using convolutions, resulting in the smoothing condition reduced by a factor of about $\sqrt{2}$. They also present a CDT sampling algorithm with reduced table size; [25,30] proposed a more efficient and more secure Gaussian sampling algorithm by using KL-divergence.

3.3 Rényi Divergence

Definition 5. *For any two discrete probability distribution P and Q such that $Supp(P) \subseteq Supp(Q)$ and $a \in (1, +\infty)$, we define the Rényi divergence of order a by*

$$R_a(P\|Q) = \left(\sum_{x \in Supp(P)} \frac{P(x)^a}{Q(x)^{a-1}}\right)^{\frac{1}{a-1}}.$$

We omit the a subscript when $a = 2$. We define the Rényi divergences of order 1 and $+\infty$ by

$$R_1(P\|Q) = \exp\left(\sum_{x \in SuppP} P(x)\log\frac{P(x)}{Q(x)}\right) \quad and \quad R_\infty(P\|Q) = \max_{x \in Supp(P)} \frac{P(x)}{Q(x)}.$$

As we can see, the divergence R_1 is the (exponential of) the KL-divergence.

Similarly, replacing the statistical distance can reduce the required parameter s for the smoothing parameter by a factor of $\Theta(\sqrt{\lambda})$. [2] analyzed the BLISS sampler using Rényi divergences, and specifically the divergence of order infinity is closely related to the relative error discussed in [47]. Again, see Table 1 for using divergence in discrete Gaussian sampling.

3.4   Max-Log Distance

The above measures either do not have strong security or depend on some specific conditions. Micciancio and Walter [39] discussed the properties of a useful or efficient measure in a cryptographic scheme, and proposed a new notation, namely, max-log distance.

Definition 6. *The max-log distance between two distributions P and Q over the same support S is*

$$\Delta(\mathcal{P}, \mathcal{Q}) = \max_{x \in S} |\ln \mathcal{P}(x) - \ln \mathcal{Q}(x)|.$$

[39] performed a detailed analysis of ML-distance that satisfies three useful properties, including probability preservation, sub-additivity, and data processing inequality. They call any measure that satisfies these three properties a useful measure. Furthermore, a measure will be called λ-efficient measure if it satisfies λ-pythagorean property. The following lemma shows that max-log distance is more competitive than other measures.

Lemma 5 [39, *Lemma 3.3*]. *Let $S^{\mathcal{P}}$ be a standard cryptographic scheme with oracle to a probability distribution ensemble $\mathcal{P}_\theta$. If $S^{\mathcal{P}}$ is k-bit secure and $\delta(\mathcal{P}_\theta, \mathcal{Q}_\theta) \leq 2^{-k/2}$ for some $2^{-k/2}$-efficient measure δ, then $S^{\mathcal{Q}}$ is $(k-3)$-bit secure.*

According to Lemma 5, we can build a 128-bit secure encryption scheme but only need to store data in variables with 63-bit precision. For more details we refer the reader to [39] and list papers that use different measures in recent years, see Table 1.

4   Samplers

Now we know what a discrete Gaussian distribution over the integers or a lattice is, we will review the current sampling algorithms. Such algorithms are known as Gaussian samplers, and there were two main types of Gaussian samplers, including rejection samplers and inversion samplers. Finally, we discuss the hybrid sampler, which is closely related to lattice-based cryptographic schemes, such as improving the efficiency of lattice signatures.

4.1   Rejection Sampler

The basic rejection sampling is as follows: sampling $x \in S$ from some easy distribution (typically the uniform or exponential distribution), where S is a set, and then accepting the sample within the probability proportional to $\rho_{s,c}(x)$ (otherwise rejecting). We survey several variants of rejection sampling and give more details below.

4.1.1   Klein's Sampler

Klein's sampler was first introduced in [33] and used in a cryptographic context for the first time by Gentry, Peikert and Vaikuntanathan [23]. Algorithm 1 describes the details of the sampler, which is a subroutine of the lattice Gaussian sampler in [23], namely a randomized rounding according to a discrete Gaussian over $\mathbb{Z}$.

Algorithm 1. Klein's Sampler

Output: a sample value $x \in D_{\mathbb{Z},\sigma,c}$
1: **do**
2:     $x \leftarrow \mathbb{Z} \cap [c - \tau\sigma, c + \tau\sigma]$
3:     $y \in [0, 1)$ uniformly at random
4: **while** $y < \rho_{\sigma,c}(x)$
5: **return** x

The above algorithm is simple and intuitive and does not require a pre-computed table. Thus, its memory consumption is independent of the parameters. However, since the algorithm needs to consume a lot of resources to compute the transcendental function e, and involves arbitrary precision operations; the rejection rate of Klein's sampler is so high that it is rarely used directly in the practical scheme of lattice-based cryptography.

Ducas and Nguyen [16] found that in most cases the most significant bits are enough to reject the samples. Their algorithm uses floating point numbers to compute transcendental functions, and the laziness technique they proposed can significantly speed up sampling algorithms. Specially, in NTRUSign lattice, laziness can decrease the complexity of preimage sampling function from $\widetilde{\mathcal{O}}(n^3)$ to $\widetilde{\mathcal{O}}(n^2)$ or even $\widetilde{\mathcal{O}}(n)$.

4.1.2   Discrete Ziggurat Sampler

Buchmann et al. [8] adapted the continuous Ziggurat algorithm to the discrete case. The discrete Ziggurat algorithm first generates multiple adjacent rectangles with the same area from top to bottom, the y-axis is the left side of the rectangle, the lower right corner of the rectangle is on the Gaussian distribution function, and the coordinates (x_i, y_i) of the lower right corner of the rectangle are stored in pre-computation table. When sampling, the algorithm picks a rectangle R_i uniformly at random and then samples an x coordinate inside the rectangle also uniformly at random. Rectangle R_i can be split into a left rectangle R_i^l that lies completely within the area of the probability density function (PDF) and a right rectangle R_i^r that is only partially covered by the PDF. If the coordinate x is in the left rectangle R_i^l, then it is accepted as a sample. Otherwise, we perform rejection sampling in the right rectangle R_i^r. Algorithm 2 shows the full sampling process.

Algorithm 2. Discrete Ziggurat Sampler

Input: $m, \sigma, \lfloor x_1 \rfloor, \cdots, \lfloor x_m \rfloor, \bar{y}_0, \bar{y}_1, \cdots, \bar{y}_m, \omega$
Output: a sample value $x \in D_{\mathbb{Z},\sigma,c}$
1: **while** true **do**
2:     $i \xleftarrow{\$} \{1, \cdots, m\}, s \xleftarrow{\$} \{-1, 1\}, x \xleftarrow{\$} \{0, \cdots, \lfloor x_i \rfloor\}$
3:     // choose rectangle, sign and value
4:     **if** $0 < x \leq \lfloor x_{i-1} \rfloor$ **then return** sx;
5:     **else**
6:         **if** $x = 0$ **then**
7:             $b \xleftarrow{\$} \{0, 1\}$
8:             **if** $b = 0$ **then   return** sx;
9:             **else**
10:                 continue;
11:             **end if**
12:         **else**
13:             //in rejection area R_i^r now
14:             $y' \xleftarrow{\$} \{0, \cdots, 2^\omega - 1\}, \bar{y} = y' \cdot (\bar{y}_{i-1} + \bar{y}_i)$;
15:             **if** $\bar{y} \leq 2^\omega \cdot (\bar{\rho}_\sigma(x) - \bar{y}_i)$ **then**
16:                 **return** x
17:             **end if**
18:         **end if**
19:
20:     **end if**
21: **end while**
22: **return** x

The expensive part of Algorithm 2 is computing $\rho_\sigma(x)$ if x does not in R_i^l. If we use more rectangles, the ratio between the left and the right rectangle becomes comparatively bigger. Hence, we accept an x without computing $\rho_\sigma(x)$ with higher probability. The discrete Ziggurat sampler provides a time-memory trade-off by controlling the number of rectangles used (more rectangles, larger memory requirement). Compared with other sampling algorithms, Algorithm 2 can only sample from a discrete Gaussian with a fixed center and is not resistant to side-channel attacks. Howe et al. [25] presented the first hardware implementation of a discrete Gaussian ziggurat sampler. They achieved constant time by controlling signals through a state machine to ensure that all comparisons were performed, with only a few extra clock cycles. Since the original ziggurat algorithm changes its time-memory requirement takes about 1000 s seconds, More and Katti [40] proposed an improved ziggurat algorithm, which can eliminate this large computational overhead and switch different "time-memory" options on the fly by storing a minimal number of extra points $(x_i, \rho(x_i))$.

4.1.3   Karney's Sampler

Karney's sampler [32] is essentially a rejection method which uses von Neumann's algorithm to sample from the exponential distribution. Intuitively, this algorithm

---

Algorithm 3. Karney's Sampler

Output: a sample $x \in$ normal distribution $\phi(x)$
 1: **Step1.**[Sample integer part of deviate k] Select integer $k \geq 0$ with probability $\exp\left(-\frac{1}{2}k\right)(1 - 1/\sqrt{e})$
 2: **Step2.**[Adjust relative probability of k by rejection.]Accept k with probability $\exp(-\frac{1}{2}k(k - 1))$; otherwise go to **Step1.**
 3: **Step3.**[Sample fractional part of deviate x.] Set $x \leftarrow U$, where U is a uniform deviate $U \in (0, 1)$
 4: **Step4.**[Adjust relative probability of x by rejection.]Accept x with probability $\exp(-\frac{1}{2}x(2k + x))$; otherwise go to **Step1.**
 5: **Step5.**[Combine integer and fraction.]Set $y \leftarrow k + x$
 6: **Step6.**[Assign a sign.]With probability $\frac{1}{2}$,set $y \leftarrow -y$
 7: **Step7.**[Return result.] Set $N \leftarrow y$

---

requires neither pre-computed tables nor floating point arithmetic. All the steps can be carried out exactly. It is a very nice property since most sampling algorithms require floating-point arithmetic, which is difficult to run on constrained devices. Overall, the probability of success in the **Step2** is $(1 - 1/\sqrt{e})G \approx 0.690$, where $G = \sum_{k=0}^{\infty} \exp\left(-1/2k^2\right) \approx 1.753$ and **Step4** succeeds with probability $\sqrt{\pi/2}/G \approx 0.715$. Therefore, **Step1** is executed $\sqrt{2/\pi}/(1 - 1/\sqrt{e}) \approx 2.03$ time on average. Du et al. [12] study the computational complexity of Karney's exact sampling algorithm under the random deviate model. They give an estimate of the expected number of uniform deviates used by Karney's algorithm, and present an improved algorithm with 2.018 uniform deviates rather than 2.194, which has better actual performance than Karney's algorithm. Although Algorithm 3 can only sample from the normal distribution, Du et al. [13] can achieve an off-centered discrete Gaussian distribution in combination with the exact property, see Sect. 4.3.1.

4.1.4   Rounded-Gaussian Sampler

Hülsing et al. [28] proposed to replace discrete Gaussian with a different distribution, namely the rounded Gaussian distribution. This distribution has the same benefits as the discrete Gaussian, but the security analysis of using rounded Gaussian in Lyubashevsky's scheme [34] is more involved than discrete Gaussian.

Formally, the rounded Gaussian distribution is obtained by rounding samples from a continuous Gaussian distribution to the nearest integer x_i. To compute the probability at an integer x_i, we compute the integral over the interval $(x_i - \frac{1}{2}, x_i + \frac{1}{2}]$.

Definition 7. *The rounded Gaussian distribution over $\mathbb{Z}^m$ centered at some $v \in \mathbb{Z}^m$ with parameter σ is defined for $x \in \mathbb{Z}^m$ as*

$$R_{v,\sigma}^m(x) = \int_{A_x} \rho_{v,\sigma}^m(s)ds = \int_{A_x} \left(\frac{1}{\sqrt{2\pi\sigma^2}}\right)^m \exp\left(\frac{-\|s-v\|^2}{2\sigma^2}\right)ds$$

where A_x denotes the area defined by $[x_1 - 1/2, x_1 + 1/2) \times \cdots \times [x_m - 1/2, x_m + 1/2)$. A very efficient and easy way to generate samples from the continuous Gaussian distribution is based on the Box-Muller transform.

Algorithm 4. Rounded-Gaussian Sampler

Input: The required number of samples $m = 2n$ and parameter σ
Output: m independent rounded Gaussian distribution integers $z_0, \cdots, z_{2n-1}$ with
    parameter σ
1: **for** i=0 **do** n-1
2:     Generate two uniform random numbers u_1, u_2
3:     $x_1, x_2 \leftarrow BoxMuller(u_1, u_2)$
4:     $z_{2i} \leftarrow \lfloor x_1 \cdot \sigma \rceil$
5:     $z_{2i+1} \leftarrow \lfloor x_2 \cdot \sigma \rceil$
6: **end for**
7: **return** $(z_0, \cdots, z_{2n-1})$

Hülsing et al. [28] show that it is secure enough to use rounded Gaussian, while the resulting rejection rate is identical to before. The implementation of the sampling algorithm is within less than 40 lines of C++ source code. Brannigan et al. [5] presented the first secure algorithm for implementing the Box-Muller Gaussian sampling algorithm. Recently, Zhao et al. [52] implemented an arbitrary-centered discrete Gaussian sampling algorithm over integers based on [28]. Compared to previous arbitrary-centered discrete Gaussian sampling techniques, their algorithm does not require any pre-computations and only requires a low number of trials close to 2 per sample on average.

4.2 Inversion Sampler

The inversion method is based upon the following theorem:

Theorem 1 [9, *Chapter 2*]. *Let F be a continuous distribution function on R with inverse F^{-1} defined by $F^{-1}(u) = \{x : F(x) = u, 0 < u < 1\}$. If U is a uniform [0,1] random variable, then $F^{-1}(U)$ has distribution function F.*

4.2.1 CDT Sampler
The cumulative distribution table (CDT) sampler was first proposed by Peikert [41]. The algorithm needs to compute the discrete Gaussian distribution $p_z \in Pr(x \leq z; x \leftarrow D_\sigma)$, and store the p_z in the cumulative distribution table. Since

the distribution is symmetric about the y-axis, taking $z \in [0, \tau\delta]$ can save half of the storage space, generally the required storage space is about $\lambda\tau\delta$ bits. We can sample directly from discrete Gaussian distribution by choosing a uniformly random $x \in [0, 1)$ and performing a binary search through the table for the $\tilde{z} \in \mathbb{Z}$ such that $x \in [p_{\tilde{z}-1}, p_{\tilde{z}})$.

The CDT algorithm avoids the exponential function and floating-point arithmetic, but due to the whole distribution table, it needs a lot of storage. Because precomputing the CDT needs to know the center c, the CDT algorithm is usually used as an offline phase. The variant [16] of Peikert's offline algorithm, by using laziness techniques, runs in average time $\tilde{O}(n)$ in some ring setting (where n is the lattice dimension). Du et al. [10] further optimized the CDT sampler. They found that when comparing two large random bits (such as 112 bits), the size of the two random numbers can often be determined by comparing the first 8 bits, thus saving $112 - 8 = 104$ random bits are used, and the remaining bits need to be compared only if the current 8 bits are the same. Melchor et al. [36] proposed a Twin-CDT algorithm, which can sample from a non-centered discrete Gaussian by precomputing the CDT for a relatively small number of centers. They decreased the number of pre-computed CDTs by using a Taylor expansion rather than the laziness technique. Aguilar-Melchor and Ricosset [1] use Rényi divergence to improve the Twin-CDT algorithm, that is, only double precision can be used for the usual lattice signature parameters and fixing the issue where prior construction is not constant-time. Karabulut et al. [29] propose a more efficient, flexible, constant-time Gaussian sampler combined with fusion trees. The results show that the size of the cumulative distribution table can be reduced by up to 86%, and the parameters are suitable for post-quantum digital signature schemes such as qTesla, Falcon, etc.

4.2.2   Knuth-Yao Sampler

Dwarakanath et al. [18] first considered using the Knuth-Yao algorithm for discrete Gaussian sampling. This algorithm is based on a discrete distribution generating (DDG) tree which is constructed from a probability matrix, where the probability matrix is denoted by $P_1, P_2, \cdots P_n$, while each sample can be represented as a binary expansion of λ bits, the probability matrix P can be written as a $N \times \lambda$ binary matrix. The DDG tree contains two types of nodes, namely internal nodes, and terminal nodes. The number of terminal nodes in the i-th level of the tree is equal to the number of non-zeros in the i-th column of the probability matrix. Each terminal node is marked as the row number of matrix P. The sampling process is a random walk from the tree root to the terminal node. When it hits the terminal node, it stops walking and outputs the sampling result. Algorithm 5 formally describes this process. From the perspective of information theory, the algorithm is perfect, it requires random input bits that are only 2 larger than the entropy of the distribution.

Roy et al. [45] used hardware to construct the Knuth-Yao sampler for the first time. They optimized the structure of the DDG tree. It is not necessary to store the entire DDG tree. Instead, one just stores the node of the current level and the

---

Algorithm 5. Knuth-Yao Sampler

Require: Three integers d, hit and ctr;
1: Discrete samplers of Gaussian distribution as matrix P with $N \times \lambda$ dimension and $N = \tau \times \sigma$;
2: Sample bits uniformly in $\{0,1\}$, store in array r;
3: Column-wise Hamming distance of P, i.e., $h\_dist[j] = \sum_{i=0}^{N} P[i][j]$;
Ensure: $d \leftarrow 0; hit \leftarrow 0; ctr \leftarrow 0$;
4: **for** int $col \leftarrow 0; col < \lambda; col \leftarrow col + 1$ **do**
5:     $d \leftarrow 2d + (!r[ctr++]) - h\_dist[col]$;
6:     **if** d<0 **then**
7:         **for** int $row \leftarrow 0; row < N; row \leftarrow row + 1$ **do**
8:             $d \leftarrow d + P[row][col]$;
9:             **if** d == 0 **then**
10:                $hit \leftarrow 1$;
11:                **break;**
12:            **end if**
13:        **end for**
14:        **if** hit **then**
15:            **break;**
16:        **end if**
17:    **end if**
18: **end for**
19: **return** $(-1)^{r[ctr++]}.\textbf{row}$

---

information of the next level; from this information, it is simple to construct the full tree. [25,30,31,44] all improve the problem that the Knuth-Yao operation is non-constant time. To achieve time-independent, [25] use a simple shuffler to shuffle discrete Gaussian samples after the generation of a complete block. [30] proposed a bit-slicing Knuth-Yao algorithm, which is 2.4 times faster than the shuffle-based constant-time implementation and consumes significantly less memory. [44] observed an interesting property of the mapping from input random bit strings to samples and proposed an efficient method to minimize the Boolean expression of the mapping. The overall performance of the signature algorithm drops by up to 33% due to the additional overhead of "constant-time" sampling.

4.3   Hybrid Sampler

The samplers we introduced above are either sampled over the integers or a single algorithm. In this section, we summarize the samplers actually used in lattice-based cryptography, which are efficient, generic, and secure at the same time. We also introduce some accelerated methods at the end, which have performed well in recent NIST submissions.

4.3.1   Bernoulli-Type Sampler

Ducas et al. [14] first proposed the Bernoulli-type sampler, which combines rejection sampling and inversion sampling, and applied it to BLISS digital signature scheme. This algorithm uses rejection sampling from the binary discrete Gaussian distribution, denoted by $D_{\mathbb{Z}+,\sigma_2}$. Firstly, Sampling $x \in \mathbb{Z}^+$ from $D_{\mathbb{Z}+,\sigma_2}$ can be very efficient because the pre-computed table for $\sigma_2 = \sqrt{1/(2 \cdot \ln 2)}$ is small. Secondly, it samples $y \in \mathbb{Z}$ uniformly in $\{0, 1, 2, \cdots, k+1\}$ and accepts $z = kx+y$ with probability $\exp -(y^2 + 2kxy)/2k^2\sigma_2^2$. Finally, it outputs a signed integer, z or $-z$, with equal probabilities. Algorithm 6 gives a detailed description.

Algorithm 6. Bernoulli-Type Sampler

Require: An integer $k \in \mathbb{Z}(\sigma = k\sigma_2)$
Ensure: An integer $z \in \mathbb{Z}^+$ according to D_σ^+
  1: sample $x \in \mathbb{Z}$ according to $D_{\sigma_2}^+$
  2: sample $y \in \mathbb{Z}$ uniformly in $\{0, \cdots, k-1\}$
  3: $z \leftarrow kx + y$
  4: sample $b \leftarrow \mathcal{B}_{\exp(-y(y+2kx)/(2\sigma^2))}$
  5: **if** $\neg b$ **then** restart
  6:    **return** z
  7: **end if**

A complete analysis of Algorithm 6 is given by Ducas et al. [14] Compared with the original rejection sampling algorithm, the average number of rejections is smaller than 1.47, so this is a very practical algorithm. The disadvantage of the Bernoulli-type sampling algorithm is that it is centered and not constant time. A lot of work has proposed improvements based on this algorithm, such as [3,11,25,27,43,53] to compensate for the security of the sampler; [13,46,49] to improve the efficiency and generality. [3,27] found that a polynomial approximation of the transcendental function could be used to achieve constant time. For sampling from the binary distribution, both need to look up the full CDT. To achieve constant-time, the FACCT method [53] used floating point multiplications instead to compute the exponential. Otherwise, the GALACTICS method [3] used integer polynomials to avoid floating operations. Howe et al. [27] show that their sampler is isochronous, i.e. running time is independent of the inputs σ, c and of the output z. Isochrony is weaker than being constant-time, but it suffices to argue security against timing attacks. More precisely, they used a base sampler and Bernoulli rejection sampler, in which the base sampler needs to look up the entire CDT to achieve isochronous, and the Bernoulli rejection sampler approximates the transcendental function by using the GALACTICS method [3]. Du et al. [11] proposed a constant-time algorithm, which requires no precomputation storage and its entropy consumption is smaller than that of the full-table access algorithm. Replacing the binary sampling with Karney's algorithm [32], Xie et al. [49] proposed a new algorithm without floating-point arithmetic, which supports a variable center of precision up to 20 bits. [46] constructed a Gaussian sampler that is generic, efficient, and resistant to timing attacks. Compared with the polynomial approximation method, their algorithm reduces the floating-point multiplications significantly.

4.3.2   Convolution-Like Sampler

There are two strategies to design generic Gaussian samplers. One is based on rejection sampling, and another is based on the convolution-like technique of discrete Gaussian distributions. The convolution-like technique was first applied to lattice Gaussian sampling by Peikert [41], and [38] used this technique to build a very efficient trapdoor for the lattice scheme. All convolution-like samplers invoke the following theorem.

Theorem 2. *Let* $\Sigma_1, \Sigma_2 > 0$ *be positive difinite matrices, with* $\Sigma = \Sigma_1 + \Sigma_2 > 0$ *and* $\Sigma_3^{-1} = \Sigma_1^{-1} + \Sigma_2^{-1} > 0$. *Let* Λ_1, Λ_2 *be lattices such that* $\sqrt{\Sigma_1} \geq \eta_\epsilon(\Lambda_1)$ *and* $\sqrt{\Sigma_3} \geq \eta_\epsilon(\Lambda_2)$ *for some positive* $\epsilon \leq 1/2$, *and let* $c_1, c_2 \in \mathbb{R}^n$ *be arbitrary. Consider the following probabilistic experiment:*

$$Choose \ x_2 \leftarrow D_{\Lambda_2 + c_2, \sqrt{\Sigma_2}}, then \ choose \ x_1 \leftarrow x_2 + D_{\Lambda_1 + c_1 - x_2, \sqrt{\Sigma_1}}.$$

The marginal distribution of x_1 *is within statistical distance* 8ϵ *of* $D_{\Lambda_1 + c_1, \sqrt{\Sigma}}$. *In addition, for any* $\bar{x}_1 \in \Lambda_1 + c_1$, *the conditional distribution of* $\bar{x}_2 \in \Lambda_2 + c_2$ *given* $x_1 = \bar{x}_1$ *is within statistical distance* 2ϵ *of* $c_3 + D_{\Lambda_2 + c_2 - c_3, \sqrt{\Sigma_3}}$, *where* $\Sigma_3^{-1} = \Sigma_1^{-1} \bar{x}_1$

Micciancio and Walter [39] adapt the above theorem to get a generic integer sampler, which can generate a relatively small number of samples coming from a discrete Gaussian distribution for a fixed small deviation, and then recombine them into arbitrary standard deviation s and center c. [38] constructed a gadget trapdoor, which is divided into two phases: an offline phase and an online phase. The perturbation vector is obtained by sampling in the offline phase, and the target vector is obtained by sampling in the online phase. The convolution theorem ensures that the target vector does not reveal the key or trapdoor information. Recently, the gadget trapdoor has attracted great interest due to its simplicity and parallelization. For example, [22] developed a new algorithm for the off-line perturbation sampling phase of [38] in the ring setting. Their algorithm is based on a variant of the Fast Fourier Orthogonalization (FFO) algorithm (we will talk about in the next section), but avoids the need to pre-compute and store the FFO matrix; Bert et al. [4] presented the first efficient implementation of a lattice-based signature scheme in the standard model by generalizing the work of [38] and [22]; to avoid using floating-number arithmetic in the perturbation sampling, [50] exploit an integral matrix decomposition which is inspired by [44]. Recently, Karabulut et al. [29] significantly optimize CDT sampling, combining convolution techniques and fusion tree searching, resulting in smaller table size and comparator size. And then, Verilog was used to achieve constant time.

4.3.3   Fast-Fourier Sampler

The fast Fourier sampler was first proposed by Ducas and Prest [17]. The sampler, which combines the quality of Klein's algorithm and the efficiency of Peikert's algorithm, improves the nearest plane algorithm through fast Fourier transformation and can be implemented on the NTRU lattice. Falcon [21] is the result of combining GPV framework, NTRU lattices, and Fast Fourier sampling. Falcon was accepted in NIST third-round submission, and it has the smallest total size among all the post-quantum digital signature schemes at the same security level. The Fast Fourier sampling was employed by Falcon for the phase of key generation. Algorithm 7 shows the detailed process of Falcon's fast Fourier sampling.

Algorithm 7. ffSampling$_n$(t,T)

Require: $\mathbf{t} = (t_0, t_1) \in \text{FFT}(\mathbb{Q}[x]/(x^n + 1)^2)$, a FALCON tree T. All polynomials are in FFT representation

Ensure: $\mathbf{z} = (z_0, z_1) \in \text{FFT}(\mathbb{Z}[x]/(x^n + 1)^2)$

1: **if** $n == 1$ **then**
2:   $\sigma' \leftarrow \mathbf{T}.\text{value}$ ▷ It is always the case that $\sigma' \in [\sigma_{\min}, \sigma_{\max}]$
3:   $z_0 \leftarrow \text{SamplerZ}(t_0, \sigma')$ ▷ Since $n = 1, t_i = \text{invFFT}(t_i) \in \mathbb{Q}$ and
                  $z_i = \text{invFFT}(z_i) \in \mathbb{Z}$
4:   $z_1 \leftarrow \text{SamplerZ}(t_1, \sigma')$
5:   **return** $\mathbf{z} = (z_0, z_1)$
6: **end if**
7: $(\ell, \mathbf{T}_0, \mathbf{T}_1) \leftarrow (\mathbf{T}.\text{value}, \mathbf{T}.\text{leftchild}, \mathbf{T}.\text{rightchild})$
8: $\mathbf{t}_1 \leftarrow \text{splitfft}(t_1)$ ▷ $t_0, t_1 \in \text{FFT}\left(\mathbb{Q}[x]/(x^{n/2} + 1)\right)^2$
9: $\mathbf{z}_1 \leftarrow \text{ffSampling}_{n/2}(\mathbf{t}_1, T_1)$ ▷ First recursive call to ffSampling$_{n/2}$
10: $z_1 \leftarrow \text{mergefft}(\mathbf{z}_1)$ ▷ $\mathbf{z}_0, \mathbf{z}_1 \in \text{FFT}\left(\mathbb{Z}[x]/(x^{n/2} + 1)\right)^2$
11: $t'_0 \leftarrow t_0 + (t_1 - z_1) \odot \ell$
12: $\mathbf{t}_0 \leftarrow \text{splitfft}(t'_0)$
13: $\mathbf{z}_0 \leftarrow \text{ffSampling}_{n/2}(\mathbf{t}_0, \mathbf{T}_0)$ ▷ Second recursive call to ffSampling$_{n/2}$
14: $z_0 \leftarrow \text{mergefft}(\mathbf{z}_0)$
15: **return** $\mathbf{z} = (z_0, z_1)$

When sampling a short vector, ffSampling is invoked twice for each leaf of the LDL* tree. Each invocation should produce an integer value from a Gaussian distribution that is centered on a value μ and with a standard deviation σ. In Algorithm 7, splitfft is a subroutine of the inverse fast Fourier transform, more precisely the part which from FFT(f) computes two FFT's twice smaller. mergefft is a step of the fast Fourier transform: it is the reconstruction step that from two small FFT's computes a larger FFT.

Note that the sampler execution time in the original Falcon is not constant, so it is hard to protect against the timing and side-channel attacks. We can see that in Algorithm 7 because samplerZ determines the security of sampling, Howe et al. [27] propose a constant-time samplerZ algorithm that uses a CDT sampler and Bernoulli rejection sampling.

5   Conclusion

Discrete Gaussian sampling plays an essential role in lattice-based cryptography. Many works in recent years have focused more on constant-time implementations and generic constructions. On the one hand, discrete Gaussian sampling needs to comply with NIST's standards for resisting side-channel attacks if it is used in lattice cryptographic schemes. On the other hand, the variable-parameter sampler can be applied to more schemes since it is easy to adjust and the efficiency will not decrease too much. This paper is devoted to summarizing the progress of discrete Gaussian samplers in measures, efficiency, generality, and security. And how to make discrete Gaussian samples more efficient and practical is still an open problem.

References

1. Aguilar-Melchor, C., Ricosset, T.: Cdt-based gaussian sampling: From multi to double precision. IEEE Trans. Comput. **67**, 1610–1621 (2018)
2. Bai, S., Lepoint, T., Roux-Langlois, A., Sakzad, A., Stehlé, D., Steinfeld, R.: Improved security proofs in lattice-based cryptography: using the rényi divergence rather than the statistical distance. J. Cryptol. **31**, 610–640 (2017)
3. Barthe, G., Belaïd, S., Espitau, T., Fouque, P.A., Rossi, M., Tibouchi, M.: Galactics: Gaussian sampling for lattice-based constant- time implementation of cryptographic signatures, revisited. In: Proceedings of the 2019 ACM SIGSAC Conference on Computer and Communications Security (2019)
4. Bert, P., Eberhart, G., Prabel, L., Roux-Langlois, A., Sabt, M.: Implementation of lattice trapdoors on modules and applications. In: Cheon, J.H., Tillich, J.-P. (eds.) PQCrypto 2021 2021. LNCS, vol. 12841, pp. 195–214. Springer, Cham (2021). https://doi.org/10.1007/978-3-030-81293-5_11
5. Brannigan, S., O'Neill, M., Khalid, A., Rafferty, C.: A secure algorithm for rounded gaussian sampling. In: Krenn, S., Shulman, H., Vaudenay, S. (eds.) CANS 2020. LNCS, vol. 12579, pp. 593–612. Springer, Cham (2020). https://doi.org/10.1007/978-3-030-65411-5_29
6. Brannigan, S., et al.: An investigation of sources of randomness within discrete gaussian sampling. IACR Cryptol. ePrint Arch. **2017**, 298 (2017)
7. Brannigan, S.: Secure Gaussian sampling for lattice-based signatures: new directions for reaching high standard deviation. Ph.D. thesis, Queen's University Belfast (2021)
8. Buchmann, J.A., Cabarcas, D., Göpfert, F., Hülsing, A., Weiden, P.: Discrete ziggurat: a time-memory trade-off for sampling from a gaussian distribution over the integers. IACR Cryptol. ePrint Arch. **2013**, 510 (2013)
9. Devroye, L.: Non-uniform random variate generation (1986)
10. Du, C., Bai, G.: Towards efficient discrete gaussian sampling for lattice-based cryptography. In: 2015 25th International Conference on Field Programmable Logic and Applications (FPL), pp. 1–6 (2015)
11. Du, Y., Fan, B., Wei, B.: A constant-time sampling algorithm for binary gaussian distribution over the integers. Inf. Process. Lett. **176**, 106246 (2022)
12. Du, Y., Fan, B., Wei, B.: An improved exact sampling algorithm for the standard normal distribution. Comput. Stat. **37**, 721–737 (2022)
13. Du, Y., Wei, B., Zhang, H.: A rejection sampling algorithm for off-centered discrete gaussian distributions over the integers. Sci. China Inf. Sci. **62**, 1–3 (2017)
14. Ducas, L., Durmus, A., Lepoint, T., Lyubashevsky, V.: Lattice signatures and bimodal gaussians. IACR Cryptol. ePrint Arch. **2013**, 383 (2013)

15. Ducas, L., Galbraith, S., Prest, T., Yu, Y.: Integral matrix gram root and lattice gaussian sampling without floats. In: Canteaut, A., Ishai, Y. (eds.) EUROCRYPT 2020. LNCS, vol. 12106, pp. 608–637. Springer, Cham (2020). https://doi.org/10.1007/978-3-030-45724-2_21

16. Ducas, L., Nguyen, P.Q.: Faster gaussian lattice sampling using lazy floating-point arithmetic. In: Wang, X., Sako, K. (eds.) ASIACRYPT 2012. LNCS, vol. 7658, pp. 415–432. Springer, Heidelberg (2012). https://doi.org/10.1007/978-3-642-34961-4_26

17. Ducas, L., Prest, T.: Fast fourier orthogonalization. In: Proceedings of the ACM on International Symposium on Symbolic and Algebraic Computation (2015)

18. Dwarakanath, N.C., Galbraith, S.D.: Sampling from discrete gaussians for lattice-based cryptography on a constrained device. Appl. Algebra Eng. Commun. Comput. **25**, 159–180 (2014)

19. Espitau, T., et al.: MITAKA: a simpler, parallelizable, maskable variant of FAL-CON. In: Dunkelman, O., Dziembowski, S. (eds.) EUROCRYPT 2022. LNCS, vol. 13277, pp. 222–253. Springer, Cham (2021). https://doi.org/10.1007/978-3-031-07082-2_9

20. Folláth, J.: Gaussian sampling in lattice based cryptography. Tatra Mount. Math. Publ. **60**, 1–23 (2014)

21. Fouque, P.A., et al.: Falcon: Fast-Fourier lattice-based compact signatures over NTRU (2019)

22. Genise, N., Micciancio, D.: Faster gaussian sampling for trapdoor lattices with arbitrary modulus. In: Nielsen, J.B., Rijmen, V. (eds.) EUROCRYPT 2018. LNCS, vol. 10820, pp. 174–203. Springer, Cham (2018). https://doi.org/10.1007/978-3-319-78381-9_7

23. Gentry, C., Peikert, C., Vaikuntanathan, V.: Trapdoors for hard lattices and new cryptographic constructions. In: Proceedings of the fortieth Annual ACM Symposium on Theory of Computing, pp. 197–206 (2008)

24. Gür, K.D., Polyakov, Y., Rohloff, K.R., Ryan, G.W., Savaş, E.: Implementation and evaluation of improved gaussian sampling for lattice trapdoors. In: Proceedings of the 6th Workshop on Encrypted Computing & Applied Homomorphic Cryptography (2017)

25. Howe, J., Khalid, A., Rafferty, C., Regazzoni, F., O'Neill, M.: On practical discrete gaussian samplers for lattice-based cryptography. IEEE Trans. Comput. **67**, 322–334 (2018)

26. Howe, J., O'Neill, M.: GLITCH: a discrete gaussian testing suite for lattice-based cryptography. In: SECRYPT (2017)

27. Howe, J., Prest, T., Ricosset, T., Rossi, M.: Isochronous gaussian sampling: from inception to implementation. In: Ding, J., Tillich, J.-P. (eds.) PQCrypto 2020. LNCS, vol. 12100, pp. 53–71. Springer, Cham (2020). https://doi.org/10.1007/978-3-030-44223-1_4

28. Hülsing, A., Lange, T., Smeets, K.: Rounded gaussians - fast and secure constant-time sampling for lattice-based crypto. IACR Cryptol. ePrint Arch. **2017**, 1025 (2017)

29. Karabulut, E., Alkim, E., Aysu, A.: Efficient, flexible, and constant-time gaussian sampling hardware for lattice cryptography. IEEE Trans. Comput. **71**, 1810–1823 (2022)

30. Karmakar, A., Roy, S.S., Reparaz, O., Vercauteren, F., Verbauwhede, I.M.R.: Constant-time discrete gaussian sampling. IEEE Trans. Comput. **67**, 1561–1571 (2018)

31. Karmakar, A., Roy, S.S., Vercauteren, F., Verbauwhede, I.M.R.: Pushing the speed limit of constant-time discrete gaussian sampling. a case study on the falcon signature scheme. In: 2019 56th ACM/IEEE Design Automation Conference (DAC), pp. 1–6 (2019)

32. Karney, C.F.F.: Sampling exactly from the normal distribution. ACM Trans. Math. Softw. (TOMS) **42**, 1–14 (2016)

33. Klein, P.N.: Finding the closest lattice vector when it's unusually close. In: SODA 2000 (2000)

34. Lyubashevsky, V.: Lattice signatures without trapdoors. In: Pointcheval, D., Johansson, T. (eds.) EUROCRYPT 2012. LNCS, vol. 7237, pp. 738–755. Springer, Heidelberg (2012). https://doi.org/10.1007/978-3-642-29011-4_43

35. Lyubashevsky, V., Prest, T.: Quadratic time, linear space algorithms for gram-schmidt orthogonalization and gaussian sampling in structured lattices. IACR Cryptol. ePrint Arch. **2015**, 257 (2015)

36. Aguilar-Melchor, C., Albrecht, M.R., Ricosset, T.: Sampling from arbitrary centered discrete gaussians for lattice-based cryptography. In: Gollmann, D., Miyaji, A., Kikuchi, H. (eds.) ACNS 2017. LNCS, vol. 10355, pp. 3–19. Springer, Cham (2017). https://doi.org/10.1007/978-3-319-61204-1_1

37. Micciancio, D., Regev, O.: Worst-case to average-case reductions based on gaussian measures. In: 45th Annual IEEE Symposium on Foundations of Computer Science, pp. 372–381 (2004)

38. Micciancio, D., Peikert, C.: Trapdoors for lattices: simpler, tighter, faster, smaller. IACR Cryptol. ePrint Arch. **2011**, 501 (2011)

39. Micciancio, D., Walter, M.: Gaussian sampling over the integers: efficient, generic, constant-time. IACR Cryptol. ePrint Arch. **2017**, 259 (2017)

40. More, S., Katti, R.S.: Discrete gaussian sampling for low-power devices. In: 2015 IEEE Pacific Rim Conference on Communications, Computers and Signal Processing (PACRIM), pp. 181–186 (2015)

41. Peikert, C.: An efficient and parallel gaussian sampler for lattices. In: Rabin, T. (ed.) CRYPTO 2010. LNCS, vol. 6223, pp. 80–97. Springer, Heidelberg (2010). https://doi.org/10.1007/978-3-642-14623-7_5

42. Pöppelmann, T., Ducas, L., Güneysu, T.: Enhanced lattice-based signatures on reconfigurable hardware. IACR Cryptol. ePrint Arch. **2014**, 254 (2014)

43. Prest, T., Ricosset, T., Rossi, M.: Simple, fast and constant-time gaussian sampling over the integers for falcon (2019)

44. Roy, S.S., Reparaz, O., Vercauteren, F., Verbauwhede, I.M.R.: Compact and side channel secure discrete gaussian sampling. IACR Cryptol. ePrint Arch. **2014**, 591 (2014)

45. Sinha Roy, S., Vercauteren, F., Verbauwhede, I.: High precision discrete gaussian sampling on FPGAs. In: Lange, T., Lauter, K., Lisoněk, P. (eds.) SAC 2013. LNCS, vol. 8282, pp. 383–401. Springer, Heidelberg (2014). https://doi.org/10.1007/978-3-662-43414-7_19

46. Sun, S., Zhou, Y., Ji, Y.S., Zhang, R., Tao, Y.: Generic, efficient and isochronous gaussian sampling over the integers. Cybersecurity **5**, 1–22 (2021)

47. Walter, M.: Sampling the integers with low relative error. In: Buchmann, J., Nitaj, A., Rachidi, T. (eds.) AFRICACRYPT 2019. LNCS, vol. 11627, pp. 157–180. Springer, Cham (2019). https://doi.org/10.1007/978-3-030-23696-0_9

48. Weiden, P., Hülsing, A., Cabarcas, D., Buchmann, J.A.: Instantiating treeless signature schemes. IACR Cryptol. ePrint Arch. **2013**, 65 (2013)

49. Xie, S., Zhuang, S., Du, Y.: Improved bernoulli sampling for discrete gaussian distributions over the integers. Mathematics **9**, 378 (2021)

50. Zhang, S., Yu, Y.: Towards a simpler lattice gadget toolkit. In: Hanaoka, G., Shikata, J., Watanabe, Y. (eds.) PKC 2022. LNCS, vol. 13177, pp. 498–520. Springer, Cham (2021)
51. Zhao, K.: Efficient Implementation Techniques for Lattice-based Cryptosystems. Ph.D. thesis, Monash University (2022)
52. Zhao, R.K., Steinfeld, R., Sakzad, A.: COSAC: COmpact and scalable arbitrary-centered discrete gaussian sampling over integers. In: Ding, J., Tillich, J.-P. (eds.) PQCrypto 2020. LNCS, vol. 12100, pp. 284–303. Springer, Cham (2020). https://doi.org/10.1007/978-3-030-44223-1_16
53. Zhao, R.K., Steinfeld, R., Sakzad, A.: FACCT: fast, compact, and constant-time discrete Gaussian sampler over integers. IEEE Trans. Comput. **69**, 126–137 (2020)

Hierarchical Identity Based Inner Product Functional Encryption for Privacy Preserving Statistical Analysis Without q-type Assumption

Anushree Belel[✉], Ratna Dutta, and Sourav Mukhopadhyay

Indian Institute of Technology Kharagpur, Kharagpur 721302, West Bengal, India
anubelel@gmail.com, {ratna,sourav}@maths.iitkgp.ac.in

Abstract. Statistical analysis is a popular research tool used by scientists, industries, and governments to summarize data in a meaningful way. It is an interesting problem to explore how statistical analysis could be performed in a hierarchical environment while preserving the privacy of individuals' data. *Hierarchical identity-based inner product functional encryption* (HID-IPFE), introduced by Song et al. (Information Sciences 2021), is a promising cryptographic primitive with applications in the context of privacy-preserving statistical analysis in a hierarchical system. Song et al. provided the construction of a *selective chosen-plaintext attack* (CPA) secure HID-IPFE scheme in the public key setting based on the *q-decisional bilinear Diffie-Hellman exponent* (q-DBDHE) problem in the standard model. Motivated by the goal to design HID-IPFE with minimal security assumption, we remove stronger q-type non-standard assumption and propose a *selective* CPA secure HID-IPFE scheme from the standard *decisional bilinear Diffie-Hellman* (DBDH) assumption. Our scheme provides stronger security guarantees against selective CPA adversaries compared to the existing q-DBDHE assumption based HID-IPFE. We support the conjectured security of our construction by proper security analysis in the existing security model. Moreover, our scheme offers favorable results in terms of online computation expenses when contrasted with the previous work.

Keywords: Identity-based encryption · Hierarchical identity · Inner product functional encryption

1 Introduction

Privacy of users' data is a major concern in data outsourcing. We store encrypted data on a cloud server as data may contain sensitive information such as medical data, organizational secrets, and personal conversations. To facilitate computation on encrypted data by the cloud server without compromising the data, we need rich cryptographic primitives as traditional public-key encryptions

© The Author(s), under exclusive license to Springer Nature Switzerland AG 2022
J. Chen et al. (Eds.): EISA 2022, CCIS 1641, pp. 108–125, 2022.
https://doi.org/10.1007/978-3-031-23098-1_7

are insufficient for such tasks. *Functional encryption* (FE) is a novel paradigm enabling general circuit computation on encrypted data while protecting the privacy of users' original data. FE has huge applications in privacy-preserving cloud computing [14] such as data mining [26], forensic image recognition [11], financial and medical privacy [21], consumer privacy in advertising [19] and many more. Given the rapidly expanding set of FE applications, there has been a trend to design lightweight FE schemes with simple functionalities. *Inner product functional encryption* (IPFE) is a special case of FE that executes the computation for inner product on encrypted data. Briefly, encryptor generates a ciphertext $\mathsf{CT}_{\vec{x}}$ corresponding to a vector $\vec{x}$, and a decryptor is able to compute the inner product $\langle \vec{x}, \vec{y} \rangle$ from the ciphertext $\mathsf{CT}_{\vec{x}}$ if the secret key $\mathsf{SK}_{\vec{y}}$ is given for a chosen value $\vec{y}$. As the inner product corresponds to the weighted mean, IPFE has direct applications in the field of privacy-preserving statistical analysis and allows to delegate the expensive computations to the untrusted server. However, general IPFE does not support a hierarchical system where higher-level users can generate secret keys for lower-level users. To resolve this issue, Song et al. [23] proposed the notion of hierarchical identity-based IPFE (HID-IPFE) by introducing an additional Delegate algorithm in IPFE. Precisely, an encryptor takes recipient hierarchical identity HID as an additional input to generate ciphertext $\mathsf{CT}_{\vec{x},\mathsf{HID}}$ corresponding to a vector $\vec{x}$, a user with hierarchical identity $\widehat{\mathsf{HID}}$ owning a secret key $\mathsf{SK}_{\vec{y},\widehat{\mathsf{HID}}}$ can execute Delegate algorithm to generate secret key $\mathsf{SK}_{\vec{y},\mathsf{HID}'}$ for a lower level user with hierarchical identity $\mathsf{HID}' = \widehat{\mathsf{HID}} \cup \mathsf{ID}$ and a decryptor is able to compute the inner product $\langle \vec{x}, \vec{y} \rangle$ from the ciphertext $\mathsf{CT}_{\vec{x},\mathsf{HID}}$ if it possesses the secret key $\mathsf{SK}_{\vec{y},\mathsf{HID}}$ or can derive $\mathsf{SK}_{\vec{y},\mathsf{HID}}$ from its secret key $\mathsf{SK}_{\vec{y},\widehat{\mathsf{HID}}}$ where $\widehat{\mathsf{HID}}$ is a prefix of HID. The inner structure of most organizations and enterprises is hierarchical. Here HID-IPFE can be used to support privacy-preserving statistical analysis using the hierarchical identity. For instance, consider Institution A having 10 departments: Mathematics, Physics, Chemistry, and many more where there are many professors in each department. This institution has advertised internships and asked participants to encrypt grades for the skills of technical writing, academics, and programming. Let a student Alice outside this institution has received the following grades – for technical writing 80, for academics 70, for programming 60 from a skill assessment center. This can be seen as a vector $\vec{x} = (80, 70, 60)$ which is considered private information (plaintext) of Alice. Suppose that Alice wants to join as an intern under the guidance of professor X in the Mathematics department. Alice encrypts the vector $\vec{x}$ using the recipient hierarchical identity HID = "Institution A, Mathematics department, Professor X". Now Professor X of the Mathematics department is granted a secret key $\mathsf{SK}_{\vec{y},\mathsf{HID}}$ corresponding to weight vector $\vec{y} = (25\%, 35\%, 40\%)$ that assigns weights $25\%, 35\%$ and 40% for technical writing, academics, and programming respectively. Alice desires that only Professor X or his superiors (i.e. institute head or head of the Mathematics department) who issued a private key to Professor X should learn $\langle \vec{x}, \vec{y} \rangle$. The primitive HID-IPFE fulfills this requirement perfectly. We discuss another example of a medical application. Consider a hospital B including Neurology, Cardiology, Psychology section, etc. Several senior specialist doctors are there in each section, and many junior doctors work under each senior specialist doctor. Suppose the hospital authority has asked patients to encrypt age, reading of blood sugar, blood pressure, weight, and heart rate for consultation. Let a patient Bob suspect a heart disease and prefer consulting junior doctor Z working under senior specialist doctor Y at the Cardiology section in Hospital B. Bob encrypts his private vector $\vec{x}$ using the recipient hierarchical identity HID = "Hospital B, Cardiology Section, Senior specialist doctor Y, Junior doctor Z". Now Junior doctor Z is granted a secret key $\mathsf{SK}_{\vec{y},\mathsf{HID}}$ corresponding to a weight vector $\vec{y}$. Similar to the above example, in this case also only Junior doctor Z or his superiors (i.e. Hospital authority or Cardiology head or Senior specialist doctor Y) who issued a private key to Junior doctor Z should learn $\langle \vec{x}, \vec{y} \rangle$ so that only they can predict the likelihood of certain disease. HID-IPFE perfectly fits in this scenario as well.

IPFE. IPFE enables computation of inner product on encrypted data while protecting the privacy of the user's original data (plaintext). IPFE was formally introduced by Abdalla et al. [1] in 2015 with beautiful application in privacy-preserving statistical analysis followed by a vast literature in various flavours ([1]- [6–8,15,22]). Also, IPFE enables the computation of conjunctions, disjunctions, and polynomial evaluations. The primitive IPFE can be categorized into two different classes, namely *public key* IPFE (PK-IPFE) and *secret key* IPFE (SK-IPFE). In PK-IPFE ([1,2,6,7]) framework, an encryptor uses public key to encrypt a vector whereas master secret key is used to encrypt a vector in SK-IPFE ([8,15,22]) setting. A bit more formally, the PK-IPFE scheme consists of a tuple of algorithms (Setup, Encrypt, KeyGen, Decrypt). In the Setup phase, a trusted authority generates a public key, master secret key, makes public-key public and keeps the master secret key secret to itself. An encryptor encrypts a vector $\vec{x}$ to generate ciphertext $\mathsf{CT}_{\vec{x}}$ using the public key in Encrypt algorithm. The trusted authority issues $\mathsf{SK}_{\vec{y}}$ to a legitimate decryptor corresponding to a vector $\vec{y}$ using the public key and the master secret key by invoking the algorithm KeyGen. In Decrypt algorithm, a decryptor can compute the inner product $\langle \vec{x}, \vec{y} \rangle$ from the ciphertext $\mathsf{CT}_{\vec{x}}$ if it possesses the secret key $\mathsf{SK}_{\vec{y}}$. The setting of SK-IPFE is the same as that of PK-IPFE except the fact that in Encrypt algorithm, the trusted authority is the encryptor as the master secret key belongs to him. In 2015, Abdalla et al. [1] introduced FE for inner product functionality (particularly PK-IPFE) and provided very simple and efficient selective secure construction from the *decisional Diffie-Hellman* (DDH) problem. Subsequently, in 2016, Abdalla et al. [2] presented a generic PK-IPFE construction secure against adaptive adversaries. Specifically, they provided three instantiations based on the DDH assumption, the *decisional composite residuosity* (DCR) assumption, and the *learning with errors* (LWE) assumption. In 2016, Agrawal et al. [6] presented a fully secure construction of PK-IPFE and provided two instantiations. One is based on the hardness of the DDH problem utilizing *hash proof systems* [13] and the other builds on the *dual Regev encryption* scheme of Gentry et al. [18] under the hardness of the LWE problem. Later, in the year 2017, Benhamouda et al. [7] proposed a generic construction of *chosen ciphertext attack* (CCA) secure PK-

IPFE from *projective hash functions* [13]. In 2015, Bishop et al. [8] constructed an efficient SK-IPFE based on the *symmetric external Diffie-Hellman* (SXDH) assumption that satisfies weakly function-hiding property. In 2016, Datta et al. [15] improved the work of Bishop et al. [8] and came up with a construction that achieves the strongest indistinguishability-based notion of full function privacy. Later, in 2018, Kim et al. [20] improved the efficiency of both works [8,15] by proving security in the *generic group model*. Tomida et al. [24] first proposed the concept of *unbounded* IPFE (UIPFE) in 2018 which can handle vectors with unbounded lengths. More precisely, they provided two instantiations based on the SXDH assumption. The first scheme SK-UIPFE is in the secret key setting with full function hiding and the second scheme PK-UIPFE is in the public key setting with adaptive security. Concurrently, Sans et al. [17] also presented the UIPFE scheme with succinct keys. Recently, in 2020, Do et al. [16] proposed *traceable* IPFE by combining the IPFE of Abdalla et al. [1] with the traitor tracing scheme of *Boneh-Franklin* [10].

HID-IPFE. General PK-IPFE does not support a hierarchical system where higher-level users generate secret keys for lower-level users. Very recently, in 2021, Song et al. [23] addressed this problem and came up with the notion of *hierarchical identity-based* IPFE (HID-IPFE) in public key setting by introducing the Delegate algorithm in PK-IPFE along with a formal security model. This primitive consists of a tuple of algorithms (Setup, Encrypt, KeyGen, Delegate, Decrypt). The Setup algorithm is the same as that in PK-IPFE. The algorithm Encrypt takes recipient hierarchical identity HID as an additional input to generate ciphertext $\mathsf{CT}_{\vec{x},\mathsf{HID}}$ corresponding to a vector $\vec{x}$. The algorithm KeyGen issues secret key $\mathsf{SK}_{\vec{y},\mathsf{HID}'}$ corresponding to a vector $\vec{y}$ taking recipient hierarchical identity HID′ as an additional input. A higher-level user with hierarchical identity $\widehat{\mathsf{HID}}$ owning a secret key $\mathsf{SK}_{\vec{y},\widehat{\mathsf{HID}}}$ can execute the Delegate algorithm to generate secret key $\mathsf{SK}_{\vec{y},\mathsf{HID}'}$ for a lower-level user with hierarchical identity $\mathsf{HID}' = \widehat{\mathsf{HID}} \cup \mathsf{ID}$. In the Decrypt algorithm, a decryptor on input PK, $\mathsf{CT}_{\vec{x},\mathsf{HID}}$, $\mathsf{SK}_{\vec{y},\mathsf{HID}'}$ obtains the inner product $\langle \vec{x}, \vec{y} \rangle$ if HID = HID′. Note that $\mathsf{SK}_{\vec{y},\mathsf{HID}'}$ is generated by either algorithm KeyGen corresponding to hierarchical identity HID′ and vector $\vec{y}$ or by algorithm Delegate on input a hierarchical identity $\widehat{\mathsf{HID}}$ and secret key $\mathsf{SK}_{\vec{y},\widehat{\mathsf{HID}}}$ where $\widehat{\mathsf{HID}}$ is a prefix of HID′. If HID = HID′, the former represents the case where the intended recipient is decryptor, and the latter models the case where a delegator is decryptor.

A closely related topic to the notion of HID-IPFE is *hierarchical inner product encryption* (HIPE) proposed by Abdalla et al. [3] in 2012. They extended the lattice-based *inner product encryption* (IPE) scheme by Agrawal et al. [5] to the hierarchical setting by utilizing the basis delegation techniques of Agrawal et al. [4]. Subsequently, in 2013, Xagawa et al. [25] improved the efficiency of the work [3]. The primitive HIPE has applications to build chosen-ciphertext secure IPE and wildcarded identity-based encryption schemes.

Our Contribution: The challenge lies in designing cryptographic primitives from minimal security assumptions. To the best of our knowledge, the only

Table 1. Comparison of storage overhead and communication bandwidth

Scheme	Storage				Communication
	$|PK|$		$|MSK|$	$|SK|$	$|CT|$
Song et al. [23]	$(d+n+3)|\mathbb{G}|$		$|\mathbb{Z}_p|$	$(l+n)|\mathbb{Z}_p| + (d-l+2)|\mathbb{G}|$	$l|\mathbb{Z}_p| + n|\mathbb{G}_t| + 2|\mathbb{G}|$
Our	$(d+2)|\mathbb{G}| + (d+2)|\widehat{\mathbb{G}}| + (n+1)|\mathbb{G}_t|$	$n|\widehat{\mathbb{G}}|$		$(l+n)|\mathbb{Z}_p| + (l+1)|\widehat{\mathbb{G}}|$	$l|\mathbb{Z}_p| + n|\mathbb{G}_t| + (l+1)|\mathbb{G}|$

$|PK|$ = public key size, $|MSK|$ = master secret key size, $|CT|$ = ciphertext size, $|SK|$ = secret key size, $|\mathbb{G}|$ = bit size of an element of $\mathbb{G}$, $|\widehat{\mathbb{G}}|$ = bit size of an element of $\widehat{\mathbb{G}}$, $|\mathbb{G}_t|$ = bit size of an element of $\mathbb{G}_t$, $|\mathbb{Z}_p|$ = bit size of an element of $\mathbb{Z}_p$, l = depth of the hierarchical identity, d = maximum depth of the hierarchical identity, n = length of the vector

Table 2. Comparison of computation cost

Scheme	Total # exp	Total # pair
Song et al. [23]	$(n+l+2d+9)|\mathbb{G}| + (3n+2)|\mathbb{G}_t|$	$(n+3)$
Our	$(2l+d+2)|\mathbb{G}| + (6l+2n+d+4)|\widehat{\mathbb{G}}| + (4n+1)|\mathbb{G}_t|$	$(l+2)$

exp = number of exponentiations, # pair = number of pairings, l = depth of the hierarchical identity, d = maximum depth of the hierarchical identity, n = length of the vector

work on HID-IPFE in the public-key setting is the work of Song et al. [23] that achieves selective CPA security in the standard model under the hardness of *q-decisional bilinear Diffie-Hellman exponent* (*q*-DBDHE) problem. The concept of *q*-type assumptions is that given *q* solutions of the underlying problem, it is not possible to produce a new solution. During simulation, these *q* solutions are utilized by the simulator to answer the queries by an adversary and then convert the adversary's forgery into a new solution of the problem. Generally, as *q* becomes larger the assumption gets stronger, and a scheme based on it becomes more vulnerable. Moreover, the *q*-type assumptions (and also the associated schemes) suffered a special attack presented by Cheon et al. [12]. This somewhat unsatisfactory state of affairs motivates us to design HID-IPFE in the public key setting in the standard model without relying on any *q*-type assumption. Our construction of HID-IPFE utilizes the technique of Boneh et al. [9] and is proven to be *selectively* secure against CPA adversary under the hardness of the *decisional bilinear Diffie-Hellman* (DBDH) problem in an asymmetric bilinear setting. We emphasize that unlike the existing work of Song et al. [23], our scheme is designed under a standard assumption instead of a stronger *q*-type non-standard assumption. Specifically, we prove the following theorem.

Theorem 1. *(Informal) Assuming the hardness of the* DBDH *problem, our* HID-IPFE = (Setup, Encrypt, KeyGen, Delegate, Decrypt) *is selectively secure against* CPA *adversary.*

We briefly summarize the comparison of storage and communication bandwidth of our HID-IPFE in reference to the existing approach of Song et al. [23] in Table 1 and computation cost in Table 2. We note the following.

- In our design, we use asymmetric bilinear pairing $e : \mathbb{G} \times \widehat{\mathbb{G}} \to \mathbb{G}_t$ where $\mathbb{G}, \widehat{\mathbb{G}}, \mathbb{G}_t$ are cyclic groups of prime order p while Song et al. [23] uses symmetric bilinear pairing $e : \mathbb{G} \times \mathbb{G} \to \mathbb{G}_t$. As exhibited in Table 1, size of master secret key is more in our design as compared to that in [23] and ciphertext length is $(l-1)$ more than that of [23] where d is depth of the hierarchical tree and $l \leq d = \lceil \log_2(N+1) \rceil - 1$ (if we consider the hierarchical tree as a perfect binary tree with N nodes). For instance if we take $n = 100$, $d = 15$, $l = 7$ our public key size $|\mathsf{PK}| = 17|\mathbb{G}| + 17|\widehat{\mathbb{G}}| + 101|\mathbb{G}_t|$ while that of [23] is $118|\mathbb{G}|$, our master secret key size is $100|\widehat{\mathbb{G}}|$ while that of [23] is $|\mathbb{Z}_p|$, our secret key size $|\mathsf{SK}| = 107|\mathbb{Z}_p| + 8|\mathbb{G}|$ whereas that of [23] is $107|\mathbb{Z}_p| + 10|\mathbb{G}|$, our ciphertext size $\mathsf{CT} = 7|\mathbb{Z}_p| + 100|\mathbb{G}_t| + 8|\mathbb{G}|$ while that of [23] is $7|\mathbb{Z}_p| + 100|\mathbb{G}_t| + 2|\mathbb{G}|$. As d and l are logarithmic in N and if $n >> d$, then length of public key, secret key and ciphertext are $\mathcal{O}(n)$ each in our scheme as well as in [23]. However, our master secret key is of $\mathcal{O}(n)$ whereas that of [23] is constant (only 1). With this trade off, we achieve HID-IPFE from standard well-studied assumption.

- Our offline exponentiation cost is $(d + 1)|\mathbb{G}| + (n + d + 1)|\widehat{\mathbb{G}}| + (n + 1)|\mathbb{G}_t|$, pairing computation is 1 which are done only once in Setup phase. Our online exponentiation cost is $(2l + 1)|\mathbb{G}| + (6l + n + 3)|\widehat{\mathbb{G}}| + 3n|\mathbb{G}_t|$ − algorithm Encrypt requires $(2l + 1)|\mathbb{G}| + 2n|\mathbb{G}_t|$, algorithm KeyGen requires $(3l + n)|\widehat{\mathbb{G}}|$, algorithm Delegate requires $(3l + 3)|\widehat{\mathbb{G}}|$ and algorithm Decrypt requires $n|\mathbb{G}_t|$. Offline exponentiation cost of [23] is 1, pairing computation is 0. Online exponentiation cost of [23] is $(n + l + 2d + 8)|\mathbb{G}| + (3n + 2)|\mathbb{G}_t|$ − algorithm Encrypt has $(l + 2)|\mathbb{G}| + 2n|\mathbb{G}_t|$, algorithm KeyGen has $(n + d + 3)|\mathbb{G}|$, algorithm Delegate has $(d + 3)|\mathbb{G}|$ and algorithm Decrypt has $(n + 2)|\mathbb{G}_t|$. One of the appealing feature of our design compared to [23] is that our scheme requires $(l + 1)$ online pairing computations in Decrypt algorithm where $l \leq \lceil \log_2(N + 1) \rceil - 1$. On the other hand, scheme of [23] performs $(n + 1)$ pairing computations in Encrypt algorithm and 2 pairing computations in Decrypt algorithm. For $n = 100$, $d = 15$, $l = 7$ our online pairing computation cost is only 8 while that of [23] is 103, our online exponentiation cost is $15|\mathbb{G}| + 145|\widehat{\mathbb{G}}| + 300|\mathbb{G}_t|$ while that of [23] is $145|\mathbb{G}| + 302|\mathbb{G}_t|$. Thus, our construction provides low cost online computation as compared to [23].

2 Preliminaries

2.1 Notation

Let λ denote the security parameter. By $x \xleftarrow{u} S$ we mean that x is chosen uniformly from the set S. Let $[n]$ represent the set $\{1, 2, \ldots, n\}$ for any $n \in \mathbb{N}$. We say $f : \mathbb{N} \to \mathbb{R}$ is a *negligible* function of n if it is $\mathcal{O}(n^{-c})$ for all $c > 0$ and we use $\mathsf{negl}(n)$ for negligible function of n. Let the symbol $\perp$ indicate failure or null value and $\langle \cdot, \cdot \rangle$ represent inner product of two vectors.

2.2 Hierarchical Identity-Based Inner Product Functional Encryption

In this section, we recall the syntax and security of Hierarchical Identity-based Inner Product Functional Encryption (HID-IPFE) from the work of Song et al.

[23]. An HID-IPFE scheme consists of a tuple of polynomial time algorithms HID-IPFE = (Setup, Encrypt, KeyGen, Delegate, Decrypt) defined as follows.

- Setup $(1^\lambda, n, d) \rightarrow$ (PK, MSK) : A trusted authority runs this probabilistic algorithm on input the security parameter λ, length of the vector n, maximum depth d of the hierarchical identity and generates the public key PK and the master secret key MSK. It publishes PK and keeps MSK secret to itself.
- Encrypt (PK, $\text{HID}_l, \vec{x}) \rightarrow \text{CT}_{\vec{x},\text{HID}_l}$: An encryptor on input the public key PK, a hierarchical identity $\text{HID}_l = (\text{ID}_1, \text{ID}_2, \ldots, \text{ID}_l)$ of depth $l \leq d$, a vector $\vec{x}$ of length n, computes a ciphertext $\text{CT}_{\vec{x},\text{HID}_l}$ and makes it public.
- KeyGen (PK, MSK, $\text{HID}_l, \vec{y}) \rightarrow \text{SK}_{\vec{y},\text{HID}_l}$: The trusted authority takes input the public key PK, the master secret key MSK, a hierarchical identity $\text{HID}_l = (\text{ID}_1, \text{ID}_2, \ldots, \text{ID}_l)$ of depth $l \leq d$, a vector $\vec{y}$ of length n and generates a secret key $\text{SK}_{\vec{y},\text{HID}_l}$. It sends $\text{SK}_{\vec{y},\text{HID}_l}$ to the user with hierarchical identity HID_l through a secure channel between them.
- Delegate (PK, $\text{HID}_l, \text{SK}_{\vec{y},\text{HID}_l}, \text{ID}) \rightarrow \text{SK}_{\vec{y},\text{HID}_{l+1}}$: A user with hierarchical identity HID_l runs this algorithm on input the public key PK, a secret key $\text{SK}_{\vec{y},\text{HID}_l}$ corresponding to its hierarchical identity HID_l of depth $l < d$ and vector $\vec{y}$, a sub-identity ID and generates a secret key $\text{SK}_{\vec{y},\text{HID}_{l+1}}$ associated with a level $l+1$ identity $\text{HID}_{l+1} = \text{HID}_l \cup \text{ID}$ and vector $\vec{y}$.
- Decrypt (PK, $\text{CT}_{\vec{x},\text{HID}}, \text{SK}_{\vec{y},\text{HID}'}) \rightarrow \langle \vec{x}, \vec{y} \rangle / \perp$: On input the public key PK, ciphertext $\text{CT}_{\vec{x},\text{HID}}$, secret key $\text{SK}_{\vec{y},\text{HID}'}$, a decryptor obtains the inner product $\langle \vec{x}, \vec{y} \rangle$ or $\perp$.

Correctness. For correctness, we require that for all (PK, MSK) $\leftarrow$ Setup $(1^\lambda, n, d)$, $\text{CT}_{\vec{x},\text{HID}} \leftarrow$ Encrypt(PK, HID, $\vec{x}$), $\text{SK}_{\vec{y},\text{HID}'} \leftarrow$ KeyGen(PK, MSK, HID', $\vec{y}$)/ Delegate (PK, $\widehat{\text{HID}}, \text{SK}_{\vec{y},\widehat{\text{HID}}}, \text{ID}$) where $\widehat{\text{HID}}$ is a prefix of HID' and HID' = $\widehat{\text{HID}} \cup \text{ID}$, return $\perp$ if HID $\neq$ HID'. Otherwise,

$$\text{Decrypt}(\text{PK}, \text{CT}_{\vec{x},\text{HID}}, \text{SK}_{\vec{y},\text{HID}'}) = \langle \vec{x}, \vec{y} \rangle$$

where $\langle \vec{x}, \vec{y} \rangle$ is from a fixed polynomial range of values.

Security. We describe below the *selective security* model of HID-IPFE against *chosen plaintext attack* (CPA) which is modeled as a game between an adversary $\mathcal{A}$ and a challenger $\mathcal{C}$.

- **Init**: The adversary $\mathcal{A}$ submits a challenge hierarchical identity $\text{HID}^\star$ and two challenge vectors $\vec{x}_0^\star, \vec{x}_1^\star$ $(\vec{x}_0^\star \neq \vec{x}_1^\star)$ to the challenger $\mathcal{C}$.
- **Setup**: The challenger $\mathcal{C}$ generates (PK, MSK) $\leftarrow$ Setup$(1^\lambda, n, d)$ and provides PK to $\mathcal{A}$.
- **Query phase 1**: The adversary makes polynomially many private key queries $\text{SK}_{\vec{y},\text{HID}}$ to $\mathcal{C}$. In response to the query on $(\vec{y}, \text{HID})$ where $\vec{y}$ is a vector, HID is a hierarchical identity, $|\text{HID}| \leq |\text{HID}^\star|$ (where $|\text{HID}|$ denotes depth of HID), the challenger $\mathcal{C}$ responds with $\text{SK}_{\vec{y},\text{HID}} \leftarrow$ KeyGen(PK, MSK, HID, $\vec{y}$). Here the restriction on $(\vec{y}, \text{HID})$ is that if $\langle \vec{x}_0^\star - \vec{x}_1^\star, \vec{y} \rangle \neq 0$, then HID must not be a prefix of $\text{HID}^\star$. If $|\text{HID}| > |\text{HID}^\star|$, the challenger $\mathcal{C}$ computes $\text{SK}_{\vec{y},\text{HID}''} \leftarrow$

KeyGen(PK, MSK, HID'', $\vec{y}$) where HID'' is the prefix of HID with $|HID''| = |HID^\star|$, obtains $SK_{\vec{y},HID}$ by invoking algorithm Delegate repeatedly ($|HID| - |HID^\star|$) times starting from $SK_{\vec{y},HID''}$ and provides $SK_{\vec{y},HID}$ to $\mathcal{A}$.

- **Challenge**: The challenger $\mathcal{C}$ flips a random coin $\beta \in \{0,1\}$, computes $CT_{\vec{x}^\star_\beta,HID^\star} \leftarrow$ Encrypt(PK, HID*, $\vec{x}^\star_\beta$). The challenger $\mathcal{C}$ sends the challenge ciphertext $CT_{\vec{x}^\star_\beta,HID^\star}$ to the adversary $\mathcal{A}$.
- **Query phase 2**: Same as Query phase 1.
- **Guess**: Finally, $\mathcal{A}$ outputs a guess bit β' and wins the game if $\beta' = \beta$.

Advantage of $\mathcal{A}$ in this game is defined as:

$$\mathsf{Adv}^{sCPA}_{HID-IPFE,\mathcal{A}}(\lambda) = \left| \Pr[\beta' = \beta] - \frac{1}{2} \right|$$

We say that an HID-IPFE scheme is selectively CPA-secure if

$$\mathsf{Adv}^{sCPA}_{HID-IPFE,\mathcal{A}}(\lambda) \leq \mathsf{negl}(\lambda)$$

We clarify the reason for setting the restriction in the Query phase 1. If the restriction is not there, the adversary $\mathcal{A}$ will obtain a secret key $SK_{\vec{y},HID}$ where $\langle \vec{x}^\star_0, \vec{y} \rangle \neq \langle \vec{x}^\star_1, \vec{y} \rangle$ and HID is a prefix of HID*. Therefore, $\mathcal{A}$ executes the Delegate algorithm itself to generate $SK_{\vec{y},HID^\star}$ and obtains $\langle \vec{x}^\star_\beta, \vec{y} \rangle$ by running the Decrypt algorithm on input $CT_{\vec{x}^\star_\beta,HID^\star}$ and $SK_{\vec{y},HID^\star}$. At the end, $\mathcal{A}$ outputs a bit 0 if $\langle \vec{x}^\star_\beta, \vec{y} \rangle = \langle \vec{x}^\star_0, \vec{y} \rangle$ and outputs a bit 1 if $\langle \vec{x}^\star_\beta, \vec{y} \rangle = \langle \vec{x}^\star_1, \vec{y} \rangle$. Thus, $\mathcal{A}$ trivially wins the game without the above mentioned restriction.

2.3 Asymmetric Bilinear Map and Hardness Assumption

Definition 1 (Asymmetric Bilinear Map). *Let* $\mathbb{G}, \widehat{\mathbb{G}}, \mathbb{G}_t$ *be multiplicative cyclic groups of prime order* p. *Let* g, $\widehat{g}$ *be generator of* $\mathbb{G}, \widehat{\mathbb{G}}$ *respectively. An asymmetric bilinear mapping* $e : \mathbb{G} \times \widehat{\mathbb{G}} \to \mathbb{G}_t$ *is a function having the following properties.*

1. $e(u^a, v^b) = e(u, v)^{ab} \; \forall \; u \in \mathbb{G}, v \in \widehat{\mathbb{G}}, a, b \in \mathbb{Z}_p$.
2. *The map is non degenerate, i.e.,* $e(g, \widehat{g})$ *is a generator of* $\mathbb{G}_t$.
   The tuple $(p, \mathbb{G}, \widehat{\mathbb{G}}, \mathbb{G}_t, e)$ *is called a prime order asymmetric bilinear group system.*

Definition 2 (Decisional Bilinear Diffie-Hellman (DBDH) Problem). *Let* $\mathbb{G}, \widehat{\mathbb{G}}, \mathbb{G}_t$ *be cyclic groups of prime order* p *and* $e : \mathbb{G} \times \widehat{\mathbb{G}} \to \mathbb{G}_t$ *be an asymmetric bilinear pairing generated by a bilinear group generator on input a security parameter* λ. *Let* $a, b, c \xleftarrow{u} \mathbb{Z}_p$, g *be a random generator of* $\mathbb{G}$, $\widehat{g}$ *be a random generator of* $\widehat{\mathbb{G}}$, $z_1 = (g, g^a, g^c, \widehat{g}, \widehat{g}^a, \widehat{g}^b) \in \mathbb{G}^3 \times \widehat{\mathbb{G}}^3$ *and* $z_2 \xleftarrow{u} \mathbb{G}_t$. *Given* (z_1, z_2), *the DBDH problem is to determine whether* z_2 *is* $e(g, \widehat{g})^{abc}$ *or a random element of* $\mathbb{G}_t$. *The advantage of a distinguisher* $\mathcal{A}$ *is defined as*

$$\mathsf{Adv}^{DBDH}_{\mathcal{A}}(\lambda) = |\Pr[\mathcal{A}(z_1, e(g, \widehat{g})^{abc}) \to 1] - \Pr[\mathcal{A}(z_1, z_2) \to 1]|$$

3   Construction of HID-IPFE

Our construction described below HID-IPFE = (Setup, Encrypt, KeyGen, Delegate, Decrypt) uses hierarchical identity space $\mathbb{Z}_p^l$ for some $l \leq d$, a vector space $\mathbb{Z}_p^n$ and asymmetric bilinear setup where l, d, n are positive integers, p is a large prime.

- Setup $(1^\lambda, n, d) \rightarrow (\mathsf{PK}, \mathsf{MSK})$: A trusted authority takes as input the security parameter λ, length of the vector n, maximum depth of the hierarchical identity d and proceeds as follows.
  - Generates an asymmetric bilinear pairing $e : \mathbb{G} \times \widehat{\mathbb{G}} \rightarrow \mathbb{G}_t$ where $\mathbb{G}, \widehat{\mathbb{G}}, \mathbb{G}_t$ are cyclic groups of prime order $p > 2^\lambda$ and chooses random generators $g, \widehat{g}$ of $\mathbb{G}, \widehat{\mathbb{G}}$ respectively.
  - Randomly selects $a, \{\delta_i \in \mathbb{Z}_p\}_{i \in [d]}$ and computes $u = e(g, \widehat{g}), g_1 = g^a, \widehat{g}_1 = \widehat{g}^a, \{h_i = g^{\delta_i}\}_{i \in [d]}, \{\widehat{h}_i = \widehat{g}^{\delta_i}\}_{i \in [d]}$.
  - Picks randomly $b, \{\gamma_i\}_{i \in [n]} \in \mathbb{Z}_p$ and computes $\{\widehat{g}_{0,i} = \widehat{g}_1^{b\gamma_i}\}_{i \in [n]}, v = u^{ab}, \{w_i = v^{\gamma_i}\}_{i \in [n]}$.
  - Sets the public key PK and master secret key MSK as

$$\mathsf{PK} = (e, \mathbb{G}, \widehat{\mathbb{G}}, \mathbb{G}_t, p, g, g_1, \{h_i\}_{i \in [d]}, \widehat{g}, \widehat{g}_1, \{\widehat{h}_i\}_{i \in [d]}, u = e(g, \widehat{g}), \{w_i\}_{i \in [n]})$$

$$\mathsf{MSK} = (\widehat{g}_{0,1}, \widehat{g}_{0,2}, \ldots, \widehat{g}_{0,n})$$

  - Finally it publishes PK and keeps MSK secret to itself.
- Encrypt $(\mathsf{PK}, \mathsf{HID}_l, \vec{x}) \rightarrow \mathsf{CT}_{\vec{x}, \mathsf{HID}_l}$: On input the public key

$$\mathsf{PK} = (e, \mathbb{G}, \widehat{\mathbb{G}}, \mathbb{G}_t, p, g, g_1, \{h_i\}_{i \in [d]}, \widehat{g}, \widehat{g}_1, \{\widehat{h}_i\}_{i \in [d]}, u = e(g, \widehat{g}), \{w_i\}_{i \in [n]}),$$

a recipient hierarchical identity $\mathsf{HID}_l = (\mathsf{ID}_1, \mathsf{ID}_2, \ldots, \mathsf{ID}_l) \in \mathbb{Z}_p^l$ with $l \leq d$ and a vector $\vec{x} = (x_1, x_2, \ldots, x_n) \in \mathbb{Z}_p^n$, an encryptor performs the following steps.
  - Chooses $s \xleftarrow{u} \mathbb{Z}_p$, extracts $g, g_1, u, \{w_i\}_{i \in [n]}, \{h_i\}_{i \in [l]}$ from PK and computes

$$E_i = u^{x_i} w_i^s , \, i \in [n], C_0 = g^s, C_k = (g_1^{\mathsf{ID}_k} h_k)^s , \, k \in [l]$$

  - Sets $\mathsf{CT}_{\vec{x}, \mathsf{HID}_l} = (\mathsf{HID}_l, \{E_i\}_{i \in [n]}, C_0, \{C_k\}_{k \in [l]})$ and publishes CT.
- KeyGen $(\mathsf{PK}, \mathsf{MSK}, \mathsf{HID}_l, \vec{y}) \rightarrow \mathsf{SK}_{\vec{y}, \mathsf{HID}_l}$: Taking input the public key PK, master secret key MSK, a recipient hierarchical identity $\mathsf{HID}_l = (\mathsf{ID}_1, \mathsf{ID}_2, \ldots, \mathsf{ID}_l) \in \mathbb{Z}_p^l$, a vector $\vec{y} = (y_1, y_2, \ldots, y_n) \in \mathbb{Z}_p^n$, the trusted authority executes the steps described below.
  - Chooses $r_1, r_2, \ldots, r_l \xleftarrow{u} \mathbb{Z}_p$, extracts $\widehat{g}, \widehat{g}_1, \{\widehat{h}_k\}_{k \in [l]}$ from PK, $\{\widehat{g}_{0,i}\}_{i \in [n]}$ from MSK and computes

$$D_0 = \prod_{i=1}^n \widehat{g}_{0,i}^{y_i} \prod_{k=1}^l (\widehat{g}_1^{\mathsf{ID}_k} \widehat{h}_k)^{r_k}, D_i = \widehat{g}^{r_i}, \, i \in [l]$$

  - Sets the secret key $\mathsf{SK}_{\vec{y}, \mathsf{HID}_l} = (\mathsf{HID}_l, \vec{y}, D_0, \{D_i\}_{i \in [l]})$ and issues $\mathsf{SK}_{\vec{y}, \mathsf{HID}_l}$ to the user with hierarchical identity HID_l through a secure channel between them.

- Delegate $(\mathsf{PK}, \mathsf{HID}_l, \mathsf{SK}_{\vec{y},\mathsf{HID}_l}, \mathsf{ID}) \rightarrow \mathsf{SK}_{\vec{y},\mathsf{HID}_{l+1}}$: A user with hierarchical identity $\mathsf{HID}_l = (\mathsf{ID}_1, \mathsf{ID}_2, \ldots, \mathsf{ID}_l)$ performs the following steps on input the public key PK, secret key $\mathsf{SK}_{\vec{y},\mathsf{HID}_l} = (\mathsf{HID}_l, \vec{y}, D_0, \{D_i\}_{i \in [l]})$ associated with its hierarchical identity and vector $\vec{y}$, a sub-identity ID.
  - Picks randomly $\{r'_i\}_{i \in [l+1]} \in \mathbb{Z}_p$, extracts $\widehat{g}, \widehat{g}_1, \{\widehat{h}_k\}_{k \in [l+1]}$ from PK and computes

$$D'_0 = D_0 \prod_{k=1}^{l} (\widehat{g}_1^{\mathsf{ID}_k} \widehat{h}_k)^{r'_k} (\widehat{g}_1^{\mathsf{ID}} \widehat{h}_{l+1})^{r'_{l+1}}$$

$$= \prod_{i=1}^{n} \widehat{g}_{0,i}^{y_i} \prod_{k=1}^{l} (\widehat{g}_1^{\mathsf{ID}_k} \widehat{h}_k)^{r_k + r'_k} (\widehat{g}_1^{\mathsf{ID}} \widehat{h}_{l+1})^{r'_{l+1}}$$

$$D'_i = D_i \, \widehat{g}^{r'_i} = \widehat{g}^{r_i + r'_i}, \ i \in [l]$$
$$D'_{l+1} = \widehat{g}^{r'_{l+1}}$$

  - Sets the secret key

$$\mathsf{SK}_{\vec{y},\mathsf{HID}_{l+1}} = (\mathsf{HID}_{l+1} = (\mathsf{ID}_1, \mathsf{ID}_2, \ldots, \mathsf{ID}_l, \mathsf{ID}), \vec{y}, D'_0, \{D'_i\}_{i \in [l+1]})$$

  associated with depth $(l + 1)$ identity $\mathsf{HID}_{l+1} = \mathsf{HID}_l \cup \mathsf{ID} = (\mathsf{ID}_1, \mathsf{ID}_2, \ldots, \mathsf{ID}_l, \mathsf{ID})$ and vector $\vec{y}$.
  - Provides the secret key $\mathsf{SK}_{\vec{y},\mathsf{HID}_{l+1}}$ to the user with hierarchical identity HID_{l+1} through a secure communication channel between them.
- Decrypt $(\mathsf{PK}, \mathsf{CT}_{\vec{x},\mathsf{HID}}, \mathsf{SK}_{\vec{y},\mathsf{HID}'}) \rightarrow \langle \vec{x}, \vec{y} \rangle / \perp$: On input the public key

$$\mathsf{PK} = (e, \mathbb{G}, \widehat{\mathbb{G}}, \mathbb{G}_t, p, g, g_1, \{h_i\}_{i \in [d]}, \widehat{g}, \widehat{g}_1, \{\widehat{h}_i\}_{i \in [d]}, u = e(g, \widehat{g}), \{w_i\}_{i \in [n]})$$

ciphertext
$$\mathsf{CT} = (\mathsf{HID}, \{E_i\}_{i \in [n]}, C_0, \{C_i\}_{i \in [l]})$$

secret key
$$\mathsf{SK} = (\mathsf{HID}', \vec{y} = (y_1, y_2, \ldots, y_n), D_0, \{D_i\}_{i \in [l']})$$

where depth of $\mathsf{HID}, \mathsf{HID}'$ are l, l' respectively, a decryptor proceeds as follows.
  - Checks whether $\mathsf{HID} = \mathsf{HID}'$. If not, outputs $\perp$.
  - Otherwise, computes

$$A_1 = \prod_{i=1}^{n} E_i^{y_i}$$

$$A_2 = \prod_{k=1}^{l} e(C_k, D_k)$$
$$A_3 = e(C_0, D_0)$$

and recovers

$$u^{\langle \vec{x}, \vec{y} \rangle} = e(g, \widehat{g})^{\langle \vec{x}, \vec{y} \rangle} = \frac{A_1 A_2}{A_3}$$

Now, it finds a certain $M \in T$ (where T is a polynomial-sized subset of $\mathbb{Z}_p$) satisfying

$$e(g, \widehat{g})^{\langle \vec{x}, \vec{y} \rangle} = e(g, \widehat{g})^M$$

and outputs M.

Note that, the Decrypt algorithm runs in polynomial time as it is restricted to check a fixed polynomial size range of possible values for M.

Correctness. Let $\mathsf{HID} = \mathsf{HID}' = (\mathsf{ID}_1, \mathsf{ID}_2, \dots, \mathsf{ID}_l)$ and $\mathsf{SK}_{\vec{y}, \mathsf{HID}'} \leftarrow \mathsf{KeyGen}$ $(\mathsf{PK}, \mathsf{MSK}, \mathsf{HID}', \vec{y})$. Then the correctness follows as

$$A_1 = \prod_{i=1}^{n} E_i^{y_i} = \prod_{i=1}^{n} u^{x_i y_i} w_i^{s y_i} = e(g, \widehat{g})^{\sum_{i=1}^{n} x_i y_i} \prod_{i=1}^{n} w_i^{s y_i} = e(g, \widehat{g})^{\langle \vec{x}, \vec{y} \rangle} \prod_{i=1}^{n} w_i^{s y_i}$$

$$A_2 = \prod_{k=1}^{l} e(C_k, D_k) = \prod_{k=1}^{l} e\left((g_1^{\mathsf{ID}_k} h_k)^s, \widehat{g}^{r_k} \right) = \prod_{k=1}^{l} e(g_1^{\mathsf{ID}_k} h_k, \widehat{g})^{s r_k}$$

$$A_3 = e(C_0, D_0) = e\left(g^s, \prod_{i=1}^{n} \widehat{g}_{0,i}^{y_i} \prod_{k=1}^{l} (\widehat{g}_1^{\mathsf{ID}_k} \widehat{h}_k)^{r_k} \right)$$

$$= e(g^s, \prod_{i=1}^{n} \widehat{g}_{0,i}^{y_i}) \, e\left(g^s, \prod_{k=1}^{l} (\widehat{g}_1^{\mathsf{ID}_k} \widehat{h}_k)^{r_k} \right) = e(g, \widehat{g})^{abs \sum_{i=1}^{n} \gamma_i y_i} \prod_{k=1}^{l} e\left(g, \widehat{g}_1^{\mathsf{ID}_k} \widehat{h}_k \right)^{s r_k}$$

$$= \prod_{i=1}^{n} w_i^{s y_i} \prod_{k=1}^{l} e\left(g, \widehat{g}^{a \mathsf{ID}_k + \delta_k} \right)^{s r_k} = \prod_{i=1}^{n} w_i^{s y_i} \prod_{k=1}^{l} e\left(g^{a \mathsf{ID}_k + \delta_k}, \widehat{g} \right)^{s r_k}$$

$$= \prod_{i=1}^{n} w_i^{s y_i} \prod_{k=1}^{l} e(g_1^{\mathsf{ID}_k} h_k, \widehat{g})^{s r_k}$$

$$\frac{A_1 A_2}{A_3} = \frac{e(g, \widehat{g})^{\langle \vec{x}, \vec{y} \rangle} \prod_{i=1}^{n} w_i^{s y_i} \prod_{k=1}^{l} e(g_1^{\mathsf{ID}_k} h_k, \widehat{g})^{s r_k}}{\prod_{i=1}^{n} w_i^{s y_i} \prod_{k=1}^{l} e(g_1^{\mathsf{ID}_k} h_k, \widehat{g})^{s r_k}} = e(g, \widehat{g})^{\langle \vec{x}, \vec{y} \rangle}$$

Let $\mathsf{HID} = \mathsf{HID}' = (\mathsf{ID}_1, \mathsf{ID}_2, \dots, \mathsf{ID}_l)$ and

$$\mathsf{SK}_{\vec{y}, \mathsf{HID}'} = (\mathsf{HID}', \vec{y}, D_0', \{D_i'\}_{i \in [l]}) \leftarrow \mathsf{Delegate}(\mathsf{PK}, \widehat{\mathsf{HID}}, \mathsf{SK}_{\vec{y}, \widehat{\mathsf{HID}}}, \mathsf{ID})$$

where $\widehat{\mathsf{HID}} = (\mathsf{ID}_1, \mathsf{ID}_2, \dots, \mathsf{ID}_{l-1})$, $\mathsf{ID} = \mathsf{ID}_l$, $\mathsf{HID}' = \widehat{\mathsf{HID}} \cup \mathsf{ID}_l$. Then the correctness follows as

$$A_1 = \prod_{i=1}^{n} E_i^{y_i} = \prod_{i=1}^{n} u^{x_i y_i} w_i^{s y_i} = e(g, \widehat{g})^{\sum_{i=1}^{n} x_i y_i} \prod_{i=1}^{n} w_i^{s y_i} = e(g, \widehat{g})^{\langle \vec{x}, \vec{y} \rangle} \prod_{i=1}^{n} w_i^{s y_i}$$

$$A_2 = \prod_{k=1}^{l} e(C_k, D_k') = \prod_{k=1}^{l-1} e\left((g_1^{\mathsf{ID}_k} h_k)^s, \widehat{g}^{r_k + r_k'}\right) e\left((g_1^{\mathsf{ID}_l} h_l)^s, \widehat{g}^{r_l'}\right)$$

$$= \prod_{k=1}^{l-1} e\left(g_1^{\mathsf{ID}_k} h_k, \widehat{g}\right)^{s(r_k + r_k')} e\left(g_1^{\mathsf{ID}_l} h_l, \widehat{g}\right)^{sr_l'}$$

$$A_3 = e(C_0, D_0') = e\left(g^s, \prod_{i=1}^{n} \widehat{g}_{0,i}^{y_i} \prod_{k=1}^{l-1} (\widehat{g}_1^{\mathsf{ID}_k} \widehat{h}_k)^{r_k + r_k'} (\widehat{g}_1^{\mathsf{ID}_l} \widehat{h}_l)^{r_l'}\right)$$

$$= e\left(g^s, \prod_{i=1}^{n} \widehat{g}_{0,i}^{y_i}\right) e\left(g^s, \prod_{k=1}^{l-1} (\widehat{g}_1^{\mathsf{ID}_k} \widehat{h}_k)^{r_k + r_k'}\right) e\left(g^s, (\widehat{g}_1^{\mathsf{ID}_l} \widehat{h}_l)^{r_l'}\right)$$

$$= e(g, \widehat{g})^{abs \sum_{i=1}^{n} \gamma_i y_i} \prod_{k=1}^{l-1} e\left(g, \widehat{g}_1^{\mathsf{ID}_k} \widehat{h}_k\right)^{s(r_k + r_k')} e\left(g, \widehat{g}_1^{\mathsf{ID}_l} \widehat{h}_l\right)^{sr_l'}$$

$$= \prod_{i=1}^{n} w_i^{sy_i} \prod_{k=1}^{l-1} e\left(g, \widehat{g}^{a\mathsf{ID}_K + \delta_k}\right)^{s(r_k + r_k')} e\left(g, \widehat{g}^{a\mathsf{ID}_l + \delta_l}\right)^{sr_l'}$$

$$= \prod_{i=1}^{n} w_i^{sy_i} \prod_{k=1}^{l-1} e\left(g^{a\mathsf{ID}_K + \delta_k}, \widehat{g}\right)^{s(r_k + r_k')} e\left(g^{a\mathsf{ID}_l + \delta_l}, \widehat{g}\right)^{sr_l'}$$

$$= \prod_{i=1}^{n} w_i^{sy_i} \prod_{k=1}^{l-1} e\left(g_1^{\mathsf{ID}_k} h_k, \widehat{g}\right)^{s(r_k + r_k')} e\left(g_1^{\mathsf{ID}_l} h_l, \widehat{g}\right)^{sr_l'}$$

$$\frac{A_1 A_2}{A_3} = \frac{e(g, \widehat{g})^{\langle \vec{x}, \vec{y} \rangle} \prod_{i=1}^{n} w_i^{sy_i} \prod_{k=1}^{l-1} e\left(g_1^{\mathsf{ID}_k} h_k, \widehat{g}\right)^{s(r_k + r_k')} e\left(g_1^{\mathsf{ID}_l} h_l, \widehat{g}\right)^{sr_l'}}{\prod_{i=1}^{n} w_i^{sy_i} \prod_{k=1}^{l-1} e\left(g_1^{\mathsf{ID}_k} h_k, \widehat{g}\right)^{s(r_k + r_k')} e\left(g_1^{\mathsf{ID}_l} h_l, \widehat{g}\right)^{sr_l'}}$$

$$= e(g, \widehat{g})^{\langle \vec{x}, \vec{y} \rangle}$$

4   Security Analysis

Theorem 2. *Our hierarchical identity-based inner product functional encryption (HID-IPFE) is selectively* CPA *secure in the security model presented in Sect. 2 assuming the hardness of the* DBDH *problem.*

Proof. Let $\mathcal{A}$ be a PPT adversary that can break the CPA security of our scheme with non-negligible advantage ϵ. We show below how to construct a simulator $\mathcal{B}$ that interacts with $\mathcal{A}$ in order to solve the DBDH problem.

- **Init**: On receiving an instance

$$z_1 = (g, g^a, g^c, \widehat{g}, \widehat{g}^a, \widehat{g}^b) \in \mathbb{G}^3 \times \widehat{\mathbb{G}}^3, z_2 \in \mathbb{G}_t$$

of DBDH problem, the simulator $\mathcal{B}$ has to decide whether z_2 is $e(g, \widehat{g})^{abc}$ or random utilizing the adversary $\mathcal{A}$. Here $\mathbb{G}$, $\widehat{\mathbb{G}}$, $\mathbb{G}_t$ are cyclic groups of prime order p, g is a random generator of $\mathbb{G}$, $\widehat{g}$ is a random generator of $\widehat{\mathbb{G}}$, a, b, c are uniformly chosen from $\mathbb{Z}_p$. The PPT adversary $\mathcal{A}$ submits a challenge hierarchical identity $\mathsf{HID}^\star = (\mathsf{ID}_1^\star, \mathsf{ID}_2^\star, \ldots, \mathsf{ID}_{l^\star}^\star)$ $(l^\star \leq d)$ and two challenge vectors $\vec{x}_0^\star = (x_{0,1}^\star, x_{0,2}^\star, \ldots, x_{0,n}^\star), \vec{x}_1^\star = (x_{1,1}^\star, x_{1,2}^\star, \ldots, x_{1,n}^\star)$ with $\vec{x}_0^\star \neq \vec{x}_1^\star$ to the simulator $\mathcal{B}$. If $l^\star < d$, then $\mathcal{B}$ appends to $\mathsf{HID}^\star$ a suffix of $d - l^\star$ zeroes to make $\mathsf{HID}^\star$ a vector of length d where d is maximum depth of the hierarchical identity.
- **Setup**: The simulator $\mathcal{B}$ sets $g_1 = g^a, \widehat{g}_1 = \widehat{g}^a, \widehat{g}_2 = \widehat{g}^b, g_3 = g^c$, chooses randomly $\alpha_1, \alpha_2, \ldots, \alpha_d \in \mathbb{Z}_p$ and defines for $i \in [d]$

$$h_i = g_1^{-\mathsf{ID}_i^\star} g^{\alpha_i} \in \mathbb{G}, \quad \widehat{h}_i = \widehat{g}_1^{-\mathsf{ID}_i^\star} \widehat{g}^{\alpha_i} \in \widehat{\mathbb{G}}$$

It computes $u = e(g, \widehat{g}), v = e(g_1, \widehat{g}_2) = e(g^a, \widehat{g}^b) = e(g, \widehat{g})^{ab} = u^{ab} \in \mathbb{G}_t$, chooses $\gamma \xleftarrow{u} \mathbb{Z}_p$ and sets $w_i = v^{\gamma_i}$ where $\gamma_i = \gamma(x_{0,i}^\star - x_{1,i}^\star)$ for $i \in [n]$. The simulator $\mathcal{B}$ provides

$$\mathsf{PK} = (e, \mathbb{G}, \widehat{\mathbb{G}}, \mathbb{G}_t, p, g, g_1, \{h_i\}_{i \in [d]}, \widehat{g}, \widehat{g}_1, \{\widehat{h}_i\}_{i \in [d]}, u, \{w_i\}_{i \in [n]})$$

to the adversary $\mathcal{A}$. The corresponding master secret key is implicitly set by $\mathcal{B}$ as

$$\mathsf{MSK} = (\widehat{g}_{0,1}, \widehat{g}_{0,2}, \ldots, \widehat{g}_{0,n})$$

where $\widehat{g}_{0,i} = \widehat{g}^{ab\gamma(x_{0,i}^\star - x_{1,i}^\star)}$ for $i \in [n]$. Note that the distribution of PK is the same as that in Setup algorithm in the real protocol.
- **Query phase 1**: The adversary $\mathcal{A}$ makes polynomially many private key queries $\mathsf{SK}_{\vec{y}, \mathsf{HID}}$ to $\mathcal{B}$. For the sake of clarity, we assume that the depth of the hierarchical identity $\mathsf{HID} = (\mathsf{ID}_1, \mathsf{ID}_2, \ldots, \mathsf{ID}_l)$ be $l \leq l^\star$. (If $l > l^\star$, $\mathcal{B}$ computes $\mathsf{SK}_{\vec{y}, \mathsf{HID}''} \leftarrow \mathsf{KeyGen}(\mathsf{PK}, \mathsf{MSK}, \mathsf{HID}'', \vec{y})$ where HID'' is prefix of HID with $|\mathsf{HID}''| = l^\star = |\mathsf{HID}^\star|$, obtains $\mathsf{SK}_{\vec{y}, \mathsf{HID}}$ by executing $\mathsf{Delegate}$ algorithm repeatedly $(l - l^\star)$ times starting from $\mathsf{SK}_{\vec{y}, \mathsf{HID}''}$ and issues $\mathsf{SK}_{\vec{y}, \mathsf{HID}}$ to $\mathcal{A}$). For a query on $(\mathsf{HID}, \vec{y})$, $\mathcal{B}$ first performs the following validity checks.
  1. If the tuple $(\mathsf{HID}, \vec{y})$ has been asked before, then the check returns 0.
  2. If $\langle \vec{x}_0^\star - \vec{x}_1^\star, \vec{y} \rangle \neq 0$ and HID is the prefix of $\mathsf{HID}^\star$, then the check returns 0.
  3. If the above checks passed but provided no return, then the check returns 1.

The simulator $\mathcal{B}$ then proceeds as follows.
  1. If the validity check returns 0, $\mathcal{B}$ refuses to answer this query and continues to listen to the next secret key query from $\mathcal{A}$.

2. If the validity check returns 1 and $\langle \vec{x}_0^* - \vec{x}_1^*, \vec{y} \rangle \neq 0$ then HID $= (\mathsf{ID}_1, \mathsf{ID}_2, \ldots, \mathsf{ID}_l)$ is not a prefix of $\mathsf{HID}^* = (\mathsf{ID}_1^*, \mathsf{ID}_2^*, \ldots, \mathsf{ID}_{l^*}^*)$ which in turn implies that there exists at least one $j \in [l]$ such that $\mathsf{ID}_j \neq \mathsf{ID}_j^*$. The simulator $\mathcal{B}$ first computes the private key $\mathsf{SK}_{\vec{y}, \mathsf{HID}_j} = (\mathsf{HID}_j, \vec{y}, D_0, \{D_i\}_{i \in [j]})$ for the hierarchical identity $\mathsf{HID}_j = (\mathsf{ID}_1, \mathsf{ID}_2, \ldots, \mathsf{ID}_j)$ by selecting randomly $r_1, r_2, \ldots, r_j \in \mathbb{Z}_p$ and computing

$$D_0 = \widehat{g}_2^{\frac{-\alpha_j \gamma \langle \vec{x}_0^* - \vec{x}_1^*, \vec{y} \rangle}{\mathsf{ID}_j - \mathsf{ID}_j^*}} \prod_{k=1}^{j} (\widehat{g}_1^{\mathsf{ID}_k} \widehat{h}_k)^{r_k}, D_k = \widehat{g}^{r_k} \; ; \; k \in [j-1],$$

$$D_j = \widehat{g}_2^{\frac{-\gamma \langle \vec{x}_0^* - \vec{x}_1^*, \vec{y} \rangle}{\mathsf{ID}_j - \mathsf{ID}_j^*}} \widehat{g}^{r_j}$$

Following it, $\mathcal{B}$ generates a private key for the requested HID $= (\mathsf{ID}_1, \mathsf{ID}_2, \ldots, \mathsf{ID}_l) = (\mathsf{ID}_1, \mathsf{ID}_2, \ldots, \mathsf{ID}_j, \ldots, \mathsf{ID}_l)$ by repeatedly applying the algorithm Delegate $(l - j)$ times starting from the secret key $\mathsf{SK}_{\vec{y}, \mathsf{HID}_j} = (\mathsf{HID}_j, \vec{y}, D_0, \{D_i\}_{i \in [j]})$.

Let us now establish the fact that $\mathsf{SK}_{\vec{y}, \mathsf{HID}_j} = (\mathsf{HID}_j, \vec{y}, D_0, \{D_i\}_{i \in [j]})$ as defined above is correctly distributed.

Let $\widetilde{r}_j = r_j - \frac{b\gamma \langle \vec{x}_0^* - \vec{x}_1^*, \vec{y} \rangle}{\mathsf{ID}_j - \mathsf{ID}_j^*}$. As $\widehat{g}_2 = \widehat{g}^b, \widehat{g}_1 = \widehat{g}^a, \widehat{h}_j = \widehat{g}_1^{-\mathsf{ID}_j^*} \widehat{g}^{\alpha_j}$ and

$$\left(\widehat{g}^{a(\mathsf{ID}_j - \mathsf{ID}_j^*)} \widehat{g}^{\alpha_j} \right)^{\frac{-b\gamma \langle \vec{x}_0^* - \vec{x}_1^*, \vec{y} \rangle}{\mathsf{ID}_j - \mathsf{ID}_j^*}} = \widehat{g}^{-ab\gamma \langle \vec{x}_0^* - \vec{x}_1^*, \vec{y} \rangle} \widehat{g}^{\frac{-ba_j \gamma \langle \vec{x}_0^* - \vec{x}_1^*, \vec{y} \rangle}{\mathsf{ID}_j - \mathsf{ID}_j^*}}$$

We get

$$\widehat{g}_2^{\frac{-\alpha_j \gamma \langle \vec{x}_0^* - \vec{x}_1^*, \vec{y} \rangle}{\mathsf{ID}_j - \mathsf{ID}_j^*}} (\widehat{g}_1^{\mathsf{ID}_j} \widehat{h}_j)^{r_j} = \widehat{g}^{\frac{-b\alpha_j \gamma \langle \vec{x}_0^* - \vec{x}_1^*, \vec{y} \rangle}{\mathsf{ID}_j - \mathsf{ID}_j^*}} (\widehat{g}^{a(\mathsf{ID}_j - \mathsf{ID}_j^*)} \widehat{g}^{\alpha_j})^{r_j}$$

$$= \widehat{g}^{ab\gamma \langle \vec{x}_0^* - \vec{x}_1^*, \vec{y} \rangle} \left(\widehat{g}^{a(\mathsf{ID}_j - \mathsf{ID}_j^*)} \widehat{g}^{\alpha_j} \right)^{r_j - \frac{b\gamma \langle \vec{x}_0^* - \vec{x}_1^*, \vec{y} \rangle}{\mathsf{ID}_j - \mathsf{ID}_j^*}}$$

$$= \prod_{i=1}^{n} \widehat{g}_{0,i}^{y_i} (\widehat{g}^{a(\mathsf{ID}_j - \mathsf{ID}_j^*)} \widehat{g}^{\alpha_j})^{\widetilde{r}_j}$$

$$= \prod_{i=1}^{n} \widehat{g}_{0,i}^{y_i} (\widehat{g}_1^{\mathsf{ID}_j} \widehat{h}_j)^{\widetilde{r}_j}$$

where $\widehat{g}_{0,i} = \widehat{g}^{ab\gamma(x_{0,i}^* - x_{1,i}^*)}$, $i \in [n]$ as set implicitly by $\mathcal{B}$.
Then

$$D_0 = \prod_{i=1}^{n} \widehat{g}_{0,i}^{y_i} \prod_{k=1}^{j-1} (\widehat{g}_1^{\mathsf{ID}_k} \widehat{h}_k)^{r_k} (\widehat{g}_1^{\mathsf{ID}_j} \widehat{h}_j)^{\widetilde{r}_j}, \; D_k = \widehat{g}^{r_k}; k \in [j-1],$$

$$D_j = \widehat{g}^{-\frac{b\gamma \langle \vec{x}_0^* - \vec{x}_1^*, \vec{y} \rangle}{\mathsf{ID}_j - \mathsf{ID}_j^*} + r_j} = \widehat{g}^{\widetilde{r}_j}$$

where the exponents $r_1, r_2, \ldots, r_{j-1}, \widetilde{r}_j$ are uniform and independent in $\mathbb{Z}_p$. Consequently, the distribution of the private key is identical to that generated by the algorithm KeyGen in the real protocol.

3. If the validity check returns 1 and $\langle \vec{x}_0^\star - \vec{x}_1^\star, \vec{y} \rangle = 0$, then the simulator $\mathcal{B}$ computes private key $\mathsf{SK}_{\vec{y},\mathsf{HID}} = (\mathsf{HID}, \vec{y}, D_0, \{D_i\}_{i \in [l]})$ by selecting randomly $r_1, r_2, \ldots, r_l \in \mathbb{Z}_p$ and computing

$$D_0 = \prod_{k=1}^{l}(\widehat{g}_1^{\mathsf{ID}_k}\widehat{h}_k)^{r_k}, D_1 = \widehat{g}^{r_1}, \ldots, D_l = \widehat{g}^{r_l}$$

Note that,

$$\prod_{i=1}^{n}\widehat{g}_{0,i}^{y_i} = \prod_{i=1}^{n}\widehat{g}^{ab\gamma(x_{0,i}^\star - x_{1,i}^\star)y_i} = \widehat{g}^{ab\gamma\sum_{i=1}^{n}(x_{0,i}^\star - x_{1,i}^\star)y_i} = \widehat{g}^{ab\gamma\langle\vec{x}_0^\star - \vec{x}_1^\star, \vec{y}\rangle} = 1$$

as $\langle \vec{x}_0^\star - \vec{x}_1^\star, \vec{y} \rangle = 0$ in this case. Thus we can write,

$$D_0 = \prod_{i=1}^{n}\widehat{g}_{0,i}^{y_i}\prod_{k=1}^{l}(\widehat{g}_1^{\mathsf{ID}_k}\widehat{h}_k)^{r_k}, D_i = \widehat{g}^{r_i} \;:\; i \in [l]$$

as in the real protocol. Thus the distribution of the private key $\mathsf{SK}_{\vec{y},\mathsf{HID}}$ matches with that by the algorithm KeyGen.

- **Challenge**: The simulator $\mathcal{B}$ flips a coin $\beta \in \{0,1\}$ and encrypts the vector $\vec{x}_\beta^\star = (x_{\beta,1}^\star, x_{\beta,2}^\star, \ldots, x_{\beta,n}^\star)$ with the hierarchical identity $\mathsf{HID}^\star = (\mathsf{ID}_1^\star, \mathsf{ID}_2^\star, \ldots, \mathsf{ID}_{l^\star}^\star)$ to generate the challenge ciphertext

$$\mathsf{CT}_{\vec{x}_\beta^\star,\mathsf{HID}^\star} = (\mathsf{HID}^\star, \{E_i\}_{i\in[n]}, C_0, \{C_k\}_{k\in[l^\star]})$$

where $E_i = u^{x_{\beta,i}^\star}z_2^{\gamma_i}$ for $i \in [n]$, $C_0 = g_3 = g^c$ and $C_k = g_3^{\alpha_k}$ for $k \in [l^\star]$. Implicitly setting $s = c$, we observe that the simulation of $\mathsf{CT}_{\vec{x}_\beta^\star,\mathsf{HID}^\star}$ is correct if $z_2 = e(g,\widehat{g})^{abc}$ as

$$(g_1^{\mathsf{ID}_k^\star}h_k)^c = (g_1^{\mathsf{ID}_k^\star}g_1^{-\mathsf{ID}_k^\star}g^{\alpha_k})^c = (g^c)^{\alpha_k} = g_3^{\alpha_k} = C_k$$

and $u^{x_{\beta,i}^\star}w_i^c = u^{x_{\beta,i}^\star}(v^{\gamma_i})^c = u^{x_{\beta,i}^\star}e(g_1,\widehat{g}_2)^{\gamma_i c}$
$= u^{x_{\beta,i}^\star}e(g^a,\widehat{g}^b)^{\gamma_i c} = u^{x_{\beta,i}^\star}e(g,\widehat{g})^{abc\gamma_i} = u^{x_{\beta,i}^\star}z_2^{\gamma_i} = E_i$ for $i \in [n]$.
- **Query phase 2**: Same as Query phase 1.
- **Guess**: At the end, $\mathcal{A}$ outputs a guess bit β'. If $\beta' = \beta$ then $\mathcal{B}$ outputs 1 to indicate that $z_2 = e(g,\widehat{g})^{abc}$. Otherwise, $\mathcal{B}$ outputs 0 to indicate that z_2 is a random element of $\mathbb{G}_t$.

For instance, if $z_2 = e(g,\widehat{g})^{abc}e(g,\widehat{g})^r$ for some $r \xleftarrow{u} \mathbb{Z}_p^\star$ then

$$\begin{aligned}
E_i &= u^{x_{\beta,i}^\star}z_2^{\gamma_i} \\
&= e(g,\widehat{g})^{x_{\beta,i}^\star}e(g,\widehat{g})^{abc\gamma_i}e(g,\widehat{g})^{r\gamma_i} \\
&= e(g,\widehat{g})^{x_{\beta,i}^\star + r\gamma_i}e(g,\widehat{g})^{abc\gamma_i} \\
&= u^{x_{\beta,i}^\star + r\gamma_i}w_i^c
\end{aligned}$$

and thus the simulated ciphertext becomes encryption of the vector

$$\vec{x'} = (x^{\star}_{\beta,1} + r\gamma_1, x^{\star}_{\beta,2} + r\gamma_2, \ldots, x^{\star}_{\beta,n} + r\gamma_n)$$

instead of the challenge vector $\vec{x}^{\star}_{\beta} = (x^{\star}_{\beta,1}, x^{\star}_{\beta,2}, \ldots, x^{\star}_{\beta,n})$. As r is chosen randomly, $\vec{x'} \neq \vec{x}^{\star}_{\beta}$ with overwhelming probability. The simulator $\mathcal{B}$ fails to simulate $\mathsf{CT}_{\vec{x}^{\star}_{\beta}, \mathsf{HID}^{\star}}$ if z_2 is random. In this case, the message $\vec{x}^{\star}_{\beta}$ is completely hidden. Thus, we have

$$\Pr[\mathcal{B}(z_1, z_2) \to 1] = \frac{1}{2}$$

If $z_2 = e(g, \widehat{g})^{abc}$, then $\mathcal{B}$ gives perfect simulation of ciphertext. In this case, we have

$$\Pr[\mathcal{B}(z_1, e(g, \widehat{g})^{abc}) \to 1] = \frac{1}{2} + \epsilon$$

Thus the simulator $\mathcal{B}$ can solve the DBDH problem with advantage

$$\mathsf{Adv}^{\mathsf{DBDH}}_{\mathcal{B}}(\lambda) = \left| \Pr[\mathcal{B}(z_1, e(g, \widehat{g})^{abc}) \to 1] - \Pr[\mathcal{B}(z_1, z_2) \to 1] \right| = \left| \frac{1}{2} + \epsilon - \frac{1}{2} \right| = \epsilon$$

which is non-negligible.

5   Conclusion

In this work, we have designed a *selective* CPA secure HID-IPFE from a *weaker* hardness assumption. We presented real-life scenarios that require this cryptographic primitive. We eliminate the q-type assumption following the technique of Boneh et al. and analyze the security in the *standard* model under the hardness of well studied DBDH problem. Moreover, our scheme outperforms the prior work in terms of online computation cost.

References

1. Abdalla, M., Bourse, F., De Caro, A., Pointcheval, D.: Simple functional encryption schemes for inner products. In: Katz, J. (ed.) PKC 2015. LNCS, vol. 9020, pp. 733–751. Springer, Heidelberg (2015). https://doi.org/10.1007/978-3-662-46447-2_33
2. Abdalla, M., Bourse, F., De Caro, A., Pointcheval, D.: Better security for functional encryption for inner product evaluations. IACR Cryptol. ePrint Arch. **2016**, 11 (2016)
3. Abdalla, M., De Caro, A., Mochetti, K.: Lattice-based hierarchical inner product encryption. In: Hevia, A., Neven, G. (eds.) LATINCRYPT 2012. LNCS, vol. 7533, pp. 121–138. Springer, Heidelberg (2012). https://doi.org/10.1007/978-3-642-33481-8_7
4. Agrawal, S., Boneh, D., Boyen, X.: Efficient lattice (H)IBE in the standard model. In: Gilbert, H. (ed.) EUROCRYPT 2010. LNCS, vol. 6110, pp. 553–572. Springer, Heidelberg (2010). https://doi.org/10.1007/978-3-642-13190-5_28

5. Agrawal, S., Freeman, D.M., Vaikuntanathan, V.: Functional encryption for inner product predicates from learning with errors. In: Lee, D.H., Wang, X. (eds.) ASIACRYPT 2011. LNCS, vol. 7073, pp. 21–40. Springer, Heidelberg (2011). https://doi.org/10.1007/978-3-642-25385-0_2

6. Agrawal, S., Libert, B., Stehlé, D.: Fully secure functional encryption for inner products, from standard assumptions. In: Robshaw, M., Katz, J. (eds.) CRYPTO 2016. LNCS, vol. 9816, pp. 333–362. Springer, Heidelberg (2016). https://doi.org/10.1007/978-3-662-53015-3_12

7. Benhamouda, F., Bourse, F., Lipmaa, H.: CCA-secure inner-product functional encryption from projective hash functions. In: Fehr, S. (ed.) PKC 2017. LNCS, vol. 10175, pp. 36–66. Springer, Heidelberg (2017). https://doi.org/10.1007/978-3-662-54388-7_2

8. Bishop, A., Jain, A., Kowalczyk, L.: Function-hiding inner product encryption. In: Iwata, T., Cheon, J.H. (eds.) ASIACRYPT 2015. LNCS, vol. 9452, pp. 470–491. Springer, Heidelberg (2015). https://doi.org/10.1007/978-3-662-48797-6_20

9. Boneh, D., Boyen, X.: Efficient selective identity-based encryption without random oracles. J. Cryptol. **24**(4), 659–693 (2011). https://doi.org/10.1007/s00145-010-9078-6

10. Boneh, D., Franklin, M.: An efficient public key traitor tracing scheme. In: Wiener, M. (ed.) CRYPTO 1999. LNCS, vol. 1666, pp. 338–353. Springer, Heidelberg (1999). https://doi.org/10.1007/3-540-48405-1_22

11. Bösch, C., Peter, A., Hartel, P., Jonker, W.: SOFIR: securely outsourced forensic image recognition. In: 2014 IEEE International Conference on Acoustics, Speech and Signal Processing (ICASSP), pp. 2694–2698. IEEE (2014)

12. Cheon, J.H.: Security analysis of the strong Diffie-Hellman problem. In: Vaudenay, S. (ed.) EUROCRYPT 2006. LNCS, vol. 4004, pp. 1–11. Springer, Heidelberg (2006). https://doi.org/10.1007/11761679_1

13. Cramer, R., Shoup, V.: Universal hash proofs and a paradigm for adaptive chosen ciphertext secure public-key encryption. In: Knudsen, L.R. (ed.) EUROCRYPT 2002. LNCS, vol. 2332, pp. 45–64. Springer, Heidelberg (2002). https://doi.org/10.1007/3-540-46035-7_4

14. Dahbur, K., Mohammad, B., Tarakji, A.B.: A survey of risks, threats and vulnerabilities in cloud computing. In: Proceedings of the 2011 International Conference on Intelligent Semantic Web-services and Applications, pp. 1–6 (2011)

15. Datta, P., Dutta, R., Mukhopadhyay, S.: Functional encryption for inner product with full function privacy. In: Cheng, C.-M., Chung, K.-M., Persiano, G., Yang, B.-Y. (eds.) PKC 2016. LNCS, vol. 9614, pp. 164–195. Springer, Heidelberg (2016). https://doi.org/10.1007/978-3-662-49384-7_7

16. Do, X.T., Phan, D.H., Pointcheval, D.: Traceable inner product functional encryption. In: Jarecki, S. (ed.) CT-RSA 2020. LNCS, vol. 12006, pp. 564–585. Springer, Cham (2020). https://doi.org/10.1007/978-3-030-40186-3_24

17. Dufour-Sans, E., Pointcheval, D.: Unbounded inner-product functional encryption with succinct keys. In: Deng, R.H., Gauthier-Umaña, V., Ochoa, M., Yung, M. (eds.) ACNS 2019. LNCS, vol. 11464, pp. 426–441. Springer, Cham (2019). https://doi.org/10.1007/978-3-030-21568-2_21

18. Gentry, C., Peikert, C., Vaikuntanathan, V.: Trapdoors for hard lattices and new cryptographic constructions. In: Proceedings of the Fortieth Annual ACM Symposium on Theory of Computing, pp. 197–206 (2008)

19. Jeckmans, A., Peter, A., Hartel, P.: Efficient privacy-enhanced familiarity-based recommender system. In: Crampton, J., Jajodia, S., Mayes, K. (eds.) ESORICS 2013. LNCS, vol. 8134, pp. 400–417. Springer, Heidelberg (2013). https://doi.org/10.1007/978-3-642-40203-6_23

20. Kim, S., Lewi, K., Mandal, A., Montgomery, H., Roy, A., Wu, D.J.: Function-hiding inner product encryption is practical. In: Catalano, D., De Prisco, R. (eds.) SCN 2018. LNCS, vol. 11035, pp. 544–562. Springer, Cham (2018). https://doi.org/10.1007/978-3-319-98113-0_29

21. Naehrig, M., Lauter, K., Vaikuntanathan, V.: Can homomorphic encryption be practical? In: Proceedings of the 3rd ACM Workshop on Cloud Computing Security Workshop, pp. 113–124 (2011)

22. Ramanna, S.C.: More efficient constructions for inner-product encryption. In: Manulis, M., Sadeghi, A.-R., Schneider, S. (eds.) ACNS 2016. LNCS, vol. 9696, pp. 231–248. Springer, Cham (2016). https://doi.org/10.1007/978-3-319-39555-5_13

23. Song, G., Deng, Y., Huang, Q., Peng, C., Tang, C., Wang, X.: Hierarchical identity-based inner product functional encryption. Inf. Sci. **573**, 332–344 (2021)

24. Tomida, J., Takashima, K.: Unbounded inner product functional encryption from bilinear maps. Jpn. J. Ind. Appl. Math. **37**(3), 723–779 (2020). https://doi.org/10.1007/s13160-020-00419-x

25. Xagawa, K.: Improved (hierarchical) inner-product encryption from lattices. In: Kurosawa, K., Hanaoka, G. (eds.) PKC 2013. LNCS, vol. 7778, pp. 235–252. Springer, Heidelberg (2013). https://doi.org/10.1007/978-3-642-36362-7_15

26. Yang, Z., Zhong, S., Wright, R.N.: Privacy-preserving classification of customer data without loss of accuracy. In: Proceedings of the 2005 SIAM International Conference on Data Mining, pp. 92–102. SIAM (2005)

AutoRoC-DBSCAN: Automatic Tuning of DBSCAN to Detect Malicious DNS Tunnels

Thi Quynh Nguyen[1,2(✉)], Romain Laborde[1], Abdelmalek Benzekri[1],
Arnaud Oglaza[1], and Mehdi Mounsif[2]

[1] University Paul Sabatier, 31000 Toulouse, France
thi-quynh.nguyen@irit.fr
[2] MODIS, 31300 Toulouse, France

Abstract. Domain Name System (DNS) is one of the core services of the Internet. Whereas it was created to associate domain names and IP addresses, modern attacks, such as Advanced Persistent Threats, use tunneling techniques over the DNS protocol to build covert channels in order to infiltrate the local network or exfiltrate data while bypassing security systems. Unsupervised machine learning techniques, and more specifically, Density-Based Spatial Clustering of Applications with Noise (DBSCAN), can achieve good results in detecting simple malicious DNS tunnels. However, DBSCAN requires manually tuning two hyperparameters, whose optimal values can be different depending on the dataset. In this article, we propose an improved algorithm called AutoRoC-DBSCAN that can automatically find the best hyperparameters, in order to automate the detection of malicious DNS tunnels in a completely new dataset.

Keywords: DNS tunneling · APT · Unsupervised machine learning · DBSCAN

1 Introduction

Domain Name System (DNS) is an important part of the internet, providing a way to map a human-friendly name of a website to its Internet Protocol (IP) addresses. It is a crucial protocol that every company and organization must enable in their network.

By taking advantage of the DNS protocol, highly-skilled attackers can use some complex tunneling techniques, such as Advanced Persistent Threats (APTs) [1], to avoid being detected by security systems. APT attacks differ from traditional web application threats in that they do not attack the system immediately when it is infiltrated, but they just gain access to the network and stay there undetected for a long time.

Once the attackers plant malware on compromised machines, a DNS tunnel will be established as a channel to communicate with a command-and-control (C&C) server. The attackers can use this channel to exfiltrate information out of the organization's network, and to manage or update the malware remotely.

The complexity of APTs attacks makes them very difficult to identify [2]. However, in our previous work [3], we have shown that machine learning (ML) techniques can help with this complex detection task. Given the tremendous amount of work and high

© The Author(s), under exclusive license to Springer Nature Switzerland AG 2022
J. Chen et al. (Eds.): EISA 2022, CCIS 1641, pp. 126–144, 2022.
https://doi.org/10.1007/978-3-031-23098-1_8

cost needed to build and label the training data set for a supervised ML approach, we decided to try several unsupervised ML algorithms, such as Density-Based Spatial Clustering of Applications with Noise (DBSCAN), Isolation Forest, One-class Support Vector Machine (One-class SVM), and Local Outlier Factor (LOF).

Among them, DBSCAN has been the most effective in detecting DNS tunneling attacks. However, DBSCAN requires experimentally finding the values of two hyper-parameters. In addition, a manual post-analysis was needed to reduce the false positive rate. This manual intervention prevents the automatic detection of malicious DNS traffic in a completely new dataset.

Therefore, we propose in this article an improved algorithm called AutoRoC-DBSCAN that can automatically tune its hyper-parameters. We then compare its performance with 3 other unsupervised ML algorithms (mentioned above) on a new dataset that we created ourselves due to the lack of quality DNS tunneling datasets available on the internet.

The rest of the article is as follows: In Sect. 2, we give a quick introduction to the malicious DNS tunneling techniques and tools. In Sect. 3, we describe our method to automatically find the best hyper-parameters for DBSCAN. In Sect. 4, we present the DNS tunnels dataset we created and how we use it to evaluate the performance of the algorithm. Then, in Sect. 5, we present the related work. Finally, Sect. 6 concludes the article and indicates possible future works.

2 Domain Name System Tunnels

In this section, we introduce the DNS protocol and how attackers use DNS tunnels to communicate with infected machines.

2.1 DNS Tunneling Techniques

The DNS protocol is an application-layer protocol encapsulated inside the User Datagram Protocol (UDP). Highly skilled attackers can employ DNS tunneling techniques to avoid being detected by security systems (Fig. 1).

DNS tunnel traffic is very similar to genuine DNS traffic as it uses the same port 53 and respects the DNS message structure. DNS tunneling encodes specific messages inside the fields of the DNS queries or responses.

To transfer information from the infected machine to the C&C server, the malicious agent on the infected machine only needs to make a DNS request to a specific domain name controlled by the attackers (for instance, XYZ.attacker.fr) and dispatch the message to hide data inside different fields of the DNS query. The DNS resolver of the attacked organization will get the IP address of the DNS server managing the domain name, which is actually the C&C server.

To transfer orders from the C&C server, the fake DNS server just has to send them through a DNS response message, thus hiding the C&C message inside different fields. As a consequence, exfiltrating data out of an organization will be as simple as sending one or more DNS queries.

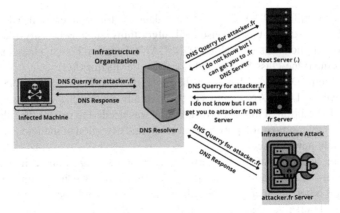

Fig. 1. Malicious DNS tunnel process

Remotely controlling or updating the malware is done by hiding C&C commands inside the DNS responses. In this case, infected machines are required to send beacon messages in the DNS queries to make these responses not suspicious. Figure 2 is an example of a beacon message sent by the Pisloader malware [4]. It is composed of a random 4-byte uppercase string that is used as the payload. The C&C server responds by an order to the infected machine inside a TXT record.

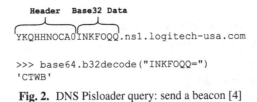

Fig. 2. DNS Pisloader query: send a beacon [4]

Figure 3 shows one example of the order: "sifo", which means collecting the infected system's information. The C&C server can send many other kinds of orders, such as: "drive" to list drives on the infected machine, "list" to list file information of a specific directory, or "upload" to upload a file to the infected machine, etc. After receiving the order, the infected machine will perform the operation requested by the C&C server.

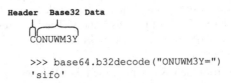

Fig. 3. DNS Pisloader response: TXT response by the C&C [4]

2.2 DNS Tunneling Tools

Several DNS tunneling utilities have been implemented such as:

- Dnscat2 [5] creates an encrypted C&C channel over the DNS protocol. It can tunnel any data: upload and download files, run a shell. Dnscat2 contains 2 parts: the client and the server. The client runs on a compromised machine, and it can run on most operating systems without any special installation. The server can run on an authoritative DNS server. However, it requires a domain where it will listen for connections from clients. When it receives traffic for this domain, it attempts to establish a logical connection.
- Dns2tcp [6] is a tool for relaying TCP connections over DNS. No specific driver is needed because encapsulation is done over TCP. Dns2tcp contains two parts: the client and the server. The server has a list of resources specified in a config file. The client listens on a predefined TCP port and relays each incoming connection through DNS to the final service. When connections are received on a specific port, all TCP traffic is sent to the remote dns2tcp server and forwarded to a specific host and port.

3 Automated Tuning of DBSCAN

In this section, after describing our high-level strategy to detect malicious network traffic, we will introduce DBSCAN and its limitation. Then, we propose our algorithm called AutoRoC-DBSCAN as an improved version of it.

3.1 Our High-Level DNS Tunnel Detection Approach

Our proposed approach consists in detecting DNS tunnels using an outlier detection method. To do that, multiple phases need to be performed under 2 hypotheses. The first hypothesis is that highly skilled attackers are trying to control their malicious traffic to go under the radar of a security system or firewall; thus, the percentage of DNS tunnel traffic is low (e.g., less than 2% or 3% of the traffic). Indeed, if the malicious traffic is higher, we consider that traditional detection systems can detect it. The second hypothesis states that detecting outliers requires comparing similar entities to detect anomalies. Thus, we need to separate the traffic into different network services (such as DNS) before applying the outlier detection method.

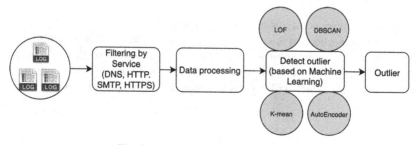

Fig. 4. Phases of the proposed solution

Figure 4 shows 3 phases of our detection process:

1. From the event logs, separate the network traffic by service like DNS, HTTPS, etc.
2. For each service, use CICFlowMeter [7] to extract features.
3. Apply an unsupervised machine learning algorithm to detect outliers.

3.2 Density-Based Spatial Clustering of Applications with Noise

Density-Based Spatial Clustering of Applications with Noise (DBSCAN) [8] clusters points together and identifies any points not belonging to a cluster as outliers. In order to run DBSCAN, we must provide two parameters:

- *minPts*: the minimum number of points required to form a dense region (a cluster).
- *eps* (ε): the maximum distance between 2 points for them to be considered neighbors.

Based on these 2 parameters, DBSCAN labels data points as core points, border points, or outliers (Fig. 5). A point is a core point if it has at least *minPts* points in its *eps* distance (red points). A point is a border point if it is not a core point and lies within the *eps* distance of any core point (yellow points). Outlier points are those that are neither core points nor border points (blue points).

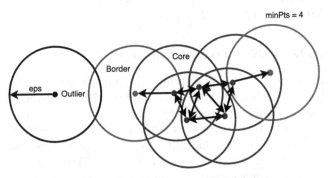

Fig. 5. DBSCAN clusters and outliers (Color figure online)

DBSCAN is composed of 3 steps:

1. Takes an arbitrary point that has not been visited.
2. The *eps* neighborhood of this point is extracted. If it contains enough points (*minPts*), then this point is a core point, and a cluster is formed. Otherwise, this point is labeled as noise (outlier). However, this point might also be found in an *eps* neighborhood of another point, which will make it a border point and a part of another cluster.

3. If a point is a part of a cluster, its *eps* neighborhood is also a part of that cluster. This process continues until all points are visited.

DBSCAN is a density-based clustering algorithm that is very effective in finding high-density regions and outliers. It does not require to specify number of clusters and it performs well with arbitrary-shape clusters. But determining the value of *MinPts* and *eps* is not easy. If the value of *minPts* is too large, DBSCAN will detect anomalies but with a high false positive rate. Otherwise, if it is too small, the detection rate will be impacted. Similarly, if the value of *eps* is too high, the clusters will merge, and DBSCAN cannot detect all anomalies. While if it is too small, a large part of the data will not be clustered and will be considered outliers. Thus, the false positive rate will be high. Therefore, selecting good values for these parameters is very important.

3.3 AutoRoc-DBSCAN

In order to select the best value of *minPts* and *eps* for DBSCAN, we need to have a certain understanding of the dataset. A specific value of *minPts* and *eps* may give good results in one dataset but may give bad results in the others. Tuning these parameters often requires looking deeper into the dataset and performing a lot of manual experiments, which somehow reduces the benefit of using unsupervised ML. Therefore, in this section, we will propose a method to automatically find the best value for them.

The first parameter, *minPts,* is the number of data points required to form a cluster. It is actually related to the expected attack rate in the network. Since the number of attacks is also the number of expected outliers in DBSCAN, we presume that all normal clusters should have more points than this number. In case of DNS tunnels, we consider the percentage of attacks to be at most 3% of the traffic. Therefore, the value of *minPts* can be chosen as 3% of the number of data points in the dataset.

The harder problem now will be determining the value of *eps*, which is the maximum distance between 2 points in the same cluster. We will solve this with the help of the K-nearest neighbors (KNN) algorithm [9]. The basic idea is to: first, calculate the average distance between each point and its K-nearest neighbors (stage 1), and then calculate the rate of change on these distances (stage 2) to find the optimal value of *eps*. It is often the point where there is a sudden and significant change in the distance values.

There are 2 parameters that must be predetermined in our algorithm:

- K: is the number of neighbors in the KNN algorithm used in stage 1. Since the minimum number of points required to form a cluster is *minPts*, we can easily see that the minimum number of neighbors of each point in the cluster is *minPts-1*. For a large dataset, it can be considered the same as *minPts*. Therefore, the value of K can be set to *minPts*, or 3% of the dataset in our case.

- Delta: is the number of points in each range of values that will be used to calculate the rate of change in stage 2. A too small value of Delta will degrade the capability to detect change points since the value of points that are close to each other does not change much. Conversely, if the value of Delta is too high, we might miss the optimal change point if it is inside the large range of values. A good balance value for Delta is around 10% of *minPts*, or 0.3% of the dataset. This value was obtained experimentally on a specific dataset that is different from the one we used for performance evaluation.

Our algorithm to find the best value of *eps* consists of 7 steps, divided into 3 main parts:

Part **1**: Calculate the curve of the distances based on KNN algorithm (Fig. 6).

1. For each point x in the dataset, run KNN algorithm with $K = minPts = 3\%$ of the dataset, then calculate the average distance between x and its K nearest neighbors.

$$mean_x^{KNN} = mean(KNN(x, K = 3\%)) \tag{1}$$

2. Sort the dataset with respect to $mean_x^{KNN}$ to produce *sortedDistanceList*.

Algorithm 1: AutoRoc-DBSCAN

Part 1: Calculate the curve of the distances based on KNN algorithm;
Data: n: number of data in dataset X;
K: number of neighbors;
$K = minPts = 0.03 * n$;
$KNNdistances = \emptyset$;
for x *in* X **do**
　　$KNNdistances = KNNdistances \cup (x, calculateKNN(x, X$ with number of
　　neighbors $= K))$;　　　　　　　　　　　　　　　/* Step 1 */
end
$meanDistanceList = \emptyset$;　　　　　　　　　　　　　　/* Step 2 */
for $(x, distances)$ *in* $KNNdistances$ **do**
　　$meanDistanceList = meanDistanceList \cup (calculateMean(distances))$;
end
$sortedDistanceList = sort(meanDistanceList)$;

Fig. 6. AutoRoc-DBSCAN part 1

Part 2: Find the points with large changes in value (Fig. 7).

3. Calculate the slope of a data interval. We do not calculate the slope between adjacent points because the difference between them will be too small to detect a high change. Thus, we define the data interval as Delta = 0,3% of the dataset. For each point y in *sortedDistanceList*, calculate the slope between that point and a point which is Delta points away from it and add to *slopeList*.

$$slope_y = sortedDistanceList_{y+\Delta} - sortedDistanceList_y \tag{2}$$

$$slopeList = \{slope_y\} \tag{3}$$

4. Calculate average slopes per block of size Delta. For scalability, we need to reduce the number of points to be considered. Thus, we group the slopes per block of size Delta and calculate the mean of each group and add them to the *meanSlopeList*.

$$meanSlope_a = \frac{1}{\Delta} \sum_{i=a}^{a+\Delta} slopeList_i \tag{4}$$

$$meanSlopeList = \{meanSlope_a\} \tag{5}$$

5. Calculate the percentage of difference between the average of a block and the average of the previous block and add to *diffPercentageList*.

$$diffPercentage_a = \frac{(meanSlopeList_a - meanSlopeList_{a-1})*100}{meanSlopeList_{a-1}} \tag{6}$$

$$diffPercentageList = \{diffPercentage_a\} \tag{7}$$

6. Calculate the difference between the percentage of change between two adjacent blocks and the average of all the previous percentage of changes. If this difference is more than 3 times, there is a big change in value at this block. We add the first point of this block to *largeChangeValuePointDict* with the key being the corresponding data point.

$$avgDiffPercentageList_a = \frac{1}{(a-1)} \sum_{i=0}^{a-1} diffPercentageList_i \tag{8}$$

$$difference_a = \frac{diffPercentageList_a}{avgDiffPercentageList_a} \tag{9}$$

$$pointNumber = a*Delta \tag{10}$$

If *difference$_a$* ≥ 3 Then:

$$largeChangeValuePointDict[pointNumber] = difference_a \tag{11}$$

Algorithm 1: AutoRoc-DBSCAN

Part 2: Find the points with large changes in value;

Data: n: number of data in dataset X;

Delta: number of points in each range of values in the rate of change;

$Delta = minPts * 0.1 * n = 0.003 * n$;

$slopeList = \emptyset$;

for *index* $i = 0$ *to (length(sortedDistanceList) - delta)* **do**

   | $delta_i = i + delta$;   /* Step 3 */

   | $slopeList = slopeList \cup (sortedDistanceList[delta_i] - sortedDistanceList[i])$

end

$meanSlopeList = \emptyset$;

for *index* $j = 0$ *to length(slopeList-delta), j+delta)* **do**

   | $delta_j = j + delta$;   /* Step 4 */

   | $meanSlopeList =$
   | $meanSlopeList \cup (calculateMean(slopeList[j], ..., slopeList[j + delta]))$;

end

$diffPercentageList = \emptyset$;

$avgDiffPercentageList = \emptyset$;

$largeChangeValuePointDict = \emptyset$;   /* Step 5 and 6 */

for *index* $k = 1$ *to length(meanSlopeList)* **do**

   | $avgDiffPercentageList_k = calculateMean(diffPercentageList)$;

   | $differentValue_k = meanSlopeList[k] - meanSlopeList[k - 1]$;

   | $differentPercentage_k = absolute(differentValue_k * 100/meanSlopeList[k - 1])$;

   | $diffPercentageList = diffPercentageList \cup differentPercentage_k$;

   | $difference_k = differentPercentage_k/avgDiffPercentageList_k$;

   | **if** $difference_k >= 3$ **then**

       | $largeChangeValuePointDict =$
       | $largeChangeValuePointDict \cup (k * Delta, difference_k)$;

   | **end**

end

Fig. 7. AutoRoc-DBSCAN part 2

Part **3**: Find the first maximum value change point among the listed points in *largeChangeValuePointDict* (Fig. 8).

7. Apply method *find_peaks* [10] to find a list of peaks and choose the value of the first peak to be the value of *eps* for DBSCAN. *Find_peaks* is a method of *scipy* library to search for peaks (local maxima) based on simple value comparison of neighboring samples and returns those peaks. If the *largeChangeValuePointDict* is an ascending list, we cannot find a peak. In this case, we calculate the difference between each pair of adjacent values. Then we choose the point with the biggest difference.

Algorithm 1: AutoRoc-DBSCAN

Part 3: Find the first maximum value change point among the listed points in Part 2;
$peakList = \emptyset$;
$pointListValue = largeChangeValuePointDict.values()$
$peaksList = findPeaks(pointListValue)$;   /* Step 7 */
if $peaksList \neq \emptyset$ **then**
    $pointValue = pointListValue[peaksList[0]]$;
    for key in largeChangeValuePointDict **do**
        if $largeChangeValuePointDict[key] = pointValue$ **then**
            $point = key$;
            $epsilon = sortedDistanceList[point]$;
        end
    end
end
if $peaksList = \emptyset$ **then**
    $dif = 0$;
    for index $i = 0$ to length(pointListValue)-1 **do**
        $j = i + 1$;
        $difNew = pointListValue[j]/pointListValue[i]$;
        if $difNew > dif$ **then**
            $dif = difNew$;
            $point = largeChangeValuePointDict.keys()[j]$;
            $epsilon = sortedDistanceList[point]$;
        end
    end
end

Fig. 8. AutoRoc-DBSCAN part 3

4   Performance Evaluation

Unsupervised machine learning algorithms do not need a training phase. However, a labeled dataset is required to evaluate their performance. In our prior work [3], we used the Botsv1 provided by Splunk, which includes both genuine and malicious DNS traffic. However, this dataset has some drawbacks. It contains only Splunk log files without the initial raw data, and the process to calculate the features is not described. The architecture and tools used to generate the traffic are missing as well. In addition, the number of features is limited. Consequently, it is not possible to reproduce or improve this dataset to compare the performance of outlier detection algorithms. Therefore, we decided to create our own dataset.

4.1   A New DNS Tunneling Dataset

To construct a dataset of both normal and tunnel DNS traffic, we create a virtual machine infrastructure that contains all the required components to perform a DNS tunneling connection. The network topology used to capture the traffic is presented in Fig. 9. First, normal traffic is generated by normal web browsing activity. We use Chrome and Firefox to randomly access a list of 100 different websites. Then, malicious DNS traffic is generated by a combination of tools, such as Dnscat2 and Dns2tcp. For example, we execute a basic software available in the infected machine like "exec cal", or we upload/download a file from the infected machine. The quantity of each type can be seen in Table 1.

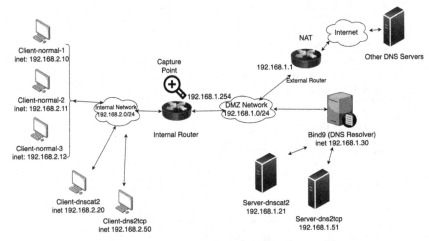

Fig. 9. The network topology used to capture traffic

We set up an internal local network that contains both normal and compromised clients and a DMZ network that contains a DNS Resolver. For simplicity, the Dnscat2 and Dns2tcp C&C servers are also deployed in the DMZ. This does not impact the quality of the dataset because the network traffic is captured at the internal router.

Normally, an attacker registers a real domain that points to the attacker's C&C server, where a tunneling malware program is installed. In our case, all traffics are generated in the virtual machine infrastructure; thus, we configured the DNS Resolver to forward DNS requests about the attackers' domains to the associated C&C servers. Requests to other domain names are redirected to the real network.

Since all traffic goes through the DNS Resolver, the destination IP address that we captured is always the DNS Resolver's, so we did not include it in our dataset. This approach allows anyone to easily build their own dataset by manipulating the raw data files to fit their own purpose.

Table 1. Quantity of each type of traffic

	Chrome	Firefox	Dnscat2	Dns2tcp
Number of records	124158	223858	353604	445097

4.2 Preparation

We use CICFlowMeter [7, 11], to build network traffic flows by grouping packets according to the source IP address, destination IP address, source port, and destination port. Looking at these flows, one might think that it is easy to identify the DNS tunnels by observing the number of bytes exchanged. As shown in Table 2, the number of bytes of normal DNS flow ranges from 70 to 790, while the number of bytes of Dnscat2 attack traffic is huge, ranging from 241 to 126479. The difference between normal DNS flow and Dns2tcp attack is not as clear as Dnscat2, but the maximum number of bytes is still distinguishable.

However, this result can be explained by the fact that the Dnscat2 and Dns2tcp clients use the same source port for different DNS queries. This behavior can be easily changed by modifying the Dnscat2 and Dns2tcp clients to use a different source port for each DNS request, making the analysis of the number bytes of flows useless.

To confirm that, we have modified CICFlowMeter to include one more parameter when grouping packets to build network traffic flows: the transaction ID. Attackers cannot spoof this value because it is simple to implement a rule on the Firewall that would drop packets with a mismatched transaction ID. By analyzing the result in Table 2, we see that the number of Dnscat2 and Dns2tcp records has increased due to the split by transaction ID. But at the same time, the maximum number of bytes has decreased significantly, which makes it impossible to differentiate between normal DNS requests and malicious attacks. This confirms the need to implement a behavioral analysis of the network with ML algorithms.

Table 2. Normal, Dnscat2, and Dns2tcp number of bytes

	Original CICFlowMeter		Modified CICFlowMeter	
	No. records	No. bytes	No. records	No. bytes
Chrome (normal)	124158	Min: 81 Max: 663	124158	Min: 81 Max: 663
Firefox (normal)	223858	Min: 70 Max: 790	223858	Min: 70 Max: 790
Dnscat2 (attack)	1967	Min: 241 Max:126479	353604	Min: 108 Max: 1830
Dns2tcp (attack)	406352	Min: 94 Max: 2941	445097	Min: 94 Max: 618

We use the modified CICFlowMeter to extract 36 network traffic features from TCPDump raw capture files. Then from the timestamps, we extracted 3 more sub-features: hour, minute, and week number (0–4: weekday, 5–6: weekend). After selecting and preparing these 39 features, we labeled the dataset using the DNS-attack logs.

In order to evaluate how machine learning algorithms can detect abnormal DNS traffic with different attack percentages, we generated 12 sub-datasets of 100,000 records each, which respectively contains 0.1%, 0.5%, 1%, 2%, 3%, 4%, 5%, 6%, 7%, 8%, 9%,

10% of attacks. In each sub-dataset, we set the percentages of the two attack types (Dnscat2 and Dns2tcp) to be almost equal.

4.3 Results

We compared the performance of our DBSCAN-based algorithm on the generated DNS dataset with 3 other outlier detection algorithms: Isolation Forest [12] is a tree-based algorithm, One-class SVM [13] and Local Outlier Factor (LOF) [14] are density-based algorithms. All 4 algorithms were tuned according to the maximum attack percentage (3%). The *eps* is set to the value obtained by our AutoRoC-DBSCAN algorithm.

We use the detection rate (DR) and the false positive rate (FPR) metrics to evaluate the performance of the algorithms. The DR is the number of attacks detected by the system divided by the number of attacks in the dataset. The FPR is the number of normal traffic that are misclassified as attacks divided by the number of normal connections in the dataset. A good algorithm should achieve a high DR while keeping the FPR low.

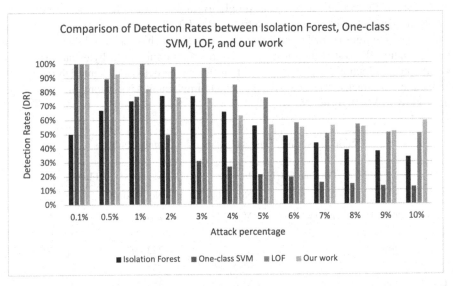

Fig. 10. Detection rate comparison

Figure 10 and Fig. 11 show the DR and the FPR of the 4 algorithms for the 12 sub-datasets. Isolation Forest has the DR ranging from 33.38% to 77.05%, and the FPR ranges from 7.28% to 9.95%. One-class SVM achieves a small FPR from 1.95% to 2.9%, but the DR varies from 12.29% to 100%. LOF gives the DR ranging from 50.2% to 100%, but its FPR is still high, from 5.53% to 9.9%. Our AutoRoC-DBSCAN obtains the best results, with the DR ranging from 51.58% to 100% and the FPR from 0.6% to 1.83%. When the attack percentage increases, the FPR decreases a little, but the DR decreases a lot.

We also calculate the Area Under Curve - Receiver Operating Characteristics (AUC-ROC) [15], which is a performance metric for binary classification problem. ROC is

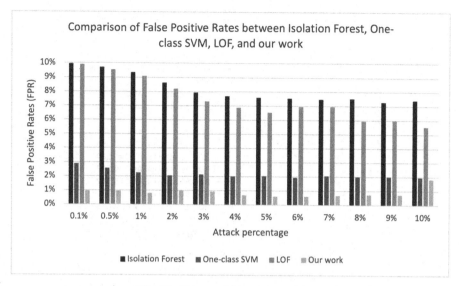

Fig. 11. False positive rate comparison

a probability curve that demonstrates the performance of models in distinguishing 2 classes. The whole area underneath the ROC is the AUC, whose value ranges from 0 to 1. The bigger area is, the higher AUC and the better the model is.

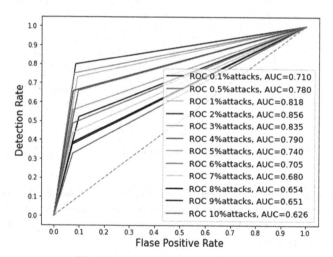

Fig. 12. Isolation forest – ROC curves

Figures 12, 13, 14 and 15 display the AUC of 4 algorithms. When attacks percentages increases, the AUC of Isolation Forest decreases from 0.71 to 0.626, One-class SVM decreases from 0.985 to 0.552, LOF decreases from 0.95 to 0.72, and AutoRoc-DBSCAN decreases from 0.995 to 0.787.

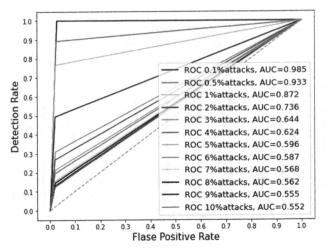

Fig. 13. One-class SVM – ROC curves

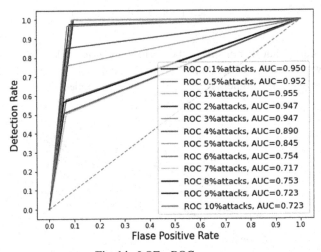

Fig. 14. LOF – ROC curves.

The results are better when the attack percentage is less than 3%. Indeed, the algorithms that we used to detect outliers work best when outliers are rare. If the attack percentage is large, it is no longer considered an outlier, so the algorithms does not detect them well anymore.

5   Related Work

In this section, we summarize some of the previous methods to determine DBSCAN parameters automatically, and also some of the other machine learning approaches to detect abnormal DNS traffic, especially DNS tunnels.

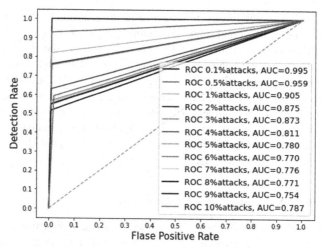

Fig. 15. AutoRoC-DBSCAN – ROC curves

5.1 Methods for Automatically Tuning DBSCAN

Starczewski et al. [16] proposed a method that determines the parameters of DBSCAN for different kinds of clusters: spirals, eyes, squares, triangles, wave shapes, etc. This method used a function called k_{dist} to compute the distance between each element of a dataset and its k-th nearest neighbor. Then they sorted the distances and determined the size of the "knee" by the number of distances generated by k_{dist} function and the size of the dataset. The MinPts parameter is calculated by the size of this knee. They also found a point that has sharp increases in distances. Based on this point and the size of the knee, the value of Eps is calculated. They evaluated their method on several 2-dimensional and 3-dimensional datasets with different sizes and shapes. All results confirmed the high efficiency of the proposed approach.

Falahiazar et al. [17] introduced a hybrid algorithm that uses the multi-objective genetic algorithm (MOGA) to determine the parameters of DBSCAN automatically. They used the Delaunay triangulation algorithm to determine the initial bounds of the DBSCAN parameters. Then they used the internal indices (Silhouette, Dunn indices) as the objective functions to choose a set of values for Eps and MinPts parameters. A new internal index named Outlier-index is proposed to provide more diversity and quality in the solution. They compared the results of MOGA-DBSCAN with the best results obtained from DBSCAN and those of SOGA-DBSCAN on five datasets (aggregation, spiral, flame, compound, path-based) by six external indices. The results of MOGA-DBSCAN, which determines the parameters automatically, are close to the best results of DBSCAN clustering.

Karami and Johansson [18] presented a hybrid clustering method, named BDE-DBSCAN, that combines Binary Differential Evolution and DBSCAN algorithm to simultaneously quickly and automatically specify appropriate parameter values for Eps and MinPts. This method executed the Differential Evolution algorithm several times to find a set of values for Eps and MinPts parameters. Then Tournament Selection method is also employed to find the best value of Eps and MinPts. The proposed algorithm is evaluated on nine 2D artificial data sets as Cluster-inside-Cluster ($K = 3$ and 5), Corners, Crescent Full Moon, Half Kernel, Pinwheel, Semi Circular ($K = 4$ and 8), Outlier and Aggregation, Compound and Path-based datasets. The results of the proposed algorithm provide optimal accuracy with the purity ranging around 99.4% and 100%.

The problem of automatically choosing parameters of the DBSCAN algorithm has been a great challenge. Other researchers have proposed different methods to find these parameters for small datasets with only a few dimensions, e.g., in the spiral dataset, there are only 3 clusters and 2 dimensions. This is not scalable and not suitable for detecting attacks on networks with high DNS traffic. Our method is efficient in identifying outliers in larger datasets with 39 dimensions.

5.2   DNS Based C&C Communication Detection

Jitesh Miglani and Christina Thorpe [19] proposed an active approach of detecting DNS tunneling by capturing all packets in a local network and employing machine learning models to detect tunneled data. In the first phase, they collected data and created a dataset. To diversify the dataset, they use different application layer protocols over the DNS tunnel to collect tunneled DNS queries, including HTTP, HTTPS, FTP and UDP. They use a packet capture of the first day in 10 Days DNS Network Traffic from April-May 2016 [20] as legitimate DNS queries. They evaluated 4 supervised machine learning classifiers (Decision Tree, Random Forest, Gradient Boosting, and AdaBoost). Out of these 4 models, all except Decision Tree were Ensemble learning techniques. Decision tree had the lowest performance. AdaBoost gave the best result, with detection rate from 99% to 100%.

Almusawi et Amintoosi [21] introduced a multilabel classification using kernel SVM that can differentiate not only the legitimate and tunneling traffics but also the types of tunneling (HTTP, HTTPS, FTP, POP3). They benchmark the performance of two models (the proposed kernel SVM and the multilabel Bayesian classifier) on a DNS tunneled traffic dataset which has been created from iodine and dns2tcp DNS tunneling tools. The results showed that the proposed kernel SVM performed better than the Bayes classifier, with a detection rate between 62.7% and 97.5%.

Franco Palau et al. [22] proposed a detection approach based on a Convolutional Neural Network (CNN) with minimal architecture complexity. They used a traditional Grid Search on a training set to find the optimal parameters. The best model was evaluated on a self-created testing dataset containing attacks from 5 well-known DNS tunneling tools: iodine, dns2tcp, dnscat2, tuns, and DNSexfiltrator. The detection rate is 92%, and the false positive rate is 0.8%.

Different researchers proposed to use supervised ML techniques to detect DNS tunneling. They achieved good detection results, with the majority of detection rates greater than 90%. However, these methods require a labeled training dataset, which is costly to build. Our approach uses unsupervised ML techniques, so it is not subject to this issue and easier to generalize. In addition, most of the related works use non-public datasets, making it difficult to replicate the experiments.

6   Conclusion

Detecting complex attacks requires considering a massive amount of indicators of compromise. Machine learning techniques can help in such tasks. In a previous article, we proved that unsupervised machine learning algorithms and, more specifically, DBSCAN can help security investigators to detect malicious DNS tunnels. However, many manual steps were required.

In this paper, we present AutoRoC-DBSCAN, an efficient algorithm that automatically determines the hyperparameters of DBSCAN. We also produced our own dataset to evaluate the detection rate and false positive rate of the algorithm by comparing it with several other state-of-the-art unsupervised ML algorithms. AutoRoC-DBSCAN obtains the best results, especially when the attack percentage is less than 3%, with DR from 75.33% to 100%, and FPR from 0.8% to 1%.

In the future, we need to consolidate these results. First, we envision to validate the detection of DNS tunnel on real world data. A first approach could be to initiate DNS tunnels inside a network infrastructure of a company during a specific period. This assessment will validate the scalability of our approach. Furthermore, we plan to investigate the capability of our approach to detect other types of tunnels, such as DNS over HTTPS, to broadening the scope of our approach.

References

1. Anatomy of an APT attack: Step by step approach, Infosec Resources. https://resources.inf osecinstitute.com/topic/anatomy-of-an-apt-attack-step-by-step-approach/. Accessed 24 Aug 2021
2. Benzekri, A., Laborde, R., Oglaza, A., Rammal, D., Barrere, F.: Dynamic security management driven by situations: an exploratory analysis of logs for the identification of security situations. In: 3rd Cyber Security in Networking Conference (CSNet 2019), Quito, Ecuador, p. 66 (2019). https://doi.org/10.1109/CSNet47905.2019.9108976
3. Nguyen, T.Q., Laborde, R., Benzekri, A., Qu'hen, B.: Detecting abnormal DNS traffic using unsupervised machine learning. In: 2020 4th Cyber Security in Networking Conference (CSNet), pp. 1–8 (2020). https://doi.org/10.1109/CSNet50428.2020.9265466
4. New Wekby Attacks Use DNS Requests As Command and Control Mechanism, Unit42, 24 May 2016. https://unit42.paloaltonetworks.com/unit42-new-wekby-attacks-use-dns-req uests-as-command-and-control-mechanism/. Accessed 18 Jan 2022
5. Ron: Introduction, 24 August 2021. https://github.com/iagox86/dnscat2. Accessed 25 Aug 2021.
6. dns2tcp|Kali Linux Tools, Kali Linux. https://www.kali.org/tools/dns2tcp/. Accessed 07 Feb 2022
7. Habibi Lashkari, A., Seo, A., Gil, G., Ghorbani, A.: CIC-AB: online ad blocker for browsers, pp. 1–7 (2017). https://doi.org/10.1109/CCST.2017.8167846
8. DBSCAN Clustering Algorithm in Machine Learning, KDnuggets. https://www.kdnuggets.com/dbscan-clustering-algorithm-in-machine-learning.html/. Accessed 01 July 2020
9. Cunningham, P., Delany, S.: k-Nearest neighbour classifiers. Mult. Classif. Syst. **54** (2007). https://doi.org/10.1145/3459665
10. scipy.signal.find_peaks—SciPy v1.8.0 Manual. https://docs.scipy.org/doc/scipy-1.8.0/html-scipyorg/reference/generated/scipy.signal.find_peaks.html#scipy.signal.find_peaks. Accessed 08 Feb 2022

11. Hieu, L.: cicflowmeter: CICFlowMeter V3 Python Implementation. https://gitlab.com/hie ulw/cicflowmeter. Accessed 24 Aug 2021
12. Liu, F.T., Ting, K., Zhou, Z.-H.: Isolation forest, pp. 413–422 (2009). https://doi.org/10.1109/ ICDM.2008.17
13. Schölkopf, B., Williamson, R., Smola, A., Shawe-Taylor, J., Platt, J.: Support vector method for novelty detection, vol. 12, pp. 582–588 (1999)
14. Breunig, M.M., Kriegel, H.-P., Ng, R.T., Sander, J.: LOF: identifying density-based local outliers, p. 12 (2000)
15. Bradley, A.P.: The use of the area under the ROC curve in the evaluation of machine learning algorithms. Pattern Recognit. **30**(7), 1145–1159 (1997). https://doi.org/10.1016/S0031-320 3(96)00142-2
16. Starczewski, A., Goetzen, P., Er, M.J.: A new method for automatic determining of the DBSCAN parameters. J. Artif. Intell. Soft Comput. Res. **10**(3), 209–221 (2020). https:// doi.org/10.2478/jaiscr-2020-0014
17. Falahiazar, Z., Bagheri, A., Reshadi, M.: Determining the parameters of DBSCAN auto-matically using the multi-objective genetic algorithm. J. Inf. Sci. Eng. **37**, 157–183 (2021)
18. Karami, A., Johansson, R.: Choosing DBSCAN parameters automatically using differential evolution. Int. J. Comput. Appl. **91**(7), 1–11 (2014). https://doi.org/10.5120/15890-5059
19. Miglani, J., Thorpe, C.: Employing machine learning paradigms for detecting DNS tunneling (2021)
20. Singh, M., Singh, M., Kaur, S.: 10 Days DNS Network Traffic from April-May, 2016, vol. 2, May 2019. https://doi.org/10.17632/zh3wnddzxy.2
21. Almusawi, A., Amintoosi, H.: DNS tunneling detection method based on multilabel support vector machine. Secur. Commun. Netw. **2018**, 1–9 (2018). https://doi.org/10.1155/2018/613 7098
22. Palau, F., Catania, C., Guerra, J., Garcia, S., Rigaki, M.: DNS tunneling: a deep learning based lexicographical detection approach (2020). http://arxiv.org/abs/2006.06122. Accessed 24 Aug 2021

HBMD-FL: Heterogeneous Federated Learning Algorithm Based on Blockchain and Model Distillation

Ye Li[1], Jiale Zhang[1]($\boxtimes$) (iD), Junwu Zhu[1], and Wenjuan Li[2]

[1] Yangzhou University, Yangzhou 225127, China
{jialezhang,jwzhu}@yzu.edu.cn
[2] The Hong Kong Polytechnic University, Hong Kong SAR 999077, China
wenjuan.li@polyu.edu.hk

Abstract. Federated learning is a distributed machine learning framework that allows participants to keep their privacy data locally. Traditional federated learning coordinates participants collaboratively train a powerful global model. However, this process has several problems: it cannot meet the heterogeneous model's requirements, and it cannot resist poisoning attacks and single-point-of-failure. In order to resolve these issues, we proposed a heterogeneous federated learning algorithm based on blockchain and model distillation. The problem of fully heterogeneous models that are hard to aggregate in the central server can be solved by leveraging model distillation technology. Moreover, blockchain replaces the central server in federated learning to solve the single-point-of-failure problem. The validation algorithm is combined with cross-validation, which helps federated learning to resist poison attacks. The extensive experimental results demonstrate that HBMD-FL can resist poisoning attacks while losing less than 3% of model accuracy, and the communication consumption significantly outperformed the comparison algorithm.

Keywords: Federated learning · Blockchain · Heterogeneous · Model distillation

1 Introduction

In recent years, the popularity of smart devices has led to an explosion of data growth, accelerating the development of machine learning and big data technologies. However, under the traditional centralized machine learning framework, participants need to upload local data to a central server for training, which

This work is partially supported by Natural Science Foundation of China (62206238), Natural Science Foundation of Jiangsu Province (Grant No. BK20220562), Natural Science Foundation of Jiangsu Higher Education Institutions of China (Grant No. 22KJB520010), Future Network Scientific Research Fund Project (FNSRFP-2021-YB-47), Yangzhou City-Yangzhou University Science and Technology Cooperation Fund Project (YZ2021158).

J. Chen et al. (Eds.): EISA 2022, CCIS 1641, pp. 145–159, 2022.
https://doi.org/10.1007/978-3-031-23098-1_9

leads to the leakage of participants' private information. To address the potential privacy leakage problem of centralized machine learning, Google proposed the concept of federated learning [1] in 2017 to provide a feasible solution for privacy-preserving machine learning. Traditional federated learning relies on a global model created by a central server, which has remarkable performance in the IID environment. However, the model's performance significantly decreased the non-IID environment. A natural solution for the non-IID problem is to use heterogeneous models, where different models are trained for different participants to fit their local data situation.

There are some existing works devoted to this problem which are mainly based on multi-task learning [2,3], meta learning [4–6] and model distillation [7–9]. First, multi-task learning is considered an effective way to solve the heterogeneous model problem. For example, Smith et al. [2] proposed MOCHA which combines multi-task learning and federated learning for the first time to realize personalized model architecture in federated learning. However, MOCHA does not support non-convex models, which limits the application in general machine learning tasks. After that, Corinzia et al. [3] extended the federated multi-task learning to general non-convex models by leveraging Bayesian methods based on the MOCHA. However, this approach may have a considerable computation overhead in complex scenarios. In addition to multi-task learning, meta-learning is a feasible solution to the heterogeneous model problem. Jiang et al. [4] combined meta-learning with federated learning to produce a global model that can be easily personalized when the federated learning is completed. However, this approach only optimizes the global model's accuracy, compromising the model's effectiveness for local data.

Furthermore, to meet the need for the independent design of local models by users, some researchers have proposed to apply model distillation techniques in federated learning, i.e., combining knowledge distillation techniques with federated learning to solve the problem of heterogeneous models in federated learning [7–9]. For example, Li et al. [7] proposed FedMD, allowing participants to use a fully independent model to participate in federated learning. Shen et al. [9] proposed FML where local models learn the knowledge of the global model in federated learning by using knowledge distillation techniques to solve the heterogeneity problem in federated learning. Compared with multi-task learning and meta-learning, model distillation allows participants have completely independent control over the local model, making the local models better perform their local tasks. However, there remain the following problems in some existing works: the central server of federated learning is vulnerable to attacks, thus leading to server failure, which affects the following training process, i.e., single-point-of-failure problem [12]; Moreover, the poisoning attacks implemented by malicious participants in untrustworthy environments can also significantly reduce the model accuracy. In FedMD, 30% of malicious participants replace their uploads with gaussian noise resulting in more than 25% reduction in the model's accuracy in the IID environment.

To solve the problems above, we proposed HBMD-FL: a federated learning algorithm based on blockchain and model distillation. First, we leverage model distillation to resolve the problem of fully heterogeneous models are hard to aggregation in central server. Then, we introduce blockchain technology [13] to replace the traditional central server and integrate the verification algorithm into the cross-validation phase, thus overcome the single-point-of-failure problem and poisoning attacks problem at the same time. The main contributions of this paper are summarized as follows:

- We propose a federated learning algorithm, named HBML-FL, based on blockchain and model distillation. HBMD-FL utilizes model distillation to solve the problem of the heterogeneous model in federated learning. Furthermore, HBMD-FL introduces blockchain technology, makes federated learning have the ability to resist the single-point-of-failure and makes federated learning has the properties of traceable and tamper-proof.
- We present a verification mechanism to validate the logits uploaded by the participants. It prevents poisoning attacks by a certain percentage of malicious participants and prevents malicious participants from gaining into the blockchain system while ensuring the security of federated learning.
- We implement the HBMD-FL algorithm on the CIFAR-10 and CIFAR-100 datasets. Experimental results show that HBMD-FL can solve the heterogeneous model aggregation problem while keeping the accuracy loss within 4.7% in the IID environment and 5.4% in the non-IID environment compared with the traditional centralized learning. Moreover, in the case of 30% malicious participants, the proposed HBMD-FL algorithm improves the average accuracy by 30% and 24% in IID and non-IID environments, respectively.

The remainder of this paper is organized as follow. Section 2 reviews the work on heterogeneous models in federated learning and the existing applications of blockchain in federated learning; Sect. 3 gives an overview of the HBMD-FL; Sect. 4 describes the experiments and parameter settings of HBMD-FL and shows the experimental results; Sect. 5 concludes the paper.

2   Related Work

2.1   Federated Learning

Federated learning is proposed by McMahan et al. [1] which leverages the federated averaging algorithm (FedAVG) to train a powerful global model and keeps data of participants locally. This approach prevents the privacy leakage problems caused by traditional centralized machine learning that uploads private data to a central server [8,12,14–17]. However, the development of federated learning faces the challenge of the non-IID problem, which caused by the distribution of participants in federated learning is not IID in real scenarios. In order to overcome this problem, Wang et al. [18] modified the model sharing to share the global model in layers to solve the heterogeneity problem. Li et al. [19] improved the results under heterogeneous data by introducing model comparison loss and correcting the local training update direction. Wu et al. [20] proposed a personalized federated learning framework, named PerFit, as a solution for heterogeneity problems in the IoT environment. Fallah et al. [21] proposed to borrow ideas from MAML to find an initial shared model in which the participants of federated learning can easily adapt to their private data by performing a few epochs of gradient descent. Arivazhagan et al. [22] proposed FedPer, where only the personalized layer is changed and the base layers are frozen on the local devices.

2.2 Model Distillation

Compared with the works above, which optimizes the global model to perform federated learning better in the non-IID environment. Another more natural solution for the non-IID problem is training a unique model for each participant, which is different from others. Since the concept of knowledge distillation was proposed by Hinton [23], student models obtain better performance via soft labels, which are generated by the teacher model, than directly using hard labels [24]. Several works consider this approach as a solution to the heterogeneous model aggregation problem associated with non-IID. Li et al. [7] designed a communication protocol by leveraging knowledge distillation and transfer learning, which realized the knowledge exchange among models with different architectures. Jong et al. [8] proposed federated distillation, which transmits the logits vectors by categories. Using global logits to train local models after global aggregating by the central server. Shen et al. [9] applied regularization between local and global models, using the output of the homogeneous model used for exchange as the output of the teacher side in knowledge distillation to train heterogeneous models. Mo et al. [10] proposed a communication-effective federated distillation method: FedDQ, which introduces a controlled averaging algorithm and soft-labels quantization and coding to reduce communication frequency and communication overhead. Sattler et al. [11] proposed CFD, which leverages a new quantization mechanism and delta coding method to compress the soft-labels and utilizes a dual distillation technique to resolve the problem of compressing downstream communication.

2.3 Blockchain

Blockchain technology is introduced in federated learning to resolve the single-point-of-failure and lack of incentive mechanism. Blockchain technology's traceable, auditable and tamper-proof nature also assists in a more transparent tracking of the federated learning process [12,25–32]. Kim et al. [12] designed the first blockchain-based federated learning framework, which leverage blockchain to exchange and validate the updates of participates. In this framework, the Proof-Of-Work mechanism is used as the consensus mechanism. Awan et al. [29] proposed Poster, a blockchain-based privacy-preserving federated learning framework that uses the immutability and decentralized features of the blockchain to protect model updates. Majeed et al. [31] leveraged global model state trie for secure storage of global models. Li et al. [32] proposed a blockchain-based federated learning framework with committee consensus. A federated chain with node access control and smart contract is leveraged to enable decentralized federated learning.

3   Preliminary

In this section, we briefly explain the concepts of federated learning, model distillation and blockchain technology.

3.1   Federated Learning

Federated learning is a privacy-preserving distributed machine learning paradigm. Taking the classic federated learning algorithm FedAVG for example, in which M participants train a powerful global model without sharing their local private data collaboratively.

For communication round t, $m = 1, 2, \ldots, M$ indicates the index of participants, and each of them holds a local dataset $D_m = \{(x_k, y_k)\}_{k=1}^{N_m}$ which is utilized for model training. In detail, m downloads the latest global model w^t from the central server at the beginning of the $t - th$ round and perform local training on their local dataset. Then, we denote η as the learning rate, ∇ is the gradient operation and the local model update in round t of participant m is given as:

$$w^{t+1} \leftarrow w^t - \eta \nabla \mathcal{F}_t(w^t), \ \mathcal{F}(w^t) = \frac{1}{|D_m|} \sum_{(x_k, y_k) \in D_m} f(w, x_k, y_k) \tag{1}$$

where $f(w, x_k, y_k)$ represents the sample-wise loss function on $k - th$ sample, it normally is the empirical risk. After all the participants upload their model, the central server incorporates these updates and updates the global model uses for communication round $t + 1$ using specific algorithms. For example, in federated averaging, the central server leverages the following equations to generate the global model w_{global}^{t+1}.

$$w_{global}^{t+1} \leftarrow \sum_{m=1}^{M} \frac{n_m}{n} w_m^{t+1} \tag{2}$$

3.2   Model Distillation

Recently, Li et al. [7] proposed federated model distillation (FedMD), which leverages knowledge distillation and transfer learning to develop a framework that enables participants of federated learning designing heterogeneous models with fully different architectures to collaborate train their models without sharing private data. The main difference between FedAVG and FedMD is that participants of FedMD upload the predictions of model (i.e. *logits*) on the specific dataset not the local model. More specificly, the central server selects a subset of the public dataset $D_t \in D_{public}$ in round t. Participant uploads the predictions of D_t, denotes as $w_m(D_t) = logits_m$. The central server aggregates the logits according the equation as follows, and broadcasts it to all participants.

$$logits_{r+1}^{global} = \frac{1}{|M|} \sum_k logits_k \tag{3}$$

Then, participants train their local models on D_t to approach $logits_{r+1}^{global}$ by leveraging the loss function as:

$$\mathcal{F} = \frac{1}{N_{D_t}} \sum_k |logits_k - w(x_k)| \tag{4}$$

3.3   Blockchain

Blockchain is a distributed ledger technique with the characteristic of decentralized, traceable, and tamper-resistant. As the name implies, a blockchain is a chain linked by pre-defined blocks and leverages various consensus algorithms to accomplish data consistency. Each block of blockchain normally contains the hash value of the previous block, transaction information, a timestamp, and others. Varieties of consensus algorithms have been proposed, e.g., the PoW, the PoS, and the PBFT. Besides that, mechanisms such as incentive mechanisms and smart contracts are also applied in the blockchain system.

4   HBMD-FL

In this section, we present a heterogeneous federated learning algorithm based on blockchain and model distillation, HBMD-FL, to achieve the fully model heterogeneous decentralized federated learning.

4.1   Overview of HBMD-FL

Figure 1 illustrates the overview of HBMD-FL, which consists two types of participating components: workers $d_i \in \mathcal{D}$ and miners $m_j \in \mathcal{M}$. Workers train models and upload prediction results of public dataset, after that, miners validate those logits and package them into blocks. In the following, we will introduce each component in detail.

Workers: Each worker $d_i \in \mathcal{D}$ holds a unique local model which has a fully different architecture from other workers to perform image classification tasks and there are two datasets, public dataset D_{public} and private dataset $D_{private}^i$, for model training to get better performance. Note that, the public dataset is much larger than the private dataset. Worker d_i trains w_i on D_{public} and leverages transfer learning trains it on $D_{private}$. Then, d_i uploads the prediction results $w_i(D_{public})$ to the miner associated with it and waits for the generated blocks. After receiving the latest block, d_i computes the global logits locally and continues training the local model.

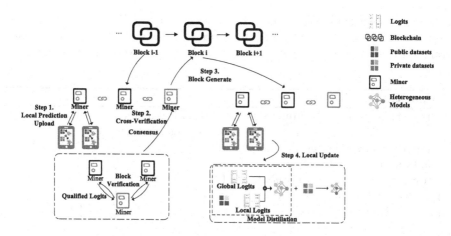

Fig. 1. HBMD-FL

Miners: For miner m_j which is associated with d_i, it broadcast the uploads of d_i to all the miners. After receiving all the uploads, m_j validates those logits, packages the validation results into its candidate block, and broadcasts to other miners. Then, it selects the qualified candidate block, adds it to the blockchain, and broadcasts it to workers associated with it.

4.2   Workflow of HBMD-FL

In HBMD-FL, workers design their model locally and pre-train it on both D_{public} and $D_{private}$. The workers upload $w(D_{public}) = \{logits_k\}_k^N$ to miners. Miners validate those logits and broadcast the validation results to other miners. After that, miners package the results of all miners into their candidate blocks, select a block according to the consensus algorithm and add it to the blockchain. The details are as follows.

Initialize: In initial phase, worker $d_i \in \mathcal{D}$ downloads the public dataset D_{public} and trains model w_i which on D_{public} until convergence and continues training on $D_{private}$ until convergence.

Local Predictions Upload: After finishing the initialization, worker d_i associates with a miner $m_j \in \mathcal{M}$ in the blockchain system randomly and uploads transaction $trans_{i,j}^r$ to m_j. The transaction contains the prediction results of w_i on D_{public} which records as $w_i(D_{public}) = \{logits_1, logits_2, \cdots logits_N\}$, expects stakes $stake_{d_i}^r$, signature for this transaction $sig_{i,j}^r$ and other informations.

Cross-Verification: Miners broadcast transactions they received to other miners for a comprehensive evaluation to the logits uploaded by workers. When m_j

collectes enough transactions, i.e., $|trans\_recivied_j^r| = |\mathcal{D}|$, m_j starts to verify the validity of the signature of those transactions and obtains the qualified transaction set $trans\_verified_j^r$, after which m_j starts verifying the quality of those logits.

Algorithm 1: HBMD-FL

Input: Worker set $\mathcal{D}$. Miner set $mathcalM$. Public dataset D_{public}. Private datasets $D_{private}$. Models of each worker $\mathcal{W}$.

Output: Models after training $\mathcal{W}$.

1 initialization
2 **for** *each communication round* $r \in (1, 2, \cdots, R)$ **do**
3   **for** *each device* $d_i \in \mathcal{D}$ **do**
4   Transmits $trans_{i,j}^r \leftarrow \{w_i(D_{public}); expect\_stake_i^r; sig_i\}$ to m_j
5   **end**
6   **for** *each miner* $m_i \in \mathcal{M}$ **do**
7   **for** *each sample* $k \in D_{public}$ **do**
8   **if** $w_i(k) = label_k$ **then**
9                 $validate\_result_k^i = True$
10   **else**
11                 $validate\_result_k^i = False$
12   **end**
13   **end**
14   **for** *each* $trans_i^r \in trans_j$ **do**
15             $outlier_i = \dfrac{\sum_{w_i(D_{public})}^{k} validate\_result_k^i = False}{|w_i(D_{public})|}$
16   **if** $outlier_i \geq threshold$ **then**
17                 $validate\_result_{j,i} = True$
18   **else**
19                 $validate\_result_{j,i} = False$
20   **end**
21   **end**
22   Broadcast $\{candidate\_Block_j^r, sig_j\}$
23   Add $Block_j^r$ to Blockchain, and broadcast this block to workers
24   **for** *each worker* $d_i \in \mathcal{D}$ **do**
25   Add $Block_j^r$ to Blockchain
26             $global\_logits_i^r = 1/|logits| \cdot \sum_j w_i(D_{public})$
27   Train w_i on D_{public} for few epochs to approach $global\_logits_i^r$
28   Train w_i on $D_{private}$ for few epochs
29   **end**
30   **end**
31 **end**

---

m_j takes out the prediction results $logits_{i,k}$ of d_i in $trans\_verified_j^r$ for sample k in turn, compares it with the logits of other workers, note that we directly compare the prediction result with other logits. After that, m_j obtains the validation results $validation\_result^i_k = (True/False)$. When all logits are validated, m_j computes the outlier of each worker according to Eq. 5.

$$outlier_i = \frac{\sum_{w_i(D_{public})}^k validation\_result^i_k = False}{|w_i(D_{public})|} \tag{5}$$

Once the outlier calculation is finished, m_j derive $validation\_result_{j,i}$ which represents the final validation result of m_j to the logits of d_i according to Eq. 6 and broadcast it to other miners.

$$validation\_result_{j,i} = \begin{cases} True & outlier_i \geq threshold \\ False & outlier_i > threshold \end{cases} \tag{6}$$

Block Generates: When finishing cross-verification, m_j packages $w_i(D_{public})$ and $validation\_result^r_j$ into its $candidate\_block^r_j$ and broadcasts it to other miners with other block informations. m_j selects the candidate block which miner has the highest stakes, adds it to their blockchain, and broadcasts it to the workers associated with it. When a new block is added, the blockchain system allocates stakes based on the contributions (i.e., Eq. 7) made by the participants in the current round.

$$\begin{cases} stake\ of\ worker = \lambda \times |D_{private}| \times local\_training\_epochs \\ stake\ of\ miner = 5 \times |trans^r_{i,j}| + 3 \times |trans^r_{i,j}|, k \in \mathcal{M} - j \end{cases} \tag{7}$$

where λ is incentive weights.

Local Update: Worker d_i aggregates the $global\_logits^r_i$ according to the qualified logits in the latest block. In detail, worker d_i leverages the logits of each worker $w(D_{public})$ and validation results of each miner $validation\_result^r$ computes $global\_logits^r_i$ according to Eq. 8.

$$global\_logits^r_i = \frac{1}{|logits|} \cdot \sum_j w_j(D_{public}) \tag{8}$$

Note that, the validation result of worker m is denoted as $validation\_result^r_m$, we specify that only $w_m(D_{public})$ satisfies $|validation\_result^r_m = Ture| \geq |validation\_result^r_m = False|$, i.e., such logits will be used to compute the $global\_logits^r_i$.

After $global\_logits^r_i$ is computed, let w_i trains on D_{public} for few epochs to approach $global\_logits^r_i$, and then trains on $D_{private}$ for few epochs.

Repeat the communication until all models converge or reaches the specified number of communication rounds.

5   Experiment

To evaluate the effectiveness of our approach, we implement HBML-FL on a federated learning prototype and further discuss the experimental results on the aspects of accuracy and communication cost.. The experiment is conducted in both IID and non-IID environments and we select CIFAR-10 and CIFAR-100 image classification datasets [33] as the public dataset and private dataset for each worker. More details are shown in the following.

5.1 Experiment Setup

We built the prototype of HBMD-FL based on Python-3.7.6 and Tensorflow-2.5.0. In this prototype we set 10 workers and 3 miners to collaborate training their models which is used for image classification tasks to improve local models accuracy. The models of 10 workers have fully different architectures and the detail parameters of those models are shown in Table 1. The parameters used in model training and logits match shows in Table 2. The CIFAR-10 is utilized as the D_{public} and the $D_{private}$ is a subset of the CIFAR-100 which has 20 superclasses and 100 classes. In both two environments, the private dataset for each worker is randomly chosen from the selected sample classes. In the IID environment, each worker has 5 samples per superclass. The number is 20 from one random subclass of the superclass in the non-IID environment. When testing in the IID environment, the model of each worker should classify test images into correct classes. In the non-IID environment, models need to classify test images into correct superclasses. For example, a worker uses bottles to train a model. When testing, it should have the ability to classify "cups" into "food containers".

In order to reduce the communication cost of exchange logits, 5000 samples are used in communication instead of the whole dataset. In addition, the threshold of outlier is set to 0.75, the incentive weight $\lambda = 1$ under IID environment and $\lambda = 0.2$ under non-IID environment. We utilize the testset of CIFAR-100 to evaluate the accuracy of models under the situations of no malicious workers and 30% malicious workers, respectively. The higher the accuracy, the better the effectiveness of our algorithm. After that, we compare communication cost with FedAVG, which is the original federated learning algorithm.

Table 1. Model parameters.

Model	Layers	n1	n2	n3	Dropout rate	Upper bound (IID\non-IID)
0	2	64	256	None	0.2	0.811\0.617
1	2	128	384	None	0.2	0.825\0.578
2	2	128	512	None	0.2	0.76\0.572
3	2	256	512	None	0.3	0.829\0.563
4	2	256	784	None	0.4	0.836\0.554
5	3	64	128	256	0.2	0.805\0.653
6	3	128	192	256	0.2	0.835\0.658
7	3	128	256	512	0.2	0.826\0.652
8	3	192	256	512	0.3	0.834\0.661
9	3	256	512	784	0.3	0.839\0.672

Table 2. Training parameters.

	Batch size	Epochs	Optimizer	Learning rate	β_1	β_2	ϵ
Pre-training	128	20	Adam	0.001	0.9	0.999	1e−8
Private training	32	5					
Logits match	128	3					

5.2   Results

Accuracy. Figures 2(a) and 3(a) illustrate that the accuracy of 10 heterogeneous models improved by different magnitudes after 20 rounds of collaborative training with an average accuracy improvement of 13% in the IID case and 18% in the non-IID case. To compare with the theoretical upper bounds in two cases, we pooled the private data of 10 workers to train models separately. The results show that the average accuracy is only 4.9% higher than collaborative training and the improvement is 5.4% in the non-IID case.

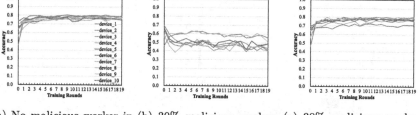

(a) No malicious worker in IID environment

(b) 30% malicious workers in IID environment

(c) 30% malicious workers with validation algorithm in IID environment

Fig. 2. Accuracy in IID environment

Then, we set the uploads of 3 workers as random Gaussian noise to simulate poison attacks and do not validate the upload of workers, which means the malicious will be treated as normal workers. The accuracy of the other 7 remaining models show a huge drop from before. In the IID case (shown in Fig. 2(b)), the average accuracy reduces over 13%, with a maximum reduction of 23.5% compared with the initial accuracy and the average accuracy reduction is 30%, the maximum reduction is 36% compare with no malicious. In the non-IID case (shown in Fig. 3(b)), the average reduction is 5.7% compared with the initial accuracy, 24.1% compared with the no malicious and the maximum reduction is 27%.

Finally, we apply validation algorithm in blockchain system, and the results in IID and non-IID cases are shown in Figs. 2(c) and 3(c), respectively. In the IID case, the average accuracy of the remaining models is 29.6% higher than without

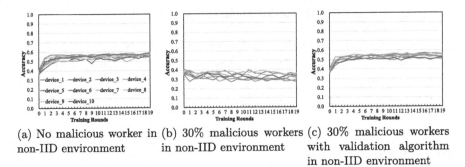

(a) No malicious worker in non-IID environment

(b) 30% malicious workers in non-IID environment

(c) 30% malicious workers with validation algorithm in non-IID environment

Fig. 3. Accuracy in non-IID environment

the validation algorithm. It is only 0.8% lower than no malicious situation. The increase is 21.4% in the non-IID case and 2.8% lower than before. To summarize the above, HBMD-FL has the efficiency to resist poisoning attacks.

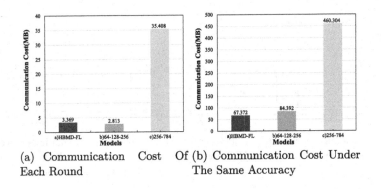

(a) Communication Cost Of Each Round

(b) Communication Cost Under The Same Accuracy

Fig. 4. Communication cost

Communication Cost. In this section, we compare the communication cost of HBMD-FL with FedAVG which is a classic algorithm in Federated learning. However, a direct comparison with those two algorithms is difficult because different model structures lead to different model sizes and convergence conditions, thus we select two models in the above 10 models with the maximum and minimum sizes (i.e., model 4 is the maximum and model 5 is the minimum in Table 1) for comparison. HBMD-FL finishes after 20 communication rounds with the accuracy are 76.8% of model 4 and 79.3% of model 5. In FedAVG, model 4 reaches 75.5% after 13 communication rounds and model 5 reaches 78.4% after 30% communication rounds. Figure 4(a) illustrates the communication cost of each communication round and Fig. 4(b) is the total communication cost. The comparison of communication costs clearly shows that HBMD-FL has the advantage over FedAVG in terms of communication cost.

5.3   Evaluation on the Incentive Mechanism

By utilizing the blockchain system, we not only achieve the decentralized federated learning and resistance to malicious workers but also give the solution for the incentive mechanism which motivate the worker to participant federated learning. In HBMD-FL, all workers and miners can get incentives (i.e., stakes) allocated by the blockchain system, while the malicious workers whose uploaded logits are identified as *False* will not be allocated. Figure 5 shows the allocation of stakes in the experiment above.

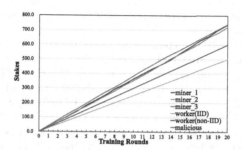

Fig. 5. The stakes of each participant in the system.

6   Conclusion

In this article, we proposed a federated learning algorithm based on blockchain and model distillation: HBMD-FL. In using model distillation to solve the problem of heterogeneous models for federated learning while introducing blockchain technology into it so that federated learning performs in decentralized ways. Meanwhile, the logits validation algorithm is integrated into the cross-validation phase to resist the poisoning attacks in federated distillation. Moreover, experiments were conducted with the CIFAR-10 dataset as a public dataset and the CIFAR-100 dataset as a private dataset. The loss of model accuracy for each worker of HBMD-FL is less than 5% compared to centralized training. In the presence of malicious workers, HBMD-FL keeps the model accuracy loss within 3% while resisting poisoning attacks by malicious workers and significantly outperforms the comparison algorithm in terms of communication cost. As for future work, we will improve the effectiveness of validation algorithm, extend HBMD-FL to diverse tasks and evaluate its performance against other attacks, such as the membership inference attack and property Inference Attacks.

References

1. McMahan, B., Moore, E., Ramage, D., Hampson, S., y Arcas, B.A.: Communication-efficient learning of deep networks from decentralized data. In: Artificial Intelligence and Statistics, pp. 1273–1282. PMLR (2017)

2. Smith, V., Chiang, C.K., Sanjabi, M., Talwalkar, A.S.: Federated multi-task learning. In: Advances in Neural Information Processing Systems, vol. 30 (2017)

3. Corinzia, L., Beuret, A., Buhmann, J.M.: Variational federated multi-task learning. arXiv preprint arXiv:1906.06268 (2019)

4. Jiang, Y., Konečný, J., Rush, K., Kannan, S.: Improving federated learning personalization via model agnostic meta learning. arXiv preprint arXiv:1909.12488 (2019)

5. Khodak, M., Balcan, M.F.F., Talwalkar, A.S.: Adaptive gradient-based meta-learning methods. In: Advances in Neural Information Processing Systems, vol. 32 (2019)

6. He, C., Annavaram, M., Avestimehr, S.: Towards non-IID and invisible data with FedNAS: federated deep learning via neural architecture search. arXiv preprint arXiv:2004.08546 (2020)

7. Li, D., Wang, J.: FedMD: heterogenous federated learning via model distillation. arXiv preprint arXiv:1910.03581 (2019)

8. Jeong, E., Oh, S., Kim, H., Park, J., Bennis, M., Kim, S.L.: Communication-efficient on-device machine learning: federated distillation and augmentation under non-IID private data. arXiv preprint arXiv:1811.11479 (2018)

9. Shen, T., et al.: Federated mutual learning. arXiv preprint arXiv:2006.16765 (2020)

10. Mo, Z., Gao, Z., Zhao, C., Lin, Y.: FedDQ: a communication-efficient federated learning approach for Internet of Vehicles. J. Syst. Archit. **131**, 102690 (2022). https://www.sciencedirect.com/science/article/pii/S1383762122001928

11. Sattler, F., Marban, A., Rischke, R., Samek, W.: CFD: communication-efficient federated distillation via soft-label quantization and delta coding. IEEE Trans. Netw. Sci. Eng. **9**(4), 2025–2038 (2022)

12. Kim, H., Park, J., Bennis, M., Kim, S.L.: Blockchained on-device federated learning. IEEE Commun. Lett. **24**(6), 1279–1283 (2019)

13. Nakamoto, S.: Bitcoin: a peer-to-peer electronic cash system. Decentralized Bus. Rev., 21260 (2008)

14. Samarakoon, S., Bennis, M., Saad, W., Debbah, M.: Distributed federated learning for ultra-reliable low-latency vehicular communications. IEEE Trans. Commun. **68**(2), 1146–1159 (2019)

15. Nishio, T., Yonetani, R.: Client selection for federated learning with heterogeneous resources in mobile edge. In: ICC 2019 IEEE International Conference on Communications (ICC), pp. 1–7. IEEE (2019)

16. Kairouz, P., et al.: Advances and open problems in federated learning. Found. Trends® Mach. Learn. **14**(1–2), 1–210 (2021)

17. He, C., et al.: FedML: a research library and benchmark for federated machine learning. arXiv preprint arXiv:2007.13518 (2020)

18. Wang, H., Yurochkin, M., Sun, Y., Papailiopoulos, D., Khazaeni, Y.: Federated learning with matched averaging. arXiv preprint arXiv:2002.06440 (2020)

19. Li, Q., He, B., Song, D.: Model-contrastive federated learning. In: Proceedings of the IEEE/CVF Conference on Computer Vision and Pattern Recognition, pp. 10713–10722 (2021)

20. Wu, Q., He, K., Chen, X.: Personalized federated learning for intelligent IoT applications: a cloud-edge based framework. IEEE Open J. Comput. Soc. **1**, 35–44 (2020)

21. Fallah, A., Mokhtari, A., Ozdaglar, A.: Personalized federated learning: a meta-learning approach. CoRR, vol. abs/2002.07948 (2020). https://arxiv.org/abs/2002.07948

22. Arivazhagan, M.G., Aggarwal, V., Singh, A.K., Choudhary, S.: Federated learning with personalization layers. CoRR, vol. abs/1912.00818 (2019). http://arxiv.org/abs/1912.00818

23. Hinton, G., Vinyals, O., Dean, J., et al.: Distilling the knowledge in a neural network. arXiv preprint arXiv:1503.02531 2(7) (2015)

24. Wang, C., Yang, G., Papanastasiou, G., Zhang, H., Rodrigues, J.J., de Albuquerque, V.H.C.: Industrial cyber-physical systems-based cloud IoT edge for federated heterogeneous distillation. IEEE Trans. Industr. Inf. **17**(8), 5511–5521 (2020)

25. Peng, Z., et al.: VFChain: enabling verifiable and auditable federated learning via blockchain systems. IEEE Trans. Netw. Sci. Eng. **9**(1), 173–186 (2021)

26. Lu, Y., Huang, X., Dai, Y., Maharjan, S., Zhang, Y.: Blockchain and federated learning for privacy-preserved data sharing in industrial IoT. IEEE Trans. Industr. Inf. **16**(6), 4177–4186 (2019)

27. Zhang, W., et al.: Blockchain-based federated learning for device failure detection in industrial IoT. IEEE Internet Things J. **8**(7), 5926–5937 (2020)

28. Nguyen, D.C., et al.: Federated learning meets blockchain in edge computing: opportunities and challenges. IEEE Internet Things J. **8**(16), 12806–12825 (2021)

29. Awan, S., Li, F., Luo, B., Liu, M.: Poster: a reliable and accountable privacy-preserving federated learning framework using the blockchain. In: Proceedings of the 2019 ACM SIGSAC Conference on Computer and Communications Security, pp. 2561–2563 (2019)

30. Chen, H., Asif, S.A., Park, J., Shen, C.C., Bennis, M.: Robust blockchained federated learning with model validation and proof-of-stake inspired consensus. arXiv preprint arXiv:2101.03300 (2021)

31. Majeed, U., Hong, C.S.: FLchain: Federated learning via MEC-enabled blockchain network. In: 2019 20th Asia-Pacific Network Operations and Management Symposium (APNOMS), pp. 1–4. IEEE (2019)

32. Li, Y., Chen, C., Liu, N., Huang, H., Zheng, Z., Yan, Q.: A blockchain-based decentralized federated learning framework with committee consensus. IEEE Netw. **35**(1), 234–241 (2020)

33. Krizhevsky, A., Hinton, G., et al.: Learning multiple layers of features from tiny images (2009)

Secure and Efficient Certificateless Authentication Key Agreement Protocol in VANET

Guoheng Wei, Yanlin Qin[✉], and Wei Fu

Department of Information Security, Naval University of Engineering, Wuhan, China
qinyanlincool@163.com

Abstract. An authentication key agreement protocol is designed to realize mutual verification and generate symmetric key shared by participants in symmetric cryptosystem. Aiming at the security problem of an authentication key agreement protocol using certificateless aggregate signature in VANET, an improved certificateless authentication key agreement protocol based on elliptic curve is proposed, and then the security of the protocol is analyzed. The analysis results show that the protocol can make up for the security loopholes of the existing schemes, meet the resistance to temporary secret key leakage, resistance to man-in-the-middle attack, the forward security, anti-impersonation attack and other security properties. Compared with the security and efficiency of congener schemes, this scheme provides higher security at the same time has the same operation efficiency of original scheme, which can be used conveniently in resource-constrained VANET.

Keywords: Symmetric cryptosystem · Certificateless public key cryptosystem · Authentication key agreement protocol · Vehicular ad hoc network · Elliptic curve

1 Introduction

Vehicular Ad hoc Network (VANET) refers to the real-time collection of road condition information by vehicle-mounted devices through wireless communication technology, effective utilization of all vehicles' dynamic information in the information network platform, and real-time navigation, collision prevention, entertainment and other functions in the operation of vehicles. To achieve secure interaction between vehicles and servers or between vehicles, secure and efficient authentication key agreement protocols for VANET are designed to realize mutual verification and generate symmetric key shared by participants in symmetric cryptosystem. Scholars have proposed various security authentication schemes for VANET based on different cryptography theories. One is the lightweight authentication scheme based on Hash function, message authentication code (MAC), password or physical unclonable function (PUF) [1–3]: Li et al. [1] proposed a cross-domain authentication and key agreement protocol in VANET using password and tamper-proof smart card. The scheme does not use traditional public key infrastructure, which can ensure high authentication efficiency, but it is difficult to resist

© The Author(s), under exclusive license to Springer Nature Switzerland AG 2022
J. Chen et al. (Eds.): EISA 2022, CCIS 1641, pp. 160–172, 2022.
https://doi.org/10.1007/978-3-031-23098-1_10

temporary key disclosure, man-in-the-middle attack and other attacks. In order to reduce the computation and communication cost of vehicle authentication and key agreement, Hou et al. [2] designed an anonymous authentication and key agreement protocol for VANET by combining Hash function, MAC and PUF, but it could not resist the temporary key disclosure attack. In order to ensure the security of the authentication scheme for VANET, many scholars proposed the authentication schemes by using the traditional public key cryptosystem and the Identity-Based Encryption [4–9]. But the management and maintenance of public key certificate library needs huge cost of calculation, communication and storage, which is not suitable for the resource-constrained environment of vehicles in VANET. Although Identity-Based Encryption avoids the use of public key infrastructure, it has the problem of private key escrow.

In order to avoid certificate management of PKI and key escrow problem of Identity-Based Encryption, Al-Riyami et al. [10] proposed Certificateless public key cryptography. Based on certificateless public key cryptography, certificateless authentication schemes for VANET are proposed [11–17]: some of the schemes use certificateless aggregate signature to realize batch authentication of vehicles [11–15], which ensure high security, but do not provide the key agreement. HAN M et al. [16] proposed an authentication key agreement protocol for VANET, but it cannot resist the temporary key leakage attack [17]. Zhang et al. [17] designed an anonymous authentication key agreement protocol using certificateless aggregate signature for cloud service oriented VANET, but the security analysis of the scheme shows that in the phase of vehicle registration and authentication key agreement between vehicle and cloud server, it can't resist impersonation and forgery attack made by adversary defined as AII in security model for Certificateless public key cryptography. At the same time, it does not meet the security properties such as anti-temporary key leakage attack, perfect forward security, anti-impersonation attack and so on. On this basis, this paper proposes an improved authentication key agreement protocol for VANET. Security analysis shows that the new protocol can resist temporary key leakage attack, meet security properties such as forward security, anti-impersonation attack and so on, and has high efficiency.

2 Security Analysis of Authentication Key Agreement Protocol for VANET Proposed by Zhang et al. [17]

Security of the authentication key agreement protocol for VANET proposed by Zhang et al. [17] is analyzed in this section. First, a brief description of the protocol is shown in Fig. 1 and Fig. 2. The protocol involves key generation center KGC, registration center TRA, vehicular unit OBU, roadside unit RSU and cloud server CS.

There are two types of adversaries attacking certificateless public key cryptography. One adversary can arbitrarily replace the public key and secret value of the user, however, the master key of the system cannot be obtained, the adversary is marked as AI; The other adversary can obtain the system master key and calculate the user's partial private key, but cannot obtain the user's secret value and cannot replace the user's public key. Therefore, this adversary is marked as AII.

Security analysis of authentication key agreement protocol for VANET proposed by Zhang et al. [17] shows that there are the following security vulnerabilities:

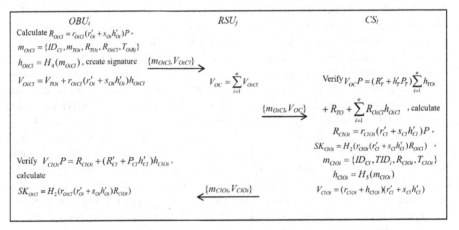

Fig. 1. Authorization and certification process between TRA and OBUi.

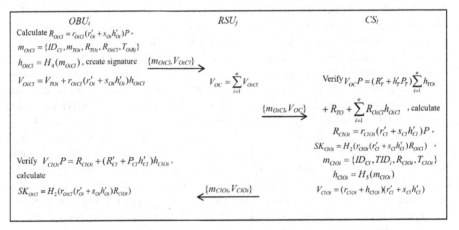

Fig. 2. Authentication key agreement protocol between CSl and OBUi

(1) In authorization and certification process between TRA and OBUi, AII can forge legitimate signature for OBUi's temporary identity generated by TRA and calculate the correct symmetric key shared between OBUi and TRA. The attack process is as follows:

① A_{II} can first randomly select $s'_T \in Z_q^*$ and replace the partial public key of *TRA* with $P'_T = h_T^{'-1}(s'_T P - R'_T)$.

② A_{II} can calculate the symmetric key $K'_{TOi} = H_2(s'_T TID_i)$, which is shared with OBU_i That's because:

$$K'_{OiT} = H_2(r_{OiT}(r'_{Oi} + s_{Oi}h'_{Oi})(R'_T + h'_T P'_T))$$
$$= H_2(r_{OiT}(r'_{Oi} + s_{Oi}h'_{Oi})(R'_T + s'_T P - R'_T))$$
$$= H_2(s'_T r_{OiT}(R'_{Oi} + h'_{Oi}P_{Oi}))$$
$$= H_2(s'_T TID_i)$$

③ After calculating the symmetric key shared with OBU_i, A_{II} can randomly select r'_{TOi}, calculate $R'_{TOi} = r'_{TOi}P$ and $h'_{TOi} = H_3(m_{TOi}, R'_{TOi})$, then generate the signature $V'_{TOi} = s'_T h'_{TOi} + r'_{TOi}$ for temporary identity of OBU_i, and the signed message is recorded as $m^*_{TOi} = \{m_{TOi}, V'_{TOi}, R'_{TOi}, T_{TOi}\}$. The shared key is then used to encrypt m^*_{TOi}, that is $e'_{TOi} = E_{K_{TOi}}(m^*_{TOi})$, and the encryption result together with TRA's identity ID_T are sent to OBU_i, the forged signature can pass OBU_i's verification. This is because:

Firstly, OBU_i uses the symmetric key K'_{OiT} to decrypt e'_{TOi} and recover $m^*_{TOi} = \{m_{TOi}, V'_{TOi}, R'_{TOi}, T_{TOi}\}$, then calculates $h'_{TOi} = H_3(m_{TOi}, R'_{TOi})$ and verifies

$$(R'_T + h'_T P'_T)h'_{TOi} + R'_{TOi}$$
$$= (R'_T + s'_T P - R'_T)h'_{TOi} + R'_{TOi}$$
$$= s'_T h'_{TOi}P + R'_{TOi}$$
$$= (s'_T h'_{TOi} + r'_{TOi})P = V'_{TOi}P$$

so the forged signature can be verified to be true.

At the same time, the signature for temporary identity of OBU_i forged by A_{II} can also pass through CS_l's authentication for the aggregation signature forwarded by the roadside unit, that is because:

$$V_{OC}P = (\sum_{i=1}^{n} V_{OiCl})P$$
$$= \sum_{i=1}^{n} (V'_{TOi} + r_{oiCl}(r'_{oi} + s_{oi}h'_{oi})h_{oiCl})P$$
$$= \sum_{i=1}^{n} (s'_T h'_{TOi} + r'_{TOi} + r_{oiCl}(r'_{oi} + s_{oi}h'_{oi})h_{oiCl})P$$
$$= \sum_{i=1}^{n} ((R'_T + h'_T P'_T)h'_{TOi} + R'_{TOi} + R_{oiCl}h_{oiCl})$$
$$= (R'_T + h'_T P'_T)\sum_{i=1}^{n} h'_{TOi} + \sum_{i=1}^{n} R'_{TOi} + \sum_{i=1}^{n} R_{oiCl}h_{oiCl}$$
$$= (R'_T + h'_T P'_T)\sum_{i=1}^{n} h'_{TOi} + R'_{TO} + \sum_{i=1}^{n} R_{oiCl}h_{oiCl}$$

(2) In the process of authentication key agreement between OBU_i and CS_l, A_{II} can also impersonate CS_l to execute the authentication key agreement with OBU_i as follows:

① Select random number $s^*_{Cl} \in Z^*_q$, and replace the partial public key of CS_l with $P^*_{Cl} = h'^{-1}_{Cl}(s^*_{Cl}P - R'_{Cl})$.

② Randomly select $r^*_{Cloi} \in Z^*_q$ for each OBU_i, calculate $R^*_{Cloi} = r^*_{Cloi}s^*_{Cl}P$ and symmetric key $SK^*_{Cloi} = H_2(r^*_{Cloi}s^*_{Cl}R_{oiCl})$.

③ Generate the message $m^*_{ClOi} = \{ID_{Cl}, TID_i, R^*_{ClOi}, T_{ClOi}\}$, calculate $h^*_{ClOi} = H_5(m^*_{ClOi})$, sign $h^*_{ClOi} = H_5(m^*_{ClOi})$ and generate $V^*_{ClOi} = (r^*_{ClOi} + h^*_{ClOi})s^*_{Cl}$, send $\{m^*_{ClOi}, V^*_{ClOi}\}$ to RSU_j, and RSU_j then forward it to OBU_i.

The above forged signature can pass OBU_i's verification. This is because:

$$R^*_{ClOi} + (R'_{Cl} + P^*_{Cl}h'_{Cl})h^*_{ClOi}$$
$$= R^*_{ClOi} + (R'_{Cl} + s^*_{Cl}P - R'_{Cl})h^*_{ClOi}$$
$$= r^*_{ClOi}s^*_{Cl}P + s^*_{Cl}h^*_{ClOi}P$$
$$= (r^*_{ClOi} + h^*_{ClOi})s^*_{Cl}P$$
$$= V^*_{ClOi}P.$$

After verifying that the signature is true, OBU_i can calculate the symmetric key $SK^*_{OiCl} = H_2(r_{OiCl}(r'_{Oi} + s_{Oi}h'_{Oi})R^*_{ClOi})$, which is the same as $SK^*_{ClOi} = H_2(r^*_{ClOi}s^*_{Cl}R_{OiCl})$ calculated by A_{II}. The symmetry can be proved as follows:

$$SK^*_{OiCl} = H_2(r_{OiCl}(r'_{Oi} + s_{Oi}h'_{Oi})R^*_{ClOi})$$
$$= H_2(r_{OiCl}(r'_{Oi} + s_{Oi}h'_{Oi})r^*_{ClOi}s^*_{Cl}P)$$
$$= H_2(r^*_{ClOi}s^*_{Cl}R_{OiCl})$$
$$= SK^*_{ClOi}.$$

(3) Except for the difficulty in resisting the above attacks launched by A_{II}, the authentication key agreement protocol between OBU_i and CS_l in reference [17] is also vulnerable to temporary private key disclosure attack as follows:

Suppose the attacker has mastered a temporary private key r_{ClOi}, which is generated by CS_l during the authentication key agreement, and intercepted signature data $\{m_{ClOi}, V_{ClOi}\}$ sent by CS_l to RSU_j. $r'_{Cl} + s_{Cl}h'_{Cl} = (r_{ClOi} + h_{ClOi})^{-1}V_{ClOi}$ can be calculated directly by using V_{ClOi}, where $h_{ClOi} = H_5(m_{ClOi})$. At the same time, using the signature data $\{m_{OiCl}, V_{OiCl}\}$, which includes R_{OiCl}, attacker can calculate the symmetric key $SK_{ClOi} = H_2(r_{ClOi}(r'_{Cl} + s_{Cl}h'_{Cl})R_{OiCl})$ of both parties.

(4) Authentication key agreement protocol in reference [17] does not satisfy perfect forward security, the attack is as follows:

Perfect forward security assumes that the attacker has the complete private keys of both sides of the communication, but cannot calculate the current shared key of both sides. In the scheme proposed by Zhang et al., it is assumed that the attacker has obtained CS_l's private key (r'_{Cl}, s_{Cl}), intercepted signature data $\{m_{ClOi}, V_{ClOi}\}$ sent by CS_l to RSU_j. $r_{ClOi} = V_{ClOi}(r'_{Cl} + s_{Cl}h'_{Cl})^{-1} - h_{ClOi}$ can be calculated directly by using V_{ClOi}, and then the symmetric key $SK_{ClOi} = H_2(r_{ClOi}(r'_{Cl} + s_{Cl}h'_{Cl})R_{OiCl})$ can be calculated by using R_{OiCl}.

Similarly, the scheme can also not resist simultaneous disclosure of one party's temporary key and the other party's long-term private key and impersonation attack. In both attacks, it is assumed that the attacker can obtain the private key of one party in the key agreement.

3 Improved Authentication Key Agreement Protocol for VANET

3.1 System Parameter Settings

(1) KGC generates a large prime number q, and selects an additive cyclic group $(G, +)$ of order q composed of points on an elliptic curve, where P is a generator of G; Selects the security hash function:

H_0: $\{0, 1\}^* \times G \times G \to Z_q^*$,
H_1: $G \to \{0, 1\}^*$,
H_2: $\{0, 1\}^* \times G \to Z_q^*$,
H_3: $\{0, 1\}^* \to Z_q^*$.

Chooses $s \in Z_q^*$, computes $P_0 = sP$, where (P_0, s) is the system master public/private key pair, and the system parameters $(q, P, P_0, H_0, H_1, H_2, H_3)$ is public, master key s is secret.

(2) Generation of user public/private key

Vehicle unit $OBU_i(I = 1, 2,...N)$ selects a random value $u_{Oi} \in Z_q^*$ as its secret value (long-term private key), calculates $U_{Oi} = u_{Oi}P$ and forwards the ID_{Oi} and U_{Oi} to KGC over a secure channel.

After receiving ID_{Oi} and U_{Oi}, which are the identity of OBU_i, KGC selects a random number $k_{Oi} \in Z_q^*$, calculates $K_{Oi} = k_{Oi}P$, $d_{Oi} = k_{Oi} + sH_0(ID_{Oi}, K_{Oi}, U_{Oi})$, then returns d_{Oi} and K_{Oi} to OBU_i over a secure channel. Then OBU_i uses (u_{Oi}, d_{Oi}) as its own complete private key, calculates $D_{Oi} = d_{Oi}P$, uses (U_{Oi}, D_{Oi}) as its own complete public key. OBU_i validates equation $K_{Oi} + H_0(ID_{Oi}, K_{Oi}, U_{Oi})P_0 = D_{Oi}$ to verify the validity of the partial private key sent by KGC.

Similarly, cloud server $CS_j(j = 1, 2, ...,k)$ and the registration centre TRA generate public/private key pairs $(U_{Cj}, D_{Cj})/(u_{Cj}, d_{Cj})$, $(U_T, D_T)/(u_T, d_T)$ in the same way.

3.2 Registration and Authorization Algorithm Between TRA and OBUi

After the temporary identity of OBU_i has been generated, OBU_i applies for registration and authorization from registration centre TRA by follow the following steps:

(1) Calculate $h_{Oi} = H_0(ID_{Oi}, U_{Oi}, D_{Oi})$ and select random number $r_{Oi} \in Z_q^*$ to construct temporary identity $LID_{Oi} = r_{Oi}(U_{Oi} + h_{Oi}D_{Oi})$, compute $h_T = H_0(ID_T, U_T, D_T)$ and $V_{OiT} = r_{Oi}(u_{Oi} + d_{Oi}h_{Oi})(U_T + h_TD_T)$, then generate a message $m_{OiT} = \{ID_{Oi}, ID_T, r_{Oi}, T\}$, where T is the timestamp.
(2) Calculate $c_{OiT} = H_1(V_{OiT}) \oplus m_{OiT}$, send LID_{Oi} and c_{OiT} to TRA.

TRA performs the following steps to authenticate OBU_i's identity:

(1) Calculate $h_T = H_0(ID_T, U_T, D_T)$ and $V_{TOi} = LID_{Oi}(u_T + d_T h_T)$,

(2) Recover $m_{OiT} = H_1(V_{TOi}) \oplus c_{OiT}$, verify whether $LID_{Oi} = r_{Oi}(U_{Oi} + h_{Oi}D_{Oi})$ is true. If the equation is true, accept OBU_i's registration application, otherwise reject it.

(3) Generate a message $m_{TOi} = \{ID_T, LID_{Oi}, T\}$.

(4) Select random value $r_{TOi} \in Z_q^*$, calculate $R_{TOi} = r_{TOi}P$ and $h_{TOi} = H_2(m_{TOi}, R_{TOi})$, then generate signature $S_{TOi} = (u_T + h_T d_T)h_{TOi} + r_{TOi}$.

(5) Calculate $c_{TOi} = H_1(V_{TOi}) \oplus (m_{TOi}||S_{TOi}||R_{TOi}||T)$, and send $\{ID_T, c_{TOi}\}$ to OBU_i.

OBU_i performs the following steps to verify signature authorization of *TRA*:

(1) Recover $m_{TOi}||S_{TOi}||R_{TOi}||T = H_1(V_{OiT}) \oplus c_{TOi}$, verify whether the timestamp T is correct;

(2) Verify whether $S_{TOi}P = (U_T + h_T D_T)h_{TOi} + R_{TOi}$ is established. If it is, OBU_i will accept the authorized signature; Otherwise refuse.

3.3 Authentication Key Agreement Algorithm Between OBUi and CSj

OBU_I performs the following steps to execute authentication key agreement with the cloud server CS_j:

(1) Select random number $k_{Oi} \in Z_q^*$, calculate $K_{Oi} = k_{Oi}(u_{Oi} + h_{Oi}d_{Oi})P$, and generate a message $m_{OiCj} = \{ID_{Oi}, m_{TOi}, R_{TOi}, K_{Oi}, T\}$.

(2) Calculate $h_{OiCj} = H_3(m_{OiCj})$, generate signature $S_{OiCj} = S_{TOi} + k_{Oi}(u_{Oi} + h_{Oi}d_{Oi}) + h_{OiCj}u_{Oi}$ and send $\{m_{OiCj}, S_{OiCj}\}$ to the roadside unit for transfer.

After receiving $\{m_{OiCj}, S_{OiCj}\}$, roadside unit will generate the aggregate signature $S_{OCj} = \sum_{i=1}^{n} S_{OiCj}$, and then forward $\{m_{OiCj}, S_{OCj}, T\}$ to CSj.

After receiving the aggregate signature, the cloud server CS_j will perform the following steps to verify the aggregate signature:

(1) Calculate $h_T = H_0(ID_T, U_T, D_T), h_{TOi} = H_2(m_{TOi}, R_{TOi})$ and $h_{OiCj} = H_3(m_{OiCj})$.

(2) Verify whether $S_{OCj}P = (U_T + h_T D_T)\sum_{i=1}^{n} h_{TOi} + \sum_{i=1}^{n} R_{TOi} + \sum_{i=1}^{n} K_{Oi} + \sum_{i=1}^{n} h_{OiCj}U_{Oi}$ is valid. If so, accept OBU_i's service request, otherwise reject it.

(3) Select random number $r_{COi} \in Z_q^*$, calculate $R_{COi} = r_{COi}(u_{Cj} + h_{Cj}d_{Cj})P$ and symmetric key $SK_{COi} = H_1(r_{COi}(u_{Cj} + h_{Cj}d_{Cj})K_{Oi})$. Generate a message $m_{COi} = \{ID_{Cj}, LID_{Oi}, R_{COi}, T\}$. Calculate $h_{COi} = H_3(m_{COi})$, generate $S_{COi} = r_{COi}(u_{Cj} + h_{Cj}d_{Cj}) + h_{COi}u_{Cj} + h_{Cj}d_{Cj}$ and calculate $C_{COi} = SK_{COi} \oplus ||m_{COi}||S_{COi})$.

(4) C_{COi} will then be sent to the roadside unit, and the roadside unit will forward it to OBU_i.

After receiving C_{COi}, OBU_i performs the following steps to verify the signature of CS_j:

(1) Calculate symmetric key shared with CS_j, that is $SK_{OiC} = H_1(k_{Oi}(u_{Oi} + h_{Oi}d_{Oi})R_{COi})$.

(2) Recover the signature $m_{COi}||S_{COi} = SK_{OiC} \oplus C_{COi}$.

(3) Calculate $h_{COi} = H_3(m_{COi})$ and $h_{Cj} = H_0(ID_{Cj}, U_{Cj}, D_{Cj})$.

(4) Verify whether the equation $S_{COi}P = R_{COi} + h_{COi}U_{Cj} + h_{Cj}D_{Cj}$ is true. If so, OBU_i will verify that the signature is true, otherwise terminate.

Correctness proof for verification equation of aggregate signature is as follows:

$$S_{OCj}P = \sum_{i=1}^{n} S_{OiCj}P = \sum_{i=1}^{n} (S_{TOi} + k_{Oi}(u_{Oi} + h_{Oi}d_{Oi}) + h_{OiCj}u_{Oi})P$$

$$= (U_T + h_T D_T) \sum_{i=1}^{n} h_{TOi} + \sum_{i=1}^{n} R_{TOi} + \sum_{i=1}^{n} K_{Oi} + \sum_{i=1}^{n} h_{OiCj}U_{Oi}.$$

The symmetry can be proved as follows:

$$SK_{COi} = H_1(r_{COi}(u_{Cj} + h_{Cj}d_{Cj})K_{Oi})$$
$$= H_1(r_{COi}(u_{Cj} + h_{Cj}d_{Cj})k_{Oi}(u_{Oi} + h_{Oi}d_{Oi})P)$$
$$= H_1(k_{Oi}(u_{Oi} + h_{Oi}d_{Oi})r_{COi}(u_{Cj} + h_{Cj}d_{Cj})P)$$
$$= H_1(k_{Oi}(u_{Oi} + h_{Oi}d_{Oi})R_{COi}) = SK_{OiC}$$

4 Security Analysis of the Improved Scheme

The following is a security proof of the improved authentication key agreement protocol for VANET:

(1) Resist A_{II}'s signature and symmetric key forgery attack: The safety analysis of the scheme proposed by Zhang et al. [17] shows that it is difficult to resist A_{II}'s signature and symmetric key forgery attack in the authentication and authorization stage between TRA and OBU_i. The main reason is the linear relation $(R'_T + h'_T P_T)$ between P_T and R'_T is contained in the calculation formula of symmetric key $K_{OiT} = H_2(r_{OiT}(r'_{Oi} + s_{Oi}h'_{Oi})(R'_T + h'_T P_T))$ and signature verification equation $V_{TOi}P = (R'_T + h'_T P_T)h_{TOi} + R_{TOi}$, where P_T is partial public key of TRA and R'_T is public key corresponding to secret value, A_{II} can use the master key of the system and partial public key P_T of TRA to eliminate the influence of R'_T included in signature verification equation and the calculation formula of the symmetric key, then eliminate the influence of the secret value r'_T of TRA, so as to successfully forge the TRA's signature and compute the shared key of both parties. Similarly, in the phase of authentication key agreement between OBU_i and CS_l, the linear relation $(R'_{Cl} + h'_{Cl}P_{Cl})$ between partial public key P_{Cl} and the public key R'_{Cl} corresponding to the secret value of CS_l is included in the signature verification equation $V_{ClOi}P = R_{ClOi} + (R'_{Cl} + h'_{Cl}P_{Cl})h_{ClOi}$ and the symmetric key calculation formula $SK_{OiCl} = H_2(r_{OiCl}(r'_{Oi} + s_{Oi}h'_{Oi})R_{ClOi})$, A_{II} can use the master key and

partial public key P_{Cl} of CS_l to eliminate the influence of R'_{Cl} included in signature verification equation and the calculation formula of the symmetric key, then eliminate the influence of the secret value r'_{Cl} of CS_l, so as to successfully forge the CS_l's signature and compute the shared key of both parties.

In the new scheme, partial public key of the user is added as the input of the hash function in $h_{Oi} = H_0(ID_{Oi}, U_{Oi}, D_{Oi})$, $h_T = H_0(ID_T, U_T, D_T)$, and $h_{Cj} = H_0(ID_{Cj}, U_{Cj}, D_{Cj})$, so as to destroy the linear relationship between partial public key and the public key corresponding to the secret value of user in the signature verification equation and the calculation formula of the symmetric key, thus resist A_{II}'s signature and symmetric key forgery attack.

(2) Anti-temporary key leakage: assume that the attacker can intercept the one-time temporary keys used by both parties, that is k_{Oi}, r_{COi}, but can't obtain private keys (u_{Oi}, d_{Oi}) and (u_{Cj}, d_{Cj}) of OBU_i and CS_j, and cannot obtain $(u_{Oi} + h_{Oi}d_{Oi})$ or $(u_{Cj} + h_{Cj}d_{Cj})$ by intercepting the signature $\{m_{OiCj}, S_{OiCj}\}$ and C_{COi} included in the public interaction between the two parties. This is because the information S_{TOi} contained in S_{OiCj} is encrypted and S_{TOi} cannot be obtained by attacker, so $(u_{Oi} + h_{Oi}d_{Oi})$ cannot be calculated by S_{OiCj}. Meanwhile, SK_{COi} is used to encrypt the generated signature S_{COi}, so that $(u_{Cj} + h_{Cj}d_{Cj})$ could not be computed from it. Therefore, the attacker cannot obtain the symmetric key even if he has obtained the temporary keys used in the interaction between the two parties.

(3) Known key security: even if an attacker has obtained a previous shared key negotiated by both parties, the current symmetric key cannot be calculated. In the improved scheme, OBU_i and CS_j both use the one-time temporary key k_{Oi}, r_{COi} in each authentication key agreement. Therefore, the leakage of the previous symmetric key does not affect the security of the current symmetric key.

(4) Forward security: ① Perfect forward security. In this scheme, OBU_i and CS_j both use the one-time temporary keys k_{Oi}, r_{COi} in each authentication key agreement, even if the attacker has obtained the complete private keys of both parties, (u_{Oi}, d_{Oi}) and (u_{Cj}, d_{Cj}), he cannot calculate SK_{OiC} or SK_{COi} if the temporary key k_{Oi}错 误!未指定书签。or r_{COi} annot be obtained.

② Master key forward security. Even if the attacker has obtained the master key of the system, the symmetric key generated in the authentication key agreement between the two parties cannot be calculated. In this scheme, even if the attacker gets the master key s of the system, because OBU_i and CS_j both use the one-time temporary keys k_{Oi}, r_{COi} and their secret values, the attacker cannot calculate the symmetric key.

(5) Resistance to simultaneous disclosure of the temporary key of one party and the complete private key of the other party: assuming that the attacker has obtained the temporary key of one party and the complete private key of the other party in the authentication key agreement, the shared key of both parties cannot be calculated. In the improved scheme, even if the attacker gets OBU_i's complete private key $(u_{Oi}, d_{Oi})$and CS_j's temporary key r_{COi}, he cannot calculate the symmetric key $SK_{OiC} = H_1(k_{Oi}(u_{Oi} + h_{Oi}d_{Oi})R_{COi})$ without k_{Oi}. According to the calculation formula of the symmetric key $SK_{COi} = H_1(r_{COi}(u_{Cj} + h_{Cj}d_{Cj})K_{Oi})$, only when the

attacker masters CS_j's temporary key and the full private key at the same time can he calculate the symmetric key.

(6) Implicit key authentication: that is, both parties involved in authentication key agreement can confirm that it is difficult for other illegal users to calculate the symmetric key. In this scheme, CS_j's private key (u_{Cj}, d_{Cj}) and $K_{Oi} = k_{Oi}(u_{Oi} + h_{Oi}d_{Oi})P$ are used in the calculation of SK_{COi}, where K_{Oi} contains The identity information and public key parameters of OBU_i, therefore CS_j can implicitly authenticate other illegal users cannot get the symmetric key except OBU_i, because only OBU_i holds the private key parameters corresponding to its public key parameters. Similarly, OBU_i can also implicitly authenticate other illegal users cannot get the symmetric key except CS_j.

(7) Anti-man-in-the-middle attack: it means that it is difficult for the attacker to replace the interactive information transmitted between the two parties of the key agreement, impersonate one party to communicate with the other party, resulting in the formation of different session keys between the two parties. Suppose an attacker intercepts $\{m_{OiCj}, S_{OiCj}\}$, selects $k'_{Oi} \in Z_q^*$, and calculates $K'_{Oi} = k'_{Oi}(U_{Oi} + h_{Oi}D_{Oi})$, because the attacker cannot get OBU_i's private key (u_{Oi}, d_{Oi}), it is difficult to generate a valid signature for $m'_{OiCj} = \{ID_{Oi}, m_{TOi}, R_{TOi}, K'_{Oi}, T\}$. After receiving a forged signature $\{m'_{OiCj}, S'_{OiCj}\}$, CS_j can detect a forged replacement attack by a middleman through the signature verification. Similarly, CS_j in this scheme signs for the message $m_{COi} = \{ID_{Cj}, LID_{Oi}, R_{COi}, T\}$ sent to OBU_i, at the same time, the shared key of both parties is used to encrypt the signature, which can effectively prevent the man-in-the-middle attack.

(8) Anti-impersonation attack: it is assumed that the attacker has mastered the long-term private key of one party (such as user B) in the key agreement, and it is difficult to impersonate the other party (such as A) to communicate with B. In the improved scheme, the attacker is assumed to have got the private key (u_{Oi}, d_{Oi}) of OBU_i, impersonate CS_j to execte authentication key agreement with OBU_i by performing the following steps: select random integer $r'_{COi} \in Z_q^*$, calculate $R'_{COi} = r'_{COi}(U_{Cj} + h_{Cj}D_{Cj})$, generate forged information $m'_{COi} = \{ID_{Cj}, LID_{Oi}, R'_{COi}, T\}$, because he cannot obtain the private key (u_{Cj}, d_{Cj}) of CS_j, the effective signature for m'_{COi} cannot be generated. Meanwhile, the attacker needs temporary key k_{Oi} used by OBU_i to calculate the symmetric key $SK'_{OiC} = H_1(k_{Oi}(u_{Oi} + h_{Oi}d_{Oi})R'_{COi})$. So after receiving forged information from the attacker, OBU_i can detect the impersonation attack of the attacker through the signature verification.

(9) No key control: it means that all participants in key agreement cannot independently calculate the symmetric key in advance. The symmetric key needs to be jointly determined by the parameters provided by all parties after data interaction. In this scheme, temporary keys k_{Oi} and r_{COi} are used, K_{Oi} and R_{COi} containing temporary keys are exchanged in the process of key agreement. The calculation of symmetric key is determined by the temporary keys used by both parties. Therefore, it is difficult for OBU_i or CS_j to generate the symmetric key separately in advance.

5 Comparison of Safety and Efficiency

The safety and efficiency of the improved scheme with the existing schemes will be compared in this section. For the convenience of comparison, SM stands for scalar multiplication operation on elliptic curve group, BP stands for bilinear pair operation, and PUF stands for physical unclonable function operation. The simulation results of the execution time of related operations [18] show that the execution time of SM, BP and PUF operations is 5.90 ms, 9.23 ms and 0.12 ms respectively. Since the time-consuming of hash function operation and point addition operation is far less than SM and BP, they are not included in the efficiency comparison. On the premise of not affecting the comparison effect, we only count the operation amount of authentication key agreement scheme between a single vehicle and another or between a vehicle and a server. Table 1 and Table 2 respectively show the security and efficiency comparison results between the proposed authentication key agreement protocol for VANET and similar schemes.

Table 1. Comparison of security between the proposed scheme and similar schemes

	Scheme in [1]	Scheme in [2]	Scheme in [16]	Scheme in [6]	Scheme in [17]	Our scheme
Anti-temporary key leakage	×	×	×	×	×	√
Known key security	√	√	√	√	√	√
Forward security	√	√	√	√	×	√
Resistance to simultaneous disclosure of the temporary key of one party and the complete private key of the other party	√	×	√	×	×	√
Implicit key authentication	√	√	√	√	√	√
Anti-impersonation attack	√	√	√	√	×	√
No key control	√	√	√	√	√	√
Anti-man-in-the-middle attack	√	√	√	√	√	√

Note: √ means the property is provided; × means not provided

Security comparison shows that compared with the similar authentication key agreement schemes for VANET, the proposed scheme can resist the temporary key leakage attack, impersonation attack, man-in-the-middle attack and other attacks, at the same time satisfy the forward security, known key security, no key control and other security features, which has obvious security advantages. The efficiency comparison shows that

Table 2. Comparison of efficiency between the proposed scheme and similar scheme

Scheme	Operation time of the initiator (OBUi)	Operation time of responder (server or OBUj)
Reference [1]	5SM = 29.5 ms	5SM = 29.5 ms
Reference [2]	2SM + 1PUF = 11.92 ms	2SM + 1PUF = 11.92 ms
Reference [16]	5SM + 2BP = 47.96 ms	4SM + 2BP = 42.06 ms
Reference [6]	5SM = 29.5 ms	5SM = 29.5 ms
Reference [17]	5SM = 29.5 ms	6SM = 35.4 ms
Our scheme	5SM = 29.5 ms	6SM = 35.4 ms

the efficiency of the proposed scheme is higher than that of the scheme using bilinear pair operation [16], and compared with the scheme without bilinear pair operation in [1, 6] and [17], the operation time is almost the same. Although the computation time of our scheme is higher than that of the lightweight authentication key agreement scheme in [2], the scheme in [2] cannot resist the temporary key leakage attack and has weak security.

6 Conclusion

The security of authentication key agreement protocol using certificateless aggregate signature for VANET proposed by Zhang et al. [17] is analyzed in this paper. Security analysis shows that the protocol is difficult to resist AII's forgery signature attack in the security model of certificateless cryptosystem, and also does not meet the anti-temporary key leakage attack, perfect forward security, anti-impersonation attack and other security features. Aiming at the above problems, an improved certificateless authentication key agreement protocol is proposed and its security is analyzed. The comparison of security and efficiency shows that this protocol is securer under the premise that the computation time is not significantly increased compared with similar schemes.

References

1. Li, X., Yang, D., Zeng, X., Zhu, X., Chen, B., Zhang, Y.: Cross-domain authentication and the key agreement protocol in VANETs. J. Xidian Univ. **48**(1), 141–148 (2021)
2. Hou, W., Sun, Y., Li, D., Cui, J., Guan, Z., Liu, J.: Anonymous authentication and key agreement protocol for 5G–V2V based on PUF. Journal of Computer Research and Development **58**(10), 2265–2277 (2021)
3. Chatterjee, U., Govindan, V., Sadhukhan, R., et al.: Building PUF based authentication and key exchange protocol for IoT without explicit CRPs in verifier database. IEEE Trans. Secure Comput. **16**(3), 424–437 (2018)
4. Wasef, A., Shen, X.: Map. IEEE Trans. Mob. Comput. (2013). IEEE Trans. Veh. AD Hoc Netw. IEEE Trans. Mob. Comput. **12**(1), 78–89 (2013)

5. Wang, S.B., Yao, N.M., Gong, N., Gao, Z.: A trigger- based pseudonym exchange scheme for location privacy preserving in VANETs. Peer-to-peer Netw. Appl. **11**(3), 548–560 (2018). https://doi.org/10.1007/s12083-017-0557-5

6. Wang, Z., Ma, Z.-F.,Luo, S.-S.: Identity- based efficient authentication and key agreement protocol for mobile internet. J. Commun. **38**(8), 19–27 (2017)

7. Chen, M.: Strongly secure anonymous implicit authentication and key agreement for roaming service. J. Comput. Res. Dev. **54**(12), 2772–2784 (2017)

8. Song, C., Zhang, M.-Y., Peng, W.-P.: Research on batch anonymous authentication scheme for VANET based on bilinear pairing. J. Commun. **38**(06), 49–57 (2017)

9. Ming, C.: Strongly secure and anonymous two-party authenticated key agreement for mobile roaming service. Acta Electron. Sin. **47**(1), 16–24 (2019)

10. Al-Riyami, S.S., Paterson, K.G.: Certificateless public key cryptography. In: Laih, C.-S. (ed.) ASIACRYPT 2003. LNCS, vol. 2894, pp. 452–473. Springer, Heidelberg (2003). https://doi.org/10.1007/978-3-540-40061-5_29

11. Yang, X., Ma, T., Chen, C., Wang, J., Wang, C.: Security analysis and improvement of certificateless aggregate signature scheme for vehicle ad hoc networks. J. Electron. Inf. Technol. **41**(5), 1265–1270 (2019)

12. Zhao, N., Zhang, G., Gu, X.: Certificateless aggregate signature scheme for privacy protection in VANET. Comput. Eng. **46**(1), 114–128 (2020)

13. Zeng, P., Guo, R., Ma, Y., Gao, Y., Zhao, G.: Provable security certificateless authentication scheme for vehicular ad hoc network. J. Electron. Inf. Technol. **42**(12), 2873–2881 (2020)

14. Liu, X., Wang, L., Huan, Li., Du, X., Niu, S.: Certificateless anonymous authentication scheme for internet of vehicles. J. Electron. Inf. Technol. X(0), 1–10 (2021)

15. Wuyi, W., Wenbo, Z.: Certificateless aggregated signature scheme for IoV. Appl. Res. Comput. **38**(7), 2158–2161 (2021)

16. Han, M., Hua, L., Ma, S.: A self-authentication and deniable efficient group key agreement protocol for VANET.KSII Trans. Internet Inf. Syst. **11**(7), 3678–3698 (2017)

17. Zhang, W., Lei, L., Wang, X., Wang, Y.: Secure and efficient authentication and key agreement protocol using certificateless aggregate signature for cloud service oriented VANET. Acta Electron. Sin. **48**(9), 1814–1822 (2020)

18. Gope, P.: PMAKE: privacy-aware multi-factor authenticated key establishment scheme for advance metering infrastructure in smart grid. Comput. Commun. **152**, 338–344 (2020)

An Efficient Federated Convolutional Neural Network Scheme with Differential Privacy

Dayin Zhang[1](✉), Xiaojun Chen[2](✉), and Jinqiao Shi[3](✉)

[1] School of Cyber Security, University of Chinese Academy of Sciences, Beijing, China
zhangdayin@iie.ac.cn
[2] Institute of Information Engineering, Chinese Academy of Sciences, Beijing, China
chenxiaojun@iie.ac.cn
[3] School of Cyberspace Security, Beijing University of Posts and Telecommunications, Beijing, China
shijinqiao@bupt.edu.cn

Abstract. Federated learning can complete the neural network model training without uploading users' private data. However, the deep leakage from gradients (DLG) and the compensatory reconstruction attack (CRA) can reconstruct the training data according to the gradients uploaded by users. We propose an efficient federated convolutional neural network scheme with differential privacy to solve this problem. By adding Gaussian noise to the fully connected layers of the convolutional neural network, the attacker cannot identify the critical gradients that cause privacy leakage. The cumulative privacy loss is tracked using the analytical moments accountant technique. We conduct extensive experiments on the MNIST and CIFAR10 datasets to evaluate our defense algorithm. After selecting appropriate parameters, the results show that our defense algorithm can defend against DLG and CRA while maintaining a high model accuracy.

Keywords: Federated learning · Differential privacy · Reconstruction attack

1 Introduction

With the accumulation of data and the improvement of hardware, artificial intelligence has become an expert in speech recognition, image recognition, and generation, assisting and even surpassing humans. The development of artificial intelligence requires a large amount of data as support. However, due to legal, security, and other reasons, it is not easy to integrate the data owned by multiple parties. Data is scattered in various institutions, which cannot be effectively

Supported by the Strategic Priority Research Program of Chinese Academy of Sciences, Grant No. XDC02040400.

utilized, resulting in the problem of data isolated islands. As a technology to solve the problem of data isolated islands, federated learning [1] has been widely concerned and applied in medical [2] and other fields. Federated learning can ensure that the data does not leave users to complete the neural network model training.

In contrast to classic centralized machine learning, users' private data does not leave the local devices during federated learning. However, recent studies have shown that due to the existence of the node of the central server, even if the user uploads only the gradients of the federated learning process, the honest but curious central server can still reconstruct the users' private training data according to the gradients [3–5].

To solve this problem, many researchers have proposed methods based on homomorphic encryption [6,7] or secure multi-party computing [8,9] to protect users' private training data. Still, these methods inevitably increase computational or communication consumption and reduce the efficiency of federated learning.

Differential privacy [10] is a method that can ensure that after a malicious adversary obtains a set of outputs, it is impossible to determine whether a specific record is in the data set. Because of the privacy issues faced by federated learning, we studied differential privacy-related technologies and proposed an efficient federated convolutional neural network scheme with differential privacy. We add Gaussian noise to the gradients of the fully connected layers, making it impossible for the server to reconstruct the user's private training data from the gradients. In the experimental part, we analyzed the defensive effect of the standard deviation of the Gaussian mechanism and the threshold of critical gradients on the attack model. Finally, it is proved that our algorithm can obtain a higher precision rate while protecting users' training data. Summarily, our contributions to this paper are as follows:

- We design a compensatory reconstruction attack, aiming at the pruning-based defense strategy. The reconstruction quality is greatly improved compared with the traditional reconstruction attack method.
- We propose a scheme for protecting users' private data during training using differential privacy in a federated convolutional neural network. Reconstruction attacks can be effectively defended by adding Gaussian noise to the critical gradients of the fully connected layers.
- We evaluate the effectiveness of defending against deep leakage from gradient attack (DLG) [4] and compensatory reconstruction attack (CRA) attacks on the MNIST and CIFAR10 datasets. The results show that our defense can provide meaningful privacy guarantees without compromising model accuracy.

This paper is structured as the following. Section 2 reviews background federated learning, differential privacy and reconstruction attack. Section 3 presents the design details of the compensatory reconstruction attack. We describe our proposed algorithm in Sect. 4. Experimental results for the proposed algorithm will be demonstrated in Sect. 5. In Sect. 6, we summarize the paper and discuss future work.

2   Background

2.1   Federated Learning

Federated learning has greatly succeeded in sentiment classification, intrusion detection, and other fields. It has become an indispensable technology and has attracted more and more researchers' attention [11–16]. In federated learning training, the central server maintains a global model. The user first downloads the global model from the central server, obtains the gradients after training with the local dataset and then transmits it back to the central server. The central server updates the global model by aggregating the gradients uploaded by the users and obtains the optimal model through multiple iterations of the above steps.

The central server has two ways of updating the global model, parameter averaging [13] and asynchronous stochastic gradient descent [14]. When the parameter averaging method is used, the update frequency must be carefully set. If it is too high, it will increase the cost of network communication and synchronization. If the frequency is too low, the difference between user parameters will increase with time and decrease model precision. The central server using asynchronous stochastic gradient descent, will update the parameters after receiving the users' gradients without waiting for other users' gradients.

[15] proposes a distributed selective stochastic gradient descent algorithm as the earliest implementation of federated learning. It distributes the task of training the neural network to a central server and multiple users. The user only uploads the gradients obtained by training the neural network on the local dataset. The central server maintains the global model and does not touch the users' local dataset. [16] uses the cyclical learning rate and the increased number of epochs for local model training to solve the problem of non-convex deep neural networks in federated learning and uses different types of data for verification.

Although federated learning makes it impossible for the central server to obtain users' private training data directly, researchers have found that if the central server is honest but curious, the user still faces the threat of reconstruction attacks. Since this paper studies architecture of the target model as a convolutional neural network, this paper focuses on the introduction of reconstruction attacks and proposes defense methods.

2.2   Reconstruction Attack

During the training process of federated learning, each user uses private data to train to get the gradients, and then upload them to the central server. As Fig. 1 presents, if the central server is honest but curious, it can reconstruct the private training data from the gradients of the user. During the attack, the central server

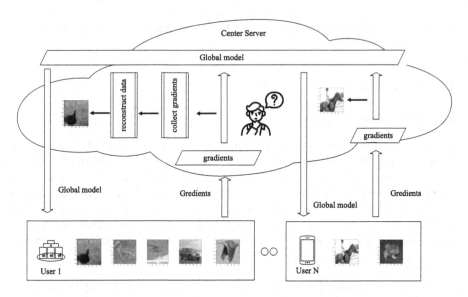

Fig. 1. Reconstruction attack

will not interfere with the federated learning algorithm. It usually collects user gradients to update the model and sends it to the user.

In the fully connected neural network training, the training data is used as input to connect to all the nodes of the first hidden layer. [6] proposes the training data as input to connect all nodes of the first hidden layer, and the similar input proportional to the original input can be obtained by dividing the partial derivative of the loss function of the neural network concerning weight by the partial derivative of the loss function concerning bias. Its use of homomorphic encryption will inevitably cause a severe burden on computing resources.

The attacker designed by [3] uses a generative adversarial network to reconstruct data similar to the training data of a particular class during the federated learning training process. However, this attack can only succeed if the same class's training data are similar.

The deep leakage from gradient attack (DLG) [4] randomly initializes dummy data and labels and inputs the dummy data into the model to obtain dummy gradients. The dummy data and labels are updated by minimizing the Euclidean distance between the dummy gradients and the real gradients, which makes the dummy data close to the private training data. Obtaining dummy data by minimizing the following objective:

$$x'^{*}, y'^{*} = \arg\min_{x',y'} \|\nabla W' - \nabla W\|^2 = \arg\min_{x',y'} \left\| \frac{\partial l(F(x';W),y')}{\partial W} - \nabla W \right\|^2 \quad (1)$$

where x' and y' are dummy inputs and labels, $F(x,W)$ is the target model, l is the loss function, and ∇W is the model gradients.

When the target model is trained with cross-entropy loss over one-hot labels in classification scenarios, the improved deep leakage from gradients attack (iDLG) [5] can certainly extract the ground-truth label from user-uploaded gradients. x is the input data, c is the corresponding ground-truth label, $y = \{y_1, y_2, \ldots\}$ is the model output, and the gradients of the loss function l for each output is:

$$g_i = \frac{\partial l(F(x; W), c)}{\partial y_i} = -\frac{\partial \log e^{y_c} - \partial \log \sum_j e^{y_j}}{\partial y_i} = \begin{cases} -1 + \dfrac{e^{y_i}}{\sum_j e^{y_j}}, & if\ i = c \\ \dfrac{e^{y_i}}{\sum_j e^{y_j}}, & else \end{cases}$$

(2)

From the partial derivative of the loss function to the output layer, it can be concluded that the gradients corresponding to the index of the ground-truth label are negative. The same applies to the fully connected layer before the output layer, and we can determine the ground-truth label by the symbol of the fully connected layer.

Aiming at the problem that federated learning faces reconstruction attacks, current researchers have proposed defense methods based on homomorphic encryption [6,7] or secure multi-party computing [8,9] and differential privacy [17,18]. Although secure multi-party computation and homomorphic encryption can achieve a high level of privacy and accuracy, the cost is high computing and communication overhead for users. It is not easy to effectively support complex scenarios such as federated learning. We study the application of differential privacy in federated learning and propose a defense method based on differential privacy.

2.3 Differential Privacy

Differential privacy is an evaluation framework proposed by [19] to evaluate the privacy guarantee provided by the protection mechanism. Introducing randomness into a learning algorithm makes it intuitively tricky for researchers to tell whether a model's behaviour comes from randomness or the training data. The related concepts are as follows:

ϵ - **Differential Privacy(ϵ - DP).** If a randomized mechanism $M : \mathcal{D} \to \mathcal{R}$ satisfies ϵ - Differential Privacy, for two adjacent dataset $D, D' \in \mathcal{D}$ and a set of output $S \in \mathcal{R}$

$$Pr\left[M(D) \in S\right] \le e^{\epsilon} Pr\left[M(D') \in S\right]$$

(3)

Parameter ϵ limits the change of output distribution caused by the random algorithm M according to the difference of adjacent datasets.

(ϵ, δ) - **Differential Privacy((ϵ, δ) - DP).** For two adjacent dataset $D, D' \in \mathcal{D}$ and a set of output $S \in \mathcal{R}$, a randomized mechanism M: $\mathcal{D} \to \mathcal{R}$ satisfies (ϵ, δ) - Differential Privacy

$$Pr\left[M(D) \in S\right] \le e^{\epsilon} Pr\left[M(D') \in S\right] + \delta$$

(4)

$(\epsilon, \delta) - DP$ indicates that the ratio of the output probabilities of the randomized mechanism in adjacent datasets D and D' is greater than ϵ is at most δ. Compared with $\epsilon - DP$, $(\epsilon, \delta) - DP$ has more flexibility when choosing a privacy protection mechanism.

Cumulative Privacy Loss. Cumulative privacy loss is the degree of privacy leakage when outputting data that meets differential privacy. $(\epsilon, \delta) - DP$ gives a strict mathematical expression. When multiple differential privacy mechanisms are used simultaneously, the cumulative privacy loss indicates the degree of final privacy leakage.

Gaussian Mechanism. Let $0 < \epsilon < 1$, $\sigma > \sqrt{(2 \ln 1.25)/\delta}$, the Gaussian Mechanism with parameter $\sigma > \Delta_2 f / \epsilon$ is (ϵ, δ) - Differential Privacy

$$G_\sigma f(x) = f(x) + \mathcal{N}(0, \sigma^2) \tag{5}$$

where $\mathcal{N}$ is the Guassian distribution, query function f's l_2 - sensitivity is defined as

$$\Delta_2 f = \max_{\|D-D'\|_2 = 1} \left\| f(D) - f(D') \right\|_2 \tag{6}$$

The Gaussian mechanism cannot satisfy $\epsilon - DP$ but can obtain a smaller privacy budget than the Laplace mechanism [19] using the advanced composition theorem. Many researchers have applied the Gaussian mechanism to the training process of neural networks.

$(\alpha, \epsilon)-$**Rényi Differential Privacy((α, ϵ)-RDP).** [20] proposes the concept of (α, ϵ) - RDP to represent the privacy guarantees of various differential privacy algorithms. Where α is the order of the Rényi divergence in the (α, ϵ) - RDP. If a randomized mechanism M: $\mathcal{D} \to \mathcal{R}$ satisfies (α, ϵ) - RDP, for two adjacent dataset $D, D' \in \mathcal{D}$

$$D_\alpha((M(D)\|M(D'))) = \frac{1}{\alpha - 1} log\mathbb{E}_{o \sim M(D')} \\ \left(\frac{M(D, o)}{M(D', o)}\right)^\alpha \leq \epsilon_M(\alpha) \tag{7}$$

[15] applies differential privacy to federated learning for the first time, but using the Laplacian mechanism will cause a large cumulative privacy loss. [17] first proposes to train differentially private generative models in federated generative networks. The private training data is distributed across multiple user devices. In each iteration, the server provides the generator and discriminator models to a subset of devices. Each user computes the discriminator gradients with its local private data and sends it to the parameter server. Cumulative privacy loss is tracked during this process using analytical moment accumulation techniques [21]. Aiming at the common imbalanced data scenarios in real life, [18]

proposes a differentially private convolutional neural network with adaptive gradient descent (DPAGD-CNN) method. It adaptively adds noise (implementing differential privacy) according to the direction of gradient descent for each user for better model performance. By combining differential privacy technology and secure multi-party computing in federated learning, [9] reduces the training time by 68% on average while keeping the model performance unchanged.

3 Compensatory Reconstruction Attack

Although current reconstruction attacks can reconstruct training data through gradients, they all use clean gradients without protection. [22] proposes that privacy leakage is essentially caused by the data representations embedded in the model updates, and the Soteria algorithm seriously degrades the reconstructed quality of the DLG [4] by pruning the data representation embedded in the gradients of the fully connected layer while ensuring the performance of federated learning. Based on the above defense methods, we believe that gradients equal to zero may be the result of user pruning, so we design an attack model called compensatory reconstruction attack (CRA) to increase the quality of reconstructed data by replacing these abnormal gradients with adjacent normal gradients.

Algorithm 1. Compensatory Reconstruction Attack (CRA)

Input: global model $F(x; W)$, global model weights W, gradients calculated by private training data ∇W, number of iterations T, learning rate η, number of adjacent gradients n.

Output: (x', y')

1: $x' \leftarrow \mathcal{N}(0, 1)$
2: $y' \leftarrow i \ s.t. \ \nabla W_L^{i}{}^T \cdot \nabla W_L^j \leq 0, \ \forall j \neq i$
3: // compensate gradients
4: **for** $i, j \leftarrow 1 \ to \ len(\nabla W)$ **do**
5:    **if** $\nabla W_{i,j} = 0$ **then**
6:       $W_{i,j} = \dfrac{W_{i,j-n/2} + \ldots + W_{i,j+n/2}}{n}$
7:    **end if**
8: **end for**
9: // reconstruct data
10: **for** $i \leftarrow 1 \ to \ T$ **do**
11:    $\nabla W' \leftarrow \dfrac{\partial l(F(x'; W), c')}{\partial W}$
12:    $L_i = \|\nabla W' - \nabla W\|_F^2$
13:    $x' \leftarrow x' - \eta \nabla_{x'} L_i$
14: **end for**

As illustrated in Algorithm 1, the compensatory reconstruction attack procedure starts with the global model $F(x; W)$ with the weights W, and the gradients calculated by private training data ∇W. The first step is to randomly initialize the dummy data $x' \leftarrow \mathcal{N}(0, 1)$, and then obtain the ground-truth labels according to the symbolic information of the gradients of the fully connected layer. The second step is traversing the fully connected layer's gradients and replacing the abnormal gradient with the adjacent gradient. Among them, i represents the number of layers of the neural network, and j represents the number of bits of the gradient vector of a particular neural network layer. To avoid the situation that the abnormal gradients have appeared in a continuous and sequential manner, we replace anomalous gradients with the average of n adjacent gradients. The third step minimizes the distance between the dummy gradients and the real gradients, and finally obtains dummy data similar to the private training data. Figure 2 shows the reconstruction of DLG and CRA when the Soteria algorithm is used in the federated convolutional neural network learning process. Although the Soteria algorithm can defend against DLG, when the server uses CRA, it cannot effectively protect the users' private training data.

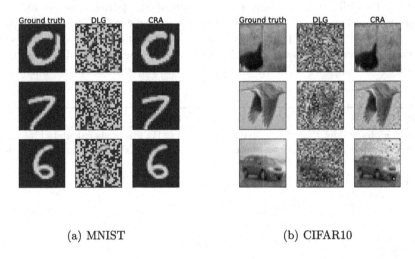

(a) MNIST   (b) CIFAR10

Fig. 2. Reconstruction of two attack models

4   Federated Convolutional Neural Network Scheme with Differential Privacy

Aiming at the problem of privacy leakage in the gradients uploaded by the user during the federated learning training process, we designed an efficient federated convolutional neural network scheme with differential privacy which is illustrated in Fig. 3. The framework of our scheme contains a server and multiple users. Similar to previous federated learning frameworks, during the federated convolutional neural network training, the central server is mainly responsible for maintaining the global model and communicating with users. The central server first sets the network structure of the target model, which is a federated convolutional neural network in this paper. After receiving the users' gradients, The central server performs an update operation on the global model and then sends the updated global model to other users. The server updates the global model using the federated averaging algorithm. Compared with the asynchronous stochastic gradient descent algorithm, the federated averaging algorithm avoids the apparent deviation of the global model due to different client capabilities.

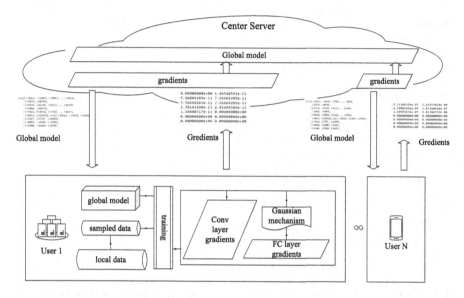

Fig. 3. Federated convolutional neural network scheme with differential privacy

Unlike previous federated learning frameworks, regardless of whether the server is honest or malicious after the user downloads the model for training, the gradients are processed and sent back to the server to prevent the server from reconstructing private data through the gradients. There are two ways for users to process gradients, the first is to add Gaussian noise to all the gradients of the fully connected layer (FC-DPSGD, Fully-Connected Layer - Differential Privacy Stochastic Gradient Descent), and the second is to add Gaussian noise to the critical gradients of the fully connected layer (CG-DPSGD, Critical Gradients - Differential Privacy Stochastic Gradient Descent).

4.1 Fully Connected Layer - Differential Privacy Stochastic Gradient Descent Algorithm

During the federated convolutional neural network training, users only upload the gradients calculated through private data. As shown in Algorithm 2, it mainly includes the steps of downloading the global model, random sample, adding noise, and calculating the cumulative privacy loss. We add Gaussian noise to the fully connected layer, making it impossible for an attacker to obtain accurate gradients.

Algorithm 2. Fully Connected Layer - Differential Privacy Stochastic Gradient Descent Algorithm (FC-DPSGD)

Input: private training dataset $\{x_1, ...x_N\}$, global model W, clip threshold C, privacy budget ϵ, sampling rate q, serial number of user I, noise scale σ, tail bound δ

Output: $g_I(x)$ and compute cumulative privacy loss ϵ_I using analytical moments accountant technique.

1: **for** $\epsilon_I \leq \epsilon$ **do**
2:     // Download global model
3:     $W_I = W$
4:     // Random sample
5:     $\mathbb{B} = q \times N$
6:     // Compute gradients
7:     For each $i \in \mathbb{B}$, compute $g_I(x_i) = \nabla loss(W_I, x_i)$
8:     // Gaussian mechanism
9:     $g_I^{FC}(x_i) = g_I^{FC}(x_i)/max(1, \dfrac{\left\|g_I^{FC}(x_i)\right\|_2}{C})$ for $i \in \mathbb{B}$
10:    $g_I^{FC} = \dfrac{1}{\mathbb{B}}\sum_{i \in \mathbb{B}} g_I^{FC}(x_i) + \mathcal{N}(0, \sigma^2)$
11: **end for**

Initialization. After the user receives the training instruction from the server, it first downloads the global model from the central server. It sets the standard deviation of Gaussian noise, privacy budget, sampling rate, and other parameters. The privacy budget is used to limit the extent of privacy leakage.

Random Sample. Users randomly select part of the data in their local dataset for training, preventing the model from overfitting and reducing the exposure of the local dataset. Then use the randomly sampled private data for training to obtain the corresponding gradients.

Gaussian Mechanism. The Gaussian mechanism can obtain a stricter cumulative privacy loss bound than the Laplacian mechanism. The Gaussian mechanism mainly includes clipping the gradients and adding noise. The threshold C needs to be used to clip the gradients to limit the influence of each set of training samples on the gradients. When the $L2$ norm of the original gradient is greater than C, it will be reduced to norm C. Make the gradients uploaded to the server meet the differential privacy guarantee. Unlike DPSGD [23] which adds Gaussian noise to all layers of the neural network, we propose a defense algorithm called FC-DPSGD (Fully Connected Layer - Differential Privacy Stochastic Gradient

Descent) against reconstruction attacks in the federated convolutional neural network. We only add Gaussian noise to the gradient of the fully connected layer to minimize the impact on the neural network model to ensure the model's accuracy.

Privacy Accounting. When the user's cumulative privacy loss ϵ_I is less than the privacy budget ϵ, it can continue to perform local training. When ϵ_I is greater than ϵ, there is a possibility of privacy leakage of user data, and training needs to be stopped immediately. We use analytical moment accounting technology [21] in the federated learning algorithm to calculate the cumulative privacy loss by giving the standard deviation of Gaussian noise σ, moments λ, tail bound δ, and sampling rate q.

$$\epsilon = \min_{\lambda} \frac{log(1/\delta) + \alpha_M(\lambda)}{\lambda} \tag{8}$$

The final cumulative privacy loss is related to the moment generating function $\alpha_M(\lambda)$. $\alpha_M(\lambda)$ is obtained by adding the moment generating functions of the privacy loss of each layer. Adding Gaussian noise to the gradients of the fully connected layers results in a more stringent cumulative privacy loss than adding Gaussian noise to the gradients of all layers.

4.2   Critical Gradients - Differential Privacy Stochastic Gradient Descent Algorithm

Since the FC-DPSGD algorithm needs to add Gaussian noise to all the gradients of the fully connected layer, we further study the algorithm to reduce the influence on the gradients of the neural network.

[22] proposes that the privacy leakage in federated learning mainly comes from the data representations in the fully connected layer. In order to prevent data representations in the model updates from leaking the user's training data, the core is to prune the critical gradients within a certain threshold. The objective function is defined as the reconstruction data and the training data being as different as possible under the premise that the perturbed data representation and the training data representation are as similar as possible, which can be expressed as follows:

$$r' = \arg\max_{r'} \|X - X'\|_2, \; s.t. \; \|X - X'\| \le \epsilon \tag{9}$$

However, the operation of pruning critical gradients is easily identified by attackers. Based on Soteria, we propose an algorithm called CG-DPSGD that adds Gaussian noise only on critical gradients. As shown in Algorithm 3, similar to the FC-DPSGD algorithm, the CG-DPSGD algorithm also includes steps such as downloading the global model, random sample, adding noise, and calculating the cumulative privacy loss. Unlike FL-DPSGD, which adds Gaussian noise to all gradients of the fully connected layer, we only add Gaussian noise to the critical gradients that cause privacy leakage, which can improve the model's accuracy while protecting user privacy.

Algorithm 3. Critical Gradients - Differential Privacy Stochastic Gradient Descent Algorithm (CG-DPSGD)

Input: private training dataset $\{x_1, ...x_N\}$, Feature extractor before FC layer $f : x_i \rightarrow r_i$, data representation $r_i \in \mathbb{R}^n$, perturbation rate p, the number of neurons in the FC layer n, global model W, clip threshold C, privacy budget ϵ, sampling rate q, serial number of user I, threshold of critical gradients τ, noise scale σ, tail bound δ

Output: g_I and compute cumulative privacy loss ϵ_I using analytical moments accountant technique.

1: **for** $\epsilon_I \leq \epsilon$ **do**
2:    // Download global model
3:    $W_I = W$
4:    //Random sample
5:    $\mathbb{B} = q \times N$
6:    // Compute gradients
7:    For each $i \in \mathbb{B}$, compute $g_I(x_i) = \nabla loss(W_I, x_i)$
8:    // Get critical gradients
9:    $\mathbb{S} \leftarrow \max_{\tau} \{\|r_i(\nabla_{x_i} f(r_j))^{-1}\|_2\}_{j=1}^n$
10:   // Gaussian mechanism
11:   $g_I^{FC_j}(x_i) = g_I^{FC_j}(x_i)/max(1, \dfrac{\left\|g_I^{FC_j}(x_i)\right\|_2}{C})$ for $i \in \mathbb{B}, j \in \mathbb{S}$
12:   $g_I^{FC_j} = \dfrac{1}{\mathbb{B}} \sum_{i \in \mathbb{B}} g_I^{FC_j}(x_i) + \mathcal{N}(0, \sigma^2)$ for $j \in \mathbb{S}$
13: **end for**

---

5   Experiments

5.1   Experiment Setup

We implemented our algorithm using PyTorch. We trained all the models on a server machine, and one central server and 100 users are simulated according to different port numbers.

Datasets. We evaluate our defense algorithm in the context of federated convolutional neural networks using the MNIST [24] and CIFAR10 [25] datasets. The MNIST dataset contains 60k training samples and 10k test samples, each with a size of 28*28. The CIFAR10 dataset contains 50k training samples and 10k test samples, each with a size of 32*32. Regardless of whether the user data is IID (Independent Identically Distribution) or non-IID, the attacks described in this paper will cause privacy leakage of user data. We construct the non-IID dataset following the configuration in [26]. There are a total of 100 users; each has two classes of data, and each class has 20 samples. Ten users are randomly sampled to update the model during training.

Target Model. Our target model adopts the network architecture used in Soteria, which consists of a convolutional neural network with four convolutional layers and one fully connected layer.

Attack Model. We evaluate defense effectiveness using two attack methods. (1) The deep leakage from gradient attack (DLG) [4] updates the dummy data by minimizing the Euclidean distance between the dummy and real gradients. (2) The compensatory reconstruction attack (CRA) adds a step of replacing abnormal gradients after collecting the users' gradients.

Defense Model. (1) BASELINE does not protect the gradient, and the user uploads the gradient directly after training. (2) Soteria algorithm [22] protects the gradient through the pruning method, and the user finds the critical gradients and prunes them before uploading the gradient. (3) Differentially private stochastic gradient descent (DPSGD) algorithm [27] protects the gradient through the differential privacy method. It adds Gaussian noise to each layer of the neural network before the user uploads the gradient. (4) Differentially private convolutional neural network with adaptive gradient descent (DPAGD-CNN) [18] adaptively adds noise according to the direction of gradient descent for each user.

Hyperparameter Configurations. Our target model optimizes model parameters using asynchronous stochastic gradient descent with a learning rate of 0.01. The attack model uses the L-BFGS optimizer. The defense uses a Gaussian mechanism with a mean of 0 and a standard deviation of less than 2.

Evaluation Metric. (1) accuracy: We use the accuracy of the global model on the test set to measure the utility of the federated learning model, with higher accuracy indicating the better performance of the model. (2) cumulative privacy loss: The cumulative privacy loss is used to control the strength of the differential privacy mechanism for privacy protection. We use the analytical moment accumulation technique to track the cumulative privacy loss of federated learning. A minor cumulative privacy loss means less privacy leakage. (3) MSE: When the mean-square error (MSE) between the reconstructed data and the private training data is larger than the boundary that the human eye can recognize, the generated data is blurry and cannot show what the private training data express. We use MSE to measure the quality of reconstructed data, and a smaller MSE indicates user privacy leakage.

5.2   Experiment Result

Reconstruction Effects. We demonstrate the effectiveness of the compensatory reconstruction attack through quantitative and qualitative results. As

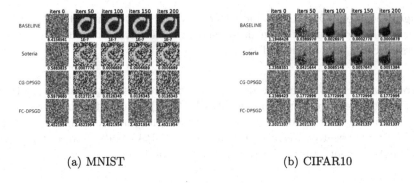

(a) MNIST   (b) CIFAR10

Fig. 4. Reconstruction of CRA on different defense models.

shown in Fig. 4(b), when training with the CIFAR10 dataset, since the BASE-LINE model does not protect the gradients, the attacker has an MSE of 0.0026 for the reconstructed and private training data after 100 iterations, and the reconstructed data is very similar to the private training data. After 200 itera-tions, the MSE of the reconstructed and private training data is 0.00008, and the user's private training data has been thoroughly leaked. When using the Soteria algorithm, after 100 iterations by the attacker, the MSE of the reconstructed data and the private training data is 0.00513, and the human eye can already recognize the reconstructed data. When using the CG-DPSGD algorithm, after 200 iterations by the attacker, the MSE of the reconstructed data and the pri-vate training data is 0.1772 and cannot be further reduced. At this time, the reconstructed data cannot be recognized by the human eye. The FL-DPSGD algorithm has a lower quality of reconstructed data due to its greater influence on the gradients. Figure 4(a) shows similar results when training with the MNIST dataset.

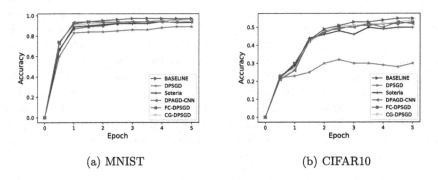

(a) MNIST   (b) CIFAR10

Fig. 5. The accuracy of defense algorithms

Model Accuracy. We compare our defense with four existing methods in terms of model accuracy. As depicted in Fig. 5(a), after five epochs, the BASELINE model achieves 97% accuracy on MNIST. Although the Soteria algorithm does not sacrifice accuracy, it cannot defend against CRA at its default setting of 1% critical gradients. The effect on the gradients is increased by increasing the threshold of critical gradients, reducing the model's accuracy by 3%. The DPAGD-CNN algorithm adaptively adds noise according to each user's direction of gradient descent and finally achieves 94% accuracy. The FL-DPSGD algorithm that adds Gaussian noise to all gradients of the fully connected layer has a larger impact on the gradients, and its accuracy is similar to Soteria. The CG-DPSGD algorithm has the least impact on the gradients, and its accuracy is close to the BASELINE model. The DPSGD algorithm needs to add Gaussian noise to all layers of the neural network, which significantly impacts the gradients and severely reduces the model's accuracy. Figure 5(b) shows similar results when training with the CIFAR10 dataset. Since the target model structure of this paper is different from that of DPAGD-CNN [18], the accuracy rate is slightly different.

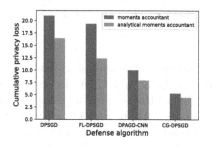
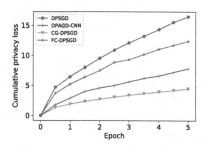

(a) Cumulative Privacy Loss   (b) Analytical Moments Accountant

Fig. 6. Cumulative privacy loss of defense algorithms

Cumulative Privacy Loss. By tracking the privacy properties of the three defense algorithms using moments accountant [27] and analytical moments accountant [21], we find that analytical moments accountant leads to a more accurate cumulative privacy loss in Fig. 6(a). The parameters of the convolutional neural network are mainly concentrated in the FC layer. FL-DPSGD and CG-DPSGD can be understood as adding noise that affects the reconstruction attack in the FC layer and then adding noise that has less effect on the gradient in other layers. As Fig. 6(b) shows, Compared with other algorithms, the CG-DPSGD algorithm only adds Gaussian noise on the critical gradient, which has less influence on the gradient. While ensuring accuracy, the standard deviation of the noise at the FC layer of the CG-DPSGD algorithm can be more significant, resulting in a minor cumulative privacy loss. The DPSGD algorithm adds

Gaussian noise with the same standard deviation to all neural network layers, and the final cumulative privacy loss is the largest. While the cumulative privacy loss can quantify the extent of privacy leakage, it is equally important to consider the attacker's ability to reconstruct the training data.

Table 1. Influence of threshold of critical gradients and standard deviation of Gaussian noise on MSE.

		MNIST		CIFAR10	
		DLG	CRA	DLG	CRA
BASELINE		9.18E–05	9.18E–05	8.78E–05	8.78E–05
Soteria	$\tau = 1$	2.60E–03	5.73E–08	7.70E–03	2.90E–03
	$\tau = 5$	2.91E–01	6.00E–04	5.38E–01	5.20E–03
	$\tau = 10$	3.99E–01	1.26E–02	8.35E–01	1.10E–01
FC-DPSGD	$\sigma = 1$	2.21E+00	1.90E+00	1.47E+00	1.25E+00
CG-DPSGD	$\tau = 1, \sigma = 1$	4.00E–04	7.80E–03	1.88E–02	1.02E–02
	$\tau = 5, \sigma = 1$	9.10E–03	4.30E–03	5.52E–02	3.54E–02
	$\tau = 5, \sigma = 2$	2.83E–02	1.29E–02	4.02E–01	5.92E–02

Table 1 shows the effect of the threshold of critical gradients and standard deviation of Gaussian noise defending against DLG and CRA. Because the BASELINE model has no protection, the MSE of the reconstructed data and the private training data is smaller. The reconstructed data is very similar to the private training data, even the pixel-level restoration. When the critical gradients threshold of the Soteria algorithm is set to 1%, it can resist DLG attack but cannot defend against CRA. Increasing the threshold of critical gradients can interfere with more gradients, making it more difficult for an attacker to reconstruct the data. When the threshold of the critical gradients is 10%, the Soteria algorithm can resist CRA, reducing the model's accuracy. Instead of pruning the critical gradients, our algorithm adds Gaussian noise to the critical gradients. When $\sigma = 2$, neither the DLG attack nor the CRA can recover the training data effectively. After adding Gaussian noise with $\sigma = 1$ to all gradients of the fully connected layer, although DLG attacks and CRA can be defended against, the cumulative privacy loss of the model is larger now.

6   Conclusions and Future Work

This paper first proposes a compensatory reconstruction attack (CRA) on a federated convolutional neural network. The honest but curious central server increases the success rate of reconstruction attacks by replacing abnormal gradients after collecting gradients uploaded by users. Compared with the deep leakage from gradient attack (DLG) [4], CRA can successfully attack the Soteria algorithm [22]. To defend against CRA, we propose an efficient federated convolutional neural network scheme with differential privacy. By adding Gaussian noise to the fully connected layers of the convolutional neural network, the attacker cannot effectively identify the critical gradients, resulting in severe degradation of the quality of the reconstructed data. We conduct extensive experiments on the MNIST and CIFAR10 datasets. The results show that our defense algorithm can provide stronger privacy guarantees with less impact on accuracy, achieving a trade-off between model accuracy and privacy.

In a convolutional neural network, the attribute features of the training data are mainly contained in the convolutional layers. We next investigate the critical gradients in convolutional layers that cause attribute leakage of training data and propose a federated learning framework to defend against attribute inference attacks.

References

1. McMahan, H.B., Moore, E., Ramage, D., Hampson, S., et al.: Communication-efficient learning of deep networks from decentralized data. arXiv preprint arXiv:1602.05629 (2016)
2. Degan, E., et al.: Application of federated learning in medical imaging. In: Ludwig, H., Baracaldo, N. (eds.) Federated Learning, pp. 483–497. Springer, Cham (2022). https://doi.org/10.1007/978-3-030-96896-0_22
3. Hitaj, B., Ateniese, G., Perez-Cruz, F.: Deep models under the GAN: information leakage from collaborative deep learning. In: 24th Proceedings of the Conference on Computer and Communications Security, pp. 603–618. ACM, New York (2017)
4. Zhu, L., Han, S.: Deep leakage from gradients. In: Yang, Q., Fan, L., Yu, H. (eds.) Federated Learning. LNCS (LNAI), vol. 12500, pp. 17–31. Springer, Cham (2020). https://doi.org/10.1007/978-3-030-63076-8_2
5. Zhao, B., Konda, R.M., Hakan, B.: iDLG: improved deep leakage from gradients. arXiv preprint arXiv:2001.02610 (2020)
6. Aono, Y., Hayashi, T., Wang, L., et al.: Privacy-preserving deep learning via additively homomorphic encryption. IEEE Trans. Inf. Forensics Secur. **13**(5), 1333–1345 (2017)
7. Zhang, Q., Jing, S., Zhao, C., Zhang, B., Chen, Z.: Efficient federated learning framework based on multi-key homomorphic encryption. In: Barolli, L. (ed.) 3PGCIC 2021. LNNS, vol. 343, pp. 88–105. Springer, Cham (2022). https://doi.org/10.1007/978-3-030-89899-1_10
8. Bonawitz, K., Ivanov, V., Kreuter, B., et al.: Practical secure aggregation for privacy-preserving machine learning. In: 16th Proceedings of the Conference on Computer and Communications Security, pp. 1175–1191. ACM SIGSAC, Dallas (2017)
9. Xu, R., Baracaldo, N., Zhou, Y., Anwar, A., Ludwig, H.: HybridAlpha: an efficient approach for privacy-preserving federated learning. In: 12th Proceedings of ACM Workshop on Artificial Intelligence and Security, pp. 13–23. ACM (2019)
10. Dwork, C., McSherry, F., Nissim, K., Smith, A.: Calibrating noise to sensitivity in private data analysis. In: Halevi, S., Rabin, T. (eds.) TCC 2006. LNCS, vol. 3876, pp. 265–284. Springer, Heidelberg (2006). https://doi.org/10.1007/11681878_14

11. Zhang, D., Chen, X., Wang, D., et al.: A survey on collaborative deep learning and privacy-preserving. In: 3th International Conference on Data Science in Cyberspace, pp. 652–658. IEEE, Guangzhou (2018)

12. Long, G., Shen, T., Tan, Y., Gerrard, L., Clarke, A., Jiang, J.: Federated learning for privacy-preserving open innovation future on digital health. In: Chen, F., Zhou, J. (eds.) Humanity Driven AI, pp. 113–133. Springer, Cham (2022). https://doi.org/10.1007/978-3-030-72188-6_6

13. McMahan, H.B., Moore, E., Ramage, D., et al.: Federated learning of deep networks using model averaging. arXiv preprint arXiv:1602.05629 (2016)

14. Zhang, S., Zhang, C., You, Z., et al: Asynchronous stochastic gradient descent for DNN training. In: International Conference on Acoustics, Speech and Signal Processing, pp. 6660–6663. IEEE, Florence (2013)

15. Shokri, R., Shmatikov, V.: Privacy-preserving deep learning. In: 22nd Conference on Computer and Communications Security, pp. 1310–1321. ACM SIGSAC, New York (2015)

16. Mi, H., et al.: Collaborative deep learning across multiple data centers. Sci. China Inf. Sci. **63**(8), 182102 (2020). https://doi.org/10.1007/s11432-019-2705-2

17. Augenstein, S., et al.: Generative models for effective ml on private, decentralized datasets. arXiv preprint arXiv:1911.06679 (2019)

18. Huang, X., Ding, Y., Jiang, Z.L., Qi, S., Wang, X., Liao, Q.: DP-FL: a novel differentially private federated learning framework for the unbalanced data. World Wide Web **23**(4), 2529–2545 (2020). https://doi.org/10.1007/s11280-020-00780-4

19. Dwork, C., Kenthapadi, K., McSherry, F., Mironov, I., Naor, M.: Our data, ourselves: privacy via distributed noise generation. In: Vaudenay, S. (ed.) EUROCRYPT 2006. LNCS, vol. 4004, pp. 486–503. Springer, Heidelberg (2006). https://doi.org/10.1007/11761679_29

20. Mironov, I.: Rényi differential privacy. In: 30th Computer Security Foundations Symposium, pp. 263–275. IEEE, Santa Barbara (2017)

21. Wang, Y.X., Balle, B., Kasiviswanathan, S.-P.: Subsampled Rényi differential privacy and analytical moments accountant. In: 22nd International Conference on Artificial Intelligence and Statistics, pp. 1226–1235. PMLR, Naha (2019)

22. Sun, J., Li, A., Wang, B., et al.: Soteria: provable defense against privacy leakage in federated learning from representation perspective. In: Proceedings of the Conference on Computer Vision and Pattern Recognition, pp. 9311–9319. IEEE, virtual (2021)

23. Brendan, M.H., Ramage, D., Talwar, K., Zhang, L.: Learning differentially private recurrent language models. In: 6nd International Conference on Learning Representations, Vancouver (2018)

24. Lecun, Y., Bottou, L.: Gradient-based learning applied to document recognition. Proc. IEEE **86**(11), 2278–2324 (1998)

25. Krizhevsky, A., Hinton, G.: Learning multiple layers of features from tiny images. Technical report, Citeseer (2009)

26. Li, A., Sun, J., Wang, B., et al.: LotteryFL: personalized and communication-efficient federated learning with lottery ticket hypothesis on non-IID datasets. arXiv preprint arXiv:2008.03371 (2020)

27. Abadi, M., et al.: Deep learning with differential privacy. In: Proceedings of the Conference on Computer and Communications Security, pp. 308–318. ACM SIGSAC, Vienna (2016)

D2CDIM:DID-Based Decentralized Cross-Domain Identity Management with Privacy-Preservation and Sybil-Resistance

Yi Xiong[ID], Shixiong Yao[⊠][ID], and Pei Li[ID]

Central China Normal University, Wuhan, China
yaosx@ccnu.edu.cn

Abstract. Most of the current decentralized cross-domain identity management frameworks are based on blockchain. In these schemes, the identity providers (IDPs) in different trust domains connect through blockchain technology. However, a single IDP in the domain is still at the risk of being compromised or corrupted. What's more, users may create redundant identities for different services but can not dominate all their identities completely. Therefore, we propose a cross-domain identity management system based on the concept of the Decentralized Identifier standard. It provides full ownership and management of identity for users. In order to reduce the burden of private key management caused by redundant identities, we present a deduplication scheme to limit the number of one user's DIDs. It can also resist the Sybil attack by real-life identity credential. Besides that, we improve the authentication efficiency by dynamic accumulator and preserve the identity privacy by the anonymous credential and zero knowledge in the cross-domain authentication scheme.

Keywords: Cross-domain · Decentralized identifier · Privacy protection · Sybil-resistance

1 Introduction

With the rapid development of information technologies such as the 5th-Generation (5G), the network cloud and the Internet of Things (IoT), more and more devices and entities will join the network and then digital identities proliferate in the future. In the existing identity management models described in [1], the Self-Sovereign Identity management model (SSI) receives great attention.

In many earlier information systems, users' identities are useful in a trust domain. While in recent years, with the development of big data, blockchain technology and so on, data sharing and cooperation among different domains prompt the development of cross-domain identity management technology.

Current cross-domain identity management frameworks mainly fall into two types, centralized and decentralized frameworks. In the former schemes, such as [2], the trust among IDPs in different domains is established through the Trusted

J. Chen et al. (Eds.): EISA 2022, CCIS 1641, pp. 191–208, 2022.
https://doi.org/10.1007/978-3-031-23098-1_12

Third-Party server (TTP). Thus, the centralized server is aware of all users' identity information in each domain. If it suffers from collapsing or single points of failure, the whole system will be down. The latter schemes mostly based on blockchain are primarily designed to solve the problems caused by centralization. Therefore, a single IDP's failure or corruption only affects identity authentication in the local domain. However, most schemes ignore the right to control users' identity information. What's more, in order to obtain application service, a user will generate redundant identities, but the consequent privacy information lacks safety management or privacy-preserving. Aimed at these issues, we propose a new fully decentralized cross-domain identity management framework based on the decentralized identifier (DID). But challenging objectives remain in DID-based cross-domain identity management systems:

Privacy Disclosure. In the cross-domain identity management, private information leak is a non-negligible issue. In this paper, privacy preservation is taken into account in each process of identity management.

Sybil attack. In the SSI ecosystem, users can create autonomously redundant DIDs for more application services. The adversary may utilize this characteristic to launch the sybil attack.

Inefficient cross-domain authentication. Under the dual pressure from the small block storage space of blockchain systems and the growing demand for cross-domain services, the high efficiency of identity authentication will be hard to achieve.

The main contributions of this paper are summarized as follows:

- At first, we propose a DID-based decentralized cross-domain identity management System (D2CDIM). It allows users to keep autonomy over their identity and thoroughly solves the issue of local single-point-of-failure in the cross-domain identity authentication scenario.
- Secondly, in order to avoid the abuse of redundant identities and resist sybil attack, each user is given a unique DID identity during the identity registration phase by attesting real-life identity.
- Lastly, we propose a practical anonymous cross-domain authentication scheme. Dynamic accumulator is utilized to achieve a fast response as well as to reduce storage space. Anonymous credentials and zero-knowledge have been introduced to achieve anonymous cross-domain authentication with privacy protection.

This paper is organized as follows. In Sect. 2, we review the techniques used in this article. The system model, threat model and design objectives are presented in Sect. 3. In Sect. 4, we give an overview of the whole system. Section 5 formally describes the system protocol. In Sect. 6, the security analysis and performance analysis of the system is given. Related work is discussed in Sect. 7. Finally, the paper is summarized.

2 Preliminaries

2.1 Decentralized Identifier Standard

In the Self-Sovereign Identity ecosystem, entities are represented by decentralized identifiers (DIDs) that are globally unique, never change, and can be generated on a ledger that is compatible with DIDs. An unlimited number of DIDs can be created by real entities. A brief introduction to the DID standard [3] is given as follows.

- DID Syntax: As shown in Fig. 1. The first part called Scheme is a Uniform Resource Name (URN), the second part called Namespace is a Universally Unique Identifier (UUID), and finally, a Namespace-specific identifier uniquely identifies an entity within the Namespace.
- DID Document: The DID is an identifier that acts as a key in the key-value schema. The value is the corresponding DID document (DDO), DDO contains information about the DID (such as the associated public key and other information).
- DID Resolver: The DID Resolver describes how to generate or resolve the DID document of a given DID.

Scheme   Namespace-specific identifier

urn:uuid:fe0cde11-59d2-4621-887f-23013499f905

Namespace

Fig. 1. The DID Syntax

2.2 Counting Bloom Filter (CBF)

Bloom filter (BF) [4] is a space-efficient random data structure that uses bit arrays to succinctly represent a set and to determine whether an element belongs to that set. The standard BF does not support deletion operations. In the counting bloom filter (CBF), each of its bits is replaced by a counter in order to support the delete operation. It is an array of m bits representing a set of n elements $S = \{x_1, x_2, \ldots, x_n\}$. Initially, all bits in the CBF are set to zero. There are k mutually independent hash functions $h_i(x)$, $1 \le i \le k$ which map $x \in S$ to uniformly distributed random numbers in the range $\{1, \ldots, m\}$ respectively. An element $x \in S$ is inserted into the CBF by adding 1 to the value at the bit $h_i(x)$, where $1 \le i \le k$. To confirm whether an element y is a member in S, we need to check each bit $h_i(y)$. If any of them is zero, y is not an element of S. When an element $z \in S$ is deleted from the CBF, the value at the corresponding bit $h_i(z)$ is subtracted by 1, where $1 \le i \le k$.

2.3   Zero-Knowledge Proof

A zero-knowledge proof is a protocol by which a prover P convinces a verifier V of the truth of a statement without revealing any specific information about the statement. In our construction, we transform it to non-interactive based on the Fiat-Shamir heuristic scheme [5]. There are three essential features of zero-knowledge proofs, namely: completeness, soundness, and zero-knowledgeness. When referring to zero-knowledge proofs, we will use the symbolic representation of Camenisch and Stadler [6]. For example, $NIZKPoK\{(x, y) : f = g^x \wedge h = g^y\}$ defines a non-interactive zero-knowledge proof of the knowledge of elements x and y, where x and y satisfy the equation $f = g^x$ and $h = g^y$.

2.4   Dynamic Accumulator

The concept of accumulator was first introduced by Benaloh and de Mare as [7], but the accumulator proposed by them was static, it could only add values to the accumulator but not delete them. The accumulator allows a large number of inputs to be hashed into a short value. The dynamic accumulator allows a value to be added or removed dynamically so that the cost of the addition or removal is independent of the number of values accumulated. The accumulator used in our solution is the dynamic accumulator [8] proposed by Camenisch and Lysyanskaya.

2.5   Anonymous Credential

The anonymous credential system [8] consists of a user and an organization. The organization only knows the user's pseudonym, and different pseudonyms from the same user cannot be linked. For example, $N_{(U,O)}$ is the pseudonym of user U to organization O. An organization issues a credential to a pseudonym, and the corresponding user can prove to another organization that she has this credential without revealing anything. The CL anonymous credential system [9] proposed by Camenisch and Lysyanskayais used in our system construction.

3   System Models

In this paper, we propose a new decentralized cross-domain identity management model as shown in Fig. 2. In this scheme, there are three types of participants: User, Identity Provider (IDP) and Service Provider (SP). The function of a traditional IDP assigned to the Committee IDPs, committee IDPs are responsible for the endorsement of identity information in the trust domain and the authentication of cross-domain user identity information, etc. SPs provide services to users. We list the notation used in our scheme in Table 1.

Table 1. Notation

Notation	Description
$(pk_U^A,\ sk_U^A)$	Public-private key pairs for users in domain A
$(pk_S^B,\ sk_S^B)$	Public-private key pair for SP in domain B
C^A, C^B	Committee IDPs Domain A, B
(pk_C^A, sk_C^A)	Public and private keys for C^A
(pk_C^B, sk_C^B)	Public and private keys for C^B
C'	Committees in which some IDPs in all domains are involved
(pk_C', sk_C')	Public and private keys for C'
$Bchain_A, Bchain_B$	Consortium blockchain in domain A, B
$Bchain'$	Master chains for cross-domain (maintained by nodes in C')
$C_i^A (1 \le i \le n_A)$	n_A nodes in C^A
$(pk_{C,i}^A, sk_{C,i}^A)$	Public and private keys of n_A nodes in C^A
$C_i^B (1 \le i \le n_B)$	n_B nodes in C^B
$(pk_{C,i}^B,\ sk_{C,i}^B)$	Public and private keys of n_B nodes in C^B
$C_i' (1 \le i \le n')$	n' nodes in C'
$(pk_{C,i}',\ sk_{C,i}')$	Public and private keys of n' nodes in C'

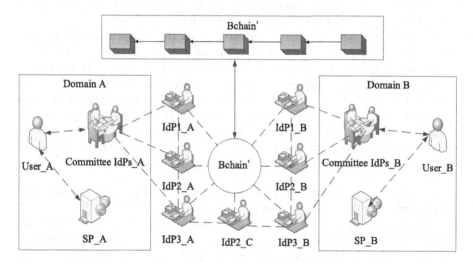

Fig. 2. System model of D2CDIM

3.1 Threat Model

In our scheme, we do not consider physical hardware attacks and software penetration. The adversary can capture the packets transmitted in the network and send the packets into the network. Firstly, we assume that SP nodes are honest-but-curious. Secondly, we assume that the IDP nodes in each committee are honest-but-curious except for those in committee C'.

3.2   Design Goals

Sybil-Resistance. Each user can get a unique DID identity during the identity
registration phase by attesting real-life identity.

Privacy Preservation. Preserve the privacy of users' identity information at
all stages of identity management.

Secure and Anonymous Authentication. Provide an efficient practical
anonymous cross-domain authentication protocol.

4   System Overview

In this section, we describe our solution in terms of the following four processes:
1) identity registration, 2) cross-domain identity authentication, 3) identity revocation, 4) identity update.

4.1   Identity Registration

In this scheme, each user can only register a unique decentralized identity DID
by binding it with a real-life legitimate identity credential (e.g. ID card) in the
identity registration phase. Then, committee C^A checks the identity credential
to determine that it has not been registered before.

We adopt the definition of a credential from the W3C Verifiable Credentials specification [10]. A credential in the identity registration phase is formally defined by C_d. It is assumed that there are k claims in the credential,
$claims = (claim_i)_{i=1}^k$, each $claim_i = \{a_i, v_i\}$, where a_i is the attribute of a
claim and v_i is the value of the attribute a_i. A series of claims are denoted as
$CS = \{claim_i\}_{i=1}^k$. C_d is denoted as $\{pk_U, ctx, CS, \delta\}$, where pk_U is an identifier
about the subject of the credential, ctx defines the circumstances and δ is the
signature of $\{pk_U, ctx, CS\}$ issued by the credential issuer. Figure 3 depicts the
identity registration process in Domain A through committee C^A.

1. *Import Identity.* Import the user's real-life legal identification credentials to
   committee C^A, e.g. (ID card), etc.
2. *Deduplication.* Committee C^A runs deduplication algorithm to check whether
   the real-life legal identity information credentials were registered already. If
   it is fresh, go to the next step, otherwise, the process is terminated.
3. *DID generation.* A generic unique identifier DID is generated on the consortium blockchain $Bchain^A$.
4. *DID Issuance and Application.* Return the DID to the user. Then the DID can
   be applied in identity authentication, identity revocation, identity update.

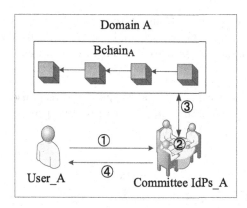

Fig. 3. Identity registration

Import Identity: We assume that the real-life identity credentials (e.g. ID card, etc.) possessed by the user are imported into our system using the Oracle system. Since our system is fully decentralized, we use the DECO protocol [11] in this step. The credential for the user is represented as $\{pk_U, ctx, CS, \delta^{Oracle}\}$. The committee is able to verify this credential with Oracle.

Deduplication: Understanding the deduplication algorithm from below:

- The nodes in committee generate a corresponding CBF based on the attribute in the user's credential claim. The CBF is stored in $Bchain'$ and it is used to record the identity v of that attribute that has been registered.
- A user shows credential C_d to nodes, the credential is about $claim = \{a, v, P\}$. For instance, $claim = \{\text{``}IDnumber\text{''}, \text{``}421023xxx\text{''}\}$.
- Nodes will check whether C_d finds a match in the CBF.
- To achieve privacy protection, this CBF store C_v. This C_v is the committed value of value v of this attribute. Afterwards, t of the n nodes all prove that C_v is not in the corresponding CBF. Each node needs to find the CBF in the blockchain and perform membership proof.

4.2 Cross-Domain Authentication

It is assumed that a user U^A in domain A requests service from SP^B in domain B. As shown in Fig. 4, the process of cross-domain authentication is described as follows.

1. *Initialize.* U^A obtains an anonymous credential *cred* from committee C^A.
2. *Upload Credential.* Nodes $\{C_i'\}_{i=1}^{n'}$ in committee C' upload the users' credential *cred* to the global accumulator GA_1 of the blockchain $Bchain'$.
3. *Requst.* U^A sends the cross-domain request to C^B to access SP^B.
4. *Obtain.* Committee C^B obtains the value of the global dynamic accumulator from the blockchain $Bchain'$.

5. *Authentication and Access.* Committee C^B authenticates whether credential *cred* is presented in the global accumulator GA_1. If authentication successes, committee C^B issues a token to U^A. Then, U^A can access the SP^B by this token.

Dynamic accumulator in this scheme speeds up response and reduce storage space. Anonymous credential is applied to preserve private information in the process of cross-domain authentication.

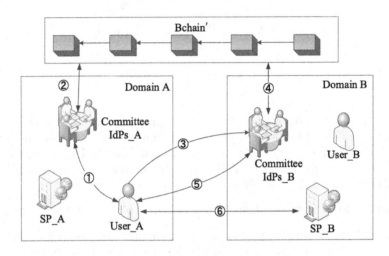

Fig. 4. Cross-domain authentication flowchart

4.3   Identity Revocation and Identity Update

Traditional PKI uses certificate revocation lists or online certificate status protocols to publish identity revocation information. The identity revocation of our scheme is divided into two steps: 1) revoking anonymous identities and anonymous certificates, 2) revoking DID identity.

Identity update includes 1) updating the DID, and 2) updating the public-private pair corresponding to DID.

5   Our Protocol Design

In this section, we formalize the algorithms mentioned above from mainly two aspects including identity registration and cross-domain authentication.

5.1   Identity Registration

Setup.   Recall that committee C^A in domain A contains n_A nodes $(C_1^A, \cdots, C_{n_A}^A)$. The threshold signature scheme $TS = (KGen, Sig, Comb, Vf)$

is used by the committee to issue credentials to users. Committee members execute a distribution protocol to generate (pk_C^A, sk_C^A). The private key of $\{C_i^A\}_{i=1}^{n^A}$ in C^A is the share $[sk_{C,i}^A]$ of sk_C^A, their public key remains pk_C^A. Each user U^A in domain A generates a public-private key pairs (pk_U^A, sk_U^A). CBF is an m-bit array that is initialized to null.

ImportIdentity. Import the real-life credentials C_d of user U^A to committee C^A. A credential $C_d = \{pk_U^A, ctx, claim, \delta^{Oracle}\}$, where $claim = (a, C_v)$, $C_v = commitment(v, r)$ (Pedersen Commitment $C_v = g^r h^v$. g is generator of order q, and k is randomly chosen by C^A, committee C^A computes $h = g^k$, then the user computes $C_v = g^r h^v$).

Algorithm 1. Deduplication

Input: $C_d = \{pk_U^A, ctx, claim, \delta^{Oracle}\}$
Output: $b \in \{0, 1\}$
    procedure $CBF_a \leftarrow SearchCBF(a)$
      $b_1 \leftarrow CheckCBF(C_v, CBF_a)$
        if $b_1 = 1$ **then return** $b = 0$
        else $\{AddCBF(C_v, CBF_a)$
            return $b = 1\}$
  end
    procedure $CheckCBF(C_v, CBF_a)$
      for $i = 1$ to k **do**
        if$(CBF_a[h_i(C_v)] == 0)$
            then return 0
            else return 1
      end for
  end
    procedure $AddCBF(C_v, CBF_a)$
      for $i = 1$ to k **do**
        if$(CBF_a[h_i(C_v)] == 1)$
          $CBF_a[h_i(C_v)] + +$
      end for
      return CBF_a
  end

Deduplication and DID Generation. The Algorithm 1 describes the deduplication process. With the input of C_d, IDPs generates the corresponding CBF_a based on a in $claim = (a, C_v)$, mapping C_v to CBF_a via a k-hash function. If Algorithm 1 output is $b = 1$, **the DID generation** process is performed. Then the DID is obtained from $Bchain_A$.

DID Issuance and Application. After committee C^A returns the DID to the user U^A, committee C^A uses the threshold signature to endorse and store the $claim = DID/pk_U^A$ of the user U^A in domain A. Then a user can apply this DID and pk_U^A interchangeably. The process is as follows:

1. The nodes $\{C_i^A\}_{i=1}^{n_A}$ find DDO associated with the DID through DID Resolver. DDO includes DID, pk_U^A and other information about U^A.
2. The user U^A proves the possession of sk_U^A corresponding to pk_U^A to the Committee by the zero-knowledge proof.
3. Nodes $\{C_i^A\}_{i=1}^{n_A}$ sign the message $m = \{pk_U^A, ctx, claim\}$ to obtain a signature share for m. Signature share $\delta_i^\pi \leftarrow TS.Sig(sk_{C,i}^A, m)$, where ctx represents the relationship DID with pk_U^A.
4. User U^A combines at least t shares to get a full signature $\delta^\pi = TS.Comb(\delta_i^\pi)$. U^A gets an endorsement $C_\pi = \{pk_U^A, ctx, claim, \delta^\pi\}$.
5. The DID and pk_U^A can interchangeably be applied in identity authentication, identity revocation, and identity update. That is, pk_U^A is equal to DID.

5.2   Cross-Domain Authentication

Setup. Recall that committee C^A is equipped with a public-private key pair (pk_C^A, sk_C^A), committee C^A contains n_A nodes C_i^A ($1 \leq i \leq n_A$). Committee C' is responsible for adding and removing dynamic accumulators. In order to trace the latest global dynamic accumulator in $Bchain'$, a parameter $GAStatus$ is defined in each block header of $Bchain'$. If $GAStatus == 1$ in a block, the global dynamic accumulator is latest and vice versa.

Initialize. In order to make user U^A obtain credentials from C^A, a decentralized CL anonymous credential deployment based on strong RSA assumptions needs to be realized on C^A, described as follows.

- $CLSetup(1^{\lambda_1}) \rightarrow params_1$. It is run by C^A to generate the system parameters $params_1$. The algorithm inputs security parameter 1^{λ_1}, C^A selects two safe prime numbers $p = 2p'+1$, $q = 2q'+1$ and computes $N = pq$, the length of N is l_n. Then C^A picks random elements $\mathfrak{a}, \mathfrak{b}, \mathfrak{c}, \mathfrak{g}, \mathfrak{h} \in QR_N$. Then the algorithm outputs $params_1 = (N, \mathfrak{a}, \mathfrak{b}, \mathfrak{c}, \mathfrak{g}, \mathfrak{h})$.
- $CommitteeKeyGen(params_1) \rightarrow (pk_C^A, sk_C^A, pk_{C,i}^A, sk_{C,i}^A)$. Committee C^A calls the algorithm to generate public-private key pair. The algorithm inputs $params_1$, C^A obtains $pk_C^A = (N, \mathfrak{a}, \mathfrak{b}, \mathfrak{c})$ and $sk_C^A = (p', q')$. Then private key $sk_{C,i}^A$ of nodes $\{C_i^A\}_{i=1}^{n_A}$ in C^A is the share of sk_C^A, their public key $pk_{C,i}^A$ remains pk_C^A.
- $UserKeyGen(pk_U^A, sk_U^A) \rightarrow (pk_U^A, sk_U^A)$. User U^A run the algorithm to set her public-private key pair. The algorithm inputs (pk_U^A, sk_U^A). The (pk_U^A, sk_U^A) of the user U^A in this phase is corresponding to (pk_U^A, sk_U^A) in the identity registration phase. And its master private key is $sk_U^A = sk_u \in (0, 2^{l_m})$. The algorithm outputs (pk_U^A, sk_U^A).

- $FormNym(params_1, sk_U^A) \rightarrow Nym_{UA}^{CA}$. User U^A and C^A run the algorithm to generate a pseudonym Nym_{UA}^{CA}. The algorithm inputs $params_1$, the user's master key $sk_U^A = sk_u$. The U^A and C^A jointly choose a random s (whose length is $l_s = l_n + l_m + l$, where l is security parameter) and compute $Nym_{UA}^{CA} = \mathfrak{a}^{sk_u}\mathfrak{b}^s$. The algorithm outputs Nym_{UA}^{CA}.

- $MintCred(params_1, Nym_{UA}^{CA}) \rightarrow cred$. User U^A and committee C^A run the algorithm to obtain an anonymous credential tuple $cred$. The algorithm inputs $params_1$ and Nym_{UA}^{CA}. The steps are as follows:

  1. The algorithm randomly select one of the nodes $\{C_i^A\}_{i=1}^{n_A}$ in C^A to generate a credential with the user, assume that the node C_t^A is selected to issue credential $cred$ for user U^A.

  2. Node C_t^A chooses a random prime e (whose length is $l_e = l_m + 2$ and e satisfies the range of accumulated values in the global accumulator GA_1 below $\mathbf{E} \in [\mathcal{A}, \mathcal{B}]$). C_t^A selects a random number c and computes the value of $\mathfrak{v}$ which satisfies $\mathfrak{v}^e = Nym_{UA}^{CA}c \equiv \mathfrak{a}^{sk_u}\mathfrak{b}^s c$. Node C_t^A issues the credential $cred$ as a tuple $(e, \mathfrak{v}, s)$.

  3. Node C_t^A create a transaction T_{cred} with the resulting credentials $cred = (e, \mathfrak{v}, s)$ and broadcast it to other nodes $\{C_i^A\}_{i=1}^{n_A}$ in $Bchain_A$.

  4. When a transaction T_{cred} is received by other nodes and verified by $VerifyCred(cred, Nym_{UA}^{CA}, pk_{C,i}^A) \rightarrow \{0, 1\}$, $VerifyCred$ verifies whether $\mathfrak{v}^e = Nym_{UA}^{CA}c$. If all nodes verify $VerifyCred$ are true, the transaction is written to the block in $Bchain_A$.

  5. The algorithm $MintCred$ outputs a legitimate credential $cred$.

UploadCred. Committee C' uploads the anonymous credential $cred$ to the global accumulator GA_1 in $Bchain'$. As we know, the accumulator values can only be prime numbers in [8]. The nodes $\{C_i'\}_{i=1}^{n'}$ in C' upload e from the anonymous credential $cred = (e, \mathfrak{v}, s)$ to the dynamic accumulator GA_1 on the blockchain $Bchain'$. We give the following algorithms.

- $AccumSetup(1^{\lambda_2}) \rightarrow (params_2, t_f)$. Committee C' runs the algorithm. The algorithm input is security parameter λ_2. The algorithm gains p, q and $N = pq$ from algorithm $CLSetup$. A seed value $u \in QR_N$ is selected, where $u \neq 1$. C' sets $t_f = (p, q)$. The algorithm outputs $params_2 = (N, u)$ and t_f.

- $ObtainAcc(\{C_i'\}_{i=1}^{n'}, Bchain') \rightarrow \mathcal{G}_A$. Run by the node $\{C_i'\}_{i=1}^{n'}$ in the committee C'. The current accumulator value of the global accumulator GA_1 can be obtained from $Bchain'$ as $\mathcal{G}_A = u^{e_1 e_2 \cdots e_i}$, where $\mathbf{E} = \{e_1, \ldots, e_i | e \in [\mathcal{A}, \mathcal{B}]\}$. The value $\mathcal{G}_A$ of the global accumulator GA_1 contains in the block whose block header parameter $GAStatus = 1$. Tracing backwards in $Bchain'$, the first block where $GAStatus = 1$ is located contains the latest global accumulator value $\mathcal{G}_A$. The algorithm outputs $\mathcal{G}_A$.

- $UploadPartCred(C', \mathbf{E}', Bchain', params_2) \rightarrow (T_{\mathcal{G}_A}, GAStatus)$. The part of credential is uploaded by committee C' to $Bchain'$. The algorithm inputs $params_2$, a set of uploaded primes $\mathbf{E}'$ including e is accumulated by committee C'. The steps are as follows:

1. $CollectAccNum(\{C_i'\}_{i=1}^{n'}, timestamp, e_i') \rightarrow \mathbf{E'}$: Run by nodes $\{C_i'\}_{i=1}^{n'}$ in committee C', these nodes $\{C_i'\}_{i=1}^{n'}$ collect uploaded prime e_i' under the current $timestamp$ in offline. This step outputs $\mathbf{E'} = \{e_1', \ldots, e_i' | e_i' \in [\mathcal{A}, \mathcal{B}]\}$, $\mathbf{E'}$ includes prime e.

2. These nodes $\{C_i'\}_{i=1}^{n'}$ obtain the current accumulator value $\mathcal{G}_A$ by running $ObtainAcc$.

3. $AccAdd(parmas_2, \mathcal{G}_A, \mathbf{E'}) \rightarrow \mathcal{G}_A$: Run by the nodes $\{C_i'\}_{i=1}^{n'}$ in the committee C', whose input is $params_2 = (N, u)$. the value $\mathcal{G}_A$ of new global accumulator GA_1 is accumulated as $\mathcal{G}_A = \mathcal{G}_A{}^{e_1'e_2'\ldots,e_i'} = u^{e_1 e_2 \ldots, e_i e_1' e_2' \ldots, e_i'}$, where $\mathbf{E} = \{\mathbf{E} \cap \mathbf{E'}\} = \{e_1, \ldots, e_i, e_1', e_2', \ldots, e_i' | e_i, e_i' \in [\mathcal{A}, \mathcal{B}]\}$. This step outputs the value of $\mathcal{G}_A$.

4. The node C_t' creates a transaction $T_{\mathcal{G}_A}$ including the value $\mathcal{G}_A$ of current global accumulator GA_1 and broadcasts $T_{\mathcal{G}_A}$ to other nodes $\{C_i'\}_{i=1}^{n'}$ where $i \neq t$ in $Bchain'$.

5. When transaction $T_{\mathcal{G}_A}$ is received by other nodes $\{C_i'\}_{i=1}^{n'}$. Nodes $\{C_i'\}_{i=1}^{n'}$ verify whether the uploaded value e_i' belongs to the latest GA_1. Each node C_i' generats a proof $w_i' = AccAdd(params_2, E\backslash\{e_i'\})$ via algorithm $GenAccWitness(params_2, e_i', \mathbf{E})$. Then C_i' uses $AccVerify(params_2, \mathcal{G}, e_i', w_i')$ to verify e_i' in $\mathcal{G}_A$, the $AccVerify()$ computes $\tilde{\mathcal{G}} = w_i'^{e_i'} \mod N$, and verifies whether $\tilde{\mathcal{G}} = \mathcal{G}$ and $e_i' \in [\mathcal{A}, \mathcal{B}]$.

6. When all the other nodes pass the $AccVerify$ validation, the transaction $T_{\mathcal{G}_A}$ including $\mathcal{G}_A$ will be stored in a new block, and the parameter $GAStatus$ is set to 1 in this block header.

7. These steps upload successfully $T_{\mathcal{G}_A}$ about value $\mathcal{G}_A$ and set $GAStatus = 1$ in $Bchain'$. The algorithm $UploadPartCred$ outputs $T_{\mathcal{G}_A}$ and $GAStatus = 1$.

Request and Obtain. User U^A uses $Nym_{U^A}^{C^A}$ to send service request to C^B. The nodes C^B obtain the value of latest global dynamic accumulator GA_1 value $\mathcal{G}_A$ from the $Bchain'$.

- $Request(Nym_U^{C^A}, C^B, SP^B) \rightarrow request$. User U^A uses the pseudonym $Nym_U^{C^A}$ to send $request$ to C^B for accessing a service provider SP^B in domain B.
- $Obtain(\{C_i^B\}_{i=1}^{n_B}, Bchain') \rightarrow \mathcal{G}_A$. Nodes $\{C_i^B\}_{i=1}^{n_B}$ run the algorithm $ObtainAcc(C_i', Bchain')$ in **step 2 UploadCred**, the accumulator value of GA_1 as $\mathcal{G}_A$ is obtained.
- Note that the some nodes $\{C_i^B\}_{i=1}^{n_B}$ belong to C' directly use $ObtainAcc(C_i', Bchain')$ in **step 2 UploadCred**, the other nodes use the API interface on $Bchain'$ to obtain GA_1.

Authentication and Access. In the phase of identity anthentication, the user utilizes his pseudonym $Nym_{U^A}^{C^A}$ to generate proof π_e with committee C^B via non-interactive zero knowledge, where the committed value of e is part of the accumulator value $\mathcal{G}_A$. And $\mathfrak{c} = \mathfrak{v}^e \left(\frac{1}{\mathfrak{a}}\right)^{sk_u} \left(\frac{1}{\mathfrak{b}}\right)^s$ is defined as the commitment of e, because value e satisfies $\mathfrak{v}^e = \mathfrak{a}^{sk_u}\mathfrak{b}^s\mathfrak{c}$.

- $GenNIZKProof(Nym_U^{C^A}, U^A) \to \pi_e$: User U^A runs the algorithm with the pseudonym $Nym_{U^A}^{C^A}$, the process generates π_e by non-interactive zero knowledge.

  • U^A chooses r_1, r_2 at random from $Z_{\lfloor n/4 \rfloor}$, and the values $\mathfrak{g}, \mathfrak{h}, \mathfrak{y}$ are quadratic residues modulo N, the user computes $\Omega_1 := \mathfrak{v}\mathfrak{y}^{r_1}$, $\Omega_2 := \mathfrak{g}^{r_1}$ and $\Omega_3 := \mathfrak{g}^e\mathfrak{h}^{r_2}$.

  • The User U^A constructs a commitment C_u to u, C_u proves that u is the e-th power root of the accumulator value $\mathcal{G}_A$. (here u is the current value $u_i = u^{\mathbf{E}\backslash e}$, i.e. $u^e = u_i^e = \mathcal{G}_A$). U^A chooses r_3, r_4, r_5 at random from $Z_{\lfloor n/4 \rfloor}$ and the elements g, h of QR_N are available such that log_g^h is not known to the committee C^B, then the user computes $C_e := g^e h^{r_3}$, $C_u := uh^{r_4}$, $C_r := g^{r_4} h^{r_5}$.
  $\pi_e \leftarrow NIZKPoK\{(\alpha, \beta, \lambda, \tau, \epsilon, \iota, \xi, \zeta, \eta, \omega, \kappa):$

$$\mathfrak{c} = \Omega_1^\alpha \left(\frac{1}{\mathfrak{a}}\right)^\beta \left(\frac{1}{\mathfrak{b}}\right)^\lambda \left(\frac{1}{\mathfrak{y}}\right)^\tau \wedge 1 \equiv \Omega_2^\alpha \left(\frac{1}{\mathfrak{g}}\right)^\tau \wedge \Omega_2 = \mathfrak{g}^\epsilon \wedge \Omega_3 = \mathfrak{g}^\alpha \mathfrak{h}^\iota \wedge$$

$$C_r = g^\xi h^\zeta \wedge C_e = g^\alpha h^\eta \wedge \mathcal{G}_A = C_u^\alpha \left(\frac{1}{h}\right)^\omega \wedge 1 = C_r^\alpha \left(\frac{1}{h}\right)^\kappa \left(\frac{1}{g}\right)^\omega \wedge$$

$$\alpha \in [\mathcal{A}, \mathcal{B}]\}.$$

- $VerifyProof(C^B, t, n_B, \pi_e) \to \{0, 1\}$. When t of n_B nodes in C^B verify that π_e passes, then output is 1, indicating that verification of π_e is successful.
- $GenToken(C^B, Nym_{U^A}^{C^A}) \to token$: When $VerifyProof$ passes successfully, C^B issues a $token$ to user U^A using pseudonym $Nym_{U^A}^{C^A}$.
- $VerifyToken(token, Nym_{U^A}^{C^A}, SP^B) \to \{0, 1\}$. Once SP^B has successfully validated the token, the user can access the SP^B service.

6 System Analysis

6.1 Security Analysis

Definition 1. *(Sybil-resistance) For a probabilistic polynomial-time (PPT) adversary $\mathfrak{A}$, it holds that given the registered real-life identity credential $C_d^{\mathfrak{A}} = \{pk^{\mathfrak{A}}, ctx^{\mathfrak{A}}, claim^{\mathfrak{A}} = \{a, C_v\}, \delta^{Oracle_{\mathfrak{A}}}\}$, Output* **Deduplication**$(C_d^{\mathfrak{A}}) = 1$, *then*

$$\Pr \begin{bmatrix} \textbf{Deduplication}(C_d) \to b = 1 \\ \textbf{Deduplication}(C_d^{\mathfrak{A}}) \to b^{\mathfrak{A}} \\ claim^{\mathfrak{A}} = claim \end{bmatrix} \leq negl(\lambda)$$

Theorem 1. *Our scheme is sybil-resistance if Deduplication scheme is completeness.*

Proof. When given the registered real-life identity credential $C_d^{\mathfrak{A}} = \{pk^{\mathfrak{A}}, ctx^{\mathfrak{A}}, claim^{\mathfrak{A}} = \{a, C_v\}, \delta^{Oracle_{\mathfrak{A}}}\}$, we perform $CBF_a \leftarrow SearchCBF(a)$ in Algorithm 1 in Sect. 5.1 to find the corresponding CBF according to attribute a in claim. Then, runing $CheckCBF(C_v, CBF_a)$ in Algorithm 1 check whether C_v in the CBF_a, $CheckCBF$ return $b_1 = 1$. If $b_1 = 1$ means that this C_v has already been registered in CBF_a. So it illustrates that the registered claims cannot be passed by the *Deduplication* algorithm, the completeness is proved.

Definition 2. *(Privacy preservation) In identity registration phase, the deduplication protocol preserved the privacy if for all PTT adversaries $(\mathfrak{A}_1, \mathfrak{A}_2)$, adversary $\mathfrak{A}_1$ outputs $\{v^{(1)}, v^{(2)}\}$, and when $\mathfrak{A}_2$ is given C_d^*, where $C_d^* = g^{r^{(b)}} h^{v^{(b)}}$ for some random bit b, $\mathfrak{A}_1$ outputs its guess b', then:*

$$\Pr\left[b = b'\right] \leq negl\,(\lambda).$$

Theorem 2. *The deduplication protocol preserves the privacy if pedersen commitment scheme have hiding property.*

Theorem 3. *Our cross-domain authentication phase is anonymous and users' private information is preserved if anonymous credential is secure and NIZKPoK scheme satisfies zero-knoledge property.*

Proof. The CL anonymous credentials is secure based on the RSA assumption. So next, we only prove the NIZKPoK scheme satisfy zero-knoledge property.

The simulator randomly picks $\{s_\alpha, s_\beta, s_\lambda, s_\tau, s_\epsilon, s_\iota, s_\xi, s_\zeta, s_\eta, s_\omega, s_\kappa \xleftarrow{R}\}$ corresponding domain, and set $c = H(\mathfrak{a}, \mathfrak{b}, \mathfrak{c}, \mathfrak{g}, \mathfrak{h}, \mathfrak{y}, g, h, n, \mathcal{G}_A, \mathfrak{t}_1, \mathfrak{t}_2, \mathfrak{t}_3, \mathfrak{t}_4, t_1, t_2, t_3, t_4)$. Then, it computes:

$$\mathfrak{t}_1 = \mathfrak{c}^c \Omega_1^{s_\alpha} \left(\frac{1}{\mathfrak{a}}\right)^{s_\beta} \left(\frac{1}{\mathfrak{b}}\right)^{s_\lambda} \left(\frac{1}{\mathfrak{y}}\right)^{s_\tau}, \mathfrak{t}_2 = \Omega_2^{s_\alpha} \left(\frac{1}{\mathfrak{g}}\right)^{s_\tau}, \mathfrak{t}_3 = \Omega_2^c \mathfrak{g}^{s_\epsilon}, \quad \mathfrak{t}_4 = \Omega_3^c \mathfrak{g}^{s_\alpha} \mathfrak{h}^{s_\iota}$$

$$t_1 = C_r^c g^{s_\xi} h^{s_\zeta}, t_2 = C_e^c g^{s_\alpha} h^{s_\eta}, t_3 = \mathcal{G}_A{}^c C_u^{s_\alpha} \left(\frac{1}{h}\right)^{s_\kappa}, t_4 = C_r^{s_\alpha} \left(\frac{1}{h}\right)^{s_\kappa} \left(\frac{1}{g}\right)^{s_\omega},$$

where they are indistinguishable from real NIZKPoK interactions. Therefore, zero-knowledge property of NIZKPoK scheme is proved.

Theorem 4. *Our cross-domain authentication is secure based RSA assumption if anonymous credential and dynamic accumulator cannot break the RSA hard problem, and NIZKPoK scheme satisty completeness property.*

Proof. We will prove this theorem from two aspects.

Firstly, the NIZKPoK protocol in Authentication is secure in cross-domain authentication, we should prove the NIZKPoK's completeness property.

$$\mathfrak{t}_1 = \Omega_1^{r_\alpha} \left(\frac{1}{\mathfrak{a}}\right)^{r_\beta} \left(\frac{1}{\mathfrak{b}}\right)^{r_\lambda} \left(\frac{1}{\mathfrak{y}}\right)^{r_\tau}, \quad \mathfrak{t}_2 = \Omega_2^{r_\alpha} \left(\frac{1}{\mathfrak{g}}\right)^{r_\tau}, \mathfrak{t}_3 = \mathfrak{g}^{r_\epsilon}, \quad \mathfrak{t}_4 = \mathfrak{g}^{r_\alpha} \mathfrak{h}^{r_\iota}$$

$$t_1 = g^{r_\xi} h^{r_\zeta}, t_2 = g^{r_\alpha} h^{r_\eta}, t_3 = C_u^{r_\alpha} \left(\frac{1}{h}\right)^{r_\omega}, t_4 = C_r^{r_\alpha} \left(\frac{1}{h}\right)^{r_\kappa} \left(\frac{1}{g}\right)^{r_\omega}$$

Table 2. Performace numbers of the cross-domain authentication phase, the values n_A, n' are the node numbers of committee C^A, C' respectively. And the arithmetic symbol exp stands for exponentiation.

Initilize	UploadCred	Rquest and obtain	Authentication anc access	Storage size
$(3n_A + 2)$ exp in QR_N	$2n'$ exp in QR_N	1 exp in QR_N	42 exp in QR_N	1 exp QR_N

Secondly, in our scheme, the anonymous credential is added into the dynamic accumulator, so we need to prove that our dynamic accumulator is still secure after adding the anonymous credential part based strong RSA assumption. It is assumed that an adversary $\mathfrak{A}$ with input $N = pq$, $u \in QR_N$ and output j prime numbers $x_1, ..., x_j \in [\mathcal{A}, \mathcal{B}]$. And $u' \in Z_n^*$ satisfies $(u')^{x'} = u^{\prod x_i}$. $\mathfrak{A}$ can utilize the value $u \in QR_n$ to break the strong RSA assumption, so $\mathfrak{A}$ have to output a value $e > 1$, where y satisfies $y^e = u = \mathfrak{a}^{sk_u} \mathfrak{b}^s \mathfrak{c}$. Attacking game is excuted as follows: challenger sends (n, u) to the adversary $\mathfrak{A}$, and suppose $\mathfrak{A}$ gives a forged $(u', x', (x_1, ..., x_j))$ such that $x = \prod_{i=1}^{j} x_i$, so we would have $(u')^{x'} = u^{\prod x_i}$.

To sum up the above two aspects proof, we know that our cross-domain authentication is secure based strong RSA assumption.

6.2   Performance Analysis

The main purpose of this paper is to propose a D2CDIM framework for user identity management, and this paper focuses more on the theoretical aspect. Therefore, the performance of the system is only analyzed qualitatively here.

The following analysis focuses on the main protocols in the identity registration phase and the cross-domain identity authentication phase.

In the identity registration phase, the performance overhead is mainly in the algorithm of deduplication. Firstly, from the storage space consideration, we assume the CBF is an array of m bits and each of its bits is replaced by a counter of b bits. So the storage size is $O(mb)$. Secondly, we analyzes $SearchCBF$, $CheckCBF()$, and $AddCBF()$ processes, the time complexities of these processes are $O(1), O(m), O(m)$ respectively, so the time complexity of this phase is $O(m)$.

In the cross-domain authentication phase, the storage size and the computation complexity of the processes **Initialize, UploadCred, Request and Obtain, Authentication and Access** are analyzed respectively, the results are exhibited in Table 2. Generally, users can complete the **Initialize** and **Upload-Cred** process in advance, so the practical cross-domain authentication for user only runs **Request and Obtain, Authentication and Access** process, the computation complexity of this phase is 43 exp in QR_N. Noted that the communication complexity is not considered.

As a result of the above system performance analysis, we believe that the cross-domain identity management system proposed in this study has the feasibility of development and implementation.

7　Related Work

We classify the current existing cross-domain identity management schemes [12–24] into centralized and distributed.

Table 3. Comparison of identity management system

	Decentralization	User ownership and management	Privacy-preservation	Sybil-resistance	Anonymity
[12, 13]	×	×	×	×	×
[16–19]	✓	×	×	×	×
[14]	✓	✓	✓	✓	×
[24]	✓	×	✓	×	✓
Our scheme	✓	✓	✓	✓	✓

Based on the system design goals and the description of some identity management schemes in this section, we present a comparison diagram of cross-domain identity management in Table 3, and this table gives us a clearer idea of what properties our solution achieves.

7.1　Centralized Schemes

In 2010, Millan et al. [12] constructed a Bridge CA (BCA) model for cross authentication in cross-domain networks. In 2015, Zhang et al. [13] proposed a virtual bridge CA-based cross-domain authentication scheme for virtual enterprises. In bridge mode, a third-party node is needed. However, when the trust central node is attacked, it is easy to break the trust chain. Therefore, these schemes have the problem of the single point of failure.

7.2　Distributed Schemes

Distributed cross-domain authentication solutions establish trust between different security domains through distributed ledgers and consensus.

CanDID [14] is the based DID identity management latest research with legacy compatibility, sybil-resistance, and accountability in SSI ecosystem, it empowers end users with the management of their credentials. As the Bitcoin project, Namecoin [15] is the first project to build an identity system using blockchain technology. Based on Namecoin, Fromknecht et al. proposed the open decentralized authentication scheme called Certcoin [16]. In addition, Certchain [17], CertLedger [18] and BCTRT [19] have introduced the distributed solution of multi-CA collaboration which can solve the single point of failure problems. However, in this cross-domain identity management, a single IDP's or single CA's failure or corruption only affects identity authentication in the local domain. And in cross-domain authentication scheme, it is not suitable to store identity data directly on the blockchain. In addition, most of these solutions [16–19] rarely have taken user privacy preservation in different security domains into consideration. And XAuth [24] propose an efficient privacy-preserving cross-domain authentication scheme called XAuth that is integrated naturally with the existing PKI and Certificate Transparency (CT) systems.

8   Conclusion

We propose a decentralized cross-domain identity management framework based on DID. The introduction of DID allows individuals to have full ownership and management of their identity, and ensures resistance to sybil attacks. And we utilize dynamic accumulators to improve the cross-domain authentication efficiency and limited block storage space. The privacy preservation and anonymity in the process of cross-domain authentication is achieved by anonymous credentials and zero-knowledge. At last, we prove the security of this scheme.

Acknowledgments. This work has been partly supported by Wuhan Knowledge Innovation Special Dawn Program under grand No. 2022010801020283, the Major project of Scientific and technological R&D of Hubei Agricultural Scientific and technological Innovation Center No. 2020-620-000-002-03 and the National Natural Science Foundation of China under grant No. 61702212, No. 62173157, No. 62172181.

References

1. Schaffner, M.: Analysis and evaluation of blockchain-based self-sovereign identity systems. Technical University of Munich, Munich (2020)
2. Fromknecht, C., Velicanu, D., Yakoubov, S.: A decentralized public key infrastructure with identity retention. Cryptology ePrint Archive (2014)
3. Reed, D., Sporny, M., Longley, D., Allen, C., Grant, R., Sabadello, M.: Decentralized identifiers (DIDs) v1. 0-data model and syntaxes for decentralized identifiers (w3c credentials community group) (2019)
4. Tarkoma, S., Rothenberg, C.E., Lagerspetz, E.: Theory and practice of bloom filters for distributed systems. IEEE Commun. Surv. Tutor. **14**(1), 131–155 (2011)
5. Fiat, A., Shamir, A.: How to prove yourself: practical solutions to identification and signature problems. In: Odlyzko, A.M. (ed.) CRYPTO 1986. LNCS, vol. 263, pp. 186–194. Springer, Heidelberg (1987). https://doi.org/10.1007/3-540-47721-7_12
6. Camenisch, J., Stadler, M.: Efficient group signature schemes for large groups. In: Kaliski, B.S. (ed.) CRYPTO 1997. LNCS, vol. 1294, pp. 410–424. Springer, Heidelberg (1997). https://doi.org/10.1007/BFb0052252
7. Benaloh, J., de Mare, M.: One-way accumulators: a decentralized alternative to digital signatures. In: Helleseth, T. (ed.) EUROCRYPT 1993. LNCS, vol. 765, pp. 274–285. Springer, Heidelberg (1994). https://doi.org/10.1007/3-540-48285-7_24

8. Camenisch, J., Lysyanskaya, A.: Dynamic accumulators and application to efficient revocation of anonymous credentials. In: Yung, M. (ed.) CRYPTO 2002. LNCS, vol. 2442, pp. 61–76. Springer, Heidelberg (2002). https://doi.org/10.1007/3-540-45708-9_5

9. Camenisch, J., Lysyanskaya, A.: An efficient system for non-transferable anonymous credentials with optional anonymity revocation. In: Pfitzmann, B. (ed.) EUROCRYPT 2001. LNCS, vol. 2045, pp. 93–118. Springer, Heidelberg (2001). https://doi.org/10.1007/3-540-44987-6_7

10. World Wide Web Consortium et al.: Verifiable credentials data model 1.0: expressing verifiable information on the web (2019). https://www.w3.org/TR/vc-data-model/?#core-data-model

11. Zhang, F., Maram, D., Malvai, H., Goldfeder, S., Juels, A.: Deco: liberating web data using decentralized oracles for TLS. In: Proceedings of the 2020 ACM SIGSAC Conference on Computer and Communications Security, pp. 1919–1938 (2020)

12. Millán, G.L., Pérez, M.G., Pérez, G.M., Skarmeta, A.F.G.: PKI-based trust management in inter-domain scenarios. Comput. Secur. **29**(2), 278–290 (2010)

13. Zhang, W., Wang, X., Khan, M.K.: A virtual bridge certificate authority-based cross-domain authentication mechanism for distributed collaborative manufacturing systems. Secur. Commun. Netw. **8**(6), 937–951 (2015)

14. Maram, D., et al.: CanDID: can-do decentralized identity with legacy compatibility, sybil-resistance, and accountability. In: 2021 IEEE Symposium on Security and Privacy (SP), pp. 1348–1366. IEEE (2021)

15. Kalodner, H.A., Carlsten, M., Ellenbogen, P.M., Bonneau, J., Narayanan, A.: An empirical study of Namecoin and lessons for decentralized namespace design. In: WEIS, vol. 1, pp. 1–23 (2015)

16. Fromknecht, C., Velicanu, D., Yakoubov, S.: Certcoin: a Namecoin based decentralized authentication system. Massachusetts Inst. Technol., Cambridge, MA, USA, Tech. Rep., vol. 6, pp. 46–56 (2014)

17. Chen, J., Yao, S., Yuan, Q., He, K., Ji, S., Du, R.: Certchain: public and efficient certificate audit based on blockchain for TLS connections. In: IEEE INFOCOM 2018-IEEE Conference on Computer Communications, pp. 2060–2068. IEEE (2018)

18. Kubilay, M.Y., Kiraz, M.S., Mantar, H.A.: CertLedger: a new PKI model with certificate transparency based on blockchain. Comput. Secur. **85**, 333–352 (2019)

19. Wang, Z., Lin, J., Cai, Q., Wang, Q., Zha, D., Jing, J.: Blockchain-based certificate transparency and revocation transparency. IEEE Trans. Dependable Secure Comput. (2020)

20. Zhang, F., Cecchetti, E., Croman, K., Juels, A., Shi, E.: Town crier: an authenticated data feed for smart contracts. In: Proceedings of the 2016 aCM sIGSAC Conference on Computer and Communications Security, pp. 270–282 (2016)

21. Zhou, Z., Li, L., Li, Z.: Efficient cross-domain authentication scheme based on blockchain technology. J. Comput. Appl. **38**(2), 316 (2018)

22. Chen, Y., Dong, G., Bai, J., Hao, Y., Li, F., Peng, H.: Trust enhancement scheme for cross domain authentication of PKI system. In: 2019 International Conference on Cyber-Enabled Distributed Computing and Knowledge Discovery (CyberC), pp. 103–110. IEEE (2019)

23. Xiao-ting, M.A., Wen-ping, M.A., Xiao-xue, L.I.U.: A cross domain authentication scheme based on blockchain technology. Acta Electron. Sin. **46**(11), 2571 (2018)

24. Chen, J., Zhan, Z., He, K., Du, R., Wang, D., Liu, F.: XAuth: efficient privacy-preserving cross-domain authentication. IEEE Trans. Dependable Secure Comput. (2021)

Link Aware Aggregation Query with Privacy-Preserving Capability in Wireless Sensor Networks

Yunfeng Cui[1,3], Wenbin Zhai[1,3], Liang Liu[1,3(✉)], Youwei Ding[2], and Wanying Lu[1,3]

[1] College of Computer Science and Technology, Nanjing University of Aeronautics and Astronautics, Nanjing, China
{cyfnuaa,wenbinzhai,liangliu,wanyinglu}@nuaa.edu.cn
[2] School of Artificial Intelligence and Information Technology, Nanjing University of Chinese Medicine, Nanjing, China
ywding@njucm.edu.cn
[3] Key Laboratory of Civil Aviation Intelligent Airport Theory and System, Civil Aviation University of China, Tianjin, China

Abstract. In wireless sensor networks (WSNs), users often submit spatial range queries to obtain statistical information of an area in the network, such as the average temperature and the maximum humidity of an area. The existing privacy-preserving aggregation query algorithms depend on pre-established network topology, and maintaining network topology requires lots of energy. In addition, these algorithms assume that the nodes between the communication radius can perform perfect communication, which is impractical. Aiming to solve these problems, this paper proposes a link aware aggregation query algorithm with privacy-preserving capability, that is, Reliable Spatial Range Data Aggregation Query with Privacy-Preserving (RPSAQ). RPSAQ first divides the query area into multiple sub-areas, and each sub-area is divided into multiple grids according to the network topology and link quality. Under the condition of ensuring node-perceived data privacy, RPSAQ collects sensing data of nodes by traversing the grids in the query area, which not only reduces the packet loss rate and energy consumption of sensor nodes, but also ensures the sensing data's privacy. The experiment results show that RPSAQ outperforms the existing privacy protection algorithms in terms of packet transmission, energy consumption and query result quality.

Keywords: Wireless sensor network · Spatial range aggregation query · Link quality · Privacy preserving

1 Introduction

Wireless sensor networks (WSNs) are data-centric, and users often submit spatial range queries to obtain statistical information of an area in the network,

© The Author(s), under exclusive license to Springer Nature Switzerland AG 2022
J. Chen et al. (Eds.): EISA 2022, CCIS 1641, pp. 209–224, 2022.
https://doi.org/10.1007/978-3-031-23098-1_13

such as the average temperature and the maximum humidity of an area in a forest. Therefore, wireless sensor networks have broad applications in the fields of national defense, military, medical and environmental monitoring.

Sensor nodes are battery powered, and the energy of the battery is limited. Also, in many cases, battery replacement is difficult. Many studies indicate that the energy consumed by sensor nodes is mainly used in data transmissions. Therefore, in order to extend the service life of WSNs, the number of data transmissions needs to be reduced. In addition, due to open deployment and wireless communication, the sensing data of nodes is at risk of being captured. In the application scenario with information confidentiality requirements, the security of the sensor network information needed to be improved. Therefore, it is necessary to study the energy-efficient and privacy-preserving spatial range aggregation query processing technique to solve these two problems.

The existing spatial range aggregation query algorithms have been proposed, which can be divided into two categories according to the topology they depend on: cluster-based and tree-based. However, these algorithms are susceptible to node movements, node failures, and the surrounding environment. Moreover, maintaining network topology incurs the energy consumption of network infrastructure due to the frequent changes of network topology.

Aiming to solve these problems, this paper proposes a link aware aggregation query algorithm with privacy-preserving capability called RPSAQ. RPSAQ is divided into three stages. First, the query message and a random number randomly generated are sent to a node in the query area using geographic routing protocol [11]. Then, the node is used as a starting node, and the query area is divided into several sub-areas. Each sub-area is dynamically divided into multiple grids according to the network topology and link quality. A query node is elected in each grid, which is responsible for sending query message to all nodes in the next grid. The nodes in the grid use the point-by-point overlay strategy to aggregate the sensing data according to the established route, and transmit the partial query result after aggregation to the node in the next grid. This above process is repeated until all nodes in the query area are accessed and the final query result is thus generated. Finally, the final aggregation result will be transferred back to the sink using geographic routing protocol.

According to the real-time network topology and link quality, RPSAQ dynamically divides the grid and selects a query node for each grid. Therefore, the impact of network topology changes on the quality of query results is avoided. Based on link quality information, RPSAQ selects communication links with low packet loss rate to distribute query information, and aggregate sensing data, which avoids multiple retransmissions of data packets and reduces energy consumption. The experiment results show that RPSAQ outperforms the existing algorithms in terms of energy consumption, the number of packet transmissions and query result quality. The main contributions of this paper are as follows:

1. We propose a route-based and infrastructure-free dynamic data collection protocol, which does not depend on the pre-established topology.

2. The method proposed in this paper only needs the nodes in the query area to participate in query processing, and does not require all nodes in the network, thus saving energy consumption.
3. The method proposed in this paper provides efficient data aggregation and takes link quality into account.

The organization of this paper is as follows. Section 2 summarizes the related work, and Sect. 3 introduces the preliminaries. Section 4 proposes a link aware aggregation query algorithm with privacy-preserving capability. An analysis of our work and experimental results is presented in Sect. 5. Section 6 summarizes the paper and presents future research directions.

2   Related Works

The window aggregation query has been extensively studied, and the existing algorithms can be divided into two categories. (1) Tree-based algorithms [2,4,5,8]: these algorithms rely on preconfigured topology and assume that communication between nodes is safe. (2) Route-based algorithms [7,22,23,25]: the query route of these algorithms is dynamically generated in the query process, which reduces the impact of network topology changes on query processing, but they assume that the communication model of the node is an ideal disk graph.

Because WSNs have the characteristics of self-organization and multi-hop, the extensive application of wireless sensor faces serious data leakage problems. Limited resources also bring a series of challenges for the extensive application of wireless sensor network. Data aggregation is an important way to reduce energy consumption. In recent years, many secure data aggregation schemes have been proposed.

Some existing schemes [9,19–21,24] take their base station (BS) as the root node and organize their nodes into a tree structure. In [9], He et al. proposed data aggregation privacy protection technology called SMART based on data fragmentation. Each node divides its sensing data into several fragments to hide its original sensing data and sends the data fragments to different intermediate nodes. After distributing the data fragmentation, the final aggregation result is finally derived at the base station. Considering that the data sent by the non-leaf node to its parent node is the result of the aggregation of the sub-tree where it is rooted rather than the original data, there is no need to protect the privacy of the data sent by the non-leaf node. On the basis of SMART, Wang et al. [21] proposed a method for fragmenting the sensing data of the leaf nodes called PECDA. The data fragments of the leaf nodes are sent to the neighbor nodes through the secure channel to protect the privacy of the leaf nodes.

In order to avoid data loss, some schemes [16,26] adopt a ring topology or a layered model, and group nodes into one layer or in the same ring according to the number of hops of the node to the BS. By grouping the nodes of layer x, their grouping is then sent to any node of layer $x - 1$ in their transport range. Therefore, there are multiple parent nodes between nodes and BS, and there are multiple paths between nodes and BS.

In addition, encryption strategy is often used in wireless sensor network to protect the sensing data. In order to protect the privacy of the original data, the data is encrypted and then transmitted to the next hop node [13]. After arriving at the next hop node, the encrypted data will be decrypted and then the aggregation operation will be completed with the sensing data of the next hop node. This process is repeated until it reaches BS. Since the encrypted data will be decrypted in each hop, the intermediate node can easily get the original sensing data, and there is a security threat in the way of hopping encryption. In order to overcome this shortcoming, some schemes [1,12,14,15,18,20,27] proposed that aggregation nodes use homomorphic encryption strategy to directly aggregate ciphertext data, and other nodes cannot decrypt in the transmission process. And all nodes in the sensor network encrypt the sensing data using the secret key shared with the sink node.

The privacy protection strategy in the case of tree-based data aggregation relies on the constructed distribution routing tree. When the node moves, the network topology changes frequently, which lead to an increase in the cost of maintaining the routing tree. The application of encryption strategy reduces the dependence on topology and increases the resource consumption. Both assume that the query area is a full network.

Both tree-based and itinerary-based spatial range queries assume that communication between nodes is secure. The tree-based query scheme relies on the constructed topology. Although the itinerary-based query scheme avoids the dependence on the topology, the algorithm assumes that the communication model of nodes is an ideal disk graph.

Aiming to solve these problems, this paper proposes a link aware aggregation query algorithm with privacy-preserving capability called RPSAQ. According to the real-time network topology and link quality, RPSAQ dynamically generates query routes. By using link quality information, links with low packet loss rate are selected to distribute query information and aggregate perceived data, which avoids multiple retransmissions of data packets and reduces energy consumption.

3   Preliminaries

3.1   IWQE Protocol

Itinerary-based Window Query Execution (IWQE) [25] is an itinerary-based spatial range aggregation query processing algorithm. As shown in Fig. 1, IWQE divides the entire query area $ABCD$ into two sub-areas $AEFD$ and $EBCF$. And an itinerary is built to traverse all the nodes in these sub-areas. The nodes on the query itinerary are query nodes (such as $S_1, S_2, \cdots, S_9$). Each query node is responsible for collecting the sensing data of its neighbors, and sending query messages and partial query results to the next query node. Nodes other than query nodes in the query area are data nodes (such as a and b) Each data node is responsible for sending its local sensing data to their query nodes (such as the temperature and humidity of the query area). The detailed process of IWQE is as follows:

1. Once receiving a query request submitted by a user, the sink S sends the query message Q_m to the first query node S_1 within the query area using geographic routing protocol [11].
2. Node S_1 broadcasts the query message Q_m to its neighbors after receiving it.
3. The neighbors of node S_1 in the query area send their sensing data to S_1 successively after hearing the query message.
4. After receiving all the sensor data of its neighbors in the query area, node S_1 aggregates them with its local data to calculate partial query result, which will be sent to the next query node of S_1. And S_1 selects S_2 from its neighbors to be the next query node.
5. The process is repeated by other query nodes in the query area. When it stops at node S_9 which is the last query node, S_9 will calculate the final query result and return it back to the sink using geographic routing protocol.

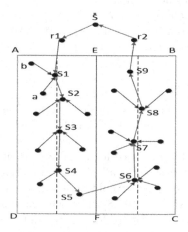

Fig. 1. The IWQE.

IWQE dynamically generates query itinerary according to the real-time network topology, which weakens the impact of network topology changes on query processing. However, IWQE assumes that wireless communication between nodes is the ideal disk model, which is impractical. And this assumption brings several problems: (1) The communication cost between query node S_i and its next query node S_{i+1} is high. As shown in Fig. 1, the node S_1 chooses S_2 from its neighbors as the next query node, which is the furthest one in the vertical direction. In the real network, the greater the distance between nodes, the poorer the link quality. Therefore, in order to send partial query results and query messages to S_2, node S_1 needs continuous retransmissions due to the lossy communication link between node S_1 and S_2, which brings a large amount of energy consumption. (2) Collecting the sensing data of neighbor nodes consumes a large amount of energy. The distance between node a and node b is denoted as $Dist(a,b)$ and

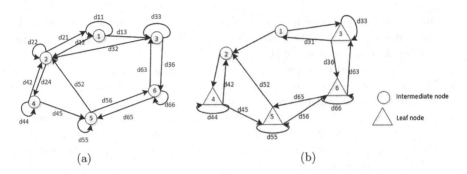

Fig. 2. The process of the improved algorithms & the process of SMART

the probability that node a successfully transmits messages to node b is denoted as $P(a, b)$. In Fig. 1, data node a is in the communication range of both S_1 and S_2. And $Dist(a, S_1) \gg Dist(a, S_2)$, $P(a, S_1) \ll P(a, S_2)$. In IWQE, the sensing data of node a is collected by query node S_1. However, if node S_2 collects the sensing data of node a, the energy consumption can be significantly reduced.

3.2 SMART Protocol

In [9], He et al. proposed the privacy protection protocol SMART based on data slicing. Figure 2(a) shows the process of SMART, which can be divided into three stages: data slicing, data mixing, and data aggregation. Each node slices its own data into three pieces, keep a piece for itself, and then transmits the rest two pieces to its neighbor nodes. After all pieces are received, each node mixes its own piece and the received pieces to obtain a new result.

On the basis of SMART, [6, 10, 28] proposed some improved sensor network privacy protection protocols. Figure 2(b) shows the process of these improved algorithms. They do not need to slice all the nodes in the query region. Only the leaf nodes fragment their data in the data slicing stage. As shown in Fig. 2(b), the leaf node n_3 slices its own data into three pieces: d_{31}, d_{33} and d_{36}. Node n_3 keeps d_{33} for itself, and transmits d_{31} and d_{31} to n_1 and n_6 respectively.

Above privacy-preserving data aggregation algorithms can aggregate sensing data to obtain the desired query results without compromising the privacy of sensing data. However, these algorithms all rely on pre-established topology trees. Because the corresponding topology will change frequently due to node failures and node movements, maintenance of the topology will incur additional energy consumption.

4   RPSAQ

4.1   Basic Idea

Suppose all sensor nodes can get their own locations through localization algorithm, and they broadcast their location information regularly. Therefore, all nodes can get the location information of their neighbor nodes. And each node uses link estimation algorithm to calculate the link quality between the node and all its neighbor nodes.

As shown in Fig. 3, RPSAQ divides the query area into several grids, and selects a query node in each grid, which is responsible for broadcasting query messages to all nodes in the next grid. Based on the link quality between nodes, RPSAQ sets the grid size and the query node reasonably to reduce the packet loss rate and the energy consumption of distributing the query message, and ensures the quality of the query results. The query processing of RPSAQ can be divided into three stages:

1. The query message and a random number randomly generated are sent to a node in the query area using geographic routing protocol which takes link quality into account.
2. The query message is sent to all grids in the query region, and the sensing data of all nodes in the query region is collected and aggregated to generate the final aggregation result.
3. The final query results generated in the second stage are returned to the sink through the geographic routing protocol which takes link quality into account.

The detailed process of RPSAQ is shown in Fig. 3. It is assumed that RPSAQ is used to calculate the average temperature of area Q_a. Without loss of generality, the query area is a rectangle. After receiving the query request from the user, the sink sends the query message Q_m and the random number γ to the query area Q_a through multiple relay nodes by using geographic routing protocol which takes link quality into account [17]. The last relay node R_1 selects node q_1 from its neighbor nodes as the first query node of the query region Q_a. After Q_m and γ arrive at node q_1, γ is added to q_1's sensing data D_{q_1} to obtain D'_{q_1}. Then node q_1 sets the size of grid g_2 and selects the query node q_2 in grid g_2 (referring to section $IV.B$). Also, node q_1 sends the query message Q_m to all nodes in grid g_2 and select node a from its neighbor nodes as the starting node of grid g_2. After receiving the query message Q_m and partial aggregation result D'_{q_1}, node a adds D'_{q_1} to its sensing data D_a to obtain D'_a and sends partial aggregation result D'_a to the next node in grid g_2. This process is repeated until node c's partial aggregation result D'_c arrives at the query node q_2 in grid g_2. Then query node q_2 add D'_c to its sensing data D'_{q_2} to obtain partial aggregation result D'_{q_2}, and sets the size of grid g_3 and selects the query node q_3 in the grid g_3. Also, node q_2 sends the query message Q_m to all nodes in grid g_3 and select node e from its neighbor nodes as the starting node of grid g_3. After receiving the query message Q_m and partial aggregation result D'_{q_2}, node e repeats what node a does in grid g_2 until partial aggregation result reaches the query node q_3. This process is repeated until the last query node q_n in the query area Q_a obtains the final aggregated result D'_{q_n}. Finally, node q_n sends D'_{q_n} back to the sink via the geographic routing protocol. The sink subtracts the random number γ from the returned aggregation results D'_{q_n} to obtain the real aggregation results in the query region.

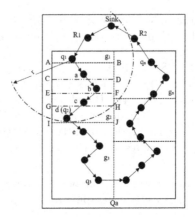

Fig. 3. The execution procedure of the RPSAQ algorithm

The entire dynamic query process of RPSAQ does not depend on the pre-constructed topology, which aggregates the sensing data while ensuring the privacy of the nodes' sensing data. Taking node q_0 as an example, the data sent by node q_0 to node a is D'_{q_1}, and node a cannot infer the sensing data of node q_0 because of random number γ.

4.2   How to Set the Grid Size and the Query Node

Suppose RPSAQ divides the query area into n grids $g_i (i \in [1, n])$, the set of nodes in grid g_i is denoted as $NS_i (i \in [1, n])$, the corresponding query node in g_i is $q_i (i \in [1, n])$, the number of nodes in g_i is represented by $|NS_i|$. The query node $q_{i-1} (i \in [2, n])$ selects its neighbor nodes along the data transmission direction as next potential query nodes for grid g_i and the set of potential next query nodes is denoted as ξ_i. For example, in Fig. 3, node a, b, c, d, R_1 and the sink are neighbor nodes of the query node q_1 and node a, b, c and d are along the transmission direction of q_1's sensing data. Therefore, the set of q_1's potential next query nodes is $\xi_2 = \{a, b, c, d\}$. In addition, to ensure normal communication between neighbor nodes, we define as follows: $Dist(q_{i-1}, q_i) \leq r, \forall i \in [2, n]$, which refers to that the distance between each query node q_{i-1} and the next query node q_i is less than or equal to the maximum communication radius of the node r.

Based on the constructed link model, this paper proposes a distributed heuristic Grid Setup Algorithm (GSA) to set the grid size and select the query node for each grid. In GSA, we define the average energy consumption to aggregate all sensing data in grid g_i to the next query node q_i as follows:

$$F(g_i, q_i) = \frac{E_c(g_i, q_i)}{|NS_i|} \tag{1}$$

$E_c(g_i, q_i)$ refers to the total energy consumption to aggregate all sensing data in grid g_i to the next query node q_i, which includes two parts: (1) the total energy consumption that each node in grid g_i receives the query message Q_m

broadcasted by the query node q_{i-1}; (2) the total energy consumption that each node in grid g_i calculate partial aggregation result and sends it to the next node.

In *GSA*, the query node q_{i-1} constructs the set of potential next query nodes ξ_i = $\{\alpha_j\}, j \in [1, \gamma]$. If node α_j is selected as the next query node by node q_{i-1}, then the corresponding grid g_{α_j} is also determined. Based on $F(g_i, q_i)$ and ξ_i, the query node q_{i-1} respectively evaluates the average energy consumption to aggregate all sensing data in grid g_i to each potential query node α_j. If $\min F_i(g_{\alpha_j}, \alpha_j), \alpha_j \in \xi_i$, then the query node q_{i-1} will select node α_j as the next query node q_i and its corresponding grid is g_{q_i}. Take Fig. 3 as an example, the query node q_1 constructs the set of potential next query nodes $\xi_2 = \{a, b, c, d\}$. And the grids corresponding to node a, b, c and d are $g_a = ABCD$, $g_b = ABEF$, $g_c = ABGH$ and $g_d = ABIJ$ respectively. Then based on $F(g_i, q_i)$ and ξ_2, the query node q_1 respectively evaluates the average energy consumption to aggregate all sensing data in grid g_2 to each node in ξ_2. If $F(g_d, d) < F(g_i, i), \forall i \in [a, b, c]$, then q_1 will select node d as the next query node q_2 and its corresponding grid $g_2 = ABIJ$.

4.3   Method of Handing Voids

As shown in Fig. 4, after the query node a collects the sensing data of the node in the grid $ABCD$, it needs to send the query message Q_m and partial query results D'_a to the nodes in region $EFGH$. As the region $CDEF$ under the grid $ABCD$ does not have the neighbor nodes of node a, $CDEF$ becomes a void region, which leads to the interruption of query processing. To avoid this problem, a geographic routing protocol is used to bypass the void region.

As shown in Fig. 4, the query node of grid $ABCD$ is a. The region $CDEF$ is characterized as a void region because a has no neighbors in $CDEF$, which will interrupt RPSAQ algorithm at node a. In order to address this issue, after data collection is finished in grid $ABCD$, its query node a will take the center of rectangular region $EFGH$ as the target location (where the distance between E and G) and use the geographic routing protocol to send the partial result and the query message to a node in $EFGH$.

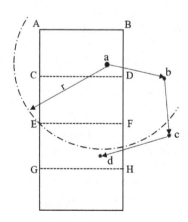

Fig. 4. Bypassing the void region

4.4   Privacy Analysis

The existing spatial range aggregation query algorithms usually utilize key mechanism to protect the privacy of sensing data. According to Eschenauer and Gligor [6], assume there are K secret keys in the secret key pool, and each sensor node in the sensor network randomly selects k secret keys from the pool. The probability of at least one identical key between any two neighbors is defined as $P_{connect} = 1 - \frac{((K-k)!)^2}{(K-2k)!2K!}$ and the probability that the third party has the same key is defined as $P_{overhear} = \frac{k}{K}$.

In the SMART protocol, when establishing a secure connection, node a and b can establish a secure connection because a and b have the same secret key value d_{ij}. The privacy leakage of sensing data mainly includes two aspects: (1) The third-party node has the same secret key with the probability $P_{overhear}$; (2) During the secret key preallocation stage, each node randomly selects k secret keys from the secret key pool with K secret keys and then establishes a connection if the adjacent nodes have the same secret keys. The third party can guess the secret key, and the correct guess is $\frac{1}{C_K^k}$. Therefore, SMART and PECDA have the possibility of privacy data leakage during data aggregation. In RPSAQ, if an attacker wants to get the original data of node a, it needs to get the aggregation result sent to the node a and the data transmitted to a's next node after node a completes the aggregation. However, RPSAQ adopts a route-based dynamic aggregation method, which increases the difficulty of the attacker guessing the next routing node and avoids the problem of sensing data leakage caused by secret key leakage in SMART and PECDA.

5   Analysis of Experimental Results

This section analyzes our proposed RPSAQ through simulation experiments. RPSAQ, SMART and PECDA are implemented in the simulator [3]. The geographic routing protocol which takes link quality into account [17] is used to

Table 1. Link model parameters

Parameter	Value
p	1
f	50 byte
P_t	0 dBm
d_0	1 m
$PL(d_0)$	55 dBm
η	4
σ	4
P_n	−105 dBm

Table 2. Simulation parameters

Parameter	Value
Area covered	$100\,\text{m} \times 100\,\text{m}$
Node communication radius	$11\,\text{m}$
Number of nodes	640
Sensing data size	110
Query data size	22

send the query message to the query area and return the final query result to the query origination node.

According to the literature [29], the typical *MICA2* mote satisfies the following log normal path loss model.

$$ppr(d) = \left(1 - \frac{1}{2} e^{-10\left(\frac{r(d)}{10}\right) \times \frac{1}{1.28}} \right)^{p \times 8f}$$

$$r(d) = P_t - PL(d_0) - 10\eta \lg\left(\frac{d}{d_0}\right) + N(0, \sigma) - P_n \tag{2}$$

where $ppr(d)$ means the proportion of successful packet transmissions when the distance between the sending node and the receiving node is d. p denotes the coding rate and f is the size of the data frame. $r(d)$ denotes the *SNR*(signal to noise ratio) of the receiving node when the distance between the sending node and the receiving node is d. P_t is the transmit power of the sending node. $PL(d_0)$ represents the power loss for the referenced distance d_0. η is the path loss exponent. $N(0, \sigma)$ represents the Normal Random Variable with expectation 0 and variance σ. P_n is the noise floor. The parameters of *LNM* link quality model in our experiments are shown in Table 1. The link qualities between nodes in our experiments are all generated by *LNM* model. In addition, Table 2 summarizes the default parameters used in our simulations.

5.1   Energy Consumption

This set of experiments analyzes the effects of node density and different topologies on the energy consumption of RPSAQ, SMART and PECDA. Since the link quality is not taken into account in SMART and PECDA, the data sent by the data node to the query node is not retransmitted when the sensing data is lost. In order to make there algorithms comparable, a retransmission mechanism is introduced in SMART and PECDA.

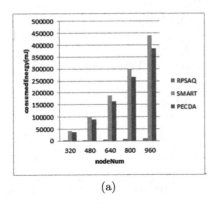
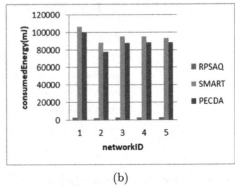

(a)   (b)

Fig. 5. Influence of the number of network nodes on energy consumption & influence of different network nodes on energy consumption

The effect of the number of network nodes on energy consumption is shown in Fig. 5(a). It can be seen that as the number of nodes in the network becomes larger, PECDA and SMART consume significantly more energy than RPSAQ. This is because SMART and PECDA are based on data slicing to protect data privacy. In SMART, each node slices its own data into three pieces, keeps a piece for itself, and then transmits the rest two pieces to its neighbor node. The energy consumed in slice data distribution takes up a large proportion of the total energy consumption. In PECDA, only the leaf nodes fragment their sensing data in the data slicing stage. However, distributing slice data also consumes energy to some extent. Moreover, RPSAQ sets the grid size and selects the query node according to the link quality in the network, which reduces the number of packet retransmission and thus saves energy.

The effect of different network topologies on energy consumption is shown in Fig. 5(b). It can be seen from Fig. 5(b) that the change of the network topology has little effect on RPSAQ and the energy consumption of RPSAQ remains low. However, the energy consumption of SMART and PECDA remain high in all cases. This is because SMART and PECDA rely on pre-constructed topologies and maintaining the topology results in a large amount of energy consumption. By contrast, route-based RPSAQ outperforms topology-dependent SMART and PECDA in terms of energy consumption.

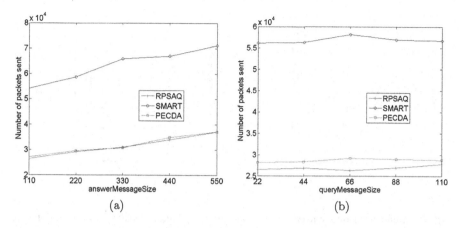

Fig. 6. Influence of sensing data size on the number of packets sent & influence of query message size on the number of packets sent

5.2 Number of Packets

This set of experiments analyzes the impact of sensing data size and query message size on the number of transmitted packets. Figure 6(a) shows the effects of different sensing data sizes on the number of packets that need to be sent. We can observe that as the size of sensing data increases, the number of packets to be transmitted by SMART, PECDA and RPSAQ increases. This is because the larger the size of sensing data, the more packets the sensing data is divided into, and the more packets are transmitted in the network. Since the RPSAQ dynamically selects the travel route according to the link quality, the nodes along the query route remain a low packet loss rate, which reduces the number of packet retransmissions. However, SMART and PECDA do not take the link quality into consideration, which increases the number of packet retransmission. Also, SMART and PECDA are based on data slicing to protect data privacy and data slice transmission also increases the number of packets transmitted in the network.

Figure 6(b) shows the effect of different query message sizes on the number of packets that need to be sent. It can be seen from Fig. 6(b) that SMART and PECDA need to send more packets than RPSAQ. On the one hand, because the link quality is not taken into account in SMART and PECDA, the retransmission of the packets increases the number of packets sent. On the other hand, as SMART and PECDA include three stages: slicing, mixing and aggregation, the transmission of data fragments also increase the number of packets that need to be sent.

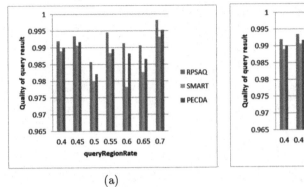
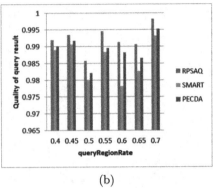

(a)   (b)

Fig. 7. Influence of query area size on the quality of query result & influence of node number on the quality of query result

5.3 Query Result Quality

This set of experiments analyzes the query result quality of SMART, PECDA and RPSAQ under different query area size. The query result quality is defined as $sr = \frac{cn}{tn}$, where cn represents the number of nodes traversed in the query area, and tn represents the total number of nodes in the query area. Figure 7(a) shows the impact of query area size on query result quality. It can be seen that when the size of query area is small, the query results of SMART, PECDA and RPSAQ are of high quality. With the increase of the size of the query area, the query result quality of SMART and PECDA decreases significantly, while the query result quality of RPSAQ remains high in all cases. This is because when the size of query area is large, Fig. 7(a) shows the impact of query area size on query result quality. It can be seen that when the query area is small, the number of nodes traversed is small, and the query results of the three algorithms are of high quality. With the increase of query area, the route with high link quality selected by RPSAQ performs query processing, while the link loss rate of SMART and PECDA is larger, so the quality of query results decreases.

6 Conclusion

The existing privacy-preserving aggregation query processing methods in sensor networks rely on pre-established network topology. Maintaining the topology results in a large amount of energy overhead. In addition, the existing privacy protection algorithms assume that the communication model between nodes is ideal, that is, the nodes within the communication radius can perform perfect communication, which is impractical. Aiming to solve these problems, this paper proposes RPSAQ, a link aware aggregation query algorithm with privacy-preserving capability. RPSAQ does not depend on the pre-constructed topology structure, and dynamically divides the query area into several grids according to the link quality, and sequentially traverses and collects the partial aggregation result of the nodes in the grid. Our proposed algorithm not only reduces the packet loss rate of nodes, but also ensures the data privacy of the sensor nodes. The experimental results show that RPSAQ outperforms the existing privacy protection algorithms in terms of energy consumption, packet transmission and query result quality.

Acknowledgments. This work was supported by the Open Fund of Key Laboratory of Civil Aviation Intelligent Airport Theory and System, Civil Aviation University of China under no. SATS202206.

References

1. Boudia, O.R.M., Senouci, S.M., Feham, M.: A novel secure aggregation scheme for wireless sensor networks using stateful public key cryptography. Ad Hoc Netw. **32**, 98–113 (2015)
2. Coman, A., Nascimento, M.A., Sander, J.: A framework for spatio-temporal query processing over wireless sensor networks. In: Proceedings of the 1st International Workshop on Data Management for Sensor Networks: in Conjunction with VLDB 2004, pp. 104–110 (2004)
3. Coman, A., Sander, J., Nascimento, M.A.: Adaptive processing of historical spatial range queries in peer-to-peer sensor networks. Distrib. Parallel Databases **22**(2), 133–163 (2007). https://doi.org/10.1007/s10619-007-7018-8
4. Demirbas, M., Ferhatosmanoglu, H.: Peer-to-peer spatial queries in sensor networks. In: Proceedings Third International Conference on Peer-to-Peer Computing (P2P2003), pp. 32–39. IEEE (2003)
5. Deshpande, A., Guestrin, C., Hong, W., Madden, S.: Exploiting correlated attributes in acquisitional query processing. In: 21st International Conference on Data Engineering (ICDE 2005), pp. 143–154. IEEE (2005)
6. Eschenauer, L., Gligor, V.D.: A key-management scheme for distributed sensor networks. In: Proceedings of the 9th ACM Conference on Computer and Communications Security, pp. 41–47 (2002)
7. Fu, T.Y., Peng, W.C., Lee, W.C.: Parallelizing itinerary-based KNN query processing in wireless sensor networks. IEEE Trans. Knowl. Data Eng. **22**(5), 711–729 (2009)
8. Goldin, D., Song, M., Kutlu, A., Gao, H., Dave, H.: Georouting and delta-gathering: efficient data propagation techniques for geosensor networks, pp. 73–95. GeoSensor Networks, Boca Raton (2005)
9. He, W., Liu, X., Nguyen, H., Nahrstedt, K., Abdelzaher, T.: PDA: privacy-preserving data aggregation in wireless sensor networks. In: IEEE INFOCOM 2007–26th IEEE International Conference on Computer Communications, pp. 2045–2053. IEEE (2007)
10. Hu, S., Liu, L., Fang, L., Zhou, F., Ye, R.: A novel energy-efficient and privacy-preserving data aggregation for WSNs. IEEE Access **8**, 802–813 (2019)
11. Karp, B., Kung, H.T.: GPSR: Greedy perimeter stateless routing for wireless networks. In: Proceedings of the 6th Annual International Conference on Mobile Computing and Networking, pp. 243–254 (2000)
12. Lin, Y.H., Chang, S.Y., Sun, H.M.: CDAMA: concealed data aggregation scheme for multiple applications in wireless sensor networks. IEEE Trans. Knowl. Data Eng. **25**(7), 1471–1483 (2012)

13. Ozdemir, S., Çam, H.: Integration of false data detection with data aggregation and confidential transmission in wireless sensor networks. IEEE/ACM Trans. Netw. **18**(3), 736–749 (2009)

14. Ozdemir, S., Xiao, Y.: Integrity protecting hierarchical concealed data aggregation for wireless sensor networks. Comput. Netw. **55**(8), 1735–1746 (2011)

15. Prathima, E., Prakash, T.S., Venugopal, K., Iyengar, S., Patnaik, L.: SDAMQ: secure data aggregation for multiple queries in wireless sensor networks. Procedia Comput. Sci. **89**, 283–292 (2016)

16. Roy, S., Conti, M., Setia, S., Jajodia, S.: Secure data aggregation in wireless sensor networks: filtering out the attacker's impact. IEEE Trans. Inf. Forensics Secur. **9**(4), 681–694 (2014)

17. Seada, K., Zuniga, M., Helmy, A., Krishnamachari, B.: Energy-efficient forwarding strategies for geographic routing in lossy wireless sensor networks. In: Proceedings of the 2nd International Conference on Embedded Networked Sensor Systems, pp. 108–121 (2004)

18. Shim, K.A., Park, C.M.: A secure data aggregation scheme based on appropriate cryptographic primitives in heterogeneous wireless sensor networks. IEEE Trans. Parallel Distrib. Syst. **26**(8), 2128–2139 (2014)

19. Singh, V.K., Verma, S., Kumar, M.: Privacy preserving in-network aggregation in wireless sensor networks. Procedia Comput. Sci. **94**, 216–223 (2016)

20. Viejo, A., Wu, Q., Domingo-Ferrer, J.: Asymmetric homomorphisms for secure aggregation in heterogeneous scenarios. Inf. Fusion **13**(4), 285–295 (2012)

21. Wang, T., Qin, X., Ding, Y., Liu, L., Luo, Y.: Privacy-preserving and energy-efficient continuous data aggregation algorithm in wireless sensor networks. Wirel. Pers. Commun. **98**(1), 665–684 (2017). https://doi.org/10.1007/s11277-017-4889-5

22. Wu, S.H., Chuang, K.T., Chen, C.M., Chen, M.S.: DIKNN: an itinerary-based KNN query processing algorithm for mobile sensor networks. In: 2007 IEEE 23rd International Conference on Data Engineering, pp. 456–465. IEEE (2007)

23. Wu, S.H., Chuang, K.T., Chen, C.M., Chen, M.S.: Toward the optimal itinerary-based KNN query processing in mobile sensor networks. IEEE Trans. Knowl. Data Eng. **20**(12), 1655–1668 (2008)

24. Xie, K., et al.: An efficient privacy-preserving compressive data gathering scheme in WSNs. Inf. Sci. **390**, 82–94 (2017)

25. Xu, Y., Lee, W.C., Xu, J., Mitchell, G.: ProcessingWindow queries in wireless sensor networks. In: 22nd International Conference on Data Engineering (ICDE 2006), p. 70. IEEE (2006)

26. Zhang, K., Han, Q., Cai, Z., Yin, G.: RiPPAS: a ring-based privacy-preserving aggregation scheme in wireless sensor networks. Sensors **17**(2), 300 (2017)

27. Zhao, X., Zhu, J., Liang, X., Jiang, S., Chen, Q.: Lightweight and integrity-protecting oriented data aggregation scheme for wireless sensor networks. IET Inf. Secur. **11**(2), 82–88 (2017)

28. Zhou, L., Ge, C., Hu, S., Su, C.: Energy-efficient and privacy-preserving data aggregation algorithm for wireless sensor networks. IEEE Internet Things J. **7**(5), 3948–3957 (2019)

29. Zuniga, M., Krishnamachari, B.: Analyzing the transitional region in low power wireless links. In: 2004 First Annual IEEE Communications Society Conference on Sensor and Ad Hoc Communications and Networks (IEEE SECON 2004), pp. 517–526. IEEE (2004)

Author Index

Printed in the United States
by Baker & Taylor Publisher Services